# God and Government
# in the Ghetto

# God and Government in the Ghetto

## THE POLITICS OF CHURCH-STATE
## COLLABORATION IN BLACK AMERICA

### Michael Leo Owens

The University of Chicago Press   CHICAGO & LONDON

MICHAEL LEO OWENS is assistant professor of political science and faculty associate of the Center for the Study of Law and Religion at Emory University. He also sits on the Board of Directors of the National Housing Institute and was senior research associate in the Urban and Metropolitan Studies Program of the Nelson A. Rockefeller Institute of Government.

The University of Chicago Press, Chicago 60637
The University of Chicago Press, Ltd., London
© 2007 by The University of Chicago
All rights reserved. Published 2007
Printed in the United States of America

16  15  14  13  12  11  10  09  08  07          1  2  3  4  5

ISBN-13: 978-0-226-64206-2 (cloth)
ISBN-13: 978-0-226-64207-9 (paper)
ISBN-10: 0-226-64206-2 (cloth)
ISBN-10: 0-226-64207-0 (paper)

Library of Congress Cataloging-in-Publication Data

Owens, Michael Leo.
God and government in the ghetto : the politics of church-state collaboration in Black America / Michael Leo Owens.
p. cm.
Includes bibliographical references (p.  ) and index.
ISBN-13: 978-0-226-64206-2 (cloth : alk. paper)
ISBN-10: 0-226-64206-2 (cloth : alk. paper)
ISBN-13: 978-0-226-64207-9 (pbk. : alk. paper)
ISBN-10: 0-226-64207-0 (pbk. : alk. paper)
1. African American churches. 2. Church and state—United States.
3. Faith-based human services—United States. 4. Community development, Urban—United States. I. Title.
BR563.N4O96 200
322'.108996073—dc22
2007000101

♾ The paper used in this publication meets the minimum requirements of the American National Standard for Information Sciences—Permanence of Paper for Printed Library Materials, ANSI Z39.48-1992.

*I dedicate this book to a psalmist and evangelist,*
MARIE ANTOINETTE MAPP OWENS, *my mom*
*(b. February 27, 1936, d. March 10, 2006)*

What is the Lord calling the churches to be and to do
in this new war on poverty? To call attention to the
neglected issues? To carry on their own war?
To enter into an alliance with . . . government?
LYLE E. SCHALLER, *The Churches' War on Poverty*

Is it the case, as some would contend, that churches
have irreversibly declined as a political force in urban
America . . . [and] are no longer significantly involved
in the governance of the nation's larger cities?
HENRY PRATT, *Churches and Urban Government
in Detroit and New York, 1895–1994*

# CONTENTS

## ACKNOWLEDGMENTS

In the late 1990s I was on the staff of the Urban and Metropolitan Studies Program at the Nelson A. Rockefeller Institute of Government, State University of New York. One of our projects included an interdisciplinary study of change and stability among black neighborhoods in the United States (Nathan, Chow, and Owens 1995; Owens and Wright 1998; Wright, Patillo, and Montiel 2006). It looked at community capacity building and social capital in the black neighborhoods of sixteen metropolitan areas. During my tenure with the study (1995–2000) and in the years after it, I traveled to eleven of the metropolitan areas discerning through conversations and observations the role of community-based organizations in the stability of and efforts to revitalize black neighborhoods, both in cities and suburbs.

During my trips, I invariably learned of African American churches, particularly those with long histories of political involvement, that were blending their resources with those of government. They worked with public agencies and used public policies and programs to wrestle with tough problems, especially in low-income black neighborhoods. Ultimately, my travels and learning influenced me to begin an independent study to examine why and how African American churches partner with government agencies, as well as the reasons that governments partner with churches. That study became this book.

My greatest appreciation and deepest gratitude are for Karen Cobham-Owens, my dear and beautiful wife, who helped me with this book. She never comes last in anything, especially not my acknowledgments. Amid the anguish of a family tragedy, we moved from New York to Georgia, a place where we never thought of residing and a part of the country where we, especially my

Bajan wife, lacked roots. Despite our sadness, Karen always found strength to support my need to travel, research, and write. I finished this book because she kept me on schedule, made me go to the office on Saturdays and Sundays to read, think, and write, and encouraged me to have fun when I required or deserved it most. Karen is the finest wife a husband could have, and she is my best friend. I am sincere when I say that this book is as much hers as it is mine.

Our book, however, would have remained an idea in my head were it not for the cooperation of the black clergy and the lay leaders of African American churches and their faith-related agencies in cities across the United States, especially New York. Numerous women and men of strong and abiding Christian faith took time from "making the Word flesh" in poor black neighborhoods to share with me their perspectives on urban politics, ministry, poverty, and neighborhood development in post–civil rights America. I am eternally grateful to them.

My appreciation is also extended to a giving group of former and current civil servants of the New York City Department of Housing Preservation and Development, who provided me with insights and unpublished data on municipal policies and neighborhood development in the Big Apple. I also thank the U.S. Department of Housing and Urban Development for a 1999 Doctoral Dissertation Research Grant (H-21182SG) and the former Ford Foundation Fellowship for Minorities Program (now the Ford Foundation Diversity Fellowships for Achieving Excellence in College and University Teaching) for a 2000 Doctoral Dissertation Fellowship that funded my initial research and writing.

From the beginning Todd Swanstrom, Richard P. Nathan, Robert Nakamura, and John DiIulio Jr. recognized the value of my project, first as a dissertation and then as a book. They aided my research and writing in immeasurable ways. Additionally, the comments and critical eyes of key colleagues in the Political Science Department at Emory University helped me improve my claims, analyses, and conclusions. Specifically, I am indebted to Micheal Giles, Clifford Carruba, Rick Doner, Donald Beaudette, Kelly Hill, Bradley Alexander, Bethany Blackstone, Katrina Gamble, and Keisha Haywood for reading my manuscript in its entirety or at pivotal points in its development. Other scholars also helped me improve the quality of my book, especially by reading drafts of chapters, commenting on conference papers, and sharing their own work with me. They include Alison Calhoun-Brown, Fredrick C. Harris, Robert A. Brown, Todd Shaw, Robert Franklin, Lester Kenyatta Spence, Laura Reese, Alton Pollard, Steve Tipton, Marion Orr, Susan Clarke,

Barbara Ferman, Arthur Farnsley, Stephen Monsma, Ange-Marie Hancock, JoAnn Rock, Jordan Yin, Bob Wineburg, Richard Roper, Said Sewell, Tamelyn Tucker-Worgs, Georgia Persons, James Jennings, Eric McDaniel, Avis Vidal, Harvey Newman, Helene Slessarev-Jamir, Brian McKenzie, Joyce Keyes-Williams, Stephanie Boddie, and Stephen Rathgeb Smith, among others. I must single out Bradford Wilcox for supreme recognition; he first suggested to Alan Wolfe the potential fit of my project within the Morality and Society series of the University of Chicago Press. (I sing praises for the Annie E. Casey Foundation, too, for bringing Brad and me together over dinner with other young scholars of social welfare policy and religion.)

The book and I benefited from the academic spaces that many of my colleagues and hospitable institutions invited me into to refine and share my research and to offer me fellowship: Michael Rich, Rudolph Byrd, Leslie Harris, Nancy Eiseland, Elizabeth Bounds, David Jenkins, Ross Rubenstein, Luis Lugo, Corwin Smidt, Richard Hula, Cynthia Jackson-Elmoore, Roland Anglin, Jeffrey Lowe, William Harris, Carole Thompson, Jo Renee Formicola, Bill Bianco, Barry Tadlock, Judith Millesen, Joanne Carmen, Ronald Walters, Wheeler Winstead, the Roundtable on Religion and Social Welfare Policy at the Rockefeller Institute of Government, the Office of University-Community Partnerships at Emory University, the Institute for Research on Poverty at the University of Wisconsin–Madison, the Program in American Democracy at the University of Notre Dame, the Scholar-Practitioner Program of the James MacGregor Burns Academy of Leadership at the University of Maryland, the Center for Research on Religion and Urban Civil Society at the University of Pennsylvania, the Andrew Young School of Policy Studies at George State University, and the Faith and the City Leadership Institute. I thank them all. I especially appreciate the invitations I received from R. Drew Smith to participate in scholarly and practitioner-oriented forums and projects that deepened my understanding of the topic of this book.

Furthermore, Amy Benson Brown, director of Emory University's Manuscript Development Program, along with three anonymous reviewers, helped me communicate my findings with strength, clarity, and style. I acknowledge their gifts of patience and compassion, the same gifts that Douglas Mitchell, Tim McGraw, and Alan Wolfe of the University of Chicago Press abundantly bestowed on me. I also thank Ruth Goring, my manuscript editor at the Press. She showed me clearer paths through the thickets of my thoughts and words, while demonstrating the wonderful truth that less really is more when writing a book.

Small portions of this book were previously published in the following:

"Contestant, Advocate, Implementer: Social Services and the Policy Roles of African American Churches," in *Long March Ahead: African American Churches and Public Policy in Post-Civil Rights America,* copyright 2004 Duke University Press; "Doing Something in Jesus' Name: Black Churches and Community Development Corporations," in *New Day Begun: African American Churches and Civic Culture in Post-Civil Rights America,* copyright 2003 Duke University Press; "Black Church–Affiliated Community Development Corporations and the Coproduction of Affordable Housing in New York City," in *Nonprofits in Urban America,* copyright 2000 Greenwood Publishing/Quorum Books; and "Which Congregations Will Take Advantage of Charitable Choice? Explaining the Pursuit of Public Funding by Congregations," *Social Science Quarterly,* no. 87 (March 2006): 55–75, copyright South Western Social Science Association.

The life and death of Reverend William Augustus Jones (1934–2006), one of my heroes of the Northern civil rights movement, influenced the choice of my book's title. Reverend Jones, the author of *God in the Ghetto,* was among the first black pastors I met who wondered aloud—mixing amazement, scorn, and hope—why African American churches would collaborate with government. But the findings and statements contained in *God and Government in the Ghetto* are mine. I claim ownership, too, of all mistakes and errors. Of course, I will accept most of the credit if this book teaches you something that you did not know about the political engagement of African American churches on behalf of black people living in the enduring ghettos of the United States.

Gang murders and brutal retributions among young black males in the low-income neighborhoods of Roxbury and Dorchester were common in Boston in the late 1980s and early 1990s. The violence held no site sacred, not even a church sanctuary. In 1992, during a funeral service at Morning Star Baptist Church for a young man killed in a drive-by shooting, a gang entered the church, shooting and stabbing mourners. "It was a wake-up call" to the Reverend Eugene Rivers, a neighborhood pastor. "If we didn't get out of the four-walled church," he realized, "the walls would collapse" (quoted in Klein 1997, 45). In response to the streets' entering the church, churches took to the streets.

African American churches formed the Boston Ten Point Coalition to reduce violent crime among black youth by working with government agencies on a voluntary basis. The churches acquired the responsibility to steer youth from prison through counseling and employment; aid the judicial system in identifying criminals, adjudicating cases, determining sanctions, and meting out punishments; and monitor the behavior of the police while seeking to improve police relations with poor black communities (Berrien, McRoberts, and Winship 2000; Winship 2001; Jennings 2005).

The agenda of the coalition was simple and clear: "Get ministers and volunteers on the streets to patrol neighborhoods and counsel gang members; cooperate with law-enforcement and criminal-justice officials to lock up the bad guys; and offer refuge and help to young people in need, including education and employment programs and mentors" (Williams 2003, 22).[1] The behavior of the churches in the coalition was historic, and it was political.

Activist African American churches across the country partner with federal, state, and local government agencies.[2] They are involved in "faith-based and community initiatives" that range from reducing welfare caseloads to facilitating the positive reintegration of ex-prisoners into society.[3] There are historical antecedents to the contemporary partnerships between activist African churches and government agencies. The phenomenon and process that many think are original to our times, presumably emerging with the presidential administration of George W. Bush in 2001 or welfare reform in 1996 in the administration of Bill Clinton, extends back further than most people recognize. At least since the War on Poverty, activist churches have partnered with public agencies to initiate neighborhood redevelopment projects and administer and implement public policy (Schaller 1967; English 1967; Fish 1973).

Today activist African American churches continue to use public-private partnerships, the coproduction of public policies, and the administration of public-funded social welfare programs to address the needs of low-income neighborhoods. In the last decade, in particular, local and state governments have contracted with activist African churches, and the federal government has directly and indirectly awarded them grants, to deliver services to the needy within their jurisdictions.[4] Such churches include Antioch Missionary Baptist Church in Chicago; Greater Allen African Methodist Episcopal Cathedral in New York City; Holy Redeemer Institutional Church of God in Christ in Milwaukee; St. Stephens Baptist Church in Louisville; West Los Angeles Church of God in Christ in Los Angeles; Allen Temple Baptist Church in East Oakland; and Zion Baptist Church in Philadelphia, to name a small set.[5] Much of the compensation for their public work is a result of or in relation to the replacement of Aid to Families with Dependent Children (AFDC) with Temporary Assistance to Needy Families (TANF) and the introduction of charitable choice as part of welfare reform in 1996.[6]

In California, for instance, FAME Renaissance, a nonprofit subsidiary of the activist First African Methodist Episcopal (FAME) Church in Los Angeles, received approximately $1 million in TANF funds to create a "welfare to wealth" program that includes job training, employment placement, debt reduction, and financial planning services (Orr n.d.). All Congregations Together, a church-associated organization supported by an alliance of churches in San Diego, whose members include Saint Stephen's Church of God in Christ, received a $316,000 contract to use vans owned by the churches to transport TANF recipients to their employers or to workfare locations (Sherman 2000). The Alameda County Social Services Agency issued a $632,318 contract to Northern California Community Development Corporation, a nonprofit organization that is associated with the Glad Tidings Church of God in Christ, to operate an "Institute for Success" that conducts job readiness training and computer classes for TANF recipients (Sherman 2000).

In New York, the New York State Department of Labor and the New York City Human Resources Administration contracted with a set of African American congregations and a faith-based nonprofit organization supported by mainly African American churches to work with TANF recipients in New York City who lost portions of their welfare benefits for failing to participate in mandatory work assignments (Rock and Roper 2001; Rock 2002). The congregations and nonprofit contacted TANF recipients and guided them in developing personalized plans for fulfilling their work obligations in return for reinstatement of their full welfare benefits. The purpose was threefold: (1) to permit TANF recipients to receive their full benefits; (2) to ensure that the city and state met its federal obligations under the Personal Responsibility and Work Opportunity Reconciliation Act (welfare reform) of 1996; and (3) to move TANF recipients closer to self-sufficiency, if not out of poverty.

There also are examples of public funding for church-based or church-backed social services delivery that go beyond (or predate) changes to the national system of welfare. Activist African American churches in Indianapolis, for instance, partnered with public agencies under the auspices of the Marion County Juvenile Court.[7] Local judges, with funds from the county government, paid clergy and church congregants to provide "home-based counseling" to youth sentenced to it (Farnsley 2003, 20). The assumption and expectation were that the churches would place positive role models with strong moral values in the lives of youth, equipping young people to make better personal and familial choices concerning their behavior and activities.

When activist African American churches partner with government, they agree with public agencies on a purpose (e.g., moving the poor from welfare to work, increasing the supply of affordable housing, decreasing youth violence and incarceration) and act jointly to achieve it.[8] The ostensible intent of activist churches' work with government agencies is to revitalize low-income neighborhoods by improving physical environments, enhancing employability, creating jobs that pay good wages, and building assets (e.g., houses). Also, all churches that partner with government interpret their actions as a means of manifesting their faith. But activist churches that work with government may also *intend* to influence, to some degree, public policy in low-income neighborhoods. For them, partnerships with government can be a means of political engagement on behalf of poor people.

I will argue in this book that church-state partnerships often constitute a

distinct type of political engagement for activist African American churches—
*collaboration with government.* Many activist churches that partner with government, especially African American churches, are participating in formal
relationships with public agencies for the *deliberate* purpose of becoming intermediaries to affect public services and public policies in their neighborhoods. They do it to win government attention and policy responsiveness to
the interests of low-income black neighborhoods.

I wrote this book to explain why and explore how activist churches, particularly African American churches, purposely partner with government to provide social welfare. I also wrote this book to analyze how church-state partnerships may affect the degree of government responsiveness in low-income
black neighborhoods. In the process, I speak to the broader relevance and
utility of political involvement by African American churches, especially in
policymaking processes on behalf of poor people in cities.

From where I sit as a scholar of American politics and public policy, the
analyses coming out of existing research on church-state partnerships have yet
to yield a comprehensive and coherent political logic of church-state partnerships, especially one that includes the perspective of activist churches. Overall, I contend that there is much we do not know about the political processes
and products of African American churches' and other religious congregations' partnerships with government, either as a complement to other political
activities or as an alternative to them. It is not because there is an absence of
scholarship on church-state partnerships.

Studies by sociologists of religion describe and explain the potential and
actual combining of churches' resources with those of public agencies and
private organizations to design and implement community development programs directed at the poor and their communities (Bartkowski and Regis
2003; McRoberts 2003; Chaves 1999; Wuthnow 2004; Roberts 2003; Cnaan
2002). They tend to explain the existence of church-state partnerships by
analyzing the correlations and probabilities of theological imperatives, religious convictions, and denominationalism's influencing faith-based poverty
relief programs, as well as how attributes and attitudes may affect the development of church-state partnerships. Other studies by sociologists, along with
social work and political science scholars, have considered why government
invites churches to partner with it or the coherence of faith-based social services in relation to the claims about government-sponsored faith-based initiatives (Cnaan 1999; Wineburg 2001; Winship 2001); determined the potential effects of church-state partnerships on national partisan elections (Black,
Koopman, and Ryden 2004; Formicola, Segers, and Weber 2003); and drawn

lessons from historical cases of patron-client relationships between political machines and politicized ministers to consider how the interaction of government agencies and churches may affect the political behavior of activist clergy and their congregants (Harris 2001 and 2005).

The analysis to date is limited, however, in its ability to improve our collective understanding of church-state partnerships as political engagement by activist churches, especially by African American churches. First, scholarship with a political focus on church-state partnerships privileges the motivations of white politicians to partner public agencies with churches. That is, it tends to ignore or discount activist churches' own political potential, rationales for, and practice of partnering with government, particularly the perspectives of clergy and lay leaders. It does not provide a convincing argument for why black clergy, for instance, assent to have their churches work with government.

Second, the political scholarship on church-state partnerships focuses too much on the national government. Most discussions about church-state partnerships in policy circles occur at the federal level or in state capitals. Yet implementation of the partnerships, and the realpolitik of them, often happens at the street level in cities. It takes place mainly through municipal governments' responding to a mix of federal, state, and local policies and working with nongovernmental organizations to improve conditions in urban neighborhoods. Third, scholarship on church-state partnerships often does not consider the direct and indirect ways government funding may influence the political practice of religious congregations or the political engagement of the local communities that are to benefit from the interactions of government agencies and churches.

My empirical examination of urban church-state partnerships, is a beginning to better understand and consider the choice, or just the thought, of collaboration with government by African American churches, particularly in relation to the choice to act politically in other ways such as electioneering and protest. And it contributes to analysis and understanding of the contemporary politics of African American churches specifically and urban black politics more generally, especially in relation to the distribution of public benefits to poor black neighborhoods.

## CHURCH-STATE COLLABORATION AS POLITICAL ACTION: A SCHOLARLY LACUNA

Though increasing numbers of churches have been working with government agencies, the topic of church-state partnerships is not a cynosure of social science, especially political science. In particular, the behavior and effects of activist African American churches that partner with government go unnoticed by most political scientists. The research, particularly the most influential and innovative studies, on the political engagement of African American churches in the post–civil rights era focuses almost exclusively on these churches as sources and sites for electoral action and ideology formation, not political engagement in policymaking processes (Reed 1986; Tate 1993; Calhoun-Brown 1996; Harris 1999; Harris-Lacewell 2004; McDaniel 2004; McClerking and McDaniel 2005; Smith and Harris 2005).[9] Scholarship does a good job of examining electoral politics by blacks and its achievements, particularly when it is based in or sustained by the resources of activist churches. Yet it does not say much about the activities of churches after the polls close, elections are decided, and triumphant politicians take their seats in office.

Alongside the electoral mobilization studies is research that addresses the role of African American churches in contentious politics. It rarely attends to the involvements of African American churches in *contemporary* protests challenging the decisions of policymakers.[10] Rather, contentious politics research on African American churches focuses on the contentious politics of blacks in the past, particularly the civil rights movement of the 1950s and 1960s (McAdam 1999; Morris 1984 and 1996). Or it explains the decline and utility of protest by blacks in the post–civil rights movement era, emphasizing the place—and absence—of churches and other institutions of black civil society (Jennings 1992; Kim 2000; Joyce 2003). But the literature is silent about the political engagement of African American churches (or other civil society institutions) after shouts cease, signs are dropped, and marches disband.

Studies of both the electoral behavior and contentious conduct of African American churches continue to be important for understanding the dynamics of black political mobilization and incorporation, especially in the lengthening shadow of the civil rights movement. But what of the political involvement of African American clergy and congregants after voters cast their ballots? What of the political activities of African American churches after protests die down?

Both election-focused and protest-oriented scholarship obscure the multiple ways that urban black clergy and congregants employ the resources of African American churches before, during, and beyond electioneering and contentious acts to participate politically. This is troublesome. Allison Calhoun-Brown, who has contributed greatly and admirably to the body of research on the electoral activism and effects of African American churches, argues that electoral and protest myopia prevents social scientists from observing "other important parts of the political process including agenda setting, interest articulation, policy formation, policy implementation, policy impact, and policy assessment—areas in which an institutional presence [by churches] may be particularly significant" (2003a, 46).

In sum, there is a dearth of scholarship and understanding about how African American churches, other than through the mobilization of their resources to affect the outcomes of elections and to support contention, may influence public policy (Smith 2004). In particular, there is much we do not know about how activist African American churches use their partnerships with government as a means of political engagement. We do not know about the political process by which they partner with government, the products of their partnerships, and the broader political implications of them. This is true despite four decades of African American churches' partnering with government to provide social services in low-income black neighborhoods.

Our shortage of knowledge about the politics of church-state collaboration is mainly because political scientists and others have ignored sound advice from scholars of religion. For instance, C. Eric Lincoln and Lawrence Mamiya comment in *The Black Church in the African American Experience* that "politics" in relation to African American churches is properly understood only when it is "broadly defined beyond electoral politics and protest politics to include community organizing and community building activities that are part of the ministry of many black clergy and churches" (1990, 234). Why? The political involvement of African American churches is about more than mobilizing individuals and groups to take to the streets as protesters and go to the polls as voters.

If the counsel of Lincoln and Mamiya is to be taken seriously, social scientists must define the political engagement of African American churches and black clergy as encompassing an assortment of ways they, alone or alongside other institutions, seek to influence public policy. Also, we must use words that more accurately reflect how organizations and citizens may and do interact with government today. This is particularly important for the study of churches in cities, given the new characteristics and forms of urban politics that have emerged over the last thirty years as a result of social movement activity, minority incorporation, and changes in governance such as the devolution of public policy, privatization, and the replacement of political machines with urban regimes (Mayer 1991; Elkin 1987; Stone 1989; Orr 1999; Hula and Jackson-Elmoore 2000; Hula, Jackson, and Orr 1997).[11] We are witnessing in cities new forms of representation and a broader incorporation of minority interests into policymaking and policy implementation (Mayer 1998; Hula, Jackson, and Orr 1997; Ferman 1996; Burns 2006).

Hence, identification and analyses of the "politics" of African American churches must include not only those activities intended to influence the selection of policymakers but also the activities intended to influence the decisions of policymakers and the means they use to administer and implement their decisions. That makes sense given contemporary examples such as the Ten Point Coalition of African American churches working with government, as well as the common practice of nongovernmental organizations' being partners with government in the delivery of public services (Salamon 1995).

While accepting the need to conceptualize the study of African American church politics more broadly than most past research has done, some may not accept my claim that social scientists should view activist African American churches' activities in partnership with government as falling within the broader scope of politics, particularly urban African American politics. Some may see African American churches' collaboration with government as apolitical. To others it may be a form of cooptation (i.e., traitorous cooperation or "selling out"). Let me address these concerns by explicating (1) what collaboration involves; (2) how collaboration creates (or is a response to) opportunities for politicized groups to possibly affect public policy, particularly at the stage of implementation; and (3) how collaboration relates to urban African Americans' historic efforts for political incorporation.

## *Defining Collaboration*

Collaboration, especially when it involves governmental and nongovernmental organizations, is a relationship of two or more actors working together to mutually achieve goals unlikely to be realized save for collective action. Moreover, collaboration involves collective action among organizations that one would normally *not* expect to act together, with groups often working across the boundaries of the public, commercial, and voluntary sectors (Fosler 2002, 19). It implies that all of the actors involved recognize that an end is important and the likelihood of achieving it is greater if they act together than alone. Collaboration, nonetheless, is "more than simply sharing knowledge and information and more than a relationship that helps each party achieve its own goals. The purpose is to create a shared vision and joint strategies to address concerns that go beyond the purview of any particular party" (Chrislip and Larson 1994, 5). For nongovernmental actors, another purpose is to gain government attention and policy responsiveness to the problems of the constituencies they represent.

*Co-optation: The Negative Face of Collaboration.* While collaboration is a process for discerning and achieving goals shared by governmental and nongovernmental actors, it does not imply that power be or is equal among participants, nor does it mean that shared visions and subsequent strategies for achieving them are determined without conflict or controversy. It is common in a collaborative relationship for one actor to possess greater resources (e.g., authority, control, and capital) than its partners. The possessor of greater resources can wield more influence than the actor with lesser resources in the design and endurance of their partnership, the selection of partner roles and functions, the achievement of their end, and the evaluation of outcomes. When government possesses greater resources than do nongovernmental actors, especially those representing groups with a history of contention and opposition toward government, we may see the negative face of collaboration—co-optation, the "process of absorbing new elements into the leadership or *policy-determining structure* of an organization as a means of averting threats to its stability or existence" (Selznick 1948, 34, emphasis added).

Government may use collaboration as a means of co-optation, to diminish the ability of its opposition to challenge the status quo, especially in terms of public policy and practice. In the process, government incorporates members of its opposition "into the legitimate structure of the negotiating process, thereby focusing and channeling opposition into a more easily controllable environment" (Murphree, Wright, and Ebaugh 1996, 451).[12] Thus co-optation can lead to the capture of nongovernmental organizations by government. Collaborators may forgo political engagement beyond collaboration in exchange for material benefits for their organization and neighborhood. They may prefer to accept from political elites what Clarence Stone terms "small opportunities" that are "not guided by a grand vision of how the world might be reformed, but by the pursuit of particular opportunities" that produce limited benefits (1989, 193).

Benefits accrue to nongovernmental organizations that assume accommodating stances toward government. Accommodation may yield resources and legitimacy for the groups in the eyes of government, as well as permit the inclusion and participation of the co-opted into a "decision-making process, [so they are] made to feel that they are participants, even though their recommendations may not affect the outcome[s]" of the processes (Murphree, Wright, and Ebaugh 1996, 455; see also Coy and Hedeen 2005). Continued receipt of governmental benefits may require "consensual approaches" by nongovernmental collaborators to the political system (Ferman 1996, 124). To get along with government, collaborators may have to go along with it, regardless of effects on their constituents.

Thus, co-optation influences nongovernmental organizations working with government to address their concerns through routine institutional processes and incremental policy change, rather than employing contention and confrontation to seek radical and immediate policy changes that would advantage, or at least not disadvantage, their constituents (Rhomberg 2004; Bockmeyer 2003; Gittell 1980; Stoecker 1994). Co-opted organizations do not view the benefits they receive from government through collaboration as their "due"; they see them as gifts or as rewards for behaving themselves. Seeing the opportunity for collaboration with government as a gift instead of a right, co-opted organizations have less freedom to act politically on behalf of their constituents. They fear that they will continue to receive public resources only if they avoid political action against government or conflict with policymakers. So co-opted organizations collaborate with government from a position of weakness rather than strength.

*Empowered Cooperation: The Positive Face of Collaboration.* Government may often have the advantage of material resources (money, personnel, and rule of law) when it collaborates with nongovernmental organizations. Yet this need not translate into dominant influence over nongovernmental organizations or into government capture of nongovernmental organizations. In short, collaboration does not always result in co-optation. It may yield empowerment.

One influential view holds that collective problem-solving is unthinkable unless public institutions rely on nongovernmental organizations to leverage the resources of government to define problems, design responses, and implement policies (Pierre and Peters 2000; Kooiman 2000; Rhodes 1997; Elkin 1987; Stone 1989).[13] It argues that problems can be effectively addressed only through strategic alliances among organizations from the public, civic, and market sectors.[14] On its own, government is hampered by fiscal, ideological, and knowledge constraints (Pierre and Peters 2000). To overcome its limits, government partners with nongovernmental organizations that possess financial, value-laden, and technical expertise or other assets (e.g., the trust of "the people") that government lacks but needs to govern effectively. For government, collaboration may yield efficient management of collective problems; reductions in the need for and costs of direct public management; expansion of social choice; advancement of citizen and ideological policy preferences;

implementation of politically motivated policies; and achievement of partisan and electoral ends (Pierre and Peters 2000; Rhodes 1996; Stoker 2000; Clarke 2000; S. Smith and Lipsky 1993; Marwell 2004).

Given that government needs the resources of nongovernmental organizations, nongovernmental organizations may collaborate with government from a position of strength. Although they may modulate their claims and change their political tactics while being "rewarded for their choice by the prospect of meaningful political access," nongovernmental organizations are not obligated to disavow their larger social change objectives (Meyer and Tarrow 1998, 21–22). In due course, nongovernmental organizations may use their position as collaborators to influence the agendas, policies, and programs of government agencies and help bring multilevel changes. Such alterations may include changed power relations among the partners; policy changes by the public partner and nongovernmental partners; and systemic changes in attitudes, institutions, and the scale of collective problems (Giugni 1998; Banaszak, Beckwith, and Rucht 2003).

When positive changes occur as a result of collaboration, nongovernmental organizations may view their participation and the resources that they receive from it as their right, given their possession and provision of other resources pivotal to effective governance. Government, therefore, should treat them as equals. Rather than being co-opted, nongovernmental organizations that collaborate with government may be empowered to maintain their political goals and act politically beyond collaboration (via protest, for example) on behalf of their constituents because government may fear losing the resources for effective governance that it derives from their collaboration (Orr 1999; Imbroscio 1997; Warren 2001).

Collaboration as empowered cooperation with government need not require nongovernmental groups to give up their political aims and interests. This is especially true if we acknowledge, as Adalbert Evers does, that collaboration "leaves enough room for the different attitudes and relationships" among nongovernmental actors and government, "which range from those that accentuate controversies (for example, over goals and ways of service delivery), to those which limit conflicts in competitive relationships and, finally to those which represent a well-tuned order of roles and responsibilities in co-operative relationships" (1995, 166). Consequently, when looked at through the lens of empowered cooperation rather than co-optation, collaboration often involves "guarded conflict" (Taylor 1997, 8).

Nongovernmental organizations may remain vigilant and constantly question the motives of government, while working with it to acquire access to policymaking processes, promote the interests of their constituents, and retain whatever public resources flow to them from collaboration. They may also remain ambivalent about "bad" public policies of government but continue to collaborate with government to implement "good" public policies.[15] Therefore, nongovernmental organizations may collaborate with government to administer public policies even where complete accord between the organizations and government is lacking (Giugni and Passy 1998).

## Collaborators as Politicized Agents of the State

Politicized groups, especially groups with histories of resisting and opposing policymakers or the decisions they make, as well as histories of pressing claims on government, need not remain outside public policy processes as opponents and claimants. They can and often do seek to incorporate themselves and their interests into policymaking systems, thus acquiring policy responsiveness. Such groups often pursue policy responsiveness by lobbying and litigating for policy change. It is also common for representatives and members of politicized groups, including politicized religious communities, to deliberately increase their numbers within government as elected and appointed administrative officials, as well as civil servants, in order to affect public policy (Viteritti 1979; Rhomberg 2004; Wald 2003).[16] There is, however, another approach available to politicized groups seeking greater policy responsiveness through the municipal bureaucracy.

Social movement scholars have observed at the national level that politicized groups seeking to transform social conditions may infiltrate the state (Giugni 1998; Giugni and Passy 1998; Banaszak 2002; Banaszak, Beckwith, and Rucht 2003). That is, some groups have identified and exploited opportunities to intentionally become agents of the nation-state in administering public policies. Their infiltration is intended to permit them to represent and incorporate their interests in not only the implementation but also the design of public programs to influence government's responsiveness to their values, interests, and needs, even if and when they are at odds with the state. To borrow from this observation and descend the layers of government with it: politicized groups may search for openings to influence city government and public policy as agents of the municipal state, just as city government and public policy may seek to influence groups and their relationships to the communities they serve or represent.

At the level of cities, as scholars of urban politics observe, politicized groups need not "simply react to market and political failures; . . . they can actively

work to restructure the [political-policy] environment in which they operate" (Jackson-Elmoore and Hula 2000, 3). They may influence policymakers
to alter public policies and programs to advantage their group. Or they may
influence public decision-making by advocating equitable policy outcomes
(Orr 1999; Ferman 1996; Imbroscio 1997).

Aside from working within the political system through voting booths, appointed boards, city councils, and courts, politicized groups may influence
governments through a "politics of administration, implementation, planning,
and economic development," one that situates political action within and in
relation to administrative agencies (Browning, Marshall, and Tabb 2003, 4).
Beyond having their voices heard or faces seen in the halls of governments,
politicized groups may also try to influence public decision making, policy
formulation, and policy execution as collaborators with government. They
may involve themselves in the politics of program design and implementation as partners of local governments and political representatives of groups
(S. Smith and Lipsky 1993; Evers 1995; Stone 1989; Mayer 1991 and 1998;
Orlebeke 1997; Cohen 2001; Rhomberg 2004).

Politicized groups in cities may select collaboration with government as
a calculated choice to influence public policy. They may act deliberately
through nongovernmental organizations to acquire governmental resources
and administrative power over public programs. The Community Action Program of the 1960s, for example, provided politicized blacks, especially those
with connections to local community-organizing campaigns and community
development organizations, access to public money and influence over its ex-
penditure (Greenstone and Peterson 1976). In the present era, this is possible
because of devolution.

Devolution involves "a transformation internal to the state that alters the
scale of activities, redefines government responsibilities for regulating civil
society, transfers authority across levels and administrative units of government, redraws the map of government costs and benefits, and changes accessi-
bility and entitlement to government services" (Kodras 1997, 81). Specifically,
three transfers occur. First, there is a shift of responsibility and authority from
the national government to state governments, primarily for the purposes of
programmatic experimentation. Second, there is a subsequent transfer of responsibility and authority from state governments to municipal governments
and nongovernmental institutions, in response to federal action. Third, there
is a shift of responsibility and authority from the national government directly
to municipal governments, again for the purposes of programmatic experimentation. The second and third shifts, in particular, create opportunities for

politicized groups to collaborate with government. This is because the shifts generally involve the transfer of responsibilities and authority over the implementation of programs from state and municipal governments to private institutions rather than public ones.

State and municipal governments depend on *private* institutions to execute *public* policy; they are "less the producer of goods and services, and more [the] supervisor of proxies who do the actual work" (Kettl 1993, 21).[17] The practice of supplying government services (i.e., the services that governments have decided to provide for their citizens) via private organizations, both commercial and nonprofit, instead of delivering the service through state or municipal workers, transfers the provision of government services from a system based on public organizations, accountability, and influence to a system with an ever-expanding role for nongovernmental organizations, as well as an ever-expanding influence of such organizations over public policies and programs (S. Smith and Lipsky 1993; Salamon 1995).[18]

Because of devolution, collaboration with local government by politicized nongovernmental groups is routine or becoming "routinized" (Howard, Lipsky, and Marshall 1994; Weir 1999).[19] Their forms of collaboration range from working loosely with government on separate activities with limited interaction between the groups and government (i.e., weak collaboration) to a tight system of collective action and power sharing by government and the groups (i.e., strong collaboration) to address collective problems (Rich, Giles, and Stern 2001).

In cities, most politicized groups that collaborate with government practice a relatively strong form of collaboration, working regularly and consistently with government to address collective problems. They behave in ways that cohere with the belief that routine access to the political system and partnership with public programs will yield increased influence within government venues and greater policy responsiveness by government to their issues. This has especially been the case for blacks seeking policy responsiveness from urban governments in the United States.

## COLLABORATION WITHIN THE CONTEXT OF URBAN AND RACIAL POLITICS

Collaboration with city government provides groups with a potential linkage for their constituents to participate in, and have their interests incorporated with, governance of collective concerns. In the process, collaboration with city government may pave for politicized groups a path to an administrative form of political enfranchisement, one that may permit them access to and influence over policymaking processes. This avenue—*bureaucratic enfranchisement*—is "a process by which the interests of a constituency are formally represented in government agencies so as to influence the manner in which electorally defined agency missions or program objectives are implemented. It is an output side process by which affected groups directly shape program strategies" (Fainstein and Fainstein 1982, 12; see also Fainstein and Fainstein 1974; Fainstein, Fainstein and Armistead 1983).

Bureaucratic enfranchisement results from groups' holding symbolic and substantive positions within policymaking arenas that allow them to voice their interests inside government and to participate in the planning and implementation of public programs. It places nongovernmental organizations "squarely in the political arena, where they must work their way through a maze of public and private centers of power" (Weir 1999, 139). Groups may bypass the electoral arena, while passing through other political arenas, namely public program development and implementation. Successful navigation of this maze offers a "resource-rich route to empowerment" (Ferman 1996, 41).

Therefore, the study of collaboration with city government as a means of political action by groups allows us to scrutinize whether partnership with public agencies provides groups with opportunities to aggregate the interests of their constituents, to position themselves better as interest representatives, and to guide the allocation of public resources in ways that accord with their interests. It permits us to examine how politicized groups that collaborate with government seek routine access to and influence in municipal government over the design and administration of programs in ways that accord with their interests and values and that meet the needs and expectations of their constituents. Through collaboration with public agencies, then, politicized groups may bring their constituents closer to government and government closer to their constituents.

Studying collaboration with government by African American churches, specifically, raises additional questions for the study of urban and racial politics.[20] May collaboration with city governments by African American churches serve to facilitate black participation in municipal policy initiatives, with the intent being greater government responsiveness to the interests of the black poor and distribution of public benefits to them? Does it help blacks in controlling, or at least sharing in, municipal decisions regarding the physical, economic, and social redevelopment of black neighborhoods? If, as Lawrence Bobo and Franklin Gilliam claim, "the black political agenda has shifted to the goal of maintaining, exploiting, and expanding the political and economic resources available to the black community" (1990, 338), is collaboration with city government a means of such maintenance, exploitation, and expansion? How might changes in mayoral administrations affect the endurance of church-state collaboration and African American churches' ability to influence the maintenance, exploitation, and expansion of political and economic resources available to the black community?

The ability of blacks, as a proxy for minority groups generally, to affect the decisions and outcomes of urban government, as well as urban government to affect blacks' acceptance of public policies and participation in policy implementation, has been the fundamental concern in the study of minority political incorporation in cities over the last thirty years (Greenstone and Peterson 1976; Browning, Marshall, and Tabb 1984, 1986, and 2003; Reed 1999; Stone 1989; Orr 1999; Henig et al. 1999; Jones-Correa 2001; Thompson 2006; Burns 2006; Marschall and Ruhil 2006). Political incorporation scholars primarily attend to assessing the openness of "governing coalitions" (strategic alliances among governmental and nongovernmental elites for deciding public issues, managing intergroup conflict, and resolving collective problems) to minorities.[21] They also identify the factors that permit the incorporation of minorities into governing coalitions, along with the limits and potential of minorities inside governing coalitions to increase accordance between government decisions and the interests and values of their constituents.

The scholarship tells us that policy responsiveness to black interests and values, which Rufus Browning, Dale Rogers Marshall, and David H. Tabb define in *Protest Is Not Enough* as "changes in city government policies [especially the distribution of public benefits] that respond to minority interests" (1984, 24), is determined by minority representatives who join governing coalitions to determine, guide, and enact public action to resolve collective problems. It also finds that minority representatives rely on community-based institutions to sustain their membership in governing coalitions and extract resources and opportunities for social change targeted at their constituents.[22] In fact, blacks have used activist African American churches as community-based organizations for participating in governing coalitions that have, in the words of Stone, the "capacity to act" (i.e., the power to make positive things happen) on behalf of their neighborhoods and their residents (Stone 1993).

When blacks via African American churches and their subsidiaries collaborate with government, however, are they actually able to support the political representation and incorporation of blacks, especially low-income blacks, in municipal politics? What degree of bureaucratic enfranchisement does church-state collaboration yield for blacks? Additionally, what are the direct (and indirect) effects of collaboration with government and bureaucratic enfranchisement, especially in exchange for public funding, on the political involvement of African American churches, particularly on behalf of the interests of low-income blacks? After all, politicians may use social welfare funds to purchase the silence of prophetic black voices on behalf of the poor, and policymakers may then reduce public responsibility for the problems the poor face in black communities.

What are the consequences of church-state collaboration for the prophetic voice and activism of the churches? How may it matter politically for the future of poor blacks? Does church-state collaboration reduce political engagement by African American churches (both as churches and through subsidiary organizations) on behalf of the interests of blacks, especially the black poor? Or does it encourage *greater* political involvement?

GLANCING FORWARD

This book has three parts. Part 1 surveys the scope and theoretical foundation of activist African American churches' collaboration with government. I claim in chapter 1 that collaboration with government is part of what my colleague Fredrick C. Harris (2001) terms the "civic tradition" of African American churches' engaging in political action, and I measure the extent of church-state partnerships today. Additionally, I explain why activist African American churches collaborate with government, why interest among African American churches in partnering with government is high, and why blacks as a group strongly support African American churches' participation in government programs to address poverty? Chapter 2 provides a theoretical consideration of collaboration with government as a mode of political engagement by African American churches, emphasizing the motives, opportunities, and means for such collaboration.

Part 2 opens my empirical study of church-state collaboration, focusing on why activist African American churches in New York City collaborate with government (see the Research Note for the reasons I chose New York City). Chapter 3, which is historically grounded, recounts the formation and decline of four black neighborhoods that became sites for church-state collaboration. It also reveals the limits of black descriptive representation in the post–World War II period and how the constraints influenced a set of churches to attempt to redevelop the four neighborhoods through the services of church-associated agencies, primarily community development corporations (CDCs), considered in chapter 4.

Part 3 looks inside the black box of church-state collaboration in New York City, especially in relation to affordable housing production. I chose affordable housing production as my policy lens because it is a domain where activist African American churches routinely collaborate with government in the United States. They often see affordable housing production as the anchor and catalyst for public and private investment in declining neighborhoods, as well as a symbol that tangible change is achievable. Furthermore, an emphasis on affordable housing production permits a clearer consideration than other policy domains (e.g., public safety, job training, or childcare) of the challenges, process, and effects of church-state collaboration. Thus part 3 examines the pushes and pulls and the process and products of church-state collaboration at the micro level. Chapter 5 shows how activist African American churches began to employ church-associated CDCs as their primary vehicles for collaborating with government, especially the municipal government, to address problems in black neighborhoods. Chapter 6 focuses on how churches, acting through CDCs, exchanged their participation in public-private partnerships to obtain resources, policy discretion from the city government, and opportunities to influence the implementation of public policy to the their advantage and that of their neighborhoods. Chapter 7 considers the act of collaboration with government in relation to the broader political engagement of the CDCs and the churches that chartered them.

The conclusion identifies new subjects for research that would advance our knowledge of church-state collaboration as political action practiced by activist African American churches. Moreover, it comments on the continued political utility of these churches on behalf of low-income black urban neighborhoods.

# * 1 *

## Scope and Theory of
## Church-State Collaboration

# The Extent and Support of African American Churches' Collaboration with Government

Wheat Street Baptist Church in Atlanta, Georgia, is "God's mighty fortress on Auburn Avenue where the doors swing back on welcome hinges." Founded by blacks in 1869, the church was elemental in the political mobilization of the city's blacks, before and during the civil rights movement. The political involvement of the church in local politics mirrored the involvement of its pastor. True to the classic definition of political participation (Verba and Nie 1972), the Reverend William Holmes Borders Sr. (pastor 1937–1988) engaged in activities directly aimed at the selection of local government officials and influencing the decisions that government officials made (Pomerantz 1996; Branch 1988).

In terms of electioneering, Borders was crucial to the inclusion of Atlanta's blacks as voters and elected officials. Recognizing that "you had to deliver to get what you wanted" from white politicians, he joined with leaders of other civic institutions (e.g., the Atlanta Urban League and Atlanta University) to initiate the historic black voter registration campaign that followed the 1946 abolition of the white primary system in Georgia by the U.S. Supreme Court (English 1967, 75; Bayor 1996). Serving on and devoting Wheat Street's resources to the All Citizen Registration Committee (ACRC), Borders participated that year in a "registration blitz" that within seven weeks added eighteen thousand new black voters to the registration rolls in Atlanta (Ferguson 2002, 254). The success of the ACRC marked what historian Clarence Bacote described as "the beginning of the period of Negro participation in Atlanta politics" (1955, 343–44). It also established blacks as the pivotal voters in citywide elections from the 1940s onward, and it increased the influence of another electoral organization that Borders belonged to, the Atlanta Negro Voters League, which vetted white and black candidates for office (Pomerantz 1996).

The electoral activities of the reverend eventually resulted in the election of blacks to public office on the local and state levels, beginning in the late 1950s.[1] In fact, Reverend Borders was instrumental in the electoral campaigns of almost every victorious black candidate, including the elections of Atlanta's first black school board member in 1953, black councilman in 1965, and black mayor in 1973.

As for protest Reverend Borders's actions at the local level were varied. He chaired the Committee of Action (COA), a group created after the 1945 lynching of four blacks, including two little girls, in Monroe, Georgia. He mobilized approximately a thousand black clergy under the banner of the COA to caravan to Monroe and deliver a message to its white political leadership: "We will not be intimidated, and we . . . petition for justice" (quoted in English 1967, 67–68). Borders also led the Triple L—"Love, Law, and Liberation"—movement to desegregate the buses of the Atlanta Transit Company in 1957 and chaired the Student Non-Violent League's Adult Liaison Committee, which financially, organizationally, and spiritually assisted youth in desegregating Atlanta's restaurants in 1961 (Bayor 1996; English 1967).

Yet the reverend did not limit his political participation, nor confine the resources of his church for political action, to electioneering and protest. Some black preachers have always known that "one way to serve their parishioners [and communities] is to be able to deliver goods and services obtainable from the political system" (Hamilton 1972, 111). In the late 1950s Reverend Borders served as a member of an urban redevelopment task force. He learned that federal policymakers had designed a new set of affordable housing production programs with financial incentives such as loans, loan guarantees, and tax credits for construction and development of affordable housing, especially in the nation's ghettoes. They also emphasized the participation of nongovernmental, community-based institutions. Specifically, the Federal Housing Administration's (FHA) Section 221(d)(3) and Section 236 programs provided 100 percent financing for development projects and government-backed construction loans to nonprofit organizations, especially churches, to develop, own, and manage affordable apartments, particularly for the elderly (Bratt 1989).

Reverend Borders thought about the utility of the affordable housing production programs for Atlanta's low-income black neighborhoods, especially those in the vicinity of his church. James English, a biographer of the reverend, describes a moment from the pastor's introspection:

> He hastened to his church study and there prayed. He prayed for guidance and the wisdom to understand this leviathan of government. With its multiple interlocking bureaus, regulations, and rulings, which so often appeared contradictory and always remained impersonal. Its bureaucratic nature aroused his suspicions, and caused him to feel that little good could come to the Negro people through this channel. . . . It was a confusing world. Yet in his conscience there spoke a small voice, warning that no promise of hope for the betterment of his people should be disregarded. (1967, 133)

Could some of the problems of low-income blacks in Atlanta be addressed via churches' working with government? Here was a chance, he reckoned, to channel the resources of government to poor black neighborhoods through the institution of the church, or at least a subsidiary of it. Such channeling held the potential to achieve a common goal of the government, the neighborhoods, and the church: the revitalization of depressed black spaces in the city. Following his reflection, Borders instructed his congregation to charter a nonprofit subsidiary, Church Homes Incorporated, to take advantage of the federal government's affordable housing programs.[2]

Through this nonprofit organization, incorporated in 1961, Wheat Street would assist the Atlanta Housing Authority to develop Wheat Street Garden Homes.[3] The homes constituted a moderate-income apartment complex located within walking distance of Atlanta's two central business districts, the black one along Auburn Avenue and the white one along Peachtree Street. Subsequently, Wheat Street Garden Homes became a pilot site for the Section 8 rent-subsidy program, another federal housing initiative that increased the supply of and access to affordable housing for low-income families. The church later used Church Homes Incorporated to develop more affordable housing through other federal programs such as the Section 202 elderly housing programs of the U.S. Department of Housing and Urban Development (HUD). All of this fit with its pastor's idea of "local productivity," the notion that blacks and their churches needed to show that they could and would bear some of the responsibility for improving conditions in their neighborhoods (English 1967, 155).

The example of Wheat Street Baptist Church is striking because its urban political history is so rich. It also reveals that the political involvement of urban activist African American churches, especially their clergy, goes beyond electioneering and protest. African American churches have lent their resources to political efforts to influence the *administration* and *implementation* of government officials' decisions. Furthermore, Wheat Street was among the first and the few activist African American churches in U.S. cities to partner with government during the nascent War on Poverty to reform conditions in low-income black neighborhoods (English 1967; Stone 1989; Pollard 2005).

The political behavior pioneered by Wheat Street endures in cities today. The resources of activist African American churches assist blacks in voting and marching against government, as well as enable them to work with government, to advance the interests and values of low-income neighborhoods. They also help blacks by seeking to ensure the delivery of public services.

## THE POLITICAL ENGAGEMENT TRADITION OF AFRICAN AMERICAN CHURCHES

The presence of activist African American churches in U.S. cities is important to the welfare of many poor blacks. Such churches provide at least emergency relief to the needy via soup kitchens, food pantries, and homeless shelters, and many offer comprehensive social welfare programs.[4] The churches hope and pray that their provisions will permit the poor to get through and maybe beyond their current impoverished circumstances, eventually living independent of alms and above the poverty line. Although munificence and missions in urban neighborhoods constitute a "civic tradition" (Harris 2001), many clergy and congregants of activist African American churches know that the provision of relief alone is insufficient.

The black faithful who question the adequacy of alms to overcome the afflictions and addictions of low-income blacks in cities view inner-city poverty as symptomatic of systemic societal wrongs that limit socioeconomic opportunity and mobility. They hold public policies and the behaviors of private institutions primarily responsible for the conditions of the urban black poor.[5] Black Christians who see the world, especially the endurance of the ghetto, through a political lens are sometimes able to move African American churches beyond benevolence. They may try to resolve race-based social inequities and encourage equality of opportunities through political action intended to change public policies. In the process, they fulfill another civic function and tradition of activist African American churches in cities: political engagement.

The tradition of political engagement by African American churches to advance the interests of and benefit black communities "stretches back to the Reconstruction era when black men first gained the right to vote" (Harris 2001, 141). It was then that activist African American churches first began to function as "political communities" that developed and transferred political messages and practices to effect individual and communal behavior directed at social change (Wald, Owen, and Hill 1998; Huckfeldt, Plutzer, and Sprague 1993). The churches became sites for political meetings and rallies, while clergy included political, even partisan, messages in their sermons, ran for elected office, and negotiated policy changes with white elites (Montgomery 1993, 153–90). "In the absence of any other grass-roots political organizations," as one history of southern African American churches during Reconstruction explains, "the churches were the only means by which political leaders could organize and mobilize constituencies" for political action (Montgomery 1993, 157). From Reconstruction onward, activist African American churches in the cities of the South and the North functioned as political communities. They still do today (Calhoun-Brown 1996; Harris 1999; Smith and Smidt 2003; Smith and Harris 2005).

"Politically speaking," however, "all African American churches are not created equal" (Calhoun-Brown 1996, 946). There has never been an expectation that all of them must be politically engaged. Many African American churches do not participate in the black political struggle for policy responsiveness.[6] This has been true for decades.

Political scientist Ralph Bunche for instance, derisively asserted at the dawning of the civil rights movement in the 1940s that African American churches "preached thunder and lightning, fire and brimstone, and Moses out of the bulrushes, but about the economic and political exploitation of . . . blacks they have remained silent" (1973, 501). Likewise, amid the demands and demonstrations of the civil rights movement in the 1960s, social psychologist Kenneth B. Clark remarked that "the black church is basically irrelevant to the hard and difficult realities of race. . . . Historically, it compromised on moral and social issues, obscuring them by abstruse theological debate" (1967, 178). Then in the 1970s one group of scholars noted, "It is generally agreed by social scientists . . . that given the black churches' vast political resources—which include a ready following, meeting facilities, and a unifying spiritualism—the average [church] has failed to realize [its] full potential as a political leader and as an inspiration for collective action in the black community" (Berenson, Elifson, and Tollerson 1976, 374).

Numerous African American churches continued their political inaction over the last decade of the twentieth century and into the next one.[7] There is even evidence that politically active African American churches have reduced their engagement: whereas 25 percent of black clergy at the beginning of 2000 described their churches as "very active" during the civil rights movement, approximately 15 percent of them described their churches as "very active" at the end of the twentieth century (Smith and Smidt 2003, 62).[8]

Even so, there has never been an expectation that politically active African American churches, or clergy serving as their proxies, would practice a particular form of political engagement. No single activity constitutes and encompasses the political tradition of African American churches (Hamilton 1972; Welty 1969; Sawyer 2001; Taylor 1994). Like U.S. churches of other stripes, African American churches and their leaders have always had choices when it comes to their political engagement (Wald 2003). But two broad categories of political engagement stand out in histories of the political tradition of African American churches, especially when we equate black clergy with their churches. The first is mobilization and the second is brokerage.

*Mobilization* refers to the process of influencing and permitting others to participate politically for themselves, with others or alone. Mobilization takes two forms, direct and indirect (Rosenstone and Hansen 1993). In direct mobilization, groups, both leaders and members, make direct contact with prospective political participants and seek to affect political attitudes and behaviors. In indirect mobilization, leaders and groups reach out to prospective political participants though their friends, families, peers, and associates to influence their political participation. Groups may employ both direct and indirect mobilization when they protest and electioneer and when they collaborate with government; for example, a group may partner with government to deliver services in a neighborhood while organizing neighborhood residents to lobby for more responsiveness.

African American churches, like all religious congregations, have two types of resources available for political mobilization: material and cultural.[9] The former are tangible, substantive, and physical assets, such as indigenous, charismatic, and skilled leaders, sites for deliberation and exchange of information, communications networks, mass memberships and volunteers, social capital, and money, that churches use to organize efforts for political action. The latter are cognitive, intangible, and rhetorical properties, such as passages from sacred narratives, songs, and texts, a theological worldview, racial and class identity and consciousness, and religious-inspired efficacy and moral imperatives, that churches use to induce and sustain political participation by their members and other audiences. Politicized African American churches have used both types of resources to mobilize blacks, both churchgoers and others, to participate politically, especially through electioneering and protest.[10]

Electioneering involves politicized groups' mobilizing their resources as a voting bloc to affect policies and social conditions through the selection of decision makers. It relies on mass mobilization through partisan means and vehicles. Needs and interests are given expression through the routine competition to acquire and hold elective office. Electioneering may yield greater descriptive representation of a group, if it brings in enough votes to grant them greater incorporation in elected bodies and administrative agencies responsible for implementing policy. Incorporation via the franchise and representation may produce policy changes that advantage a group, or at least do not disadvantage them in relation to other groups.

Protest involves politicized groups' mobilizing their resources to make public objections for the purpose of forcing decision makers to change policies and conditions. It is radical in its tenor, often seeking wholesale transformation of political structures and new distributions of public resources. Protest often requires mass mobilization (i.e., appeals to and inclusion of large numbers of actors to engage in contentious action). It expresses the needs and interests of groups through disturbance, disruption, and demand. Protest may increase descriptive representation of a group by achieving appointments of its members to administrative agencies. In turn, descriptive representation may yield substantive representation or responsiveness to the interests, values, and needs of the group through public policy.

Throughout American history, the resources of African American churches have led millions of blacks to the polls as voters and candidates and moved many to the streets as demonstrators and protesters, often motivated by moral outrage and working in alliance with other institutions of civil society.[11] This suggests that African American "churches have the capacity not only to coordinate the tangible [material] and intangible [cultural] resources needed for political action but to impact the motivations and consciousness of individuals as well" (Calhoun-Brown 1996, 951). African American churches proved it during the insurgency of the civil rights movement of the 1950s and 1960s and in the subsequent transition from protest to politics in the 1970s and 1980s (Grimshaw 1992; McAdam 1999; Morris 1984; Harris 1999; Tate 1993; Smith and Harris 2005).

There is, however, another way that some African American churches and their leaders have involved themselves politically: black pastors who favored political engagement through the resources of African American churches have selected *brokerage*. Brokerage is the process of acting politically on behalf of others by identifying, expressing, and acting on their political interests, values, and wants. In brokerage, nominated or self-appointed agents function as negotiators, arrangers, and deliverers of benefits to a group. Brokers transfer political messages from the masses to the elite and political resources (symbolic and substantive) from the elite to the masses. They often privilege elite political participation over mass participation through mobilization.

Historically, black clergy functioning primarily as brokers rather than mobilizers have preferred to represent the race rather than empower its members to represent themselves at the polls or in the streets via mobilization (Welty 1969). Their manner of politics favored accommodation and mollification, which fit with black bourgeois convention and extended the peacemaking tradition of black clergy as ambassadors to white power, which first arose under Reconstruction.[12] All of this dovetailed with "race politics," which was presumably beneficial to all blacks, though, according to Martin Kilson, "in reality it was of benefit more to the elites than to the urban Negro masses" (1971, 171). Brokerage sidelined the majority of blacks from political contests in the city, and it often retarded the development of mass-based political participation in black neighborhoods.

In the past, much of the brokerage by African American churches involved a clergyperson who individually coordinated interactions between the city government and a black community (Montgomery 1993; Sernett 1997; Wilson 1965; Kilson 1971). Black clergy served as intermediaries between government and black communities.[13] Indeed "black ministers [were] commonly designated the natural political leaders and interest brokers in the black community" (Berenson, Elifson, and Tollerson 1976, 374). Although brokerage continues today, black clergy are no longer the only brokers associated with African American churches. Nonprofit subsidiaries associated with individual African American churches or collections of them, known in present-day parlance as "faith-based organizations," are political brokers in cities, too. This is evident in the actions of churches involved in faith-based welfare reform initiatives from New York to California, as well as other cases of church-government collaboration.

Collaboration with government, again, involves groups' deliberately using their resources to work in concert with government decision makers and agencies to change a set of conditions through agreed-upon policies and programs, with the nongovernmental groups bearing much of the responsibility for implementation. It is similar to electioneering but different from protest in its core emphasis on a group's acquiring positions of authority and influence for its representatives from and within public agencies to change public policy. Collaboration is also similar to electioneering in the tenor of political struggle involved, for both are moderate forms of engagement that seek modest structural and distributive reforms, unlike traditional protest.

Whether practiced by clergy or by a faith-based organization, collaboration with government does not require mass mobilization. "Even as it comes dressed in invocations of 'the people' or 'the masses,'" Adolph Reed Jr. cautions that brokerage via collaboration with government "is not an approach that leads to popular mobilization," at least not all of the time. Rather, collaboration often relies on elite mobilization. Reed clarifies the point: "It's ultimately a form of high-level negotiation; its main practice is assuming the voice of a putatively coherent black community and projecting it toward policymakers. . . . The 'people' don't get to speak; they are spoken for" (2000, 4–5). Thus, collaboration is characterized by the routine competition of elite-led interest groups and elite-based cooperation with the public sector to coproduce programs and implement policies. Collaboration with government may augment the descriptive representation of groups, especially through their incorporation in bureaucratic bodies, which may then yield greater substantive representation of groups through bureaucratic enfranchisement.

### FROM MINISTER-MACHINE POLITICS TO CHURCH-STATE COLLABORATION

One may ask, is church-state collaboration as a form of brokerage much different from the patron-client politics of yesterday, when white politicians gave black pastors modest loans and grants to pay church debts or provided black ministers with petty patronage jobs to distribute to a few of their congregants in exchange for a predictable bloc of votes on Election Day? Certainly, minister-machine politics have not disappeared, and we might even expect to see more of it in the current age of church-state partnerships (Harris 2001 and 2005). Nevertheless, church-state collaboration is qualitatively different from the pastor-politician patronage of the past in at least three ways: the motivations of white politicians, the mix of congregations involved, and the centrality of faith-related agencies.

### *The Motivations of White Politicians*

In earlier periods, white politicians, particularly mayors, had straightforward electoral motivation for linking with African American churches: to secure black votes. In the 1960s, for example, Mayor Richard M. Daley distributed public funds to black preachers to align them politically with his machine, motivate them to endorse its candidates and campaigns, and gain black votes on its behalf. Today public funding of African American churches, both the rhetoric and the reality of it, is used by some white politicians to corral a greater proportion of black votes, as well as Latino votes, during elections. It is understudied by scholars and rarely revealed by politicians.[14] But as Stephen Goldsmith, former mayor of Indianapolis and a chief proponent of faith-based and community initiatives, writes in a study of the reasons mayors pursue partnerships with churches, "politics is surely connected to some of this type of work, even if not a primary factor" (2003, 5).

Further, though the politician may indeed be seeking black votes, the use of church-state partnerships, as well as more general compassion-based political appeals, may be a tactic to secure and retain *white* votes, especially those of conservatives and evangelical Christians and socially moderate suburban women (Kuo 2006; Formicola, Segers, and Weber 2003; Wald 2003; Wuthnow 2004; Hutchings et al. 2004). Beyond the electoral motivation, however, politicians may have an ideological motivation for supporting church-state partnerships.[15]

Social conservatives, especially self-identified evangelicals, argue that spiritual loss, religious disassociation, and a lack of ethical development are among the greatest obstacles to self-sufficiency among the poor (Olasky 1992 and 1997; Mead 2003; Murray 1994; Emerson and Smith 2000). In short, poverty results from moral failure. If we assume that people are poor because they possess poor values and make poor decisions, we may conclude that the involvement of value-bearing and value-enforcing institutions such as congregations in public-funded social welfare programs would reduce poverty. Indeed, social services provided by religious institutions, especially congregations and church-associated nonprofits, might succeed where government failed in transitioning the poor to self-sufficiency. This leads back to the electoral motivation of white politicians.

Defining urban poverty in terms of moral values and behaviors and proposing faith-based and community initiatives as a policy solution may lay the groundwork for fiscal reductions in government programs for the poor. The potential reduction in public outlays appeals to conservative, as well as libertarian, voters, while the emphasis on religious institutions as partners of government appeals broadly to public opinion and narrowly to evangelical Christians (Pew Research Center for the People and the Press 2001a). That is, the electorate generally favors the promotion of religion in the public square and public subsidies of religious groups.[16]

None of this is to deny that church-state partnerships may be intended to secure or control black votes. Instead, it is to point out that the political and ideological motivations behind church-state partnership differ somewhat from the reasons that white politicians favored minister-machine politics in the past.

## *The Congregational Mix*

The types of African American churches and black clergy likely to engage in church-state collaboration, directly through their congregations or indirectly through church-associated entities, generally diverge from those that were likely to maintain patronage relationships with white politicians in the past. In *Negro Politics,* James Q. Wilson reported that the urban African American churches likely to seek and receive public resources from political machines in the 1950s and 1960s were large congregations, "characteristically Baptist or Pentecostal, with large followings among lower-income Negroes. Another group of ministers, often better-educated and with wealthier congregations, [were] suspicious of [patron-client relationships] in particular and of politics in general" (1965, 127).

Contemporary studies of congregations generally, regardless of racial composition, are inconclusive regarding whether larger congregations, especially megachurches, are more likely to partner with public agencies than smaller ones (Chaves 1999; Owens 2006; Tucker-Worgs 2002). Many small and medium-sized congregations are in alliance with each other or with larger congregations and jointly operate organizations that collaborate with government to yield tangible benefits for their communities (Clemetson and Coates 1992). An illustration of this is the development of twenty-three hundred units of affordable housing in the East New York section of Brooklyn by the Nehemiah initiative of a multiracial, multiethnic alliance of small to medium-sized congregations under the banner East Brooklyn Congregations (Freedman 1993; Ross 1996).

As for denomination, Methodist congregations are as likely as, if not more than, Baptists and Pentecostals to seek and receive public aid to operate social welfare programs, especially through church-associated organizations (Tucker-Worgs 2002; Frederick 2001; Billingsley 1999). Concerning the class of congregations, middle-class congregations seem more likely than congregations of poorer blacks to pursue collaborations with government agencies (Tucker-Worgs 2002; Frederick 2001; Billingsley 1999). That is, resource-rich churches may be most likely to seek government funding (Bositis 2006). As for clergy, educational attainment may not predict whether black clergy or their churches will support church-state collaboration. Clergy with college degrees and professional training may be as likely as, if not more than, those with lower levels of educational attainment to pursue collaborations with government agencies.

## *The Centrality of Faith-Related Agencies*

Pastors and politicians are the central figures in patron-client politics. In contrast, clergy are not necessarily the primary participants when churches collaborate with public agencies, although the opinions and guidance of the clergy may inform and influence the partnerships. Church-state collaboration is professionalized and relies on "faith-related agencies," not clergy and often not congregations (S. Smith and Sossin 2001).[17] Faith-related agencies are distinct from congregations. The former are groups with "a formal funding or administrative arrangement with a religious authority or authorities; a historical tie of this kind; a specific commitment to act within the dictates of a particular established faith; or a commitment to work together that stems from a common religion" (S. Smith and Sossin, 2001, 652). Congregations are collectives of individuals brought together for the practice and promotion of religious worship and education (Chaves 2004).

Faith-related agencies are often the primary means by "which congregations do their work in the community" (Ammerman 2002, 147). They include nonprofit subsidiaries of individual congregations and faith-based social service coalitions, with the coalitions sometimes being ecumenical institutions but almost always possessing resources and governance structures distinct from congregations, partnering with secular groups and agencies, and pursuing and receiving government funding to operate their programs (Ebaugh, Chafetz, and Pipes 2005). In exchange for public contracts and grants to deliver social welfare, faith-related agencies permit government oversight of their finances and public regulation of their services.[18]

## THE MEASUREMENT AND SCALE OF COLLABORATION WITH GOVERNMENT

*All churches that collaborate with government involve partnerships with government, but not all partnerships with government equal churches collaborating with government.* Whether a church receives funds from government agencies to provide or expand social services programs is the conventional metric for measuring the proportion of congregations that partner with government to provide social welfare services (Chaves 1998 and 2004; Bositis 2006). It is the measure I use to estimate the extent of church-state collaboration by African American churches over time. However, it is an indirect and less than ideal measure of collaboration with government as a form of political engagement by activist African American churches.

Gauging the proportion of activist African American churches that collaborate with government (i.e., deliberately use their partnerships to attempt to affect policy and responsiveness) and whether it is increasing is difficult. The standard metric does not control for the intentions behind churches' receiving public money to provide social services. For my purposes, collaboration is a political act, and for a church's partnership with government to be called collaboration, there must be a conscious intent to affect public policy in some way.

African American churches that receive public funding may or may not be concerned with affecting government responsiveness to low-income neighborhoods. They may intend only to serve their members; they may want to merely increase the revenue of their church; or they may fail to conceive of the possibility that they could use their position as agents of the state to try to affect government responsiveness (McRoberts 2003; Laudarji and Livezey 2000; Pattillo-McCoy 1998). Accordingly, the measure may overstate the proportion of churches that collaborate with government.

Additionally, the measure does not differentiate between churches directly receiving public funding to provide services and churches indirectly receiving it through faith-related agencies, particularly a church-associated subsidiary such as Wheat Street's Church Homes Incorporated. Many churches, in fact, prefer not to receive public money in their coffers. This preference is common among African American churches: they favor directing public funding to and through faith-related agencies chartered by and standing legally and financially separate from their congregation (Watkins 1998; Reed 1994; W. T. Walker 1994; D. Walker 2001).[19]

Plus, the metric is inappropriate for measuring the proportion of churches that ally with each other to operate a single faith-related agency (e.g., East Brooklyn Congregations) to receive public funding and potentially affect the design and implementation of "public" services. Therefore, the measure may actually undercount the number of churches that collaborate with government, especially given that faith-related agencies are pivotal to the partnerships between churches and government agencies and that alliances of churches may create such agencies. So the study of activist African American churches collaborating with government often requires one to concurrently keep in view two units of analysis—churches and faith-related agencies.

The metric, furthermore, ignores those churches that partner with government for free. Not all church-state partnerships involve money. Arguably, much church-state interaction is voluntary, with churches acting for free. Much of the work performed by African American churches in support of government objectives involves the recruitment of volunteers to provide services that require consistent commitment (e.g., ministering to inmates, fixing meals, and being available to youth) but do not require a great deal of planning, concern about financial sustainability, or reliance on many volunteers (Chaves 2004; Chaves and Tsitsos 2001; Barnes 2004; Owens and Smith 2005; Laudarji and Livezey 2000). Their most common types of services involve relief (e.g., food for the hungry), redemption (e.g., ministering to the incarcerated), and recreation (e.g., youth activities). Consequently, churches may provide services without government funding, but their provision is in accordance with government objectives and publicly legitimated by government through acknowledgment and accolades. Again, this means that our broad-brush criterion would understate the extent of partnerships between churches and government agencies.

Finally, the measure does not distinguish among the faces of collaboration. It does not draw a distinction between collaboration as co-optation and collaboration as empowered cooperation. Some churches that partner with government may find themselves captured by it and weakened in their ability to represent the interests of their community. Other churches may maintain their independence to advocate for their community's interests and may gain the ability to work with government from a strengthened position because of their possession of pivotal resources.

Beyond the challenges posed by the metric for measuring church-state collaboration, datasets containing the metric are problematic. Survey data on the political involvement of African American churches tend to come from samples biased toward activist churches and churches affiliated with denominations. Much of the bias is attributable to the undetermined universe of African American churches and the lack of comprehensive mailing and telephone calling lists for them.[20] Therefore, depending on the dataset, we may be able to make only tentative statements about the degree to which African American churches receive public funding, let alone the extent to which they collaborate with government, as defined above.

Keeping in mind the aforementioned measurement and methodological caveats regarding determining the extent of collaboration with government by churches, what proportion of African American churches *might* be using their partnerships with government as opportunities to possibly influence policy, as gauged by their receipt of public funding? Data from two sources, the Joint Center for Political and Economic Studies and the Public Influences of African American Churches Project, which are the most recent and best attempts to derive national data on African American churches, suggest that between 11 and 24 percent of African American churches receive public funding to operate social welfare programs (Bositis 2006; Smith and Smidt 2003).[21]

Are some activist African American churches more likely than others to collaborate with government? Is collaboration with government a function of church size, whether measured by memberships or by financial resources? Does denomination affect the volition of churches to collaborate with government? Social scientists' ability to determine which types of activist African American churches are most likely to collaborate with government, let alone partner with government, is constrained; we lack nationally representative or public data with variables measuring church-state collaboration and including a sufficient sample of African American churches.[22]

Still, should we expect a larger proportion of African American churches to collaborate with government in the future, *if* the opportunity is available to them? Yes, for many more African American churches at the close of the 1990s wanted to partner than could. Data from the 1996 National Congregations Study, which relies on a random sample of congregations in the United States, reveal that almost three-quarters (71 percent) of clergy leading majority-black churches say that their churches would apply for government money to provide social welfare services in their neighborhood (Chaves 1998). Moreover, when other factors are held constant, African American churches are more likely than other congregations to claim that they would pursue public funding to provide social services for the poor, if there were opportunities to obtain it (Chaves 1999; Chaves and Tsitsos 2001). This finding especially holds for metropolitan areas with high concentrations of blacks and African American churches. As table 1 shows, African American churches in metropolitan Atlanta, for instance, are five times more likely than other churches to pursue public funds to operate or expand social welfare programs ($p = 0.000$).[23]

## THE BLACK POLITY AND CHURCH-STATE COLLABORATION

Within the black polity there is strong and consistent support for church-state collaboration. Compared to the general populace, blacks overwhelmingly favor churches' and faith-related agencies' collaboration with government.

TABLE 1 Determinants of the willingness of congregations to partner with government

*Logistic regression. Dependent variable: whether a congregation would apply for public funding to provide social services, if given an opportunity.*

| INDEPENDENT VARIABLES | B | S.E. | Exp(B) |
|---|---|---|---|
| **Congregation Attributes** | | | |
| Majority-black (≥50 percent of members are black) | 1.629*** | 0.403 | 5.101 |
| Denomination (reference: Baptist) | | | |
| Mainline Protestant | 1.215** | 0.429 | 3.369 |
| Catholic | 1.550 | 0.951 | 4.713 |
| Other Christian denomination | 0.677 | 0.418 | 1.969 |
| Congregation size (reference: <100 members) | | | |
| 100–499 members | −0.378 | 0.436 | 0.685 |
| 500 or more members | 0.088 | 0.490 | 1.092 |
| Clergy age | −0.034** | 0.013 | 0.967 |
| Clergy education (college-educated) | −0.671 | 0.551 | 0.511 |
| Church provides social welfare services | 0.671* | 0.323 | 1.957 |
| Church partners with secular (nongovernmental) organizations to address community problems | 1.132** | 0.403 | 3.102 |
| **Clergy Attitudes** | | | |
| Fears public funding would entangle government with religion | −0.974** | 0.327 | 0.378 |
| Fears public funding would increase competition among religious groups | −0.478 | 0.569 | 0.620 |
| Fears public funding would upset church-state separation | −0.925* | 0.411 | 0.396 |
| Hopes religion can transform the lives of the poor | 0.510 | 0.405 | 1.666 |
| Hopes congregations would provide more compassionate services than secular groups | 0.550 | 0.392 | 1.734 |
| Hopes congregations would provide more efficient services than government | 0.363 | 0.347 | 1.438 |

Constant = −0.613***; Pseudo-$R^2$ = 0.417
−2 log likelihood = 257.221
Number of cases = 274

Notes: All respondents are pastors. Entries are standardized regression estimates.
*$p \leq .05$; **$p \leq .01$; ***$p \leq .001$
Source: 2002 Faith and the City Survey of Metropolitan Atlanta Clergy

Among adult blacks, 92 percent favor congregations in their communities working with government to aid the poor, with 80 percent opining that religious organizations (congregations and faith-related agencies) should be allowed to apply for government money to provide social services (Wuthnow 2000; Pew Research Center for the People and the Press 2002).[24] Of course, not all blacks agree that churches should collaborate with government. Table 2 identifies four variables that are statistically significant predictors, after measures of religiosity, attitudes toward government and such partnerships, and demographic characteristics have been controlled for, of strong support by blacks for churches' applying for public funding to provide social services to the poor.[25]

First, blacks who attend churches that are nondenominational are ten times as likely as those who attend denominational congregations to strongly support churches' working with government ($p$ = 0.020). Second, where blacks live also influences their support for churches' partnering with government: the odds that a black adult will strongly support church-state partnerships nearly quadruples if she or he lives in a city rather than a suburban area ($p$ = 0.002). Third, blacks who believe faith-based social welfare organizations have more caring and compassionate employees than do secular (governmental and nongovernmental) organizations are seven times more likely to strongly support churches' partnering with government agencies than are other blacks ($p$ = 0.000). Finally, the belief that allowing congregations to apply for public funding would upset church-state separation by entangling government with religion decreases the odds of strong support for church-state partnerships by approximately 64 percent ($p$ = 0.001).

The strong support by blacks for church-state collaboration is informed by the ideology of community nationalism.[26] Community nationalism values community control, autonomous organizations, and self-determination; it privileges collective action and civil society as the founts of community reforms (Carmichael and Hamilton 1967; Dawson 2001; Brown and Shaw 2002; R. Bush 1999; Simpson 1998; Harris-Lacewell 2004). These values, which are as old as the oldest African American church, are rooted in the historic firmament of black uplift and have the greatest influence on black public opinion today. Furthermore, community nationalism rejects racial separatism as a means or end of black empowerment. While strongly tied to a disillusioned liberalism among blacks that stems from racism in the United States, community nationalism does not necessarily call for antiliberalism or antistatism, though it favors self-initiative (Dawson 2001; P. Smith 1999).[27]

TABLE 2 Determinants of black support for church-state collaboration

*Logistic regression. Dependent variable: Favors allowing churches and other houses of worship, along with other organizations, to apply for government funding to provide social services.*

| INDEPENDENT VARIABLES | | B | S.E. | Exp(B) |
|---|---|---|---|---|
| **Attributes** | Attends church regularly (at least biweekly) | .799 | .647 | 2.223 |
| | Attends church sometimes (monthly or less) | −.033 | .582 | .967 |
| | Attends a Baptist church | −.025 | .375 | .976 |
| | Attends a Methodist church | .004 | .579 | 1.004 |
| | Attends a nondenominational church | 2.335* | 1.007 | 10.328 |
| | Gender (female) | −.002 | .312 | .998 |
| | Age (years) | −.016 | .010 | .984 |
| | Education (≤H.S. diploma) | −.224 | .337 | .799 |
| | Resides in a city | 1.253** | .407 | 3.502 |
| | Resides in a rural area | .527 | .554 | 1.694 |
| | Moderate-income household ($20,000 < $40,000) | −.172 | .406 | .842 |
| | Middle-income household ($40,000 < $75,000) | −.300 | .565 | .741 |
| | High-income household (≥$75,000) | .856 | .916 | 2.354 |
| **Attitudes** | Believes public funding of congregations would upset separation of church and state, entangling government with religion | −1.016*** | .319 | .362 |
| | Believes faith-based organizations have more caring and compassionate employees than secular organizations (governmental and nongovernmental) | 1.993*** | .376 | 7.338 |
| **Interactions** | Attends church regularly × Middle-income household | −.403 | .682 | .668 |
| | Attends church regularly × High-income household | −1.177 | 1.064 | .308 |

Constant = −.407***; Pseudo $R^2$ = .304
−2 log likelihood = 294.466
Number of cases = 223

Notes: All respondents are blacks over the age of 18 years. Entries are standardized regression estimates.
*$p \leq .05$; **$p \leq .01$; ***$p \leq .001$
Source: 2001 Pew Forum on Religion, Religion and Public Life Survey

Self-initiative, borrowing from the conceptual argument of community development theorists Donald Littrell and Daryl Hobbs, is "based on the premise that people can, will, and should collaborate [with other individuals and institutions] to solve community problems. . . . It embodies the notion that a community can achieve greater self-determination within constraints imposed by the larger political economy in which it is embedded" (1989, 48). If day care is needed in a community, black civil society should use its resources to leverage those of other institutions in and beyond the community to open centers. Thus, *interdependence* characterizes self-initiative.[28] In the process, the conventional dichotomy—"bootstrap or government"—becomes irrelevant, for community nationalists accommodate the necessity of both for black socioeconomic advancement (Harris-Lacewell 2004, 60–62).

Community nationalism may oppose governmental interference in local decision making and neighborhood programming in black communities on the grounds of self-determination and community control, but its adherents welcome investment by government and other institutions to support their work. They are willing to leverage internal effort to secure external support, in contrast to the "self-help" efforts of separatist nationalists who ignore the potential for and avoid external support, especially from government. As Robert Brown and Todd Shaw demonstrate empirically, community nationalists are open to cooperating with "partners external to the black community" (2002, 30). They also are "attentive to [the ideology] precisely because it mixes black civil autonomy strategies with control over public institutions. [Supporters] prefer efforts at black control of public and private institutions in black communities, but not to the exclusion of strategic coalitions with other groups," including government agencies (Brown and Shaw 2002, 26). Hence community nationalism permits, even proposes, black participation and partnership with government.[29]

Some blacks are a more attentive audience for and greater supporters of community nationalism than are other blacks. Table 3, which relies on data from the 1993 National Black Politics Study, demonstrates that blacks who are members of black uplift organizations or who display the strongest form of group consciousness—linked fate[30]—are more likely to support community nationalism than blacks unaffiliated with uplift organizations or those with a weaker group consciousness.[31] Furthermore, blacks with higher family incomes support community nationalism more than blacks of lower family incomes. Also, younger blacks favor community nationalism more than older blacks do. More central to the subject of this book, *community-oriented*

TABLE 3  Predictors of community nationalism
*OLS. Dependent variable: four-item index measuring support for community nationalism.*

| INDEPENDENT VARIABLES | B | S.E. |
|---|---|---|
| Believes African American churches should be involved in political matters | .151**** | .105 |
| Attends church that provides community outreach programs | .065* | .105 |
| Black linked fate | .108** | .099 |
| Family income | .085** | .132 |
| Years of education | .025 | 1.316 |
| Age | −.099* | .242 |
| Female | −.011 | .079 |
| Respondent from South | −.054 | .074 |
| Liberal-conservative ideology (1 = strong liberal) | .054 | .107 |
| Member of black organization that works to improve the status of blacks | .083** | .086 |
| Perceived race of interviewer (1 = white or other) | −.109*** | .093 |

Adjusted $R^2$ = .110
Standard error of the estimate = .92
Number of cases = 635

Notes: All respondents are blacks over the age of 18 years. Dependent variable ranges from 0 to 1. Entries are standardized regression estimates.
*$p \le .10$; **$p \le .05$; ***$p \le .005$; ****$p \le .001$

*religiosity* and a *positive attitude toward church involvement in politics* both have positive and significant correlations with community nationalism.

It is understandable that blacks who favor church involvement in politics support community nationalism. They view the achievement of black control over the behaviors of local government and local economies in their neighborhoods as being possible mainly through churches' becoming political communities and political actors. Also, blacks who advocate the political engagement of churches find community nationalism appealing because the ethos fits with their sense of the history and presumed role of African American churches in black civil society— that they have been and should be institutions of black self-determination, fostering collective action and pursuing racial uplift.

Outreach or "institutional" churches have historically been central to and authoritative in black civil society, especially in terms of addressing negative social conditions and their effects (Mays and Nicholson 1933; Frazier 1964; Sernett 1997; Wilmore 1983; Taylor 1994; Billingsley 1999). Activist churches demonstrate community nationalism in action. Attendance at such churches positively influences attitudes regarding the need and potential of black-led institutions to address problems at the local level.

Furthermore, most activist African American churches are "mainstream" churches; they are "committed, at least in theory, to a reformist strategy of social activism that will enable African Americans to become better integrated into the political, economic, and social institutions of the larger society," not separate from them (Baer and Singer 1992, 58–59; also Harris 1999, 63–65).[32] This makes sense because a majority of blacks believe that government should do more to help needy people, even if it requires cuts in other programs or delaying tax cuts: 84 percent of blacks favor more generous government assistance to the poor (Pew Research Center for the People and the Press 2002). But blacks, along with the general public, believe that government working alone is inadequate to reduce problems in low-income neighborhoods (Pew Research Center for the People and the Press 2001a). They favor government's working in concert with civil society, particularly churches and other religious organizations.[33]

## SUMMARY

This chapter identified mobilization and brokerage as broad ways that activist African American churches have engendered political participation by blacks and used their resources politically on behalf of blacks. Collaboration with government belongs within the latter category. Having considered the percentage of African American churches that collaborate with government, I have provided evidence that there is strong support within the black polity for church-state collaboration. Certain attributes and attitudes of blacks predict strong support for church-state collaboration, particularly the overarching ideology of community nationalism. Still, while a majority of blacks support church-state collaboration, only a minority of black churches collaborate with government. Why? A mixed set of motives, opportunities, and means determines the political engagement of religious organizations in the United States (Wald 2003, 26). Churches' choice to collaborate with government is no different.

# CHAPTER TWO

# The Volition to Collaborate
# with Government

A minority of African American churches partner with government, but a majority of them *would* do it if given the chance. And a super-majority of blacks would support their doing it. Why African American churches work with government, or are willing to do so, rather than work apart from it remains a fundamental question.

One explanation is that public policies are, as a theologian puts it, "seducing the Samaritan" (Roberts 2003). The thinking is that African American churches work with government because government seeks and induces their assistance, which it does (Cisneros 1996; Bush 2001 and 2003; Goldsmith 2000; Ashcroft 2003). Another explanation of the choice by African American churches to collaborate with government is that they are responding to the enduring poverty predicament (Bartkowski and Regis 2003; Ammerman 2005). Churches located in or proximate to impoverished black neighborhoods may simply want to reform the social conditions of those neighborhoods, using any resources available. Perhaps theological and religious convictions account for much of the choice by African American churches to partner with government (Bartkowski and Regis 2003; Ammerman 2005; McRoberts 2003). American history is replete with instances of the faithful acting out of religious imperatives. We should not doubt that theology and religious belief may inform churches' choices concerning political behavior, including their choice to partner with the public sector to create opportunities to collaborate with government.

Each conventional explanation has face validity. Yet they remain inadequate individually or jointly as determinants of collaboration with government by African American churches. For instance, it is plausible that the actions of government account for why African American churches collaborate with government (Roberts 2003; Bartkowski and Regis 2003; Monsma 1996; Farnsley 2003). But the simple fact that government invites churches to participate with it does not mean that churches will accept the invitation. Thus, it is questionable whether public policy affects the social welfare activities of congregations in the United States, directly or indirectly (Wineburg 2001; Cnaan 2002).

Likewise, the scale of poverty and churches' proximity to it has little effect on the social welfare behavior of most African American churches (McRoberts 2003). If it did, we would expect to have seen most congregations in poor neighborhoods joining forces and working with government to foster neighborhood change. But most churches in poor neighborhoods do not partner with government, and many churches that provide social welfare choose to work independent of other churches (Chaves 1998; Owens and Smith 2005).

As for underscoring theological and religious convictions, such an emphasis fails to identify why churches would choose to collaborate with government versus choosing another mode of political engagement or choosing to work independently of the state to provide social welfare. Moreover, many individuals of faith are guided by religious tenets and values to remain *separate* from government. Some of the faithful even assume an oppositional stance toward the state.

To comprehend completely the choice by African American churches to collaborate with government, we need to give greater attention to (1) the goals of clergy in relation to such partnerships and (2) the occasions for and the capacity of churches to collaborate with government. In particular, the effects of changes in social welfare policies, especially in the last decade, and of institutional means for activist African American churches to partner with government must be taken into account.

## THE MOTIVES OF BLACK CLERGY

When it comes to using their material and cultural resources, African American congregations seek the wisdom of and primarily follow the leadership of their clergy. This is not a controversial statement. "Historically, black churches have been clergy-dominated," in the words of Lawrence N. Jones (1999, 586). Scholars have confirmed this (Hamilton 1972; Williams 1974; Higginbotham

1993; Freedman 1993; Franklin 1994; Mamiya 1998).[1] But how do clergy decide whether their church—indirectly through a faith-related agency, directly as a congregation, or both—should devote resources to collaborate with government to address social conditions in its neighborhood?

When facing various choices for using the resources of their churches, black clergy leading activist churches will make a decision that coheres with their own preferences and values that accord with purposeful goal seeking.[2] This is true of almost all individuals who make decisions that determine or affect collective action by a group (Arrow 1951; Chong 1991; Skocpol 1979 and 2003; Hays 1994). The goals of clergy can be divided among three categories—*political, programmatic,* and *professional.* Each class of motives contains the common hopes clergy generally have for themselves, their congregations, and their communities (Ammerman 2001; Cnaan 2002; McRoberts 2003; J. Harris 1987).[3]

Additionally, I assume that black clergy are rational actors: they seek to maximize their utility (material and nonmaterial) and use means "that are efficient and effective" in the achievement of their goals and objectives (Olson 1965, 65).[4] Also, I assume that clergy will make their decisions based on their goals as clergy, even when their preferences and values are open to influence by lay members of their congregation. Moreover, I contend that a set of consequences, assumed and actual, interact with the three sets of clergy goals and influence the decisions clergy make regarding church-state collaboration.

Together, the clergy's goals and interpretations of the consequences of collaboration affect and sustain the volition of African American churches to collaborate with government. Figure 1 illustrates how the motives of clergy and the consequences of church-state collaboration specifically and partnerships generally affect black clergy's choice for their church to collaborate with government. It identifies the political, programmatic, and professional goals that inform the assessments clergy make about church-state collaboration.

Looking at multiple sets of goals allows us to recognize the absence of groupthink among black clergy. We should not assume that black clergy that display similar behavior act on similar motivations. Their bundles of motivations may vary. Moreover, the goals of clergy may overlap, and we should not treat the sets of goals as mutually exclusive. For illustrative purposes, however, I have kept the sets of goals distinct.

## Political Goals

Black clergy who lead activist churches are motivated to call attention to salient concerns in the neighborhood of their church. In particular, a political

FIGURE 1 Church-state collaboration: the considerations of black clergy

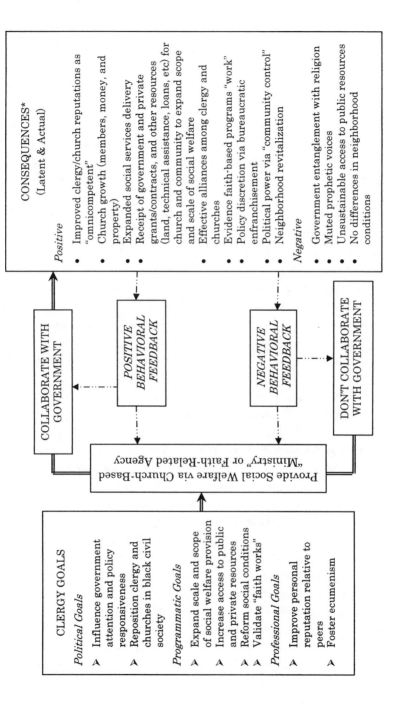

goal of activist clergy is for government to attend more to the issues and conditions of a low-income neighborhood that hosts their church or is located near it (Brazier 1969; English 1967; Hamilton 1972; Newman 1994; Freedman 1993; Jennings 2005; Day 2002; Olson 2000). One way of directing governmental attention is to voice the concerns of neighborhoods through concrete action that targets resources toward them (Orbell and Uno 1972). Thus clergy, alone or with others, may decide that addressing issues such as drug abuse, low student achievement, and a lack of affordable housing through church-based or church-associated services is appropriate. They may also make sure that their action draws the attention of government agencies to the problems and their "faith-based" approach. As policymakers observe the actions of churches serving the poor, they learn about the scale and scope of community problems. This may influence policymakers to give more attention to the neighborhoods.

Merely calling attention to issues through independent social action by activist churches, however, may be inadequate to shape and affect governmental responses. Accordingly, clergy may direct the resources of their church, alone or in alliance with other churches, toward influencing the distribution or redistribution of public resources to the advantage, or at least not the disadvantage, of their community. In the process, they may employ protest, electioneering, and collaboration with government as means of increasing and strengthening the substantive representation of their neighborhood's concerns in policymaking venues.

Black clergy leading activist churches have another political goal for themselves, their church, and their community—repositioning and improving the reputation of clergy in the leadership of black civil society. Such a goal may seem unnecessary, even peculiar, given that many churches provide social welfare services to the disadvantaged in their neighborhood, demonstrating their ability to be community-serving institutions (Chaves 1998; Billingsley 1999; Owens and Smith 2005; Lincoln and Mamiya 1990; Bositis 2006). Moreover, 84 percent of black churchgoers attend churches that provide community outreach programs that assist the poor through emergency relief, as well as social welfare services such as affordable housing, job training, and daycare intended to increase the ability of the poor to live independent of alms (Brown, Dawson and Jackson 1994). Together, these facts account for much of why blacks generally identify churches as key institutions of black civil society (Taylor 1987; Pew Research Center for the People and the Press 2002). Nevertheless, that black clergy might want to improve blacks' perceptions of them and their churches as leaders of black communities and representatives of black interests is not that odd.

*The Diminished Position of Clergy.* Through the middle of the twentieth century, black preachers were commonly designated, by blacks and by whites, as "the natural political leaders and interest brokers in the black community" (Berenson, Elifson, and Tollerson 1976, 374; also Mays and Nicholson 1933; Hamilton 1972). Since then, in the words of historian Manning Marable, society has "witnessed a gradual unmistakable decline in the political influence and social status of black ministers" (1983, 197). The decline became noticeable in cities toward the end of the civil rights movement, when preachers faced competition from civic and political professionals to represent the interests and values of black communities to white elites, as well as to procure public resources to address problems in their communities (Wilson 1960). "With professional training, administrative skills, and political sophistication," Wald (2003, 279) writes, "[professional] experts assumed some of the political and social responsibilities previously monopolized by ministers."

As black politicians and other secular elites sidelined many—but certainly not all—black clergy, political and secular authority equaled and at times replaced moral and sacred authority as the source of political claims on behalf of blacks. By the end of the 1960s, the traditional elite of urban black neighborhoods, represented largely by the clergy, was replaced by a new elite who took charge of the political course. The new elite gained its influence through a strategy of "appealing over the heads of the existing elites to the masses of potential black voters and developing entirely new leadership elements in the process" (Salamon 1973, 627).

From that point forward, "as the Civil Rights Movement was transformed from the protest to electoral politics phase, the role of the church was eclipsed by the role of politicians and political institutions," along with nonpartisan leaders of secular organizations (Assensoh and Alex-Assensoh 2003, 197). "The ministers [were] not called upon to speak, much less to lead, that [was] for the professionals and the titular heads of the civic associations" in black neighborhoods (Wilson 1960, 298).

The primary outcome of the changes in clergy standing and church position in black civil society was, according Adolph Reed Jr., "the development of a new context of political authority in the aftermath of the civil rights movement" (1986, 43). The new context included frequent substitutions of black secular elites for the clergy as "political spokespersons" (Reed 1986, 43). It influenced the behavior of black clergy and African American churches. Many of them turned to "individually producing change, rather than serving as the vanguard of any particular movement" (Calhoun-Brown 2003a, 27).

A supplemental effect was the "diminished" position and reputation of the black pulpit, particularly in the eyes of black civil society (Lincoln and Mamiya 1990, 230). By 1984, fewer than one-half (40 percent) of blacks would rate ministers as "very effective" leaders within black civil society (cited in Harris 1999, 108–9). This was to be expected, as political scientist Charles Hamilton had predicted in *The Black Preacher in America:* "Those that fail to measure up to the demands of the day will be cast aside. Many are now, and have been for a long time, anachronisms in this society. And those men simply do not have a bright, popular future in the black community. . . . They and their churches may linger for a time, even in some cases a long time, but they will not be relevant to the central thrust of social change" (1972, 230).

At the beginning of the 1990s, surveys suggested that some black clergy and their churches indeed were irrelevant. The *Detroit News,* for example, conducted a telephone survey in 1991 among a random sample of black adults in the United States. Most respondents (64 percent) strongly agreed that African American churches should spend more time addressing social and economic conditions in black communities. The implications were twofold. First, many churches and their clergy were doing too little about the conditions of black neighborhoods. Second, the socioeconomic and political struggles of black neighborhoods no longer pivoted on or were sustained by the material and cultural resources of African American churches. Black public intellectuals now asserted that black clergy and their churches were peripheral to the black quest for political, economic, and social advancement (Pinn 2002; Cohen 1999; Assensoh and Alex-Assensoh 2003; Williams 2003; Franklin 1997; Andrews 2002). It was not a new suggestion.

Periodically since emancipation, black public intellectuals' negative critique of black clergy and African American churches has entered the collective discourse of black civil society (Hamilton 1972; Clark 1967; Bunche 1973). Moreover, in the contemporary period, as William Nelson observes, "the progressive face of the Black church is still an unfinished product. Black citizens are continuing to receive mixed signals from church-based leaders, leaving them in a quandary regarding the extent to which they can trust such leaders to negotiate in their interests . . . in the policymaking process" (2000, 152).

The opinions and behaviors of clergy themselves during the 1990s may have fostered the distrust and further diminished the position and reputation of the black pulpit.[5] Approximately nine out of ten black clergy, as reported by C. Eric Lincoln and Lawrence Mamiya (1990), did not identify "civic leadership" as one of their primary "duties" as clergy. This parochial view of clergy as congregational leaders rather than civic leaders may have affected their utterances from the pulpit and reduced the likelihood that they would address civic issues relevant to contemporary life in Afro-America, especially low-income black neighborhoods.

Generally, black preachers do not use their prophetic voice during worship services to critique social inequality or to mobilize blacks to contest the racial and economic status quo in the United States.[6] Instead of a social gospel, according to Robert Franklin, a scholar of homiletics and former president of the Interdenominational Theological Center (the Atlanta-based consortium of six seminaries serving historically black religious denominations), black preachers increasingly "proclaim the gospel of health, wealth and success through personal acts of heroic faith" (1997, 70), a homiletic that ignores social injustice and does not call for collective action to address temporal needs. This fuels a "crisis of relevance and purpose" that weakens the position of African American churches in civil society (Franklin n.d.).

The "crisis" is worsened by the increased spatial disconnection of predominantly middle-class African American congregations from inner-city neighborhoods. In earlier periods, including the first two decades of the post–*de jure* segregation era, African American churches were more heterogeneous in their class composition due to their geographic proximity to poor blacks (Lincoln and Mamiya 1990, 384; McRoberts 2003). But since the 1980s, much of the black middle class has migrated away from inner-city black neighborhoods (Wilson 1987). Yet inner-city black neighborhoods continue to host many of the black middle class's churches. The migration widened the social distance between black churchgoers, especially those from the middle class, and blacks who may not attend church or attend infrequently, particularly the poor and working poor (Laudarji and Livezey 2000; Smith 2001 and 2003b; McRoberts 2003; Gramby-Sobukwe n.d.).[7]

While African American churches may "continue to speak out on behalf of the poor, they tend not to attract strong membership in the least affluent neighborhoods" (Wald 2003, 284; see also Nelsen and Kanagy 1993).[8] A pastor interviewed as part of a study of churches located in inner-city neighborhoods at the start of the millennium acknowledged this point on behalf of his peers: "There are probably very few community churches left [in the neighborhood]. Even though our members have their roots in the neighborhood, they now live in the suburbs" (quoted in Smith 2003b, 11). "When our service is over," according to another pastor, "our folks go back home [to the suburbs]. Church is over" (quoted in Smith 2003b, 11).[9]

The "churched" and the "unchurched" in poor neighborhoods may be assumed to correlate with the groups of blacks that anthropologist Elijah Anderson (1999) classifies as the "decent" and the "street." The low levels of interaction between churched and unchurched are a function of a growing black middle class whose ethics, values, and manners are assumed to differ from the culture of those who are less prosperous.[10] This notion is reflected well in the words of one inner-city pastor: "An attitude among some of my members is that they've worked hard to escape the ghetto. And to erect bridges between our congregations and the housing projects across the street means there will be more social interaction between the kids, and our kids may come under the influence of some of the things we've tried to get away from" (quoted in Smith 2003b, 12).

The perceived diminished position of clergy among the "leaders" of black neighborhoods, advanced by the social disconnection of middle-class African American churches from impoverished black neighborhoods, troubles many black pastors. It accounts for why in the late twentieth century they ranked public criticism of their leadership in community affairs among the major problems facing African American churches (Lincoln and Mamiya 1990). The perceptions of the clergy and their churches work against black pastors' being celebrated as they once were—as "omnicompetent leaders" capable of identifying, representing, and addressing the broad needs of African American neighborhoods (Wilson 1960, 277).

*Reaffirming Clergy Relevance.* Seeing a darkened image of themselves and their churches (i.e., as disengaged from the realities and struggles of blacks, especially the poor), some black pastors wish to reaffirm their relevance in the civic leadership of black communities. They seek to restore the reputation of African American churches as institutions whose resources are pivotal to black struggles for socioeconomic progress and vital to the resurrection and restoration of black neighborhoods. These clergy, many of them activists, can be found urging other leaders of African American churches to relocate themselves within the local, and even national, leadership of Afro-America.[11]

Qualitative evidence from low-income black neighborhoods in cities such as Boston, Philadelphia, Indianapolis, Milwaukee, and New York suggests that "a number of politically active ministers have taken strong steps to *reestablish* the Black church as an instrument for positive community uplift and advance-

ment" (Nelson 2000, 150, emphasis added; see also Day 2001 and 2002; Olson 2000; Crawford and Olson 2001; Freedman 1993). For instance, the Reverend Ray Hammond, chair of the board of the Boston Ten Point Coalition
and the Boston Foundation, advocates that his peers in the pulpits reestablish
their credibility and legitimacy as community leaders: "We must move to an
emphasis on what I like to call the 3 R's of community and spiritual revitalization: renewal, responsibility, and reconnection—renewal of our faith in the
fact that we can make a difference in every aspect of the lives of youth, their
families, and their communities; a willingness to take full responsibility for
our respective roles in meeting the needs of our communities; and a commitment to reconnecting and working in collaboration with other individuals and
institutions" (quoted in Jennings 2005, 86). The intent of such advocacy is for
black clergy and activist churches to regain authority in, and possibly over,
low-income black neighborhoods, an authority that is assumed to have been
lost in the decades following the civil rights movement. Moreover, they seek
to reassert the sociopolitical dominance of clergy and sectarian institutions
in relation to secular elites and institutions in the postsegregation politics of
poor black neighborhoods.

The failure of the dramatic increases of black faces in municipal places of
authority to bring significant improvements is a motivation and occasion for
activist African American churches to relocate themselves in black civil society. The wins at the polls by black politicians, especially their victories in mayoral races, provide "a psychological triumph for African Americans, but they
represent no qualitative resolution to the crises of black poverty, educational
inequality, crime, and unemployment" (Marable 1990, 20–21; also Reed 1999;
Thompson 2006). Case studies of minority-led mayoral administrations in
cities over the last twenty tears confirm the limits of black political incorporation (Reed 1999; Colburn and Adler 2001; Browning, Marshall, and Tabb
2003; Owens and Rich 2003). The inability of black electoral participation
to make a difference is a function of coalitions: the electoral coalitions that
put blacks in elected and appointed office often differ from the governing coalitions that make and execute policy, resulting in limited responsiveness to
mass black interests, despite some moments for elite black interests to have
their needs met (Stone 1989). Furthermore, some black elected officials employ a governing strategy of deracialization. Huey Perry contends that this allows black politicians to engage in "soft-pedaling or avoidance of black issues
combined with a vigorous appeal to white voters" that requires an avoidance
of mass black interests, both on the campaign trail and in office (1996, xi).
In the end, Robert Smith writes, black electoral "politics has become largely

irrelevant in terms of a politics and policies that would address effectively the problems of the [black] race in the post–civil rights era" (1996, 21–22). Much of the black polity agrees with him: 52 percent of respondents to the 1993 National Black Politics Survey answered "no" to the claim that "gaining political rights, such as the vote, has been most important for black progress" (Dawson 2001, 329).

The continuing presence of low-income neighborhoods in U.S. cities itself provides motive and occasion for African American clergy to retake leadership in black civil society. The 25 percent of blacks below the poverty line in 2004 was down from 33 percent three decades earlier, but 8.6 million blacks remained poor.[12] They accounted for approximately one quarter of the poor in the United States, and they tended be spatially concentrated. Extreme poverty areas with majority-black populations have declined in number over recent decades, but they have not disappeared (Jargowsky and Yang 2006). The enduring supply of low-income black neighborhoods yields opportunities for clergy to demonstrate leadership on neighborhood renewal and social welfare issues. Middle-class outmigration produces leadership vacuums in impoverished black neighborhoods—and thus occasions for clergy to identify themselves as and act like neighborhood leaders (Crawford and Olson 2001; Olson 2000; Day 2002).

It is not that poor black neighborhoods are necessarily leaderless, or that they will necessarily accept clergy as their representatives. Rather, the milieu of many low-income neighborhoods is marked by a social isolation that produces a dearth of a certain type of leadership. What poor black neighborhoods often lack is leadership capable of building, sustaining, and evaluating the capacity of community-based organizations to meet needs, access venues of public (and private) decision making to represent neighborhood interests, and identify and hold stakeholders accountable. They need a leadership that is capable of "creating synergy with financial and public institutions" to redevelop and revitalize them (Saegert, Thompson, and Warren 2001, 15; see also Cohen 2001; W. J. Wilson 1987 and 1996).

Neighborhoods lacking such leadership are arenas for black clergy to begin to reclaim mantles of and reputations for effective leadership. As Calhoun-Brown infers from her review of the civic engagement of African American churches since the 1960s, the authority of black clergy vis-à-vis secular leaders and organizations "may be strengthened if through [omnicompetence and social welfare] programs they can successfully demonstrate continued centrality and relevance" (2003b, 53).

## Programmatic Goals

In addition to politically advancing their communities and themselves, black clergy aspire to improve social conditions in poor black neighborhoods surrounding (or near) their church. A successful pursuit of this goal, of course, contributes to the political goal of developing and demonstrating omnicompetence by clergy and church. An approach to achieving the goal of neighborhood improvement is to expand social welfare services in both breadth (number of programs and clients) and depth (comprehensiveness of programs).

Opening public and private resources (e.g., money, land, and technical assistance) to access and administration by churches and their faith-related agencies to produce and to provide social welfare services is a supplemental means of improving black neighborhoods (Farnsley 2003).[13] It is not easy, however. For decades black clergy have attempted, often with little success, to increase funding from philanthropic foundations and government agencies to faith-based organizations to develop social welfare programs, as well as to redirect a share of the funding going to faith-related agencies associated with historically white Christian denominations (e.g., the Salvation Army, Catholic Charities, and Lutheran Family Services) to black-led agencies.[14]

Alongside expanding social welfare services and increasing access to public and private resources, black clergy have the aim of demonstrating that social change in black neighborhoods is possible. Reverend Eugene Rivers, a founder of the Boston Ten Point Coalition and pastor of the Azusa Christian Community, observes: "For us, at the end of the day, serving the needs of the poor is the priority. And that's not about religion, it's about results. It's not about proselytizing; it's about performance. And we want sacred institutions to be judged on the basis of their performance and results, not by the fact that they are religious" (2001, 95). In other words, the objective is to validate that *faith works;* religious organizations can improve the lives of the poor (Washington 1986).[15] Such a validation is relevant professionally to black clergy.

## Professional Goals

Beyond bringing the fallen to Christ and proving that the Holy Ghost operates for the good of the fallen, black clergy seek to advance their careers as pastors. They are professionals who seek to improve their reputations in relation to their peers in the pulpit. Pastors are competitors, contesting to acquire reputations equal to or greater than those of other pastors. Histories of African

American church development demonstrate that such competition has been routine among pastors (Mays and Nicholson 1933; Sernett 1997). Superior homiletics and great choirs have long been the currency used by many clergy to purchase their professional elevation, measured in terms of church memberships and revenue (Salvatore 2005; Sernett 1997). Extensive community outreach is another means pastors have used to acquire better standing for themselves, as well as their church, within the black faith sector (Washington 1986; W. T. Walker 1994; Billingsley 1999).[16]

Designing social welfare programs oriented to individuals outside their congregation broadens and strengthens the reputations of clergy and their congregations as other-regarding individuals and institutions (Sernett 1997; McRoberts 2003; Sengupta 1995; Onishi 1997). Clergy believe, in turn, that a community-oriented reputation and evidence of attending to the temporal conditions of blacks impress observers and assists the membership recruitment efforts of their church. "Some people," according to the Reverend Floyd Flake of the Greater Allen African Methodist Episcopal Cathedral (formerly Allen AME Church) in New York City, "come to the church precisely because of the community outreach programs" (quoted in Billingsley 1999, 150). This is a basic logic of church development: community-oriented service programs beget congregation growth (Barna and Jackson 2004; Stewart 1994). "And the bigger the congregation, the more likely it is to have an expanded professional staff, which in turn expands the range of activities and ministries the congregation can undertake" in its neighborhoods (Ammerman 2001, 49).[17]

Some black clergy seek to foster ecumenism among their peers and their churches, even if they are competitors (Sawyer 1994). Ecumenism is especially espoused by clergy leading congregations that are small to medium in their number of congregants and other material resources. Clergy influenced by black liberation theology, a worldview favoring cooperation among black-led institutions, also maintain ecumenism as a professional goal for themselves and their church. While acknowledging the competitive nature of the black pulpit, ecumenical clergy believe churches should cooperate more, sharing resources, risks, and rewards, especially in addressing the problems of neighborhoods they share, and they seek out opportunities to act on their beliefs.

*Consequences of Collaboration vis-à-vis Clergy Motivations*

Recall that figure 1 depicts the goals of black clergy interacting with two broad sets of consequences—positive and negative—that flow from church-state collaboration and bear on the volition of churches to provide social welfare in conjunction with government agencies. These consequences, which may be latent or actual, shape the decisions by clergy to have their churches begin or continue to collaborate with government. That is, church collaboration with government, either alone or in conjunction with other modes of political engagement, offers their clergy the potential to achieve the political, programmatic, and professional goals they have for themselves, their churches, and their communities. Moreover, collaboration with government may provide positive feedback that reinforces extant collaborations, and it can generate new partnerships between churches and public agencies. It may also give negative feedback that reinforces clergy fears of church-state collaboration, which may lead to the dissolution of extant partnerships and barriers to new ones.

*Achievement of Goals.* Collaboration with government may allow churches to engage in more community outreach and enterprise and, in turn, acquire more attenders and more money, improve clergy reputations, and foster ecumenicism. (This may not be true of other forms of political engagement by activist African American churches, at least not when practiced by themselves.) Furthermore, by collaborating with government, churches may gain access to public and private resources that enhance their income for community outreach and permit them to expand the scope and scale of their social welfare programs. As Arthur Farnsley comments, many black clergy view "recent [public social welfare funding] reforms as a chance, finally, to put funds earmarked for social services and development in the African-American community under the control of African-American [religious] organizations" (2003, 45). This may permit them to broaden the array of social services they provide and increase and diversify their clientele, as well as better the reputations and positions of clergy in relation to secular leaders of black civil society.

Additionally, collaboration, especially if it involves funding and some autonomy over program design, may permit clergy and their churches to acquire (1) influence over public policy, (2) bureaucratic enfranchisement that they could use on behalf of their communities, and (3) degrees of community control of the implementation of public policy in black neighborhoods. Subsequently, if their church demonstrates "success," or even if they "fail," the outcomes may increase government responsiveness to neighborhood issues and conditions. Collaboration with government may be one way of focusing government's attention and resources on the problems of poor black communities. Again, this can enhance the standing and location of clergy within black civil society.

*Increased Church-State Collaboration.* If collaboration results in positive outcomes (e.g., improvement of clergy reputations, acquisition of public resources, attention to group needs, expansion of the scale and scope of faith-based social welfare programming, or increased political power via community control), churches that already collaborate with government will maintain and expand their partnerships. Churches that do not collaborate with government but observe positive outcomes achieved by other churches, or merely accept the rhetoric of potential effects, may become more willing to consider collaboration. In particular, if poor black neighborhoods show physical signs of renewal through church-state collaboration, black clergy may spread their success stories to other black clergy, who then influence their own churches to adopt collaboration. Church-state collaboration does not, however, guarantee such a virtuous circle.

*Abandonment of Church-State Collaboration.* Collaboration with government may not necessarily permit clergy to accomplish their goals, especially those they have for their community, such as neighborhood revitalization. Consequently, clergy may decide to devote the material and cultural resources — time, volunteers, money, political and community legitimacy—of their church elsewhere, apart from or including political engagement. Clergy whose church has yet to collaborate with government but maintains a willingness to do it may observe the negative lessons of others and decide to devote their resources elsewhere, too.

Because collaboration with government may produce negative consequences for clergy and churches, such collaboration is a contentious issue among black clergy, even if it does elicit a clear and favorable response among their congregants and the black polity generally. While African American churches may be more willing than other congregations to seek public funding and collaborate with government, there is disagreement within the black pulpit over whether African American churches *should* partner with government. Asked as part of a survey by the Public Influences of African American Churches Study whether "the current policy context that encourages congregations to seek and use public money to deliver human and health services is useful," 52 percent of black clergy disagreed and 46 percent agreed (R. D. Smith 2005; Owens 2004b).

Also, the Faith Communities and Urban Families Project, which included an opinion survey of a random sample of clergy leading churches located in the vicinity of public housing complexes in majority-black neighborhoods in four cities (Camden, Denver, Hartford, and Indianapolis), found that 65 percent of respondents disagreed that it is "helpful that policymakers are encouraging congregations to apply for and use public funds to provide social services" (Owens and Smith 2005, 327).[18] Lastly, in a random sample of black seminarians studying at the Interdenominational Theological Center, 56 percent of respondents believed that churches should not apply for public funding.[19] Evidently, many black clergy, including those whose churches already collaborate with government, are wary of collaboration, especially if it comes with compensation for their involvement (Bositis 2006).

A strong fear that black clergy have about collaboration is that it will result in government entanglement with religion. They are concerned that church-state collaboration will result in churches' falling under the authority and scrutiny of the state, which will limit their freedom to teach and preach and design social welfare programs consonant with their religious convictions, theological imperatives, and conservative social stances (McRoberts 2003, 112). The Reverend Philip Cousin, an African Methodist Episcopal bishop, adamantly declared: "I don't want government out to dictate to faith-based institutions" (quoted in Farris 2004). Collaboration with government may muffle the prophetic voice of the black pulpit (Waldman 2001; Daniels 2001). Reverend Jeremiah Wright Jr., pastor of Trinity United Church of Christ in Chicago, has remarked: "We have pastors who will not speak to power with conviction because they have their [public-private] partnerships. . . . If they criticize too much, they risk the funding" (quoted in Hadnot 2004).

Even if church-state collaboration is successful at revitalizing low-income black neighborhoods, clergy worry that such collaboration may work against the interests of neighborhood residents. Political scientist Meredith Ramsay explains, "Some observers fear that increasing governmental reliance on the [faith] sector could further reduce the government's social welfare role, which is already minimal by standards of other industrialized democracies" (1998, 612). Moreover, black clergy fear their church's becoming agents of gentrification via public-funded neighborhood redevelopment initiatives. Sensitive to past claims that churches that collaborated with government agencies fostered displacement and "Negro removal" from potentially lucrative sections of cities, clergy may not wish to work with government in ways that could threaten the existence of black neighborhoods (English 1967; Brazier 1969).

The negative outcomes of church-state collaboration, whether latent or actual, may dissuade many clergy from employing the material and cultural resources of their church to deliver social welfare services in partnership with government, especially in return for compensation. Yet in the end, when a church does collaborate with government, the potential and actual achievement of their professional, programmatic, and political goals may deepen clergy's faith in church-state collaboration. For black clergy whose churches have yet to collaborate with government, seeing actual achievements by their peers engenders hope that they too can pursue and achieve their goals through church-state collaboration.

Both types of black clergy may remain wary of collaborating with government, grounding their wariness in theological convictions, denominational imperatives, church-state separation, and perceived failures of other churches as collaborators. Still, black clergy who are open to their church's collaborating with government tend to believe that a church-state partnership will yield much good for themselves, their church, and their community.

## OPPORTUNITIES FOR CHURCH-STATE COLLABORATION

For a church to collaborate with government, there must be opportunities for partnerships. In the last decade, government officials have spoken often and long about the potential value that religious organizations bring to public-funded social welfare initiatives and the need to elevate the position of churches and faith-related agencies to parity with, if not above, secular organizations as partners of government in the delivery of social welfare and community development services in poor neighborhoods. They also have made decisions that create openings for religious congregations of all faith traditions to partner with government. In particular, policymakers used a portion of the Personal Responsibility and Work Opportunity Reconciliation Act (PRWORA) of 1996 to design what became a collection of federal and state laws and regulations, collectively known as "charitable choice," to induce faith-based organizations to collaborate with public agencies to address the causes and symptoms of poverty.

Congregations and faith-related agencies associated with them may apply for and use public funds to foster work (job preparation, employment training, and vocational education), nutrition (emergency food distribution and subsidized meals), healthy living (drug and alcohol treatment), and human care (adoptions, foster care, orphanages) among the needy, especially working-age, nondisabled heads of poor households and their children, on behalf of government (Monsma 2004; Kennedy and Bielefeld 2006). It is not the first time the public sector has looked to congregations to address the problems of the urban poor in partnership with governments.[20] There is, however, a difference between the past and the present.

From the War on Poverty begun in 1964 until welfare reform in 1996, public policy required all congregations to establish separate faith-associated social enterprises to receive public money. They were to charter and operate secular organizations because the incorporation of religious doctrine with services the public funded was deemed unconstitutional (Monsma 1996; Lupu and Tuttle 2003). However, as a result of PRWORA and other changes in federal social welfare policy, public policy no longer mandates the creation and use of separate secular agencies by congregations. Instead, charitable choice allows states to use federal funds to contract directly with "pervasively sectarian institutions" to provide welfare-related services through purchase-of-service agreements with public welfare agencies. In sum, what is new about public funding of congregations in the current era is that churches may directly receive public funding to provide social welfare services.

Since the introduction of charitable choice, public policy directly encourages—but does not require—government agencies to award public contracts and grants to congregations and faith-related agencies to develop and administer social services that improve the personal situations and environmental conditions of the poor. There are signals that government's encouragement of church-state partnerships is leading to an increasing number of public contracts and grants to faith-based organizations, creating new opportunities or expanding extant ones for church-state collaboration.

One sign that the policy environment is becoming more "faith-friendly" is administrative. While the overall level of administrative (and legislative) change is modest, many states have long and deep histories of working with faith-based organizations to provide social services. There is no evidence that states are reducing the number of partnerships with faith-based organizations. Instead, all the evidence suggests that they are increasing them, albeit at a slow rate. Also, a scan of the states in 2005 revealed that 53 percent of state governments are "engaged in significant administrative activities to affect government partnerships with faith-based social service providers," up from 36 percent in 2003 (Ragan and Wright 2005, 29). The same survey found that more than one-half of the states had enacted legislation that improved the environment for church-state collaboration. There is evidence that some states have instituted "faith-based organization" quotas for particular programs. Florida, for instance, requires that 15 percent of its federal Workforce Investment Act monies for the labor force development of youth go to faith-based organizations (Montiel 2002, 17).

Another indication of the changed policy environment is fiscal, and it comes mainly from the federal government, even if the resources do not match the rhetoric of the "faith-based and community initiative" (Kuo 2006). In 2005, federal agencies allocated a minimum of $2.2 billion in funds to faith-based organizations (White House Office of Faith-Based and Community Initiatives 2006), a 69 percent increase from the $1.3 billion the federal government distributed to faith-based organizations in 2004 (White House Office of Faith-Based and Community Initiatives 2005).[21]

Overall, there are five points to remember about federal faith-based funding in recent years. First, the proportion of federal discretionary grants across the five core departments of what is called the federal "faith-based and community initiative" (Housing and Urban Development, Health and Human Services, Education, Justice, and Labor) going to faith-based organizations between FY 2003 and FY 2005 increased by 21 percent, rising from 8.1 percent to 10.3 percent, respectively (White House Office of Faith-Based and Community Initiatives 2006, 3). Second, the total number of discretionary grants by the five agencies to faith-based organizations grew by 38 percent, increasing from 1,634 grants in 2003 to 2,250 in 2005. Within the Department of Health and Human Services, the number of discretionary grants and dollar amounts of such grants to faith-based organizations grew by 82 percent and 64 percent, respectively, over the period (White House Office of Faith-Based and Community Initiatives 2006, 6).

Third, although there was significant growth between 2003 and 2005 in overall federal discretionary allocations to faith-based organizations, a close look reveals that the allocations among the five core departments increased only marginally from $1.1 billion to $1.4 billion (White House Office of Faith-Based and Community Initiatives 2006).[22] Fourth, 46 percent of faith-based organizations receiving federal grants, as of 2004, were "new" grantees; they did not receive a grant in years prior from the agency that funded them in 2004 (Montiel and Wright 2006, 6).[23] Fifth, the federal government does not guarantee that it will or can sustain a faith-friendly funding environment. In 2006, for instance, the Bush administration submitted to the U.S. Congress a budget that would reduce spending by many federal departments and programs that target the poor and elderly, and these tend to be the programs most likely to seek the participation of faith-based organizations as partners in delivering benefits.

Surveys of states and faith-based organizations, nevertheless, provide a sense of how changes in federal funding, especially under TANF and the Labor Department's Welfare-to-Work program, are affecting partnerships between the public and faith sectors. Attempting to assess the initial effects of charitable choice, Amy Sherman reports that "new cooperative relationships between government and the faith community that involve financial contracts or formal nonfinancial collaboration" were happening in almost one-half of the states at the end of the 1990s (2000, 6).[24] Moreover, government agencies were the primary initiators of the collaboration; that is, government sought faith-based organizations, not the other way around).

Research in fifteen states by John Green and Amy Sherman (2002) reveals that 55 percent of respondents to a survey of congregations and faith-related agencies with government contracts were "new participants" in public-funded faith-based initiatives.[25] More than half of the faith-based organizations began to partner with government in exchange for public funding *after* the federal enactment of charitable choice in 1996. Among congregations specifically, about "one-half . . . were in their first [government] contract ever, and nearly as many had [government funding] experience only back to 1996" (Green and Sherman 2002, 14).[26] All of this suggests that the policy environment for collaboration with government by activist churches, including African American churches, is good and possibly getting better.

## CAPACITY OF CHURCHES TO COLLABORATE WITH GOVERNMENT

Regardless of the policy environment that invites churches to work with government, and the openness of clergy to church-state partnerships, unless churches possess the institutional means for partnering with government, church-state collaboration is unlikely. That is, even if church-state collaboration fit with the goals of clergy, could produce positive consequences, and was an available opportunity, churches could not partner with government agencies without possessing the institutional capacity to do it. Institutional capacity "is reflected in the ability of . . . groups to carry out their functions responsively, effectively, and efficiently, connecting to larger systems, both within and beyond the community, as appropriate" (Chaskin et al. 2001, 20; see also Glickman and Servon 1998; Owens 2004a). And it is derived from three aptitudes—organizational, resource, and programmatic.[27]

*Organizational aptitude* pertains to the ability of organizations to develop their internal human resources to operate in a professional manner befitting social welfare provision. It is very important for organizations to recruit, train, and retain skilled principal and programmatic staff to manage social services for effectiveness and sustainability. *Resource aptitude* relates to the ability of organizations to obtain and manage material resources, including money (e.g., loans, contracts, and grants) and real property (land and buildings), for social welfare. It points to the obvious: social welfare organizations mortgage their ability to achieve goals and objectives to their competence to acquire financial support or leverage other resources to expand their finances. *Programmatic aptitude* denotes the ability of organizations to design and implement activities that cohere with their mission and the goals and objectives that flow from it. It corresponds to an organization's ability to plan and execute well one activity or a multiplicity of activities. Because it requires skill and expertise, organizational aptitude influences it. In terms of practice, programmatic aptitude could include an organization's ability to offer mortgage counseling, deliver addiction services, manage a charter school, operate a for-profit subsidiary such as a bookstore, or engage in all of these activities.

Given the necessity of these aptitudes, some churches, probably most, do not possess the institutional capacity to collaborate with government. This is the case for many African American churches. For this reason, black clergy over the last four decades have had their churches experiment with establishing agencies, especially community development corporations (CDCs), to assist them in developing the institutional capacity to collaborate with government (Clemetson and Coates 1992; Mares 1994; Thomas and Blake 1996). A CDC is a tax-exempt, charitable organization whose programs are intended to contribute to the general welfare of a neighborhood by serving the values, needs, and interests of stakeholders beyond the attenders of the founding congregation (D. Walker 2001). CDCs, especially those affiliated with activist African American churches, are often the loci of a church's action via public-private partnership to resurrect and redeem its low-income urban community (Thomas and Blake 1996; Clemetson and Coates 1992).

At the close of the 1990s, at least two hundred African American church–associated CDCs existed in U.S. cities (Frederick 2001).[28] Their utilities, as they relate to church-state collaboration, are manifold. Church-associated CDCs possess production utilities, generating goods (e.g., affordable housing, jobs, and social services) to better the conditions of neighborhood residents, individually and collectively (Mares 1994; Thomas and Blake 1996; Clemetson and Coates 1992). They enable churches to obtain, albeit indirectly, resources—public and private—normally unavailable to them because they are religious organizations.[29] They also ensure that the capital assets of their churches remain unaffected by the potential legal and economic liabilities inherent in collaborating with government to provide social welfare services (W. T. Walker 1994; G. Reed 1994; Mares 1994). Additionally, African American church–associated CDCs possess and exercise spiritual utilities, manifesting the core elements of Afro-Christian theology: self-determination, communication of the gospel, and application of the Golden Rule (Brazier 1969; Walker 1994; Tucker-Worgs 2002).

African American church–associated CDCs *may* also possess political utilities, serving as instruments for addressing collective problems in the neighborhood to the benefit of constituents and for influencing public policies. As quasi-administrative arms of government agencies, CDCs may allow urban blacks to affect the distribution of public resources, such as land, money, and authority, in their favor (Gilliam 1975; Cross 1984). Perhaps urban black neighborhoods benefit from African American church–associated CDCs if they function as interest groups, articulating the political values and concerns of their constituent-clients while proposing policy alternatives and influencing the delivery of collective goods and services to their neighborhood.[30]

## SUMMARY

Church-state collaboration is not simply the result of government seduction of churches. It is also not just about churches' desire to reduce poverty. It may be correlated with theological and religious convictions, but theology and religion are insufficient explanations. Instead, church-state collaboration is a rational decision by black clergy leading activist churches, a choice made to achieve a set of interrelated goals they have for themselves, their church, and their community. Their decision to collaborate with government is informed by their goals, which they seek to achieve in an environment marked by a presumed "diminished" position of clergy as effective leaders of black civil society, continued black poverty (and the inability of descriptive representation to reduce it), and changes in social welfare policy. It is also influenced by the opportunities and capacity of their church to partner with government to provide social welfare in a low-income neighborhood.

Empirically, how does the process of church-state collaboration unfold? What does it produce for churches and poor neighborhoods? Is church-state collaboration in practice a supplement or an alternative to activist churches' involvement in electioneering and protest? Does collaboration with government create opportunities for the clergy and lay leaders of activist African American churches to influence the decisions and behaviors of government in their neighborhood? How, if at all, does collaboration with government relate to the use of other modes of political engagement by African American churches and their faith-related agencies? An examination of church-state collaboration in New York City provides many answers to these questions.

# * 2 *

# The Social and Political Context
# of New York City

# CHAPTER THREE

# Public Policy and Black Neighborhood Decline

Blacks in New York City toiled hard in the political fields of Gotham during the twentieth century. Their objective went beyond the pursuit of descriptive representation: they sought substantive evidence that urban democracy could benefit them, especially in terms of improving conditions in majority-black and predominantly poor neighborhoods (Morsell 1950; Walter 1989; Taylor 1994; Green and Wilson 1992). Pursuing it required electoral and protest efforts to try to equalize opportunities and outcomes between blacks and whites in the city. Yet after decades of political struggle that began in earnest in the 1930s to eradicate slum conditions and social inequities rooted in race (Katznelson 1973; Greenberg 1991; Wilder 2000; Biondi 2003), the poorest black neighborhoods were in serious decline by the 1960s and 1970s. They lost population, commerce, vitality, and social control.

The decline of a set of black neighborhoods resulted from politics and policies. The problems of the black neighborhoods stemmed from the power of white politicians, particularly mayors and city council leaders, to neglect black interests. Further, for eight decades black politicians in New York City were weak in relation to their white peers. As a result, impoverished black spaces grew and endured. Neighborhood decline both stymied black optimism and pushed blacks, especially black clergy, to search for new political and institutional means of developing their neighborhoods. This chapter will consider the results of that quest in the final decades of the twentieth century, giving particular attention to mayoral policies and the strategies of African American clergy and congregations.

## BLACK NEIGHBORHOODS AND POLITICS
## IN NEW YORK CITY, 1960–PRESENT

The intensification of racial humiliation and white brutality under the Jim Crow system, the decimation of the southern agrarian economy by the boll weevil and soil exhaustion, and the economic inducements of industrialization and World War I pushed many southern blacks north. Initially, no city in the South or the North, not even Chicago, compared to New York City in black resettlement. The human swell of the Great Migration and its wavelets during the years 1910 to 1920 quickly increased the black population of New York City. In that decade the number of blacks in the city grew by 66 percent to approximately 150,000, transforming New York City (Osofsky 1996, 128). By 1920 New York was the epicenter of urban black residence in the United States, and zones of black settlement, absent any visible white presence, contained the bulk of its black population. This was a dramatic change in neighborhoods during earlier periods in the city, when blacks had resided in close proximity to whites.

At the end of the nineteenth century, northern cities were less segregated than they would become in the twentieth century (Spear 1967). Although there were blocks that housed relatively high numbers of blacks, the proportions of blacks among their residents rarely exceeded 30 percent, and contiguous clusters of black settlement were rare (Massey and Denton 1993, 20). While "New York had never been," in the words of historian Gilbert Osofsky, "an 'open city'—a city in which Negroes lived wherever they chose" (1996, 127), from the 1890s to the late 1900s most blacks lived in predominantly white neighborhoods. Analyses of wards at the time reveal that the isolation indices for blacks in New York City ranged from 3.6 percent in 1890 to 5 percent in 1910 (Lieberson 1980).[1]

After 1910, black residential choices were more constrained than they had been in prior decades, even years. Rates of white-black residential segregation increased appreciably in New York City during this period. Black neighborhood formation was quick and dramatic, with the isolation index for blacks climbing to 21 percent in 1920 and further upward to 42 percent by 1930. Black migration per se did not build majority-black neighborhoods. Moreover, black self-segregation played a minimal role in their formation. Instead, a developing racial-residential order, one that emerged in the 1900s and intensified in ensuing decades, explains the increasing segregation of blacks from whites during the 1920s and on in New York City.

As the black population increased, whites expressed their wishes and intentions to self-segregate from blacks through their deeds. Whites initially employed violence to communicate their antiblack sentiments and to confine black migrants to the emergent zones of black settlement. They used brutality and bloodshed to build and retain walls between white and black residential spaces during the first two decades of the twentieth century. From the 1920s forward, whites used their social capital and civil society to institute practices that steered black migrants to black residential areas.[2] The effect was to expel black settlers and to wall off black migrants from areas of white residence, directing blacks to "the slums where they belong," according to John G. Taylor, the founder of the Harlem Property Owners' Improvement Corporation (quoted in Osofsky 1996, 107).

Ultimately, white self-segregation retained white residential privilege in New York City. White self-segregation also yielded dense, large, contiguous black neighborhoods as the number of black migrants continued to increase. More than half of the city's blacks in 1920 lived in the Harlem section of Manhattan, an increase of about 80,000 from fifteen years earlier (Waldinger 1996; Greenberg 1991). Approximately 32,000 blacks also resided in Brooklyn, mainly in the vicinity of Bedford-Stuyvesant. Twice as many blacks would live there by the close of the decade. The remainder lived in the other boroughs. A decade later, the black population had grown by an additional 115 percent citywide, increasing the population densities in the original zones of black settlement. Moving forward, blacks would gain access to almost all parts of the city, but the majority of them would continue to reside in or proximate to four black neighborhoods: Harlem, Bedford-Stuyvesant, South Jamaica, and Morrisania (see figure 2).

By the 1960s, the scale of physical and socioeconomic problems in the four neighborhoods was great. Positive changes in their physical and socioeconomic conditions were negligible between the late 1930s and the late 1960s. Their impoverishment, which originated from the white imposition of a racial order of residence and relief in the early and middle decades of the twentieth century, continued into and beyond the 1960s. Political participation did little to change the conditions. It also contributed little to black representation, whether descriptive or substantive.

In the three decades following the Great Depression, political activism by blacks did not increase markedly the number of blacks elected to public office. The first black member of the modern New York City Council—the Reverend Adam Clayton Powell Jr., of Abyssinian Baptist Church—was elected in

FIGURE 2  Principal black neighborhoods in New York City, 2000

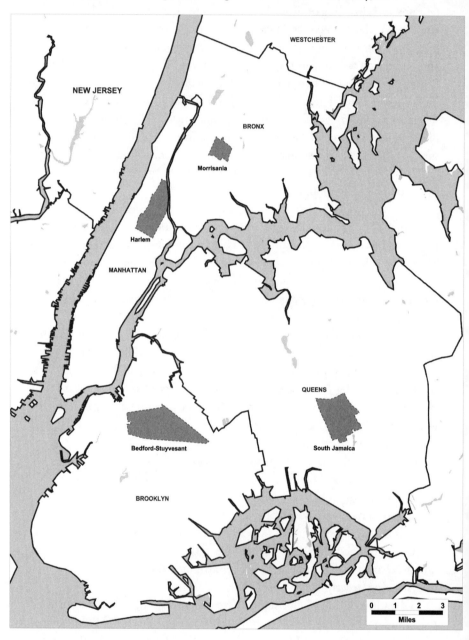

Note: Gray shadings above neighborhood names denote boundaries of neighborhoods.

Harlem in 1941. Outside Harlem, blacks were not elected to municipal office until almost two decades later. Blacks in Brooklyn and Queens, for instance, did not elect one of their own to serve on the city council until 1957 (Thompson 1990). At the state level, after the 1917 election of the first black assemblyman from Harlem, black neighborhoods in Brooklyn, the Bronx, and Queens did not send black representatives to Albany, the state capital, until 1948, 1953, and 1964, respectively (Lewinson 1974).[3] Thus, much of the black political participation before the late 1960s amounted to little more than "intense struggle for small gains" (Biondi 2003, 222).

Surveying their political progress in New York City at the end of the 1960s, blacks judged it glacial. A plurality (45 percent) of blacks in the city believed the political process to be too slow to secure equal rights (Harris and Associates 1969). Their neighborhoods confirmed the belief. Bedford-Stuyvesant illustrated the socioeconomic hardship that most black neighborhoods in New York City faced in the late 1960s.[4] A survey of its residents in 1967 reported an unemployment rate twice the rate for the city, a median household income that lagged well behind the city median, and almost one-third of households receiving welfare assistance, with women heading two-thirds of the welfare households (Center for Urban Education 1967). Opportunities for decent housing, employment, and access to good public schools were, according to the majority of its black residents, the primary needs in the neighborhood. They had been problems since the genesis of the city's zones of black settlement. Resident dissatisfaction in Bedford-Stuyvesant was expressed over lack of safety on the streets, recreational areas for children, upkeep of property (especially the stoops and curbs of brownstones), affordable groceries, and adequate police protection and medical care. Given these dissatisfactions, 50 percent of residents expressed a desire to leave Bedford-Stuyvesant and even New York City for the suburbs just beyond the city's limits.

Two years later, a citywide survey of blacks confirmed a broader displeasure with the negative conditions in New York City's black neighborhoods (Harris and Associates 1969).[5] It also identified a major cause of the problems residents faced day to day: 86 percent of blacks responding to the survey agreed that blacks as a group remained discriminated against by whites and institutions of white privilege (e.g., banks and insurance companies), especially in terms of their ability to purchase and rent decent housing, to gain employment in well-paying occupations, and to access high-quality public schools.[6] The survey revealed, too, an important finding about black New Yorkers' faith in the ability of electoral participation to produce dramatic changes on their behalf. At the time, approximately 60 percent of blacks in the

city voted, but a large minority of them failed to see how their electoral participation translated into government responsiveness. Specifically, 43 percent of
respondents stated that local politicians were not helpful in creating opportunities for black social advancement in the city.[7]

In the 1970s, the majority of New York City blacks continued to reside
mainly in the original areas of black settlement in Manhattan (Harlem),
Brooklyn (Bedford-Stuyvesant), the Bronx (Morrisania), and Queens (South
Jamaica). These were the most populous black neighborhoods, and they were
also among the poorest neighborhoods in the city. On average, according to
city records, 37 percent of persons in the four neighborhoods earned incomes
below the federal poverty level (New York City Department of City Planning
1992 and 1993). Median household income in the neighborhoods was approximately $9,000 less than the municipal median. Male unemployment in the
neighborhoods was nearly twice the city rate.

The employability of the neighborhoods' residents, measured by the proportion of high school graduates, was low: 54 percent of adults lacked a high
school diploma. Widespread poverty-level incomes, unemployment, and low
human capital yielded high welfare dependency. About one-third (32 percent)
of the residents of the four neighborhoods received public assistance income,
compared to 15 percent in the city as a whole in 1979.

Many middle-class black residents began to leave the neighborhoods for
safer majority-black areas in other parts of the city, especially newer black
neighborhoods in southeast Queens and in the north Bronx. Others escaped
to emerging majority-black suburbs east of the city on Long Island and north
of the city in Westchester County. Some working-class residents, too, left the
declining black neighborhoods. Overall, the mean rate of population decline
among the four neighborhoods was 34 percent, compared with 4 percent
population growth citywide. For those blacks left behind in Harlem, Morrisania, South Jamaica, and Bedford-Stuyvesant, tough situations endured, and
public policy worsened them.

## Black Neighborhoods and Municipal Policy

From the 1960s through the middle of the 1970s, expenditures by the city
government outpaced its revenue. As the local economy declined by 11 percent, municipal spending, because of swollen welfare rolls and growing employment in the public sector, increased by 30 percent.[8] Rather than raising
local taxes or reducing services, the municipal government led by Abraham

Beame increased municipal debt to unsound levels.[9] By 1975 Beame's mayoral administration oversaw a municipal government that had a fiscal deficit of approximately $1.5 billion, a sum viewed by the bond markets on Wall Street and in the capitals of the state and nation as profligate and untenable (Shefter 1987; Fuchs 1992).

Following state intervention, the city government was forced to implement a fiscal austerity plan. It included reforms directed at increasing the city's solvency (e.g., requiring balanced budgets and three-year financial plans), the creation of powerful extramunicipal institutions to monitor spending increases and assist in raising revenue, and "the slaughter of three sacred cows of New York politics—cheap subway fares, free tuition at the City University of New York, and low-rent housing for apartment dwellers," budgetary bovines that had greatly assisted not only the poor but also the middle class (Shefter 1987, 134).[10] In the wake of the financial crisis, the city government abandoned the fiscal and policy liberalism of mayors during the 1960s and early 1970s. Edward I. Koch, elected mayor in 1978, led the conservative shift.

*The Koch Administration, 1978–1989.* From the beginning Koch, who had been born in Morrisania when it was a Jewish enclave, was committed to further implementing the austerity measures imposed by the state government. His administration dramatically rearranged the city's budget and policy priorities. Development, not redistribution, became the priority of city hall. In 1978 the city government spent $734 million on economic development projects; four years later, approximately $1.3 billion was dedicated to such projects. The rate of municipal spending for economic growth outpaced growth in redistribution spending through welfare, human, and health services agencies (Shefter 1987, 176).

Koch eventually assessed his administration thus: "I believe that I was able to take a city on the edge of bankruptcy and make it bankable, I believe that I was able to lead a citizenry in total disarray, shaken by what had occurred in the financial debacle of 1975, without confidence in government or themselves, and turn them around so that they now have confidence in themselves and faith in their government" (1984, 346–47). Yet measured by the scope and scale of negative social conditions in Harlem and Bedford-Stuyvesant, along with South Jamaica and Morrisania, as well as the attitudes of their residents, Koch, famous for asking, "How'm I doin'?" did not do too well by the city's black neighborhoods. This assessment was captured well in a question a black teenager asked the mayor at a town hall meeting in 1980: "Mr. Koch, I have a question for you. If you're supposed to be doing something for the black community and the black neighborhoods, how come you're not doing anything? I see no progress being done" (quoted in Koch 1984, 220). Meanwhile the city was experiencing a resurgent economy, declining unemployment, and population gains (Windhoff-Heritier 1992, 49).

Scholars agree that most of the government policies during the Koch administration did not serve black neighborhoods (Mollenkopf 1994; Shefter 1987).[11] Yet there was one area where Koch would set the city government on a course to make a marked difference in some of the poorest black neighborhoods: affordable housing (Orlebeke 1997; Schill 1999). Nonetheless, in other areas there was little blacks could do for their neighborhoods under the Koch administration, especially given the limited presence of blacks inside the city government as policymakers.

Consistently, since the formation of black neighborhoods in the city, black representation in the city council had lagged behind the proportion of blacks in the city's general population, electorate, and Democratic Party (Lewinson 1974; Gelb 1970; Mollenkopf 1986). Midway through the 1980s, blacks held seven (20 percent) of the seats in the New York City Council, an improvement from the period of 1945–1968, when no more than two black members (5 percent) had held seats. Still, after decades of political action, the black legislative presence in the New York City government at that time was characterized by limited incorporation and effect, especially in comparison to other major cities in the United States such as Chicago, Atlanta, and Detroit (Kilson 1987, 523).

Low black descriptive representation in the policymaking positions of the city government yielded low policy influence—and white imposition of political limits on black politicians served to minimize their policy influence (Mollenkopf 1986 and 1994). Though black politicians were part of the majority coalition in the city due to their affiliation with the Democratic Party, white elites and the electorate routinely declined to consider and accommodate black political interests.[12] White policymakers' refusals to appoint blacks to leadership roles in the city council, white party officials' reneging on promises to back black candidates for citywide elected office, and white voters' withholding ballots from nonwhite candidates prevented blacks from placing their interests and values high on the public agenda and influencing government largesse to their benefit.

Besides the restrictions set by whites, black politicians often imposed limits on themselves. In particular, they consistently subordinated themselves to the Democratic Party and accommodated conservative municipal agendas that privileged economic growth over neighborhood equity in exchange for patronage.[13] Although some black politicians continued the traditions of reform and radicalism that had characterized the origins of black politics in New York City (Biondi 2003; Greenberg 1991; Lewinson 1974), most black councilmen aligned themselves tightly with the remnants of the Democratic machine organizations in Manhattan, the Bronx, Brooklyn, and Queens (Thompson 1990). Respecting political hierarchy and favoring partisan solidarity over racial identity, they provided political support to their white peers in exchange for low- to mid-level municipal jobs and contracts they awarded to allies in their neighborhoods.

Furthermore, in their districts, black politicians sought to quell dissent and suppress activism. To these ends, they sponsored allies, ensuring continued support from them; they made deals with opponents, and they withheld patronage from potential rivals (Quimby 1977; Hamilton 1979 and 1990; Thompson 2006). Unseating ineffective incumbents became nearly impossible. During the 1980s, incumbents consistently garnered 90 percent or more of all votes cast in the city's majority-black election districts. Ultimately, the historic efforts of blacks as a collective to debate and redefine their political interests, encourage mass political participation, and hold elected representatives accountable to their constituents ground almost to a halt.

While black councilmen, in the end, took "their slice" during the Koch administration, as John Mollenkopf remarked at the time, they were "not a powerful and independent force on the overall allocation of public benefits" (1986, 592). As a result of the patron-client politics inherent in New York City, the conditions of black neighborhoods were of low regard to the city government, and the effects were noticeable.

At the end of the 1980s, unemployment rates in Morrisania, South Jamaica, Bedford-Stuyvesant, and Harlem remained well above the city rate. In particular, the male unemployment rate across the four neighborhoods grew from 14 percent to 18 percent between 1979 and 1989. Poverty levels among individuals at the conclusion of the 1980s remained above 30 percent, the threshold for determining "poverty areas" (W. J. Wilson 1987; Jargowsky and Yang 2006). Morrisania and Harlem were *extreme* poverty areas, where poverty rates equaled or were greater than 40 percent. The proportion of families with children under eighteen years of age that earned poverty-level incomes or less was 39 percent across the neighborhoods.[14] The declining conditions motivated most of the remaining middle-class residents to flee. Many working-class families that could follow the middle class did. But hope among those that remained in the neighborhoods was buoyed in 1989 by what first appeared to be a significant political change—the election of the city's first black mayor.

*The Dinkins Administration, 1989–1993.* Following racially polarized primary and general elections, David N. Dinkins was elected mayor. His supporters assumed that he could and would change the municipal agenda in ways that would advantage black neighborhoods through city spending. Blacks, especially those in the poorest neighborhoods, expected significant changes in the governance of the city. According to Gil Noble, a local political and cultural commentator who produced *Like It Is,* a weekly televised public affairs show that emphasized black life, "among the needy and the have-nots in our community, there was one great expectation that there would be coffers opening up and things would substantially change for the better" (1992). They assumed that Dinkins would not only place their values and interests high on the municipal policy agenda but reallocate municipal funds in ways to begin a redistribution of the city's wealth and assets.

As Dinkins took office, residents of Morrisania, Bedford-Stuyvesant, South Jamaica, and Harlem faced relatively high levels of socioeconomic hardship. Median household income was $15,172 below the median of the city. Twice as many of their residents were poor (41 percent) relative to residents of the city as a whole (19 percent). Compared to 13 percent of households in the city receiving public assistance, 28 percent of households in the four neighborhoods depended on such assistance. The proportion of female-headed households with children under the age of eighteen (24 percent) was double the city rate.

Dinkins wanted to improve conditions in the city's black neighborhoods. He tried to do it. During his administration, for instance, social services spending increased annually, albeit modestly (Weikert 2001, 368). Moreover, Dinkins, like Koch, used public resources to increase and improve affordable housing; some reports claim that he spent greater than $200 million in Harlem alone (Bernstein 1994). Yet multiple factors weakened Dinkins's ability to govern in accordance with black interests.

Dinkins was mayor at a time of economic downturn. The United States was enduring a recession (Citizens Budget Commission 1997; Pagano and Barnes 1991). Locally, Dinkins inherited a $1 billion budget deficit from the Koch administration, which grew to $2.2 billion by the end of his term in office. He also took over a municipal government that was suffering declining tax revenues, along with anemic growth in employment and incomes. When Dinkins became mayor, the municipal revenue environment was characterized by the lowest income growth since 1982 and the lowest employment growth since 1980 (Thompson 2006, 200). Throughout his administration, Dinkins often reminded residents and prospective voters of the fiscal limits of the city: "My big problem has been the fiscal constraints that have seized us from day one. . . . It is my misfortune that I come to office now at a time of fiscal crisis. And so there are not the resources to address a lot of the problems. . . . And the tax base sure isn't poor folks" (1992).[15] His efforts to balance the budget in his first year included reducing municipal expenditures by $260 million and raising $453 million through new taxes, with approximately 50 percent of the new revenue coming from increased property taxes.[16] He also agreed to layoff ten thousand municipal workers, most of whom were black (Biles 2001, 146). Plus, he pledged a four-year abatement of corporate taxes (Sites 1997, 548).

Furthermore, the Dinkins administration, filled with former allies of the Koch administration, was conflicted about weighing competing demands among the bloc of voters that gave Dinkins his victory. Latinos gave Dinkins the votes he needed to beat Koch in the mayoral primary and Rudolph Giuliani in the general election in 1989. Accordingly, Latino representatives and interest groups pressed the administration to direct resources to their communities. At the same time, black representatives were pulling the mayor in the other direction. Additionally, the Dinkins administration was seemingly jinxed by racial violence and discord in the city's neighborhoods. Events such as the boycotting of Korean businesses by blacks, the accidental killing of a young black boy by Hasidim ambulance drivers, rallies by white police officers against city hall, and the murder of a rabbinical student by young black youth hampered the administration's ability to implement a more redistributive policy agenda.

Racial dynamics within the municipal bureaucracy also hindered Dinkins's ability to accord municipal priorities with black interests and values. In the 1960s, the majority of blacks employed by the city government had been semiskilled workers, clerks and secretaries, and general laborers (Wilder 2000, 225). Three decades later, the municipal government had become the core employment sector for blacks in New York City.[17] The proportion of blacks employed by the municipal government under Dinkins surpassed the proportion of blacks in the population. Nonetheless, the majority of blacks continued to occupy the ranks of frontline workers, not administrators and managers, making them the least influential actors, as well as among the lowest paid, in the bureaucracy (Waldinger 1996).[18]

In departments where blacks were visible among the highest ranks of public administrators, such as the Human Resources Administration, black officials and managers found their bureaucratic authority and discretion constrained by fiscal realities. Moreover, their positions afforded them little influence over the mayor and his deputies in strategy and decision sessions to restructure municipal priorities. Thus, black public servants were unable to use their positions to substantively change public policy, at least not to the sustained benefit of poor black neighborhoods.[19] This finding contradicts a long-standing theory that the inclusion of blacks in a dominant governing coalition positively effects "changes in city government policies [especially the distribution of public benefits] that respond to minority interests" (Browning, Marshall, and Tabb 1984, 24). Joining a dominant coalition, even one led by a black mayor supported by a strong-mayor form of government, did not necessarily improve black's ability to determine, guide, and enact public action to resolve collective problems, especially those in low-income neighborhoods (Mollenkopf 1997).

In due course, the Dinkins administration showed that, in the words of Adolph Reed Jr., in relation to "dimensions of advocacy for justice and equity, the record of black regimes is poor. They are by and large only black versions of the pro-growth regimes that they have replaced, distinguished in part by the asymmetry of their campaign rhetoric and their practice of governance" (1999, 109). For instance, Dinkins campaigned on minority access to jobs connected to economic development projects subsidized by the city, but as mayor he decided, just as Koch did, against linking public-funded economic development to minority employment (Mollenkopf 1994). "By the end of its four-year term the Dinkins administration showed few signs of having pursued a policy agenda much different from that of its predecessor" (Sites 1997, 548).

Rather, the Dinkins administration provided further evidence that when blacks govern cities, even cities where they have achieved strong political incorporation, they are no more progressive in their policy stances than whites, often because black mayors tend to lead city governments burdened by revenue shortages and financial difficulties (Reed 1999; Keiser 1997). Moreover, it proved that black mayors, like white mayors, fear that an increased municipal emphasis on redistribution in the name of equity will expel capital and jobs from their city, further weakening their local economy and tax base (Peterson 1981).

Constrained from governing New York City in accordance with the interests of his electoral coalition, particularly its black voting bloc, and dogged by accusations of inability to hold together the city's racial mosaic, Dinkins failed in his reelection bid. He lost to Rudolph Giuliani, the Republican candidate he had beat four years earlier.

*The Giuliani Administration, 1993–2001.* The Giuliani administration continued the overall trend of advancing economic development by reducing social welfare expenditures (Sites 1997). Along with seeking elimination of the municipal sales tax and ultimately reducing taxes by more than $2 billion, Giuliani pressed for municipal spending reductions regardless of the state of the local economy, seeking cuts in good times and bad times (Weikart 2001). Unlike Koch and Dinkins, however, Giuliani sought a full-scale diminution of the local welfare state's apparatus and its consumers.

Giuliani's assault on the municipal government began with cuts to affordable housing production programs and core agencies of the municipal social welfare system, agencies whose consumers and employees were predominantly black, and led by blacks installed by Giuliani himself: Human Resources Administration, Health and Hospitals Corporation, Board of Education, and Department of Housing Preservation and Development (Institute for Puerto Rican Policy 1994; Barrett 2000). At one point the Giuliani administration even lobbied the state government to reduce its allotment of welfare and Medicaid payments to the city by $1.2 billion. Journalist Wayne Barrett (2000, 309) put the mayor's lobbying in perspective: "For the first time, a New York City mayor decided that a reduction in state entitlements aid was a fiscal positive. It meant, from Rudy's perspective, that the city could slice its own entitlement expenses since it was required to match state funding. Rudy was literally discovering that less was more—less aid from the state for the city's poor allowed the city to slash its own expenditures by similar amounts" (2000, 309).

This approach fit with the Giuliani administration's interpretation of its mandate to make government more efficient and effective. In Giuliani's words, his administration was "truly an attempt to reengineer the way in which city government operates"; it was combating the "apostles of dependency" and the "old way of thinking" about government's role (quoted in Kirtzman 2000, 102, 173).[20] But as one insider in the administration remarked candidly to journalist Andrew Kirtzman, Giuliani's "guys came [into] government with . . . disdain for government" (quoted in Kirtzman 2000, 100).

Others saw the administration's behavior as expressing official disdain for the city's black neighborhoods, a disdain rooted in racism and realpolitik. "As I'm concerned primarily in New York City, I think there is the most racism that I have ever seen in all my life," according to a pastor of a church in Queens whom I interviewed. "I've been here—I'm almost seventy years old—and I've never seen this much racism directed toward [black] people." Since Giuliani did not respect blacks, especially those elected to represent black neighborhoods, and since blacks generally did not vote for Giuliani, he had no need to shift his municipal agenda to accommodate blacks in any way, unless it was about getting tougher on crime in black neighborhoods (Newfield 2002; Barrett 2000).

In the end, whether it was about reengineering, racism, or the fact that Giuliani won office without black support, the efforts of the Giuliani administration sustained a convention: from the late 1970s through the 1990s, little good came from government in relation to the interests and needs of the residents of Bedford-Stuyvesant, South Jamaica, Harlem, and Morrisania. The neighborhoods remained "filthy, crime-ridden, and neglected by city services"—a sentiment common among the city's most activist black clergy (Kirtzman 2000, 71–72). The Reverend Calvin O. Butts III of Abyssinian Baptist Church spoke earnestly about the situation during a televised public affairs program: "Right now, as things sit in my community, we've got troubles. We've got problems" (1998). The problems were unyielding.

By 2000, the mean rate of female-headed households with children in the four black neighborhoods had risen to 25 percent. The poverty rate continued to hover near 40 percent. Median household incomes in the neighborhoods still lagged behind the city median by $13,180. A survey of adults in Harlem revealed that 65 percent of residents rated the neighborhood as a fair to poor place to raise a child (Metis Associates 2003, 62). Moreover, 56 percent of respondents either expected to leave the neighborhood or were uncertain about remaining in it (Metis Associates 2003, 55). This was not surprising given that economic conditions in Harlem and the other black neighborhoods had remained virtually unchanged since the end of the Koch administration (Pristin 2000). Ultimately, the four black neighborhoods remained poor places with limited economic vitality through the end of the Giuliani administration.

North of Yankee Stadium, the extreme poverty rate in Morrisania barely declined. Instead, poverty became more concentrated as the neighborhood continued to lose working-class residents to middle-class neighborhoods. Across the East River, male unemployment had become endemic in Bedford-Stuyvesant. Squads of working-age men stood outside corner stores for hours, shooting dice, drinking forty-ounce bottles of malt liquor, and waiting for something to "jump off." In South Jamaica, far more residents rented apartments than owned homes. This was the case even though the neighborhood is adjacent to middle-class black neighborhoods and is located in Queens, the borough of homeowners.

## THE INTERSECTION OF POLITICS, POLICIES, AND NEIGHBORHOODS: THE PERSPECTIVES OF BLACK PASTORS

Black pastors of activist African American churches, especially the most politically active, in Harlem, Bedford-Stuyvesant, South Jamaica, and Morrisania knew well of the effects that politics and policies from the 1970s onward had on the city's black neighborhoods. From their unanimous standpoint, the Koch, Dinkins, and Giuliani administrations had perpetuated problems in their communities. They witnessed government's ongoing failure to change the circumstances of poor blacks in the city and, in many ways, worsening of them by reducing public spending on social services.

During an interview with me, a pastor from a Harlem church recalled the period of government retrenchment under the Koch administration and its consequences for the neighborhood:

The welfare state was anemic. It lacked vigor on behalf of the poor. So I recognized that government was no longer the answer. I knew this once the crack epidemic took off in the 1980s. Also, AFDC was keeping many of my people dependent. It gave them cash assistance, but what did it to their lives and self-esteem? The cost is immeasurable. The efforts by the city to foreclose on abandoned houses did little, at least in the beginning. Crackheads and dealers used those shells to buy and ply drugs. Don't forget the prostitutes. Man, it was sick up here. Now, I'm not laying all the blame on government, but more money, better programs, could have made a difference.

Likewise a pastor from Bedford-Stuyvesant commented on the role of government in the decline of his church's neighborhood:

Back in the eighties, the Reagan-Bush years, government pulled out very extensively in giving money to the communities in need, and you know who lived in those communities. [Interviewer: No. Who?] You're funny. All right, I'll say it—blacks. Anyway, those pullbacks hurt our communities. The programs that were in place just couldn't continue to meet the need. Reaganomics caught up with us and it was a stretch for black people. I mean federal housing dollars ceased to come into the city. I'm exaggerating, but you know what I mean. Then crack [cocaine] restructured reality. Remember the violence? Remember the boarder [abandoned, often crack-addicted] babies? It was horrible. It really was. . . . And where was government? What was government for? Where were our black tax dollars going? Elsewhere, that's where.

As for the Dinkins administration, most of the black clergy I interviewed could not summon supportive words.

During interviews, I reminded the clergy that some of their peers had tried to modulate black hopes during Dinkins's first year in office. Reverend Butts of Abyssinian Baptist Church, for instance, had cautioned the black polity about the mayor: "Dinkins is as much a machine, clubhouse politician as he is African-American" (quoted in Biles 2001, 139). In hindsight, however, they believed that symbolism got the best of them and their communities. One pastor from Bedford-Stuyvesant commented: "The presence of a black mayor had tremendous symbolic power. But we elected a person who was a traditional politician, who had no real understanding of how to make the political process responsive to the needs of the very people that he represented."[21] This feeling was widespread among black New Yorkers during Dinkins's reelection campaign, and it accounts for an important reason that Dinkins lost his bid—dissatisfaction, especially among working-class and poor blacks, over municipal policies, crime, employment, and race relations decreased black electoral turnout (Mollenkopf 1994, 214–16).

With descriptive representation unable to produce substantive representation, the dearth of political associations for electoral engagement, and black politicians resting under the thumb of the Democratic Party and often concerned more about self-preservation than about neighborhood transformation, city government remained unresponsive to most of the needs, interests, and values of black neighborhoods. When the pastors looked at the state of black neighborhoods, they recognized how palpable the limits of electoral representation were in New York City. Here are the words of a pastor from South Jamaica: "Most black officials weren't bringing any resources of any substantive nature to their communities. Our black politicians were feeble. Do you understand? Even our lone black mayor was weak."[22] That was a universal observation among the clergy I interviewed, one expressed more fully by a pastor from Harlem: "I raise my question again. Where would you go to see the stewardship evidence of . . . whoever the black officials are? Now, there may be some that exist about which I do not know, but I can't tell you where to go to find it. It would be good to ask them, 'What has your term in office produced in a tangible way to improve the life and quality of the people who elect you to term after term after term?' "

Offering a criterion for judging the effectiveness of politicians, a pastor from Bedford-Stuyvesant posited that the ability of black politicians as substantive representatives of black interests in New York City had declined over the years: "I didn't see evidences of their influence at making city government responsive to blacks. A tree is known by a fruit it bears. [Interviewer: What do you mean by that?] It's the fruit that gives validity to the tree. I'd seen a significant decline in the influence of black politicians in my thirty-seven years as a pastor in New York City. [Interviewer: When were they most influential?] Back in the sixties and in the seventies."

It was not supposed to be like this, as the pastor later acknowledged: "We thought, when we came out of the sixties revolution or people presumed . . . that our next leadership would be political leadership, effective political leadership." The pastor continued, "Our elected black officials failed [us]. They weren't worth a quarter. They did not deliver for us."²³

It was the sentiment of most black politicians, too, according to a survey I administered in 1999 to a random sample of black elected officials in New York City. I probed their satisfaction with the quantity of municipal services received by blacks. The data showed that 96 percent of respondents were dissatisfied with the level of municipal responsiveness to their neighborhoods' problems. Furthermore, the survey found that 72 percent of black elected officials deemed their group uninfluential at making the city government more responsive to the concerns of blacks.²⁴ Just 36 percent of black elected officials described their group as influential at setting and controlling the policy agenda of the city. Evidently, pastors had cause to view black politicians negatively.

As the pastors sought to account for the inability of electoral politics and elected officials to match the hopes they possessed and the optimism they had about electoral action and representatives at the end of the civil rights movement, their comments raised a supplemental theme—black leaders lacked commitment to black communities. An element of this theme was the idea that politicians cared more about reelection to public office than about resurrection of the neighborhoods as decent places to live. "They became so committed to the party to which they belonged and to their position of prestige and power," a pastor averred, "that they had largely forgotten that the people [black voters] made it possible for them to have their positions."

One pastor, somewhat facetiously, suggested that local drug dealers had more character than neighborhood politicians: "I don't know which one is worse. At least with drug dealers you can use the word *respect,* but with a politician the only word you can use is *elect.*" Attempting to be fair in his assessment, another pastor wondered aloud about the commitment of his neighborhood's elected representatives to being strong political advocates for its residents: "Black politicians were not producing justice or economic independence, or any real respect from white people for black people. Where were black politicians at the time? I don't know. I really don't know. The short and long of it is I just don't know. I guess they were somewhere. But that doesn't necessarily mean they were not doing anything. But I can't argue that they were."

Despite the dissatisfaction and reservations clergy had regarding neighborhood politicians, as well as their recognition of the overall political environment, especially the unlikelihood of blacks' interests being equated with the city's interests, their churches did not depart from the electoral arena nor abandon electoral action. Throughout the 1980s and into the 1990s, activist African American churches carried out the acts that they had historically done on the electoral stages of the Big Apple (Green and Wilson 1992; Wilson and Green 1988; Ross 1996; Owens 1997a; Freedman 1993). Their activities included, among other things, voter registration drives, the distribution of voter education guides, and invitations of electoral candidates to address their congregations. An informant from a church in Bedford-Stuyvesant, reflecting on that church's historic reputation as one of the most influential political communities in New York City, explained why African American churches like it continued to engage in electoral politics despite limited gains for blacks: "Miracles are good, but the polls matter more. . . . The African American church cannot separate itself from politics. We, too, must operate in the main. That means we must be political and seek the spoils of politics like other groups, for change takes place at the polls. It's true even if change comes slowly."

Even if electoral participation and political incorporation did not translate into dramatic changes in neighborhood conditions, retaining black faces in public places of authority yielded symbolic rewards, preserved and increased the ranks of the black middle class via municipal employment, and kept alive the idea that voting mattered, while honoring those who died to give blacks the franchise and access to the political process.[25] Still, in the 1980s and 1990s the churches did not invest all their resources in increasing black descriptive representation in government, as a pastor from South Jamaica recalled: "Now, we had to divert some of our attention away from [electoral] politics. It was a necessity. We knew that if we didn't look out for us, wasn't anybody going to look out for us. We had despaired about government programs living up to what politicians said they were going to live up to in terms of enhancing or even providing a quality of life for the citizen, especially the citizen of pigmentation. . . . But we despaired long enough. We got our act together."

Instead of lamenting the feebleness of black politicians or rethinking how to translate electoral victories into substantive rewards for their neighborhoods, pastors turned to the resources of their churches to address neighborhood needs. "We weren't interested in waiting on public officials," according to a pastor from Bedford-Stuyvesant, "because the people in public office, number one, did not have any ideas for their neighborhoods, and, two, even if they had ideas they could not get them off the ground."[26]

Summing up the opinion of the pastors I interviewed, one Morrisania pastor closed a session with me with these comments: "The churches had tried to call the politicians into action on behalf of the community, but they didn't hear us or turned a deaf ear. We pushed on without them."

## SUMMARY

The largest and poorest black neighborhoods in New York City were in socioeconomic trouble in the 1960s, and these troubles worsened in subsequent decades. Harlem, Bedford-Stuyvesant, South Jamaica, and Morrisania lost middle-class residents, along with jobs, investment, and security. Politics and policies contributed to black neighborhood decline. Activist black clergy tied the problems of the neighborhoods in the last three decades of the twentieth century to the limitations and flaws of city politics and black politicians in making government more responsive. They averred that white politicians had power and black politicians did not.

Even when black politicians assumed pivotal positions such as the city's mayorship, they were unable or unwilling to substantively represent the preferences of their districts. The interests of poor black neighborhoods were seldom recognized or addressed, or they were addressed in ways that did not reduce the scale of their most serious problems.

Activist black clergy would act, however, on behalf of the low-income neighborhoods. They would take steps that were both traditional and innovative. Redeeming the four black neighborhoods from decline became a goal for their churches.

# CHAPTER FOUR

# Faith in Action for
# Neighborhood Redemption

Despite decline, concentrated poverty, and inadequate municipal responsiveness, activist African American churches remained in Harlem, Bedford-
Stuyvesant, Morrisania, and South Jamaica. They made a deliberate choice to
stay rather than leave the neighborhoods for new locales or remain but resign
themselves to the impoverished conditions. Even as conditions worsened,
these churches never lost their faith that their resources could assist in the
redemption of the four black neighborhoods. And they deliberately put their
faith in action.

## BECAUSE JESUS COULDN'T MAKE IT

The municipal government's inability and ineffectiveness to respond to the
needs of the black neighborhoods, according to a pastor from Queens, "encouraged the increase in our churches and other religious institutions stepping up their actions and activities in the whole process of black neighborhood redevelopment." A Bronx peer of his pointed out to me, "If we had
waited for a handout, we would have waited for a long time." Of course, as was
characteristic of African American churches in New York City and elsewhere
over the sweep of black history, not all African American churches would take
the step to resurrect the neighborhoods. The conditions in Morrisania, South
Jamaica, Bedford-Stuyvesant, and Harlem presented local churches, as well as
neighborhood residents generally, with three choices—flight, resignation, or
action (Orbell and Uno 1972).

## *Flight*

Some African American churches fled from the four neighborhoods as conditions worsened. They divested from them, selling their edifices and other properties they owned. They let their leases expire and moved to new locations. Exit fit the dual traditions of African American churches' following the movements of their attenders and seeking new "religious districts" (McRoberts 2003; Sernett 1997). The pull of choosing exit over passivity and voice was great in the 1980s and 1990s in New York City. Large numbers of blacks, led by the middle class, were exiting the original nodes of black settlement (Nathan, Chow, and Owens 1995; Owens 1997b; Haynes 2001). The emigrants settled in newly forming black neighborhoods inside the city, such as those in southeast Queens (e.g., Laurelton and Cambria Heights) and the northern Bronx (e.g., Wakefield and Williamsbridge), as well as black neighborhoods in the cities and suburbs of Nassau (e.g., Hempstead), Suffolk (e.g., Wyandanch), and Westchester (e.g., Runyon Heights) counties (Haynes 2001). Many of their churches followed them.

Rising crime often made the neighborhoods unsafe for churches and their congregants. Churches were slightly less vulnerable than other types of properties to theft and arson. But they were not immune to the neighborhoods' problems. They could not provide their congregants with absolute sanctuary from evil. In the daytime church workers might be accosted by muggers. In the evenings crack addicts sometimes preyed on the elderly returning home from revivals and other church gatherings. Even on Sundays the ground outside churches could be more sacrilegious than sacred, with children leaving Sunday school trapped in the crossfire of drug gangs contesting turf and markets. Too often death literally stood outside the doors of the churches.

## *Resignation*

The majority of African American churches, however, did not flee Harlem, Morrisania, Bedford-Stuyvesant, or South Jamaica. Even though many of their congregants exited to other locales and stayed away or moved to other locales and reverse-commuted long distances for Sunday worship services, most churches stayed, and new ones appeared. Yet the majority of the churches that remained resigned themselves to worsening conditions. Instead of focusing on solving the worldly problems faced by their congregants and broader communities, most churches that chose resignation looked to just save souls.

Their choice fit another tradition of African American churches—keeping open their doors in the midst of sin, suffering, and social change to offer salvation and soul preparation for the afterlife. As others before them, pastors preached "pie in the sky," while trying, as Reverend Albert Cleage, a founder of the Black Christian Nationalist movement, once chided, to "take people to heaven one by one" (1972, 33).[1] In the process, they ignored temporal conditions outside the stained-glass windows and closed doors or burglar-barred and security-gated storefronts of their edifices.

## Action

Not all of the churches that remained in the neighborhoods resigned themselves. Some churches elected to be activist, to stand with residents amid decline, crime, and blight, giving voice to and working on the problems of the neighborhoods. Their choice of voice and action preserved the legacy of African American churches as the cornerstones of black civil society, the founts of civic, social, and political action. Among the churches that decided against departure or passivity were Abyssinian Baptist Church and Canaan Baptist Church of Christ in Harlem, Allen African Methodist Episcopal Church in South Jamaica, Bridge Street African Wesleyan Methodist Episcopal Church in Bedford-Stuyvesant, and Walker-Memorial Baptist Church in Morrisania. They had long histories of civic engagement and political engagement in and on behalf of their neighborhoods (Wilson and Green 1988; Taylor 1992 and 1994).

Scripture influenced the decisions of the churches to remain in and serve the neighborhoods. Surmising why most of the activist churches had remained in their neighborhoods, a pastor I interviewed in Morrisania about the history of his church quoted the Old Testament prophet Isaiah (58:12): "And they that shall be of thee shall build the old waste places: thou shalt raise up the foundations of many generations; and thou shalt be called the repairer of the breach, the restorer of paths to dwell in." Most pastors I interviewed, however, suggested that the basis for their churches' decisions to remain in and work with the neighborhoods rested on a liberal exegesis of the New Testament. "Monasticism and asceticism are not presented in the Gospel narratives as models of Christian witness," as the Reverend Dr. William Augustus Jones of Bethany Baptist Church in Bedford-Stuyvesant once wrote. "Jesus' hometown was the slum section of Galilee. He grew up in a ghetto. He sat and supped with sinners" (1979, 70). Every pastor who sat for an interview with me borrowed heavily from this analysis.

When I asked one pastor from Bedford-Stuyvesant to explain why his largely middle-class congregation had decided to remain in its neighborhood, he pulled from a shelf a yellowed and tattered copy of *God in the Ghetto*, one that Reverend Jones had given him years ago. He read aloud from it a portion of a letter that Jones, while staging an Operation Breadbasket sit-in, wrote to his brethren in the ministry.[2] "We are a privileged group," the pastor read. "But for millions of our brothers and sisters, hunger pains dart through their bodies. We have to be here not for our sake, but for the future's sake. I am here because Jesus couldn't make it. If He were in town, I'm convinced that He would be here with us." Putting the book down, he asked, "Need I say more, young man?" Summing up the consensus of the activist black pulpit in New York City regarding the institutional place of African American churches in poor neighborhoods, another pastor from Harlem exclaimed to me: "Read Luke 4:18! We got to preach the gospel to the poor, heal the brokenhearted, preach deliverance—physical, social, economic, and spiritual—to the captives, recover the sight of the blind, and free them that are bruised."

Collectively and independently, the activist churches that remained behind sought to improve the social, physical, and economic conditions of their neighborhoods by fulfilling a historic charge, one rooted in the social gospel movement of the early twentieth century and advocated by the Reverend Dr. Gardner Taylor, pastor emeritus of Concord Baptist Church of Christ in Bedford-Stuyvesant—"Get out of the Bible and into people's lives" (quoted in Gilbreath 1995, 26). From the pastors' perspective, effecting positive changes might be difficult for the churches, but their effort continued custom: their churches had long given succor to neighborhood residents.[3] Pastors and congregants held tightly to the original conviction of church founders that "a ministry of social service" was the primary responsibility of churches in black neighborhoods (Wilmore 1983, 160). The interviewed pastors reviewed this original intent in order to place the contemporary activities of their churches in historical context. Most of them began by revisiting the history of African American churches in New York City, beginning with the Great Depression, which they tended to parallel with the final days of the twentieth century.

*Recalling Original Intent: The Great Depression and Church Outreach.* During the economic downturn of the late 1920s, black clergy witnessed daily the swelling ranks of the black poor. From 1927 to 1930, the number of black New Yorkers receiving some form of public relief expanded from two thousand to twenty thousand (Green 1979, 361). Although the black neighborhoods needed all of black civil society's institutions engaged in addressing physical deprivations and reforming neighborhood conditions, the majority of African American churches did not struggle against the slums. This was true of African American churches in New York City as well as in cities across the nation (Lincoln and Mamiya 1990; Sernett 1997). Their clergy did not know how or did not care to make their churches socially relevant in relation to poverty. Most did what they could do best, which was also the simplest response to the temporal problems of blacks: they "retreated into enclaves of moralistic, revivalistic Christianity by which they tried to fend off the encroaching gloom and pathology of the ghetto" (Wilmore 1983, 161). Employing a sin-salvation model of ministry, they kept open the breaches among theological conservatism, a progressive social gospel, biblical fundamentalism, and scriptural interpretation (Sernett 1997, 119).

Still, out of economic despair and physical hunger, gaunt-looking families and individuals sought out the churches for assistance. And many impoverished sojourners in the black neighborhoods of New York City found useful social services behind the doors of some churches. The churches with congregation-based social services extended comfort to the afflicted and balm to the economically broken. Once inside, the fortunate found basic rations, meager monetary aid, limited but hopeful job prospects, and a good word of coming changes promised by the New Testament.

Connecting evangelism to a social gospel that focused on the temporal conditions of impoverishment, the pastor of a Harlem church explained why his church and a few others welcomed the poor at their doors by extending relief during the Depression:

> Christianity is more than preaching, praying, singing, and giving; it is all of these but a great deal more. The purpose of the Christianity of Jesus as revealed in the New Testament is to supply man's social as well as spiritual needs. . . . Very few people ask anymore what the church believes but what is the church doing for the amelioration of the condition of mankind. The majority of the people care very little about church doctrine. They are looking for a translation of the spirit of Jesus Christ in the everyday life of his professed followers. The church will never draw and hold masses by essays on faith, but by showing her faith by her works. (quoted in Clark 1978, 63)

That is, African American churches needed to "go into the highways and hedges during the week, caring for the sick, the wounded, the distressed and all that are needy" (Welty 1969, 83).

Although benevolence by African American churches at the onset of the Great Depression was insufficient to reduce poverty, the number of African American churches, especially those led by college-educated clergy, giving relief and operating uplift services on a relatively large scale increased. Activist African American churches raised contributions from congregants and local entrepreneurs to assist the economically and socially displaced (Clark 1978). They focused on meeting the economic needs of the working poor and the unemployed. Church-operated clothing pantries, soup kitchens, and emergency shelter and rent assistance covered basic needs for many among the multitudes in need. Church-funded pensions assisted some widows and the elderly. Church-run academies reduced adult illiteracy, trained for future employment, encouraged thrift, and influenced the moral character of their students, adults and adolescents alike.[4] Collectively, Gayraud Wilmore writes, they "became, in effect, social welfare agencies serving a broad spectrum of the needs of the burgeoning urban populations" (1983, 160).

*"Something in Jesus' Name."* Through the 1980s and 1990s, activist African American churches were still addressing the problems and concerns of blacks in their neighborhoods, which in some cases had lasted since the Great Depression. Some in the black pulpit expressed frustration about the enduring nature of these problems. They did not, however, convey hopelessness. The churches might not solve the neighborhoods' problems, but they could, in the words of a worshiper I conversed with before interviewing their pastor, "do something in Jesus' name that would make a difference and bring glory to God." The African American churches that remained in Harlem, Morrisania, Bedford-Stuyvesant, and South Jamaica, choosing action over resignation, sought to tackle the social, physical, and economic problems of residents of their neighborhoods.

The breadth and depth of the problems—problems the pastors blamed mainly on public policy and unresponsive mayoral administrations—demanded more than salvation and sanctification, more than prayer and benevolence. "Neighborhood resurrection," as one pastor termed it, required changes on the part of the churches. At a minimum, activist churches needed to broaden their definitions of ministry on behalf of the neighborhoods. "Used to be you could get away with tellin' folk, 'It'll be all right when you get to heaven.' [They] don't buy that no more," noted the Reverend Johnny Ray Youngblood of Saint Paul Community Baptist Church in Brooklyn; consequently, "the church has to do more than save souls" (quoted in Freedman 1993, 37; see also Youngblood 1992).

Additionally, activist churches needed to adopt a more comprehensive notion of community. The Reverend Gary Simpson of Concord Baptist Church of Christ in Bedford-Stuyvesant spoke to this requirement in conversation with another scholar: "The church has to wrestle with itself and ask, 'What do we really mean by community?' If we just mean ourselves, then we're missing it. We ought to have a broader sense of community that focuses" on neighborhoods, not just congregations (quoted in Toussaint 1999, 76). The "broader sense of community" was necessary. As Omar McRoberts (2001, 10) comments, "Churches are not necessarily neighborhood institutions." And in the black neighborhoods of New York City there were many African American churches that chose to stand apart from their neighborhoods and other "community-based" institutions, seeing their purpose as solely to serve the needs of those who came to them for salvation and sermons.

Most important, neighborhood resurrection required activist churches to go beyond emergency relief as a response to declining socioeconomic and physical conditions. The churches were competent at "programmatic religion"; they expressed well the traditions and theologies of their faith by providing food, clothing, temporary shelter, and other services to support needy individuals and families (DiIulio 2002). But many activist churches, as well as churches inclined toward becoming activist, lacked the capacity to design, implement, and, most importantly, integrate services across a spectrum of areas to increase their overall effect (Owens 2004a).

The provision of relief by activist African American churches in New York City in the last two decades of the twentieth century was not consonant with the broader problems their neighborhoods faced, such as limited educational attainment, unemployment, violence, and drug addiction. The scale of problems required a comprehensive set of services, along with greater structure and sustainability in delivery. "I said to myself and congregants," a pastor from Bedford-Stuyvesant remembered, "that good will ain't enough to run outreach ministries that affect lives on a large scale." To address neighborhood problems better and convert declining neighborhoods into "redemptive sites," churches, he contended, had to move beyond small-scale voluntarist activities such as soup kitchens and clothing pantries. They had to create organizations that could approach the fundamental problems of their neighborhoods with a higher degree of complexity and comprehensiveness in programming. In short, they needed to build their institutional capacity.

## BUILDING INSTITUTIONAL CAPACITY FOR
## COMMUNITY DEVELOPMENT

A common approach activist African American churches in New York City took to develop their institutional capacity was to work in partnership with secular nongovernmental groups. Congregational survey data from a sample of primarily activist black clergy in Gotham during the early 1980s suggest that a majority of such churches had joined with secular community-based organizations to deal with neighborhood problems (Lincoln and Mamiya n.d.).[5] A pastor of a small nondenominational church in Morrisania told me why: "We had resources among us as churches that your typical community group lacked. We believed, and still do, that cooperating with secular nonprofits is a good way to leverage those resources into tangible improvements that move us away from some of the neighborhood's problems."

The primary problems that activist churches addressed with secular groups were police-community conflict, civil rights abuses, welfare reform, and substance abuse and addictions. On the one hand, the activist churches' work alongside secular community groups did not necessarily address the problems that were most responsible for poverty and the lack of social opportunities in the neighborhoods. Limited employment, inadequate housing, and failing public schools often were ignored. On the other hand, the problems the churches attended to were among the most contentious in New York City at the time: police brutality, white racial hooliganism and homicides of blacks, cuts in public assistance spending, and the crack epidemic.

Additionally, activist African American churches addressed other needs, such as feeding the homeless, providing child care, and producing supportive housing for the elderly, through nascent collaborations with government. Available data suggest that up to 25 percent of activist African American churches in New York City in the 1980s provided a social service funded by or in conjunction with government agencies (Lincoln and Mamiya 1990).

Another approach by activist African American churches to building their institutional capacity was the chartering of faith-related agencies. By 1995 the activist African American churches I studied in depth had chartered, either independently or in cooperation with other churches, approximately thirty faith-related agencies. They included credit unions, home health agencies, senior citizens' centers, and Christian schools. Activist African American churches throughout the city created such nonprofit subsidiaries on behalf of their neighborhoods, not just their congregants. Through their faith-related agencies, the churches sought to provide the residents of Bedford-Stuyvesant, Harlem, Morrisania, and South Jamaica with the tools they needed to become self-sufficient, which included shelter, jobs, transportation to work, daycare, and even voter registration cards. A faith-related agency of Allen AME Church in South Jamaica illustrates the point.

The Allen AME Women's Resource Center (AWRC) provides temporary asylum for female victims of domestic violence and their children and receives funding from a diverse collection of government agencies. In telling the story of "Mrs. Q," Catherine Sweeting explains how the AWRC works:

> Mrs. Q., the thirty-two-year-old mother of a thirteen-year-old daughter and two sons ages twelve and eight, sought admission to the shelter to allow her to separate from her physically abusive husband, who was addicted to drugs. During their four-month stay in 1990, Mrs. Q.'s family received individual and family counseling to address their feelings of victimization. Upon discharge from AWRC, Mrs. Q. and her children were transferred to a supportive housing program developed for domestic violence survivors. Eight months later, she moved into her own private apartment. Mrs. Q. keeps in touch with AWRC staff, and she has secured employment. (Sweeting 1999, 88)

Aside from providing information on medical assistance, housing, legal assistance, and day care, the AWRC offered clients professional crisis intervention counseling. The AWRC was one among a myriad of faith-related agencies supplementing the neighborhood services of secular nonprofit organizations and public agencies. But it was not the only one.

## Churches Chartering CDCs

CDCs became one of the most important types of faith-related agencies that activist churches chartered to respond to the physical and social conditions of black neighborhoods in New York City. From 1980 to 1995, nine African American church–associated CDCs appeared in South Jamaica, Harlem, Bedford-Stuyvesant, and Morrisania: Abyssinian Development Corporation, Allen Neighborhood Preservation and Development Corporation, Bridge Street Development Corporation, Canaan Housing Development Corporation, Concord Community Development Corporation, Association of Brooklyn Clergy for Community Development, Bronx Shepherds Restora-

TABLE 4  Nine African American church–associated community development corporations in New York City

| COMMUNITY DEVELOPMENT CORPORATION • Sponsor Congregation(s) as of 2000 | NEIGHBORHOOD (Borough) | YEAR FOUNDED |
|---|---|---|
| Abyssinian Development Corporation | Central Harlem | |
| • Abyssinian Baptist Church | (Manhattan) | 1989 |
| Allen Neighborhood Preservation and Development Corporation | South Jamaica | |
| • Allen African Methodist Episcopal Church | (Queens) | 1986 |
| Association of Brooklyn Clergy for Community Development | Bedford-Stuyvesant | |
| • Alliance of 35 congregations | (Brooklyn) | 1987 |
| Bridge Street Development Corporation | Bedford-Stuyvesant | |
| • Bridge Street African Wesleyan Methodist Episcopal Church | (Brooklyn) | 1995 |
| Bronx Shepherds Restoration Corporation | Morrisania | |
| • Alliance of 55 congregations | (Bronx) | 1980 |
| Canaan Housing Development Corporation | Central Harlem | |
| • Canaan Baptist Church of Christ | (Manhattan) | 1980 |
| Concord Community Development Corporation | Bedford-Stuyvesant | |
| • Concord Baptist Church of Christ | (Brooklyn) | 1994 |
| Harlem Congregations for Community Improvement | Upper Harlem | |
| • Alliance of 109 congregations including Memorial Baptist Church | (Manhattan) | 1986 |
| Southeast Queens Clergy for Community Empowerment | South Jamaica | |
| • Alliance of 64 congregations including Bethesda Missionary Baptist Church | (Queens) | 1986 |

tion Corporation, Harlem Congregations for Community Improvement, and Southeast Queens Clergy for Community Empowerment (see table 4).[6]

Each church-associated CDC emerged from the struggles of clergy to mobilize the material and cultural resources of activist churches on behalf of black neighborhoods and in the face of neighborhood decline and inadequate government responsiveness. Their collective focus would be on affordable housing production and human and health services. A few of the CDCs also would concentrate on the development of youth and neighborhood economies.[7] No single catalyst induced activist African American churches in New York City to charter CDCs as a means of building their institutional capacity for neighborhood redemption.[8] Instead, three overlapping sets of rationales influenced the churches to charter CDCs.

*Community-Related Rationales.* Morrisania, one of the original neighborhoods that gave birth to the Bronx, underwent dramatic negative changes between 1970 and 1980. During that period its population shrank by 64 percent (New York City Department of City Planning 1992). This downward population trend had began with the introduction of the city's subway lines to the neighborhood in the 1920s, followed by public housing in the 1950s (Gonzalez 2004). Its remaining residents faced hardscrabble conditions. Historian Evelyn Gonzalez describes the transformation of Morrisania thus: "An area that was once an aspiring suburb and later a thriving residential community had become the home of a poor, minority population" (2004, 31). Here is a description of Morrisania's blighted physical environment in the 1980s: "To travel through the area brings back memories of war-torn Europe in the 1940s. In some places, where fires, vandals, and city-paid wrecking crews have done their work, neighborhoods have a more pastoral appearance. Tall trees grow up in fields that cover rubble left from four-story walkups. In other places, attractive buildings still stand, the windows of lower floors filled with cinderblocks in a fruitless effort to keep out vandals" (Tabb 1986, 103).

Nevertheless, the neighborhood, especially in its commercial corridors, continued to house a collection of African American churches. A group of clergy and lay leaders from some of them routinely convened informally over the years to deliberate about restoring the neighborhood as a place for stable and decent living, as it was when European immigrants and their offspring (including Edward I. Koch) called it home. In 1980 the group ended its deliberations and formulated an institutional response to the neighborhood's decline—Bronx Shepherds Restoration Corporation (BSRC).[9] A principal of the BSRC recounted for me why the churches allied with each other, choosing action over resignation and flight: "Thirty-member churches came together when the Bronx was burning. Ministers wanted to put out the fires. They also wanted to address the crises of shrinking congregations and the outmigration of the working- and middle-classes. They wanted to develop jobs and housing for neighborhood residents, as well as reinstall community pride." These were the objectives of activist churches in Harlem, too.

By the 1980s, the Harlem Renaissance had long given way to a nadir. One-third of neighborhood residents received public assistance income. Both male unemployment and the proportion of households with children headed by women hovered near 20 percent. Housing abandonment was rife, and facades along and off commercial corridors (e.g., 125th Street and Malcolm X Boulevard) were dilapidated. Rental housing was often squalid. Social psychologists Jacqueline Leavitt and Susan Saegert, in an analysis of grassroots movements to address affordable-housing shortages in the neighborhood, made the following observations: "On blocks where some buildings remain standing, and others demolished, nothing remains of formerly inhabited apartments except the colored walls that were once rooms. On roofs and in abandoned lots where ailanthus grows rampant, the accoutrements of daily life are also abandoned, an old fashioned bathtub with clawed legs, a rotting mattress or a rusting coffeepot, stray curtain, or a flower pot or hot plate on a window sill" (1990, 20). Like their peers in Morrisania, black clergy in Harlem were interested in identifying an institutional approach to these conditions. Among the first black clergy in Harlem to act was the Reverend Wyatt Tee Walker, pastor of Canaan Baptist Church.

Reverend Walker charged his congregation to charter a CDC in 1980 to revitalize the blocks in the vicinity of its edifice. Through Canaan Housing Development Corporation (Canaan HDC) the church would develop affordable housing, especially for the elderly. The elderly were a special focus for three reasons: they constituted a majority of the church's remaining congregants, they were least likely to want to or be able to leave the neighborhood, and they were the most likely to maintain the condition of rehabilitated and new properties. Serving them first was intended to serve the overall neighborhood, ensuring that the church would remain and the initial investments would not be wasted.

Six years later, Canaan HDC was joined by Harlem Congregations for Community Improvement (HCCI). HCCI opened its doors in Bradhurst, a forty-block area in the northeast quadrant of Harlem. Patterned on Bronx Shepherds Restoration Corporation, HCCI grew from a coalition of clerics and lay professionals that had met frequently to discuss and develop a response to neighborhood neglect. The causes of neglect, according to one of its founders, were twofold. First, in the view of the group, mayoral administrations neglected most of the public services needs of the neighborhood, especially public safety (e.g., fire and police protection and building code enforcement). Second, there was the perception that private landlords abandoned properties or speculated on them, reducing the supply of affordable housing and fostering tenant displacement from their buildings and even the neighborhood. Although HCCI would focus on Bradhurst, it also would work in other sections of Harlem and the South Bronx, developing and managing affordable housing in tandem with secular community groups and eventually government agencies. "We want to get beyond soup kitchens and care packages," one of its founders would later declare (quoted in Martin 2003).

In 1989 another church-associated CDC appeared in Harlem, Abyssinian Development Corporation (ADC). Like Canaan HDC and HCCI, ADC was a response to neighborhood divestment and decay surrounding the church's building. Congregants of Abyssinian Baptist Church, according to an ADC staff member who recounted the history of the organization to me, "were distressed by the deteriorating living condition in Harlem—the rise in homelessness, wholesale abandonment of apartment buildings by landlords, increased drug traffic on neighborhood streets and playgrounds, a lack of quality open spaces, diminished economic opportunities for residents, and the disintegration of the overall community fabric." A group of them, along with the pastor of Abyssinian Baptist Church, convened neighborhood workshops to identify community problems and build consensus around responses to them. From the workshops came the idea for a CDC. In time, ADC would become, in Reverend Butts's words, "a vehicle [for Abyssinian Baptist Church] to become actively involved in the physical as well as the spiritual redevelopment of Harlem" (quoted in Clemetson and Coates 1992, 31). It was a sentiment adopted and echoed by black clergy in Brooklyn, especially in the Bedford-Stuyvesant neighborhood.

Bedford-Stuyvesant in the 1980s was a place where scholars observed "a permanent underclass, denied access to even the lowest rungs of the employment ladder by a woefully inadequate public school system, suffer[ing] from a 'mismatch' between the supply and demand of entry-level clerical skills" (Warf 1990, 89). The neighborhood had high rates of social distress. Overall, the percent of persons earning incomes below the federal poverty level was 13 percent, but there were census tracts in the neighborhood where poverty rates exceeded 40 percent (New York City Department of City Planning 1993). Median household income was about 50 percent that of the city. Male unemployment was double the rate for the city, so a growing number of men were to be seen on street corners, and illicit activity increased. The neighborhood needed community initiatives to confront its conditions. A set of clergy acknowledged it by birthing the Association of Brooklyn Clergy for Community Development (ABCCD) in 1987.

ABCCD developed from talks among black ministers to address social conditions, worsened by housing abandonment and speculation, in the southeast section of Bedford-Stuyvesant and the northwest section of Ocean Hill–Brownsville. A few years later the collective efforts of the clergy and churches that joined together to create ABCCD to restore the abandoned spaces of the neighborhoods were supplemented by the individual efforts of two African American churches. The first was Concord Baptist Church of Christ, which chartered the Concord Community Development Corporation in 1994. The second was Bridge Street African Wesleyan Methodist Episcopal Church, which incorporated its own CDC in 1995. But these two CDCs had been preceded by two other church-associated CDCs in the Queens neighborhood of South Jamaica.

South Jamaica was one of the original black middle-class neighborhoods in New York City (Nathan, Chow, and Owens 1995; Gregory 1998). It accommodated and reproduced the middle-class blacks who fled Morrisania, Harlem, and Bedford-Stuyvesant for better neighborhoods during the 1960s and 1970s. Yet it could not hold on to its identity as a site of black middle-class residence, especially black professionals and artists. Like the other black neighborhoods, albeit to a lesser extent, in the 1980s the neighborhood suffered from commercial divestment, job losses, and the introduction of public housing.

What had been a "suburban like" neighborhood inside the city's limits became an inner-city neighborhood of "auto repair joints and used-car dealerships, a place of crowded, tumble-down wooden houses with cracked siding and broken windows" in the wake of the outmigration of middle-class blacks (White 1992, 16). An unemployment rate of 71 percent among male youth aged sixteen to nineteen contributed to the explosive trade of crack cocaine and a spate of infamous murders of police officers and civilians (New York City Department of City Planning 1993; Brown 2005). HIV/AIDS and deaths associated with the disease, which were often connected to the drug trade as well as numerous prostitution rings in the vicinity of public housing, also emerged as problems in the neighborhood.

Reacting to the conditions in and around South Jamaica, two African American church–associated CDCs appeared in 1986—Southeast Queens Clergy for Community Empowerment (SQCCE) and Allen AME Neighborhood Preservation and Development Corporation (Allen NPDC). The former had begun in 1984 as a meeting group for clergy to discuss weekly community affairs and concerns in the majority-black neighborhoods of southeast Queens. At the time the Reverend Jesse Jackson Sr. was a candidate in the New York Democratic presidential primary, along with Walter Mondale, Gary Hart, and John Glenn. Supporting Jackson's bid, the ministers' group transformed itself into a nonpartisan political organization focused on voter registration and mobilization (Owens 1997a). After the primary, the ministers incorporated their alliance as a faith-related agency to pursue a larger agenda of social services and activism. Its work complemented the preexisting activities of an SQCCE charter member, Allen AME Church. The church incorporated Allen NPDC to acquire land, build houses, and supplement commercial redevelopment in and around South Jamaica.

*Church-Related Rationales.* Beyond concentrated poverty, housing abandonment, and other troubling conditions, there were church-related catalysts for the chartering of such CDCs. In particular, the desire of clergy and congregants of activist churches to transform faith into action affected the churches' decisions to charter CDCs. CDCs provide the churches with a supplemental form of worship and means of sharing the gospel with others. Stephen Monsma clarifies the point, based on his analysis of faith-related agencies: "A sense of compulsion, of living out one's inner faith, of following the dictates of one's conscience is clearly present. . . . Religious nonprofit organizations are often concrete embodiments of certain beliefs of the religious faiths out of which they arise" (1996, 52).[10]

For the African American churches that chartered CDCs in New York City, religion absent religious indoctrination was inherent in the mission of their agencies.[11] "It's not about proselytizing the Word," one pastor from Bedford-Stuyvesant declared to me, "but showing people that you really care and that you really can make a difference." Expressing the general sentiment of the black clergy whose churches chartered their own CDCs, a pastor from Queens remarked to me that the actions of African American church-associated CDCs patterned Jesus as represented in Luke 7:21–22: " 'In that same hour, he cured many of their infirmities and plagues, and of evil spirits; and unto many that were blind he gave sight. Then Jesus answering, said unto them, Go your way, and tell John what things ye have seen and heard; how that the blind see, the lame walk, the lepers are cleansed, the deaf hear, the dead are raised, to the poor the gospel is preached.' Jesus didn't speak of the capacities of God to induce converts; he demonstrated them." Through their deeds, not their words, the pastor observed, the churches were spreading the message of their Christ by means of the CDCs. The institution of the church-associated CDC, as Alvin Mares acknowledges, allows "congregants to express their faith in a tangible and fulfilling way, in addition to giving congregants access to people who may not be willing to come to weekend church worship" (1994, 140). The works of the employees of the church-associated CDCs, especially the faithful, are a means for them to give expression to the Christian ethic of brotherly love, as well as to foster community renewal and self-initiative in a way that coheres with their sacred texts.[12]

This does raise the issue of whether the practices of the church-associated CDCs also cohere with *democratic* texts. The leaders of African American church–associated CDCs claim that participation and empowerment are fundamental to their works; they affirm participation and empowerment in their mission statements, often implying that their processes and products are the result of popular rule, consent, or support.[13] This fits with the consensus in community development circles, which for practical and ethical reasons avers that organizations "representing" low-income neighborhoods should have broad and deep resident involvement (Chaskin et al. 2001; Gittell 1980).

Practically, resident engagement is important because residents possess unique or indigenous understandings of their problems and assets, as well as how to leverage local resources to improve the design and outcomes of neighborhood-based initiatives. "Ethically," in the view of Robert Chaskin and Sunil Garg, to include residents in organizational "policymaking and program delivery is to take seriously their rights and responsibilities to have some control over [organizations] that will have an impact on their lives" (1997, 633). Furthermore, the broad engagement of low-income residents in "their" organizations is expected to develop and maintain a public focus, enhancing concerns for collective interests over individual interests. Subsequently, engagement should foster the "development of responsible social and political action on the part of the individual"; this coheres with what democratic theorists envision as the end product of political participation and the central aim of democratic societies (Pateman 1970, 24).

In the church-associated CDCs that serve Harlem, Morrisania, South Jamaica, and Bedford-Stuyvesant, however, the overwhelming majority of neighborhood residents do not have opportunities to learn civic and political skills or to enjoy the sense of efficacy that comes from working to redevelop their communities. That is, the CDCs are not necessarily community-driven organizations. While all of the African American church–associated CDCs are rhetorically attentive to resident participation and empowerment, few routinely practice these values on a broad scale. In particular, the participation of working-class residents is noticeably lacking in the organizations. Only a minority of residents are in positions to influence the direction of "their" organizations and to acquire important competencies transferable to the political arena.[14]

The church-associated CDCs, like their sponsor churches, are not necessarily representative of their neighborhoods. Rather than being democratic institutions that allow resident participation in agenda setting and decision making, they are normally undemocratic in relation to the neighborhoods where they operate. Instead of residents selected by election or appointment from the target neighborhood, unelected boards of directors, whose members often live outside the neighborhoods, set the agendas and decide the actions of the organizations.

Furthermore, middle-class professionals govern the decisions of the African American church–associated CDCs. This is because they make up the leadership and the staff of these CDCs. Unlike the majority of African American church–associated CDCs nationally (Frederick 2001), all executive directors of the nine church-associated CDCs in New York City as of 2000 possessed graduate or professional degrees. The middle-class nature of the church-associated CDCs is also evident from a review of their boards of directors. Neighborhood entrepreneurs and homeowners, along with representatives of citywide for-profits and nonprofits, account for all board members, except for those of the three CDCs that are governed solely by clergy.[15] Renters, laborers, and social services clients are absent from these boards of directors.[16]

Thus, as in their associated churches, power within the CDCs rests with a few individuals: pastors govern alliance-based CDCs, while middle-class stakeholders, especially property owners, govern independent CDCs. Such governance is rooted in the New Testament admonishment that "whosoever of you will be the chiefest, shall be servant of all" (Mark 10:44). Paradoxically, the ideal of servanthood can yield a type of organizational governance that serves others, often out of devotion to a religious creed, without regard for the debilitating effects of service on empowerment, due to the application of religious "imperatives of mission and service [that allow the 'servant'] to dominate and control" (McKnight 1989). The faith sector's elevation of stewardship and its tradition of benevolent paternalism, along with the political tradition of brokerage by church-based elites, allow those who govern African American church–associated CDCs to be guided by an assumption that they know what is best for others. Inherent in the "servanthood" model of CDC governance, unfortunately, is the possibility that an organization's agendas and activities will serve the servants more than others.

There is no unitary community or constituency in low-income neighborhoods. Instead, they contain multiple and competing "communities" and groups of stakeholders.[17] Low-income residents constitute a key constituency, and they may envision collaboration in the name of the community to benefit "all" in it, particularly themselves. This is the case in the four black neighborhoods researched here (Little 2002; Gopnik 2002; Matloff 2002). Middle-class servants, another key constituency, may also envision the church-associated CDCs as working in the name of the community to benefit "all" in it. Yet they may believe that the initial effects should preserve their constituency as anchors in their neighborhood by, for example, increasing property values, increasing numbers of owner-occupied homes, or developing areas proximate to commercial strips.

Allen NPDC, for example, strategically revitalized areas to create commercial buffers and affordable-housing transition zones between South Jamaica and more affluent black neighborhoods to its east such as St. Albans, Hollis, and Springfield Gardens (Owens 1997b). Its initial work in the neighborhood was an infill project that developed owner-occupied housing in an area just blocks from a public housing complex. Community activists charged that its decision was a response to fears of the church's middle-class congregation, which was concerned about the church's proximity to the black poor, especially public housing, and how it might result in poverty creep and declining property values. Likewise, most community activists and some long-time residents in Harlem believe that Abyssinian Baptist Church and its CDC, with their middle-class congregation and supporters, skews community development agendas away from the grassroots needs of residents and promotes values that result in the displacement of working-class interests, needs, and persons (Gopnik 2002).

At its worst, the servanthood model coupled with the lack of broad resident engagement or working-class governance produces suspicions. They include the notion that the CDCs and their sponsor churches are disinterested in redeeming their neighborhoods for the good of incumbent residents, that their work is self-serving, and that it ultimately is intended to pave the way for gentrification and displacement. Low-income residents may see physical development or services being delivered, but the beneficiaries may not be themselves, their families, or their friends. This may alter their perceptions about the churches and their "community" work.[18] Residents may perceive the projects of the CDCs, along with the bulk of benefits, to belong to the churches, not the communities that host them. Consequently, residents may dismiss collaboration as other-regarding in a negative sense—it benefits someone else. Such suspicions and dismissals may further weaken the legitimacy of the church-associated CDCs and their sponsor churches as neighborhood representatives and may make it difficult for clergy and churches to advance their positions in relation to other groups in black civil society.

Putting aside the challenges of balancing faith and democratic practice in the operation of the CDCs, activist African American churches also chartered CDCs in New York City to emulate their peers.[19] Pastors readily admitted to me that the chartering of CDCs by their churches or with other churches was often a matter of imitation, not invention. By 1980 a few African American churches in other cities had used or begun to use CDCs to physically redevelop their neighborhoods (Clemetson and Coates 1992). A pastor from South Jamaica revealed why his church and other churches formed SQCCE: "We turned to the [CDC] because we saw visible results by churches in other neighborhoods, even other cities. . . . We witnessed and believed in the good Bronx Shepherds Restoration Corporation and Canaan's CDC were doing in their communities. We believed deep in our hearts and minds that we, too, could do as much good, if not more, here in South Jamaica."

It is understandable that some churches would emulate their peers and begin their own (independent) church-associated CDCs. It is less obvious why some pastors would choose to enter their churches into an alliance like SQCCE or BSRC. At the close of the 1990s, approximately 250 churches were allied through ABCCD, BSRC, HCCI, and SQCCE. Their alliances were more than temporary unions or federations where individuals cede authority to central institutions. They were enduring associations with common objectives.[20] A brochure for ABCCD signals the intent of the alliance-based church-associated CDCs: "Prior to ABCCD's inception, member church groups strived independently for years to address critical issues confronting Black families. Some met with success; others were merely duplicating services already being provided while stretching their resources thin. Through ABCCD, member churches now launch a joint 'attack' on the socio-economic problems endemic to the African-American community." Still, why not act independently? Why privilege ecumenism and collective action among clergy and congregations, while others chose independence over alliance?

Alliance gave activist African American churches the opportunity to combine their material and cultural resources—volunteers, money, political capital, and moral authority—to increase their collective institutional capacity. Alliance also permitted smaller activist churches, especially those that lacked a political reputation or tended to avoid direct political engagement, to work with activist churches equal or greater in size and quality of activism. "There are churches that are large enough in magnitude to go their own way, and . . . I take nothing away from that model," a pastor affiliated with SQCCE remarked. His church had fewer than one hundred congregants. "That model is fine," he continued, "but I think the alliance is the best way to do it for those of us who have small churches." Alliance also created opportunities for member churches to potentially increase their political influence. A SQCCE officer put the alliance-based CDC in political perspective during one of my interviews: "We recognized that the alliance worked best [because of] numbers. Politicians look at numbers. To get elected they need numbers. So the alliance was the best way to go."

The formation of the four alliance-based CDCs is evidence that activist African American churches in New York City appreciate collective action. It also counters the stereotype of African American churches as incessantly scrimmaging over turf and competing for resources and prestige. Nevertheless, the presence of independent church–associated CDCs is evidence that not all black clergy or their congregants favor alliances with other churches to address neighborhood problems. Generally, activist churches with the largest congregations tended to charter CDCs independent of other activist churches in their neighborhoods. Their independence was pragmatic.

The success of an alliance-based CDC is a function of cooperative relationships and concentrated efforts among members: An effective alliance of activist churches pools the material and cultural resources of its member clergy and congregations and focuses them on a particular area at a particular time. For example, ABCCD is an alliance of thirty churches in Bedford-Stuyvesant. To produce noticeable and substantive differences in the neighborhood, ABCCD directs its resources and collective action to specific areas. The blocks of or near a few of its member churches usually benefit immediately. The remainder receive little, if any, of the attention and services of ABCCD. Concord Baptist Church and Bridge Street AWME Church could wait for ABCCD to focus on the problems of its neighborhood subareas, or the two churches could, as they did, act independently of the alliance-based CDC.

Despite their purposes to preach the gospel and increase the number of adherents to their faith, churches are competitive organizations. Multiple churches exist on a single block, sometimes side by side, in New York City's majority-black neighborhoods. The prevalence and proximity of the churches creates a marketplace where churches compete for attendants and their potential tithes and offerings (McRoberts 2003). The preaching ability of a pastor, as I noted in chapter 2, is one potential determinant of a congregation's membership size and money. The degree and visibility of community outreach by churches is another factor correlated with church size and growth.

"Folks in the neighborhood," according to Reverend Simpson of Concord Baptist Church, "expect much more from [churches] than a rousing sermon and a firm handshake from the pastor on the way out" (quoted in Toussaint 1999, 64). He and other pastors believe that through social action, churches develop positive reputations that impress observers and assist in recruitment of new members (Stewart 1994; W. T. Walker 199r; Billingsley 1999). In the language of one pastor from Harlem, social welfare provision influences con-

gregation size and impact: "butts in the pews and budgets for God and good-
ness in the neighborhood."

As the memberships of churches grow, revenues and operating budgets are
expected to follow, allowing churches to engage in more social action and acquire more attenders. Allying with other churches to provide social services,
however, generates a problem in this regard—the apportionment of credit.
The division of credit among alliance members could influence where prospective worshipers attend services and tithe. Thus, the clergy and the congregants of activist churches may prefer to remain independent of their peers,
even if the pooling of resources and collective delivery of social welfare services might be more efficient and effective in resurrecting neighborhoods.

*Financial Rationale.* The final rationale for activist churches' chartering
CDCs was a financial one. A pastor from Queens spoke of this as an essential consideration: "We acquired knowledge about the [community develop-
ment] funds that were available, not only the city's but also the state and the
federal governments'. We also learned that you couldn't just get the money as
a church. We needed a nonprofit to receive it on our behalf, or at least we did
back in the 1980s."

At the time his church joined others to charter a CDC, a direct flow of
public resources to churches would have conflicted with convention about
church-state separation, along with case law and a state constitutional provision against the public funding of sectarian institutions (Monsma 1996; Lupu
and Tuttle 2003). From the War on Poverty begun in 1964 until welfare reform in 1996, policymakers emphasized secular solutions to public problems.
Based on the belief that the Constitution bars church-state collaboration, and
influenced by social experiments of the 1960s, the public consensus was that
rational programs supported by public funding, rooted in secular humanism,
and implemented by social welfare professionals worked best to address the
problems of the poor.

Public policy did allow religious institutions (congregations and denominations), if they chose, to assist state and county public agencies in addressing public problems such as poverty, malnutrition, lack of affordable housing,
and even safety in public housing. To receive public funding for their efforts,
however, religious institutions were required to establish separate faith-based
nonprofits. They were to operate secular programs because the incorporation of religious doctrine with services the public funded was deemed unconstitutional. An undeterminable number of religious institutions chartered
faith-based nonprofits. Legally distinct from and independent of religious in-

stitutions in their funding, expenditures, and governance, nonprofits such as Catholic Charities, Lutheran Social Ministries, and Jewish Boards of Family and Children's Services received public funding. At government request, the faith-based nonprofits removed religious symbols from service delivery sites. They abandoned, or at least downplayed, proselytism and mandatory worship in conjunction with services they delivered on behalf of public agencies at public expense.

Leaders of activist African American churches in New York City observed how faith-related agencies such as Catholic Charities and the Salvation Army in New York City and in other cities could receive government assistance, and had received it for decades; actually the bulk of their revenue came from government (Glenn 2002).[21] Accordingly, these churches decided to charter CDCs to seek and receive government funding.[22]

Executive directors of the nine church-associated CDCs in New York City estimated for me what proportions of their external financial resources came from various sources.[23] Although the private sector, especially commercial banks, provides church-associated CDCs with financial resources, in New York City the public sector is the monetary pivot of African American church–associated CDCs.[24] Taken together, municipal contracts, grants, and loans, plus the estimated monetary value of buildings, land, and infrastructure investments, account for a plurality (49 percent) of the financial resources the CDCs rely on for their work.[25] Clearly, the municipal government is the chief benefactor of the church-associated CDCs in New York City, as it is of secular nonprofits (Arete Corporation 1997; New York City Nonprofits Project 2002; Marwell 2004).

Were it not for public funding, the African American church-associated CDCs would find it difficult to leverage the material and cultural resources of their churches to acquire private support for affordable-housing production, health and human services, and economic development. However, this presents a contradiction: municipal policy was generally perceived as antiblack but supportive of community-based organizations serving black neighborhoods. Given New York City's municipal policy history between the late 1970s and the end of the 1990s, how is it that CDCs associated with activist African American churches could rely on government support for their work?

Public sector support of the African American church–associated CDCs, as I will explain in chapters 5 and 6, happened despite the conservative municipal priorities of city hall, mainly because of the city's special history of supporting affordable housing development and community-based nonprofit housing developers (Leavitt 1980; Leavitt and Saegert 1990; Schill 1999;

J. Schwartz 1986). Moreover, beginning with the Koch administration, the municipal government implemented, and subsequent mayoral administrations furthered, a public initiative to divest the city government of property it had acquired through property tax foreclosures (Orlebeke 1997; Braconi 1999; Wylde 1999; A. Schwartz 1999).[26] Since much of this property was located in minority neighborhoods, including the four black neighborhoods of my study, the initiative, which I will detail in the next two chapters, became a significant conduit for the transfer of public resources to the church-associated CDCs.

## SUMMARY

The city's black neighborhoods, especially large swaths of Harlem, South Jamaica, Bedford-Stuyvesant, and Morrisania, became and remained impoverished places. African American churches had the choice to exit them. Yet the majority of the churches remained. While many of them resigned themselves to the conditions of their neighborhood, activist churches opted for voice and action. They chose to create and maintain faith-related agencies focused on neighborhood improvement. In particular, a collection of activist churches chartered CDCs. Their rationales fell into three broad categories—community, church, and cash. The churches chartered CDCs to address neighborhood needs; to manifest their faith, as well as to compete better in the religious marketplace; and to seek public, along with private, funding to support and expand their provision of social welfare services.

While the churches had a history of advocating direct government intervention to change the conditions of black neighborhoods, and while they had reputations for political engagement via protests and electioneering, in the 1980s and 1990s African Americans began to call for indirect government action through their churches, working in tandem with government agencies (Green and Wilson 1992; Carnes 2001). They also began to develop *with government assistance* affordable housing and commercial facilities and to foster enterprise, employment, and youth development in and on behalf of the city's poorest black neighborhoods. They would view their partnership as involving more than social service delivery: it would be collaboration with government, with the churches as intermediaries to affect public services in their neighborhoods.

# * 3 *

# *Inside Church-State Collaboration*

# CHAPTER FIVE

# Partnering with Caesar

At the start of the 1980s, the supply of affordable housing for low- and moderate-income individuals and families was one of the most pressing political and social items on the municipal agenda in New York City (Orlebeke 1997; Roistacher and Tobier 1984). The limited supply of affordable housing was consequential to the city's minorities. One writer in the 1980s observed, "In New York an address is harder and harder to find, particularly for Latinos and blacks" (quoted in Windhoff-Heritier 1992, 140). Something needed to be done. The city government was pressured to do it. Interest groups lobbied the city government to revive the affordable housing market. Grassroots activists pressed the city for more housing for the working poor and the impoverished. Consent decrees mandated that the municipal government find homes for homeless families and individuals (Thompson 1996–1997; Culhane, Metraux, and Wachter 1999). Public- and private-sector elites advocated a municipal response, too, albeit with an emphasis on stemming the middle-class outmigration they attributed to high housing costs.

The city government, beginning with the Koch administration, reacted with a long-term policy for affordable housing production. In the words of a former New York City Department of Housing Preservation and Development (HPD) commissioner who spoke to me about the initiative, the policy addressed the affordable housing crisis "by privatizing to produce better results for the public." The City of New York privatized public assets for affordable housing production, giving for-profit and not-for-profit organizations land and money to build affordable housing over the next ten years.[1] For more than a decade, then, for-profit and nonprofit organizations, which the city assumed possessed the skills, competencies, and assets to partner with it, re-vived the affordable housing market. The plan, rather than relying on public management of the redeveloped properties, disposed of land and buildings to moderate-income buyers, low- and middle-income renters, and nonprofit or-ganizations. This approach was possible at the time because Koch was at the apex of his political power (Arian et al. 1991).

Activist African American churches, acting primarily through CDCs, were among the nonprofit organizations eligible to receive land and money for re-development, as well as the management or ownership of the properties. The churches that chartered CDCs (whether independent or alliance based) in-tended for them to be their institutional means to collaborate with the city to address their neighborhoods' need for affordable housing. For some of the churches, the city's program extended an existing church-government part-nership; for other churches, it provided a mechanism for beginning such a partnership.

In many respects, the 1980s were auspicious times for activist African American churches to collaborate with the city government. The city gov-ernment introduced new opportunities for collaboration, and the churches possessed a means to collaborate with it—CDCs. The churches that eventu-ally partnered with the city viewed church-state collaboration as a method for achieving some of the goals clergy had for themselves, their churches, and their communities. In other respects, however, the times were inauspicious. Interactions between black leaders, especially clergy, and city hall were tense, and the city government had a reputation for neglecting black neighborhood interests. Despite this, a set of activist black clergy directed their churches to partner with the city government, especially for the purpose of using the mu-nicipal affordable housing initiative on behalf of their neighborhoods. This chapter explores the 1980s New York City context in some depth and pastors' reasons for embracing or eschewing the opportunity to partner with the city government to extend affordable housing.

## A DECADE OF PRIVATIZATION FOR AFFORDABLE HOUSING

The limited supply of affordable housing in New York City became an issue in the middle 1960s, a problem in the 1970s, and a crisis in the 1980s. Each decade witnessed a loss of residential properties. It was a weird phenome-non. Housing production had been adequate in the early 1960s (Salins 1999). By the 1970s, however, total production of housing had slowed; up to 19,000 fewer new units were being produced each year. One estimate is that between the 1960s and 1970s the median annual production rates dropped from 37,000 units to about 10,000 units (New York City Rent Guidelines Board 1998).

The absence of a capable and efficient affordable housing production system worsened the affordability issues. "New York's private affordable housing industry," Kathryn Wylde recalls, "all but disappeared in the 1970s, when the cost of new construction went over $35 a square foot and increasingly large numbers of city residents could no longer afford the price of an unsubsidized home or apartment" (1999, 75). Reductions in the affordable housing inventory were resulting largely from choices by property owners—that is, abandonment.[2] Static, sometimes rising, property taxes, along with outmigration of middle-class residents and rising crime, contributed to property owners' decision to abandon their buildings.[3] Boarding them up, sometimes even burning them down, many owners walked away from their properties and tax burdens.[4]

As a result of abandonment, the housing inventory in the city declined by 100,000 units between 1965 and 1968, while the number of boarded-up and abandoned buildings in 1968 stood at 7,000 (Braconi 1999, 94). Through the 1970s the city's housing inventory continued to decline. Between 1970 and 1978, 40,000 to 100,000 units were abandoned, vacated, and removed from the rental stock (Leavitt 1980, 97; Braconi 1999, 94; Salins and Mildner 1992). Later, from 1980 through 1984, the city underwent a further net loss of 23,400 housing units. Tax delinquency often followed abandonment. "As income decreased and costs increased, many owners were unable to pay the property taxes on their buildings, which ultimately led to City foreclosure" (Allred 2000, 1). This was not the best situation for the City of New York.

The city government preferred that property owners pay their taxes, retain ownership of their properties, and maintain the properties in accordance with building and housing codes. But this was not always possible, and in such cases the city took their properties. An HPD official was blunt about it to me: "We were actually taking people's property. We were taking the property. We were not selling the right to collect the taxes, which are tax lien sales. . . . What we were saying was 'Hey, if you don't pay what you owe us, we're gonna take your building.'"[5]

*The City Government Becomes the Largest Landlord*

By 1979 the city government possessed approximately 10,000 buildings containing 60,000 vacant and 40,000 occupied apartments, up from fewer than 3,000 buildings in 1976 (Bach and West 1993; Braconi 1999). Subsequently, it came to own over 100,000 tax-foreclosed properties by the middle of the 1980s, of which 64,000 were vacant buildings, making the municipal government the largest single landlord in New York City (Schwartz and Vidal 1999).[6] Not wanting to remain a landlord, the city sought to quickly sell the properties and return them to the tax rolls.

Unfortunately for the city government, the initial market for its newly acquired properties was small. The buildings were often in complete disrepair. Steep investments would be required to rehabilitate them, especially as affordable housing. Further, most of the city-owned properties (vacant and occupied) were located in declining neighborhoods. Neighborhoods like Morrisania continued to suffer population loss due to rising rates of impoverishment and its negative effects. In addition, despite the federal passage of the Community Reinvestment Act (1977) and the Home Mortgage Disclosure Act (1975), banks and insurance companies quickly redlined the neighborhoods that contained the most city-owned housing. This further destabilized the declining neighborhoods, signaling to investors that they were sites of extreme economic risk. Despite, or because of, the limited interest in the city-owned properties, the Koch administration proposed to use them to tackle the affordable housing crisis.

*The Ten Year Plan*

The Koch administration proposed a large scheme of public-private partnerships to develop 252,000 affordable housing units. The purposes of the plan were manifold: increase affordable housing supply; rehabilitate existing units; increase the supply of permanent housing for special needs constituents (e.g., the homeless and the poor with HIV/AIDS); and produce owner-occupied properties for first-time buyers (Michetti 1993). It would execute the plan through a hybrid approach to privatization.[7] Beginning in 1986, the city government deliberately mixed divestment and delegation to catalyze the production of affordable housing through transfers of tax-foreclosed city-owned properties to the private sector, especially nonprofit organizations.[8]

Seeking to relinquish its title as the largest landlord, one with an oversupply of abandoned and dilapidated properties, the city would divest itself of and delegate its responsibility for the properties by transferring its ownership of them to nongovernmental organizations and private citizens to own, rehabilitate, and manage as affordable housing or sell to middle-income and working-poor families as owner-occupied housing.[9] Beyond its transfer of land to nongovernmental organizations, the city government planned to contribute $4.2 billion in subsidies and awards of contracts for redevelopment and management services to the affordable housing production experiment. Approximately 82 percent of the amount would come from the city's capital budget (Schill et al. 2002, 535).[10]

Revenue from the economic development initiatives of the Koch administration (e.g., the development and operation of Battery Park City) provided supplemental resources, as did Wall Street's reopening of the bond markets to the municipal government. Additional subsidies for the experiment came from multiple government sources. The city government tapped its allocations of Community Development Block Grants.[11] It later drew from its federal and state allocations of Low Income Housing Tax Credits and HOME Investment Partnership funds to subsidize the production of affordable housing.[12] Also, the city government used its resources to leverage $5 billion from the private sector in the forms of construction loans, mortgages, and equity investments.[13]

Together, the land, subsidies, and private investments provided "the raw material for a giant urban housing laboratory" (Wylde 1999, 77). The Koch administration planned to experiment for a period of five years. Its successors from both political parties extended it until the city had relinquished all properties in its tax-foreclosed inventory (Schwartz 1999; Chen 2003; Steinhauer 2005).[14] Although they were less committed to it financially than the Koch administration, succeeding mayoral administrations boosted municipal spending on the experiment to $5.2 billion, $1 billion more than Koch had promised (see figure 3).[15] Aside from the fiscal inputs, the initiative known as the Ten Year Plan would owe much of its execution and eventual success to nongovernmental organizations.

### The Importance of "Third-Party Government"

Provision of public services in the United States, particularly its cities, is based largely on a system that distributes government authority over public expenditures and implementation of public programs to "third-party implementers" (Salamon 1995, 41). This was increasingly the case in the 1980s and 1990s. Governments employed nongovernmental organizations as means of facing up to a truth: "The central reality of public problem solving for the foreseeable future [was] its collaborative nature, its reliance on a wide array of third parties in addition to government to address public problems and

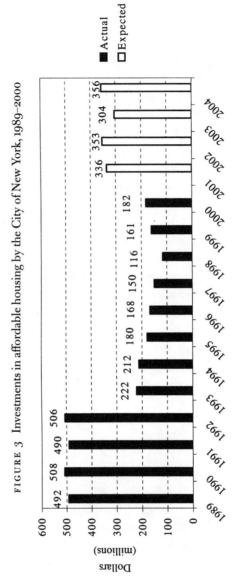

FIGURE 3 Investments in affordable housing by the City of New York, 1989–2000

Source: New York City Independent Budget Office, 2000.

pursue public purposes" (Salamon 2002, 8). During the 1980s and 1990s third-party government mushroomed, principally in municipalities (Mayer 1991; Eisinger 1998).[16]

New York City was chief among the municipalities that broadened and deepened its reliance on nongovernmental organizations (both commercial and nonprofit) rather than public institutions to address collective problems and achieve public purposes in areas ranging from social services to elementary and secondary education to criminal justice. In particular, municipal reliance on *nonprofit* organizations increased in the 1980s, especially in social welfare policy domains of aging, social services, health, youth services (e.g., foster care and adoption services), and housing (Abramson and Salamon 1986).[17] By the end of the decade, New York City spent more on the provision of public services by nonprofit organizations than other large cities spent on their total budget (Mollenkopf 1994, 156).

The delivery of public services by nonprofit organizations was routine in New York City by the 1980s, but in housing and neighborhood development the city government was still least likely to rely extensively on nonprofits.[18] The city generally relied on direct services by government agencies to address housing, above all the management of its inventory of tax-foreclosed properties. Also, the city government had often looked to commercial organizations over nonprofit ones to aid it in achieving its neighborhood improvement goals.

Nevertheless, transfers of public resources to nonprofit agencies for community development services in New York City, while modest, had been under way for a few decades. In 1972, for instance, the city government created the Community Management Program to sell moderately rehabilitated city-owned buildings to community-based organizations to manage as rental or sell as co-op apartments (Turetsky 1993; Lawson 1986).[19] If we focus less on money and more on consultation and planning, the roots of the city's partnerships with nonprofits for community development services appear older. One could locate them in the municipal decentralization, community control, and War on Poverty initiatives of the 1960s, including the city's Vest Pocket Program, which relied on community-based advisory groups to plan for targeted slum and blight removal via small-scale public housing development in low-income neighborhoods, and the housing receivership programs that entrusted the management of tax-foreclosed buildings to community-based groups (Raymond and May Associates 1968; Leavitt 1980; Leavitt and Saegert 1990; Yates 1973; Katznelson 1981; Cannato 2001).[20] The broader origins of municipal-nonprofit neighborhood redevelopment in New York City even date to the 1959 passage of the federal Section 202 Elderly Housing program, which introduced nonprofit community-based organizations in New York City to affordable housing development, both as project sponsors and as developers.[21]

During the 1980s and in the decade to follow, the city government increased its reliance on nonprofit organizations to foster neighborhood revitalization, particularly in the building and management of affordable apartments and houses in low-income neighborhoods (Turetsky 1993; Oppenheim and Sierra 1994). Nonprofits participating in the implementation of municipal policies in the 1980s and 1990s, especially those advancing the Ten Year Plan's goals, were varied. The initial execution of the plan, however, included few activist African American churches and their faith-related agencies. The small number of participants from the black faith sector gives rise to a question: why did some black clergy leading activist African American congregations decide to have their churches collaborate with government?

## CHURCHES CHOOSE TO COLLABORATE
## WITH CITY GOVERNMENT

Generally, the city government's approach created new avenues for community-based groups to work with and receive resources from the city government to serve their constituencies. In particular, the Ten Year Plan provided physical and financial resources to an array of nongovernmental organizations, especially citywide and community-based nonprofit housing organizations, to produce affordable housing. Yet the majority of activist African American churches in the city did not pursue opportunities to participate in the Ten Year Plan.

Most black pastors were neutral to the idea; they neither opposed nor supported church-state partnerships to produce affordable housing. Some pastors of activist churches held negative attitudes about collaborating with government. Yet some pastors were open to partnering their church with the city government, if they could. They looked favorably on the Ten Year Plan as a goal and a process, especially its physical and financial inducements to draw neighborhood-based nonprofit organizations into the Plan's implementation in their neighborhoods.

### *Opposition to Church-State Partnerships*

Black pastors' opposition to partnering with the city government made sense in New York City during the 1980s and 1990s—especially during the regimes of conservative white mayors whose municipal agendas were often diametrically opposed to black neighborhood interests. And it made sense beyond the fact that most activist black clergy were liberal or moderate in their politics.[22] Black clergy whose church made a conscious decision to refrain from collaborating with government counted four broad concerns—cooptation, dependency, conservative machinations, and white neglect—as their reasons.

*Fear of Co-optation.* Resistance to church-state partnership, even when such partnership might have improved physical conditions in black neighborhoods, was a way for activist African American churches to avoid government co-optation and protect their missions and objectives from the influence of government. Viewing his opposition as preservation of the prophetic voice of the black pulpit, a senior pastor of a church in Bedford-Stuyvesant, one without a CDC or ties to one, declared: "This is a church that has never accepted public funds to support any of its activities. That has been the policy of this church since I have been here, and I have been here for thirty-seven years. I do not believe you can raise the voice of prophetic protest and at the same time eat of the king's meat.[23] So I have consistently refrained [my church] from seeking any kind of public funds. Any financial support mutes the voice of the church, for he who pays the piper calls the tune." In remaining independent of government in all forms, the pastor and others with a similar attitude believed that they avoided becoming "secular minions of Caesar,"[24] which is what one pastor of a church opposed to partnership labeled churches that worked with government, especially during the Koch and Giuliani administrations.

*Preservation of Independence.* Avoiding partnership with the city government offered a means for the churches to preserve and perhaps advance the tradition of black self-reliance, which was the fount of the Black Church in the United States. Some clergy held that a church's working with the government contradicted, ideologically and practically, more than a century of black collective responsibility. "How can we say we're free and independent of white folks if we go begging to government for relief," argued a pastor who prevented his church from seeking public funding and opposed its alignment with other congregations that acted collectively through CDCs to seek partnerships with the city government. "We must do for ourselves, with our own money," he continued, "even if it means we don't solve all of the problems. We must maintain our dignity." This perspective matches the view of some other pastors I interviewed, especially one from Bedford-Stuyvesant with a history of confronting city government: "Everything we do is under our own auspices, everything. I believe the church has to remain free from all encumbrances."

*Avoiding Conservative Snares.* Resisting church-state partnerships ensured that activist African American churches did not aid in government retrenchment. Church-state partnerships could abet a conservative scheme to reduce social welfare spending and abandon public authority for poverty reduction by recruiting black organizations to assume government's responsibilities. "Government was trying to get out of spending a lot of money, balance its books, and cut taxes on the backs of the poor and the blacks," stated a pastor in Harlem. Even those clergy whose churches worked with government conceded this point. A clergyman affiliated with the Bronx Shepherds Restoration Corporation commented, "I think the problem with partnership is that it—it somehow exempts the city from its responsibility of delivering community services. So they think, 'Well, we'll just get the black guys to do that and then we'll cut spending.' " The result would be increased social hardship in black neighborhoods, not increased socioeconomic opportunities for their residents.[25]

*Wariness of White Neglect.* Opponents of church-state partnerships also perceived the prospect of public-funded, church-administered initiatives as allowing whites to ignore how structural racism was keeping black neighborhoods poor. "The city government was much more interested in funding self-help bootstrap kinds of programs," claimed a Bedford-Stuyvesant pastor from a church belonging to the Association of Brooklyn Clergy for Community Development, "because it allowed white people to abdicate their responsibilities for the production of the ghetto. With black churches working for government to correct the poor, however, they don't have to deal with racial history because the colored people is gonna get themselves together." Thus, whites could claim that they were assisting blacks to help themselves while surreptitiously making it harder for black communities to ever improve. "But inevitably, and fundamentally," another pastor opined, "inner-city neighborhoods do not just belong to black churches; they belong to the fabric of the city. It is the responsibility of others in the city to look after the well-being of those who are also the city's inhabitants."[26]

## Openness to Church-State Partnerships

Given the concern of activist black clergy to protect the prophetic voice of their churches, tied to the long-standing tradition that African American churches are the moral voice of the nation that speaks truth to power on behalf of the poor, it seemed unlikely in the 1980s and in the years after the Dinkins administration that any activist African American churches in New York City would even envision, let alone pursue, working with the city government. Additionally, fears of reduced social welfare spending and increased white neglect of problems rooted in racism, which many perceived as implicit in government calls for public-private partnerships, could have forestalled partnerships between activist African American churches and the city government.

Nonetheless, some activist African American churches from Bedford-Stuyvesant, South Jamaica, Harlem, and Morrisania did partner with the city government, even when "an explicit war-on-the-poor mayor" such as Giuliani was in office (Barrett 2000, 310). Their pastors believed that collaboration with government would help them achieve their political, programmatic, and professional goals. This belief was not lost on city policymakers. A veteran HPD official remarked to me, "In trying to promote themselves, increase their reputations in their neighborhoods, and expand their capacities, the black church–affiliated CDCs looked to the agency and its bevy of programs and resources. In trying to promote their faith [through] community outreach, the black [churches and their] church-affiliated CDCs . . . looked to HPD's programs as a means of helping their community."

Clergy who chose for their churches to work with government discounted the concerns of the critics of church-state partnerships. They believed that their collective action with government would not weaken the prophetic voice of churches, nor would it necessarily yield co-optation. Indeed they were confident that church-state partnerships would assist them in confronting and overcoming a crisis in perception and reality within their neighborhood. On the one hand, the pastors recognized that African American churches, including their own, despite their activism, were negatively perceived, even neglected, by politicians (white and black) and many neighborhood residents. On the other hand, they realized that black political incorporation through electoral action had failed to provide an adequate conduit for transferring sufficient resources from the city government to low-income black neighborhoods. Church-state partnerships, they contended, would reverse, or at least halt, declining conditions in black neighborhoods. Further, the success of partnerships might reposition African American churches and clergy as pivotal institutions and individuals in their neighborhood vis-à-vis politicians, demonstrating their relevance in the lives of low-income blacks and efforts to improve the neighborhood.

Pastors open to partnering with government saw church-state interaction as a means of further building the church's institutional capacity and actualizing their potential to accomplish community goals, especially decreasing neighborhood problems such as the lack of recreational programs for youth, the presence of hunger and homelessness, and the limited supply and quality of affordable housing. In their view, low-income black neighborhoods needed to identify ways of affecting public policy beyond electoral action, and it made sense to see whether partnerships with public agencies would prove a new vehicle for community action and self-initiative, as well as to expand the resources and maintain the strength of activist churches.

*Discounting "False Claims."* Pastors that advocated church-state partnerships disagreed with what one pastor from Morrisania called the "false claims" of their peers who opposed such partnerships. They especially disagreed with the notion that churches' receipt of public funding would enslave pastors and prevent them from publicly disagreeing with or condemning the actions of government officials that disadvantaged low-income black neighborhoods. A pastor from Harlem asserted that collaboration with government, even when it meant accepting public funding, did not restrict his political advocacy: "I've got all these city-funded dollars around here—millions of dollars—and it has not kept me from saying anything I had to say. I have not had [my voice] squelched. So what [others] says does not make any sense. There are a lot of ministers who make the claim that they need to be independent of government: They must protect their prophetic voice. It is an excuse. . . . It takes work to go after the [money for] these programs and to monitor them to see that the money is right. It has to do with how much work you want to do."

He and others were convinced that collaboration with government never affected their judgment regarding the use of political action. Neither they nor their church would deliberately limit their political action merely because they collaborated with government, even if they received public resources. For them, cooperation never meant co-optation. "I don't think the government is buying us off or doing us any favors," one informant opined.

Instead of focusing on the resources they might receive from government as payment for choosing cooperation over or alongside conflict, many pastors I interviewed, as well as executive directors and board members of CDCs, argued that observers should see their churches and church-associated CDCs as deserving the benefits. They were being rewarded for their ability to achieve agreed-upon ends that matched the needs, interests, and values of the residents of the neighborhoods they served. In particular, their neighborhoods needed and wanted affordable housing, the city wanted them to have it, and activist churches via church-associated CDCs were best positioned among civil society organizations to produce it.

These pastors saw the resources that would come to their faith-related agencies as nothing more than an equitable return of tax revenue to black neighborhoods. Indeed, they contended that the resources would be payback to blacks for decades of low government responsiveness. "When we are partners with government," one pastor argued, "we're not bought by government; we're given what we deserve to have." Pastors also saw partnership as a way to level the playing field among religious groups in the city. "We don't get our fair share. Look at Catholic Charities and the tax dollars that go to them. We still don't [receive a fair share]. But partnerships give us more than we got before."

Pastors who partnered their church with the city government acknowledged to me that churches that received public money might be in a position to assume the blame if government cut direct provision of social services by public workers and agencies. They were willing to take the risk. The pastors knew that they could not control reductions in government budgets. But they could use the available money and other resources to provide their neighborhoods with services they needed. Thus, some black pastors in New York City during the 1980s and 1990s believed, as Reverend Borders of Wheat Street Baptist Church did in the late 1950s in Atlanta, that they could not disregard opportunities to improve the lives of the black poor. "Even if you don't agree with someone's politics, per se," a pastor told me, "that does not preclude you from seeking their help." He continued, "You can still keep your integrity and at the same time get resources [for your organization and community], because that's what's important."

*"Repositioning the Body of Christ."* Following their decision to remain in their urban neighborhood, clergy who led activist African American churches sought to demonstrate that the faith sector was vital to poor blacks. Pastors sought to offer much more than spiritual succor and emergency relief in response to the high rates of abandoned property, unemployment, poverty, and crime. Consequently, activist churches created or expanded programs focused on outreach to neighborhood residents, rather than just those who attended their worship services. Their clergy were "repositioning the body of Christ in black civil society," as a pastor described the community-based work of his church. This was needed, pastors believed, because their "commanding influence" in neighborhood affairs and local politics had been diminishing (French 1988).

Pastors seemed, in the eyes of neighborhood residents and activist, disconnected from civic life and disappearing from the public square. Survey research by the International Research Institute on Values Change on the associational engagement of black pastors in New York City during the 1990s suggests that the participation of black clergy in secular groups oriented toward community change was low. Tony Carnes claims that less than one-half of black clergy belonged to groups other than religious ones: 24 percent, 19 percent, and 13 percent of black clergy participated in civic groups, neighborhood associations, and school-related groups, respectively (Carnes 2001). Moreover, less than one-tenth of black clergy were involved in political clubs (6 percent) or issue groups (4 percent). The lack of civic membership kept the clergy out of the view and lives of many individuals, especially secular leaders, in the neighborhoods of their churches.[27]

Black pastors' lack of civic engagement had lowered the regard secular leaders, especially neighborhood politicians, held them in. Over the previous two decades, some black politicians had even acted as if they could ignore black clergy as political actors. In Bedford-Stuyvesant, for example, a group of politicians in the early 1980s formed the Coalition for Community Empowerment (CCE), a political association to foster electoral action by blacks in Brooklyn. The intent was to create a new vehicle for mobilizing voters and yielding victories. It also aimed to install a new black leadership, one whose authority in the black community came from political power and nothing else.

Seeking to downplay the authority of certain types of civil society figures, especially clergy, the founders of CCE restricted membership mainly to elected officials and secular leaders (Thompson 1990). It specifically barred ministers from membership, sidelining even those pastors who were most likely to support black political action, such as Reverend Jones, an avowed Black Christian Nationalist who led Bethany Baptist Church and had been a leader of Operation Breadbasket in the 1970s. Black politicians such as those associated with the CCE believed that they were the only legitimate political actors in black neighborhoods. Politicians, not pastors, were elected to represent their neighborhoods; politicians, not pastors, spoke for the neighborhoods.[28]

A case such as the CCE does not diminish the fact that black politicians recognized the value of church-based resources to electoral politics or the historic role that clergy and churches played in the electoral mobilization of blacks. Black politicians often owed their elections and continued tenure to black clergy's enlisting the material and cultural resources of their churches. Overall, black politicians believed that churches had much to contribute to local politics. For example, 88 percent of black New York City politicians who responded to a 1999 survey I administered agreed with the normative position that churches should be involved in politics, especially neighborhood politics. They also asserted that more churches should engage in political action. Yet such agreement was affected by a pivotal factor: tenure. The longer politicians served in office the less likely they were to endorse the involvement of churches in neighborhood politics.

Self-preservation explains the inverse relationship between politicians' tenure and their support for church involvement in politics, as well as the emergence of overtly anticlergy movements like the CCE. Black politicians valued the engagement of churches in political campaigns (electoral and otherwise) to advance black interests, as long as they focused their activities against the politician's opponents or outside their district. Churches did not always comply with these preferences, and politicians knew it. Reverend Butts of Abyssinian Baptist Church, for instance, routinely condemned Harlem's politicians, from its councilmen to its congressman (anonymous 1992). Given the low opinion clergy such as Butts had of politicians in their districts, long-serving politicians preferred that churches not be too involved in neighborhood politics.

Aside from politicians' overlooking clergy, neighborhood residents had expressed disappointment that African American churches, activist or otherwise, were not helping to address everyday problems such as work, education, housing, and crime. Many residents, particularly the poor but even some of the prosperous, of South Jamaica, Bedford-Stuyvesant, Morrisania, and Harlem claimed to have no sense of the relevance of the churches in their temporal lives in the 1980s and 1990s. Neighborhood denizens asked rhetorically, according to one pastor, "What are the churches doing?"

Some clergy, such as the pastor of Concord Baptist Church of Christ in Bedford-Stuyvesant, could honestly answer, "A lot." For years Concord Baptist was among the few churches in its neighborhood that administered social welfare services oriented toward the broader community. Its Concord Family Services was a comprehensive community action agency that operated foster care and adoption, after-school, and computer literacy programs and provided low-cost health services on site. The Concord Christfund, a congregation-endowed philanthropy, had given away approximately $500,000 in grants to community-based organizations serving Bedford-Stuyvesant. The church's Concord Federal Credit Union had a membership of 5,000, and it provided loans to neighborhood residents to start businesses and make investments. The church also operated Concord Baptist Elementary School, the first Afro-Christian school certified in New York State. All the same, neighborhood residents seemed blind to the church's efforts. As Reverend

Simpson of Concord Baptist commented in an interview, "I'm sad to say that some people in this community have no idea what we do, even though they walk by this church every day" (quoted in Toussaint 1999, 76).

Pastors like Reverend Simpson who led activist churches in Bedford-Stuyvesant and in the other black neighborhoods heard from neighborhood residents that the collective Black Church was ignoring them. They also heard residents claim that the primary recipients of the churches' munificence were their members, not their broader communities.

Some residents complained about the "ungodly" amounts of money the churches took in on Sundays through tithes and offerings and the salaries they paid to their pastors. Activist pastors realized that too many neighborhood residents, in the words of Anthony Pinn, "saw no real progress, while the Black Church became richer and its ministers more comfortable with middle class status" (2002, 19), even if the churches did return some resources to the community via faith-related agencies and services.

Community activists, in particular, were down on African American churches, even the activist churches. "Trends, such as the advent of AIDS, drug epidemics, and increasing poverty and stratification within black communities, [were] beginning to make some activists question the central authority given to the church" in New York City and its vaunted position in black civil society (Cohen 1999, 278).

Pastors leading congregations that were medium or small in size commented to me that they were losing members, and such losses generated an impression that neighborhood churches overall were in decline. Some of them had lost members to outmigration by families to other black neighborhoods, and death, too, reduced membership rolls. Pastors faced difficulties in recruiting new members, often because a large proportion of residents had turned from the faith of their childhood or had never been "churched."[29]

In the face of negative perceptions of churches by residents and activists, along with direct neglect of pastors by some politicians and residents' declining participation in local church activities, the clergy of some activist churches set out to change their image, as best they could. They assumed that by delivering long-anticipated goods and services such as affordable housing, employment, and quality schools through churches or faith-related agencies, they could win positive publicity, elevate their civic prestige, and deepen their political legitimacy in the neighborhoods.

By making their church and faith-related agencies more relevant to the lived conditions in their neighborhood, especially through the acquisition of new resources, the pastors could change the position of their churches within civil society. Church-state partnerships, in particular, they reasoned, could be a means for accomplishing this. Such partnerships might provide blacks with a new medium for acting politically and a different means of self-initiative to alleviate some of the poor conditions in their neighborhoods, in the view of pastors whose churches had independent CDCs or joined with others to charter alliance-based CDCs.

*Needed: New Means of Community Action.* At the close of one of my interviews, a pastor declared that "black communities needed alternative or supplemental conduits to increase the ability of black people in New York City to acquire more public resources and influence city policy making." Partnership was necessary, other pastors averred, given the weakness of black political incorporation to produce substantive changes in the state of black neighborhoods. After two decades of increasing numbers of blacks in elected positions, as well as a national movement for social equality of opportunities and the implementation of multiple antipoverty initiatives, most black neighborhoods in New York City were in socioeconomic and physical decline, or they were devastated, like Harlem.

In the 1980s Harlem experienced the difficulties common to many black neighborhoods in New York City, ranging from abandonment to concentrated poverty to redlining. Yet unlike the other neighborhoods, it had a potentially effective political institution, the Harlem Urban Development Corporation (HUDC). Created in 1971 by the New York State Development Corporation at the urging of black politicians, HUDC's mission was to improve Harlem's local economy and strengthen its ties to the citywide economy. HUDC, however, became a tool for patronage distribution, one connected to the traditional political leaders of Harlem, especially U.S. Representative Charles Rangel.[30] As a result, "political loyalty often took precedence over community need and policy effectiveness" (Thompson 2006, 213). The infusion of millions of dollars of public funds into HUDC yielded no substantive changes in the neighborhood's conditions. In an interview with J. Phillip Thompson, the late Reverend Preston Washington, a founder and past executive director of Harlem Congregations for Community Improvement, recalled that a colleague of his, Reverend Linton Gunn, once put a set of black politicians associated with the HUDC on the spot in the 1980s, asserting to them that "our community looks like shit" (quoted in Thompson 2006, 214).[31]

The ability of black politicians to increase government responsiveness to their neighborhoods was low; white politicians discounted black votes in formulating and executing public policies affecting the advancement of black neighborhoods. Even a Democratic majority in the city council did not increase black representatives' ability to influence public agendas and policies to the advantage of black neighborhoods, contrary to the expectations of some urban politics scholars (Browning, Marshall, and Tabb 1984; Eisinger 1982a; Viteritti 1979). Hence, in and beyond Harlem many black pastors perceived politicians to be without effect.

In the end, activist black pastors concluded that collaboration with government could be as useful as, if not more than, elected representatives at addressing neighborhood problems. According to one pastor, "Political power via the ballot was important, but collaboration, as you put it, had greater potential to help our efforts and neighborhoods." Another pastor added, "We were convinced that the hope of our community could be better realized by it than by merely electing particular personalities to office." Consequently, in 95 percent of the city council and state legislative districts represented by black elected officials in New York City, African American churches, directly and through their agencies, partnered with government to deliver public benefits in 1999.

Politicians claimed that they did not mind activist churches' collaborating with government. Despite criticisms of them by local pastors, black politicians in New York City generally expressed support for the churches and their CDCs, especially their collaboration with city government. Specifically, 96 percent of black elected officials who responded to my survey supported African American churches' working with government to redevelop black neighborhoods. Furthermore, black politicians endorsed church-state partnerships regardless of the concerns some of them had that church-guided neighborhood development, especially affordable housing production, might yield a "ghetto within a ghetto" or that "preachers acting under the guise of God [were] fighting for their own agendas" (Shipp 1991).

Black politicians' support for church-state partnerships was connected to an expectation. They anticipated that they, too, would benefit from the work of the churches and their CDCs. Their logic was simple: if the neighborhoods improved, the politicians could point to the improvements as signs of *their* effectiveness, especially by arguing that they were critical to the churches and the CDCs' acquiring public resources, either by claiming that descriptive representation yielded substantive representation or that they were advocates for the agendas of the churches.

*Advancing Self-Initiative.* Church-state partnerships, along with CDCs, were to be what one pastor referred to as "positive change agents." They were to improve the physical, social, and economic environments of black neighborhoods in the city, especially by providing new links to public resources. Through formal involvement of the churches with the city government, clergy hoped to indirectly affect government responsiveness to improve neighborhood conditions. They would collaborate with government to advance the redevelopment of their neighborhood, acquire public resources, leverage private resources, and take ownership, often literally, of their neighborhood, building by building, block by block. Ultimately, the pastors believed, collaboration with government, if it produced changes in the neighborhoods, would advance black self-initiative as well as raise the stature of churches in communities.

Conceptually, there is a distinction between self-initiative and self-help, which I laid out in chapter 2. The former involves individuals and groups acting interdependently with government to address their problems. The latter is about individuals and groups acting independently of government, guided by the inherent claim that they alone own their problems and answers.

Simultaneously disassociating the term *bootstrapping* from self-help rhetoric and appropriating it to characterize the process of self-initiative, Reverend Floyd Flake of Allen AME Church distinguishes between the two concepts to explain the partnerships between his church and government agencies: "The difference between a bootstrapper and others is that they may receive government help, but they refuse to become totally dependent on it. A bootstrapper views government assistance as a leveraging tool that moves whatever he wishes to accomplish from a means to an end. . . . The Allen A.M.E. community development programs know how to leverage government resources for the good of the people and communities by building coalitions for success" (Flake and Williams 1999, 22).

A peer of Flake elaborated the distinction between self-initiative and self-help for me. "We need to do for ourselves what we can do. But we need to utilize our resources to assist the city, the state, and the federal governments to do what they ought to do." Implicit in this statement is the idea that city governments are limited in their ability and capacity to provide services to those who need them. Reverend Johnny Ray Youngblood, pastor of Saint Paul Community Baptist Church and a founder of East Brooklyn Congregations, captured much of this sentiment in a public address:

Substantive hope demands that we see the distress we are in. . . . We, who say government is the answer. We, who say privatization is the answer. Anyone who waves either wand at the distress we are in, does not see it, and does not see that they are part of the distress. . . . So seeing the distress means that we come to grips with the fact that we are in this together and that the incompetence and narrowness of the public sector and the incompetence and narrowness of the private sector are all part of the distress. . . . They [governments] need us [the churches], and we must make ourselves available that we might together save the central cities of America and the families and institutions that are so central to the central cities. (Youngblood 1992)

In the minds of such pastors, receipt of public resources does not conflict with black initiative or denote black dependency. Rather, the acceptance and use of public resources actually enhances the self-help tradition of black churches and girds up the commitment of black people to initiative and enterprise.

In the words of another pastor, the approach that Flake, Youngblood, and others advocate is "assisted self-reliance": "When we talk about self-help, what we are talking about is something we have been doing all along, and our pressure of government—on government—is another indication of our desire to help ourselves . . . . . . So, you cannot say black churches, because they accept resources from folk other than black folk, are not involved in self-help. We, as black-led organizations, mix those resources with our own resources and try to better the condition of black people and help black people to better themselves, their families, and their communities."

The pastor of a founding-member congregation of the Southeast Queens Clergy for Community Empowerment represented well the self-initiative argument for activist African American churches to partner with the city government:

The churches had the vision and the resources, and they started looking at well—they started making the noise . . . and saying our communities are deteriorating. What do we do? We could try to do for self. But that only goes so far. So we looked around. We found out there were some government programs that could be helpful, at the federal and municipal levels, and we wanted to know why those programs weren't working and whether we could make them work better. So we started pressuring the political leadership, both black and white, and that's . . . why the churches began to work with the government, instead of just looking to self-help and the old saw of "black capitalism."

In sum, some of the clergy leading activist African American churches in New York City decided that partnership with the city government, along with the federal and state governments, was a better response than self-reliance to the black condition. Public policy influenced their attitude.

*Capacity Building.* The city was moving toward a greater reliance on privatization, with nonprofits coproducing and implementing public policy, particularly affordable housing policy on the basis of the Ten Year Plan. The design and incentives of municipal policy encouraged some activist churches to pursue collaboration. At times obtaining public resources seemed, from the perspective of pastors as well as the professionals who ran the church-associated CDCs, almost as easy as putting out a hand or opening the mail. Although this is an exaggeration, access to public resources had indeed become easier, as noted by an informant who was a former leader of the Southeast Queens Clergy for Community Empowerment:

> During the 1980s, [black churches] began to see the government empowering black religious institutional actors to acquire access to public and private resources. This continued into the 1990s, you know. We also saw government, as well as private institutions, mobilize technical and financial assistance. . . . All of sudden, we started getting invited to meetings down at [the New York City Department of Housing Preservation and Development]. Contracts were put before us. Buildings were given to us. TA [technical assistance] grants were out there for us, along with subsidies of all kinds to rehab city-owned property and own it on behalf of the community.

The city government did not necessarily discriminate in terms of the types of nonprofit organizations it would work with, even if politics could pose barriers to certain groups' working with the city. Access to the city's resources, however, required that the churches join with it to implement public policy. Only collaboration with government, or so it seemed, could give the churches access to the resources necessary to better address problems in their neighborhoods.

By the time the Association of Brooklyn Clergy for Community Development (ABCCD) was fully functional as a CDC in Bedford-Stuyvesant, the city government owned 409 abandoned buildings in the neighborhood (Bach and West 1993, 20). ABCCD members learned from neighborhood politicians that the city wanted to relinquish title to these properties. They believed that it was in the interest of the neighborhood for a community-based organization, especially a faith-based agency, to reclaim the properties from the city and transfer them to "community ownership." Collectively, they approached city hall to secure the properties and acquire subsidies to convert them into decent, occupied, and affordable residences. Like other church-associated CDCs, ABCCD leveraged the resources it acquired from the municipal government to lure private financial support and foster community support for its neighborhood redevelopment agenda.

MAKING A WAY OUT OF NO WAY: THE REALPOLITIK
OF CHURCH-STATE PARTNERSHIPS

Community-based nonprofit organizations welcomed the city government's invitation to work with it to increase the supply of affordable housing. Historian Alexander von Hoffman writes: "New York's nonprofit groups clamored to be included in the great campaign to rebuild New York's inner city. [They] had earned a moral right. From the practical point of view, the groups were familiar with the neighborhoods and the people who lived in them" (2003, 54). The groups could use the subsidies and contracts involved in affordable housing development to increase their operational budgets, hiring more staff to deliver more services. Moreover, a demonstrated ability to secure public funding would increase their chances of securing private support, especially from national and local philanthropies and community development intermediaries that were seeking community-based organizations and comprehensive community initiatives to invest in New York City.

The affordable housing production experiment that the city initiated in the 1980s encouraged community development organizations and tenant associations of all stripes and from all neighborhoods with city-owned properties to pursue partnerships with City Hall. The city government did not explicitly seek to partner with activist African American churches, however, at least not initially. Though these churches' involvement was crucial, the ethnic politics of the city, personified in a battle between black clergy and a white mayor, posed a high barrier to their inclusion.

Historically, mayoral administrations had not attended much to the issues and interests of black neighborhoods. Mayors had only rarely sought to make the city's community development policies consonant with the values of such neighborhoods. Additionally, though blacks challenged incumbent politicians to match their campaign rhetoric with policy reality, sometimes embarrassing them in the process, black political influence in city policy making remained feeble. The number of black elected officials in the city continued to be small, and their ability to influence the formulation of public policies continued to be shaky, even under during the Dinkins administration. Therefore, activist African American churches and their CDCs were in a weak position to win partnerships with the Koch administration to develop affordable housing.

The story of the Harlem Congregations for Community Improvement (HCCI) and its Bradhurst Comprehensive Community Development Plan demonstrates the political realities of the time, which tended to disadvantage black community-based organizations as potential partners with the city government. It explains, too, how activist African American churches and their CDCs overcame the obstacles to establish what would become long-term formal relationships with the city government to develop affordable housing in their neighborhoods.

### *The Bradhurst Plan: A Proposal for Church-Driven Neighborhood Development*

Recall that HCCI first convened in 1986 as an ecumenical effort among clergy on the upper east side of Harlem to correct market failures that had produced an inadequate supply of affordable housing in the area known as Bradhurst. It also emerged as a church-based initiative to challenge the city government's efforts to redevelop Harlem without community participation.

At the time the Koch administration was three years from reelection, and it wanted to lock down the Harlem vote. During his first election campaign, Koch had promised to bring new housing to the neighborhood (von Hoffman 2003). The city government owned 40 percent of the neighborhood's buildings and vacant land (Plunz 1990, 325). Koch, however, wanted to work with Harlem "leaders" and groups he could control or at least whose leadership he could influence through patronage (Koch 1984).[32] Furthermore, "[taking] advantage of the political moment, Koch wanted [development projects in Harlem] to happen quickly, which predictably left the community out of the picture" (Oppenheim and Sierra 1994, 146).

Like other alliance-based church-associated CDCs that emerged in the 1980s, HCCI viewed itself first and foremost as a political coalition of congregations. Collectively, the member congregations, fulfilling the legacy of clergy-initiated brokerage, pressed the claims of neighborhood residents on the city government. In the process it morphed from a ministerial alliance for discourse about community issues into an institution for collaborating with government to advance the interests of its section of Harlem. The late Reverend Dr. Preston Washington, then senior pastor of Memorial Baptist Church and first president of HCCI, conveyed the organizational premise and political interests for HCCI in a 1987 article: "Our purpose is to advocate and agitate for low- and moderate-income housing for Harlem families. We are particularly interested in a program whereby city-owned multiple dwellings in Harlem can be renovated and turned into cooperative apartments managed by churches and community organizations. We are committed to being active participants in the struggle to revitalize the Harlem community" (quoted in Scotland 1999, 186). HCCI then set out to draw up a plan to realize the collective vision that its members had for the neighborhood—the Bradhurst Comprehensive Community Development Plan.

HCCI's plan outlined the creation of at least 2,000 housing units in ten years for low- and moderate-income residents, whether current or newcomers to the neighborhood. New social services and economic development projects were also included in the plan. The idea was to devise a comprehensive community initiative to permit individuals and families to live decent and stable lives in a decent and stable neighborhood. The plan identified city-owned property as the foundation for revitalizing Bradhurst through a mix of affordable housing and health and human services.

*Fighting Koch*

HCCI knew that it could not go to Koch with a hand out, even if the other hand held the blueprint for a sound housing plan that would catalyze neighborhood improvement. "The Koch administration," according to von Hoffman, "only liked to deal with partners who placed serious cash on the table" (2003, 56). Thus HCCI presented its plan and offered the administration a deal. HCCI would seek $57 million from the market sector through low-income housing tax credit financing and traditional commercial lenders in exchange for approximately $63 million in subsidies from the city government. This was, in the view of HCCI, more than reasonable.

Immediately, the city government dismissed the ability of HCCI to partner with it. An HCCI informant recounted to me what happened:

We gave [our plan] to Koch, because Koch—we were trying to meet with him, and he says, "You people don't have no"—"*you* people," right?— "You people don't have any experience doing housing." But Koch, in the meantime, initiated a 100,000-unit redevelopment program, because the city had all of this doggone [tax-foreclosed] housing. And [it] didn't know what to do with it, [and it] was not an efficient landlord of the space they had. It was the ugliest, most bureaucratically, dehumanizing [housing] that you've ever seen. They tried to manage the properties. They became the owners, and Koch initiated this 100,000-unit redevelopment program at the time when we presented him with [our plan]. They didn't allow us to be developers, or codevelopers, investors, and of course, when I finally realized what was going on, I said, "Dag! This is going to have to take a whole new strategy." *Boom!* We fought Koch for three years . . . to get the city to work with HCCI and to support our plan with resources. We fought to make a way, our way, out of "no way, niggers, you ain't working with the city."[33]

The involvement of HCCI, or any other African American churches and their CDCs, in the Ten Year Plan seemed, from the initial viewpoint of municipal policymakers in the Koch administration, unnatural. This was their perspective despite two facts. One, churches and faith-related agencies of Christian denominations in New York City had participated in federal affordable housing development programs since the 1970s (Gartell and Herman 1971). In the 1970s and early 1980s African American churches such as Canaan Baptist Church of Christ, Bridge Street AWME Church, Abyssinian Baptist Church, Allen AME Church, and Concord Baptist Church of Christ had participated in the development of Section 202 housing for low-income senior citizens.[34] Two, the faith-related agencies of African American churches (e.g., Allen AWRC and Concord Family Services) were among the nonprofits the city government contracted with to deliver public-funded human services in black neighborhoods, especially programs oriented toward children, the aged, and families (e.g., summer recreation, elder transportation, and foster care and adoption services).

In the end, the initial inclusion of African American churches and their CDCs in the implementation of the Ten Year Plan would be the product of political struggle. HCCI pressed Koch to include African American churches and faith-related agencies in the city's affordable housing production experiment, at least in the black neighborhoods. Mayor Koch responded with disdain. Here is how an HCCI informant recalled the initial experience with the administration: "Koch called the preachers 'poverty pimps.' He just couldn't deal with the black clergy. But he could deal with everybody else, just not the black clergy in Harlem, or elsewhere." Generally, Koch did not like agitators, particularly those from black neighborhoods, attempting to influence his decisions (Koch 1984). As social scientists, historians, and journalists, as well as Koch himself, later revealed, he was especially contemptuous of activists who, in his view, "used antipoverty funds for personal and political gain" (Shefter 1987, 179). An HCCI informant echoed this theme during an interview: "Koch was mad that black preachers acted politically in ways that potentially undercut his reelection and public image, and he did his best to weaken the commitment of our congregations to making the city government respond to us and the community by trying to ignore or inflame us. We knew that partnering with Caesar [Koch] would be hard, but I mean really, it was almost impossible."

The result was extreme bitterness and animosity between the mayor and the black pulpit in Harlem. Opposed to collaborating with "politically wired groups," the city government initially ignored Harlem, disregarding Koch's earlier campaign promise to Harlem (von Hoffman 2003, 61). Instead, it targeted resources in the predominantly Latino neighborhoods of the South Bronx.

HCCI battled the Koch administration. At one point it even aligned with a set of Harlem politicians—politicians that HCCI members generally deemed ineffectual—to block efforts by the administration to transfer the Bradhurst Plan to white for-profit developers (Thompson 2006). Reflecting on the experience, Rev. Washington was quoted in a 1991 *New York Newsday* story as saying, "Koch didn't believe that we had the capacity as churches to pull off this massive plan and he took our plan to another developer, a white developer. . . . We fought tooth and nail" (Scotland 1999, 162). A year later, in another venue, the reverend recalled, "Koch fought us like you wouldn't believe. . . . It was like a personal vendetta" (quoted in Scotland 1999, 162).

### Conflict Comes to an End

Two years after publicizing its plan, however, HCCI received word from the Koch administration that it could partner with the city, after he was no longer in office. The decision by the municipal government to work with HCCI was one of the last acts of the Koch administration. Maybe it was Koch's way of fulfilling an earlier campaign promise to build housing in Harlem. Perhaps it was a welcome gift to the Dinkins administration—after a bitter contest for the mayoralty, a peace offering to heal racial wounds reopened during the campaign. Maybe, given the horrendous financial condition of the city at Dinkins's inauguration, Koch was further boxing in Dinkins politically, forcing him to choose fiscal conservatism over liberal policy making. It may have been any and all of these things. Regardless, Dinkins honored and extended Koch's invitation to HCCI to partner with the city government. The difference in administrations was significant.

While Koch had finally been willing to give HCCI a few million dollars in public subsidies, Dinkins reserved $18.4 million for the Bradhurst Plan (Thompson 2006, 215). Later, the chairman of the board of HCCI, Canon Frederick B. Williams, rector of the Church of the Intercession, commented, "Koch and his people were not unsupportive. They were supportive, just at a minimal level. They said, 'Here's a little crumb.' David Dinkins came in and said, 'I know you can serve a banquet'" (quoted in Bernstein 1994). Eventually, however, HCCI was forced to serve a smaller "banquet" under the Giuliani administration: the Giuliani administration reduced its share of city funds to approximately $5 million (Shipp 1991; Millner 1995, 20). Following the cut, a spokesperson for the mayor affirmed, "The bottom line is the Giuliani administration is committed to the Bradhurst project." Unfortunately, the "commitment" was less than expected or adequate to fulfill the plan's goals.

Koch's decision and Dinkins's fulfillment of it, nonetheless, had a profound effect on Bradhurst. HCCI's implementation of its plan yielded approximately $200 million in investment to produce 1,500 units of affordable housing and 30 commercial sites, including a 45,000-square-foot supermarket (Strozier 1999; Moorer 2003). By 1996, HCCI owned approximately 1,000 apartments in formerly city-owned buildings and had rehabilitated them and returned them to the affordable rental housing market (Scotland 1999, 164).

But Koch's initial choice to directly partner the city with HCCI also had another effect: it opened the affordable housing-production experiment to the participation of multiple African American churches and their CDCs across the city. Unpublished records of the New York City Department of Housing Preservation and Development (HPD) show that a minimum of two hundred community-based organizations received land and money to develop affordable housing from 1987 to 1997.[35] All types of community-based organizations received them, ranging from tenant associations to secular community development corporations. Thirty of the organizations were affiliated with religious institutions. Of those, 30 percent were CDCs associated with activist African American churches in Harlem, Morrisania, South Jamaica, and Bedford-Stuyvesant.

By 1999, the opportunities for activist African American churches to acquire resources from the city through collaboration, especially with HPD, seemed abundant. A majority (80 percent) of black elected officials in my survey concurred with the statement "There are more opportunities than ever for African American churches to get public resources for neighborhood development." Most pastors, too, held that view.

## SUMMARY

On the heels of its return to fiscal solvency, the city government used city-owned land and buildings (occupied and vacant) and municipal and federal funding to catalyze an increased supply of affordable housing. The intervention, which relied on a scheme of privatization, was a response to cross-pressures on the city government to address an issue that had become a crisis. The city turned to nongovernmental organizations, mostly nonprofits, to execute what became a decade-long, $5.2 billion, public-private partnership for affordable housing production. The Ten Year Plan permitted activist African American churches to partner with the city government. Their partnerships expanded the potential of the churches to receive public funds. Yet church-state collaboration was not inevitable.

Aside from the city government's initial disinterest in working with African American churches, many black clergy opposed their church's partnering with the city government. Their opposition rested upon a set of fears. They feared that partnerships with the city government would co-opt churches, muting their individual and collective prophetic voice. Pastors also feared that church-state collaboration would make the churches dependent on public resources, which would counter and undercut African American churches' legacy as the only institutions of black civil society that were autonomous and free from government intrusion. Given the policy directions of the city government and the federal government alike, pastors presumed that church-state collaboration would reduce public sector responsibility for the poor and produce government retrenchment, all the while furthering white neglect of the ghetto.

Nevertheless, such fears posed low barriers to the cadre of pastors who directed their churches to partner with the government. Instead of focusing on the potential for harm to the churches or their communities, these activist pastors looked to the hopes of church-state partnerships. They anticipated that their involvement with the city government would reaffirm the relevance of their churches and themselves to black civil society, especially as they demonstrated that they could leverage church resources to obtain public resources and neighborhood effects beyond the normal reach of black politicians. They also believed that church-state partnerships would enable them to advance black self-initiative and retain or increase church memberships. These factors, along with the possibility for neighborhood revitalization, were sufficient for some activist black clergy to pursue the promise of collaboration with government.

From the late 1980s onward, a set of activist African American churches through their CDCs would partner with the city government, particularly the core programs that constituted its Ten Year Plan. These partnerships were but necessary preludes to something more—collaboration with government—on behalf of black neighborhoods. By sharing in the governance of black neighborhoods, especially the production of affordable housing, activist African American churches would use their CDCs to acquire resources and a degree of public power, as the next chapter reveals. They would attain less than absolute authority over affordable housing development agendas and programs of the city government, but their future roles as developers, managers, and sponsors of affordable housing would permit them to exert influence over redevelopment in their neighborhoods. Combined with the activities of other neighborhood-based organizations, church-state collaboration would begin to positively affect the physical trajectory of poor black neighborhoods, even if its capacity to improve the social and economic lives of current residents was low.

# CHAPTER SIX

# Acquiring Resources for
# Neighborhood Resurrection

The small crowd on West 138th Street was atypical for the block, let alone Harlem. It included politicians and preachers, bankers and foundation officers, public administrators and journalists. Their gathering among the residents of the block had to be for a special occasion, and it was. Monday, August 19, 2002, was the day that the Laura B. Thomas Houses, seven residential buildings that would house working-class families within a three-block radius ringing Abyssinian Baptist Church, opened. Sheena Wright, president and CEO of the Abyssinian Development Corporation (ADC), remarked that day, "For some of us the Laura B. Thomas Houses is simply one part of Harlem's beautiful landscape. But for 52 families, this is the day they get to experience Harlem's Second Renaissance for themselves" (quoted in Geto and DeMilly 2002, 1).

A modest effort among many in the city to increase the supply of decent and affordable housing, the Thomas Houses, named after an Abyssinian congregant whom Rev. Adam Clayton Powell Jr. appointed in the 1930s as the church's first social worker, are tributes to the almost century-long struggle for adequate housing in the low-income black neighborhoods of New York City. Inadequate housing—too expensive, too crowded, too dilapidated—dogged these neighborhoods from their beginnings. Over the decades activist black clergy sporadically called on the city government to improve housing conditions in these neighborhoods. Few pastors, however, paid significant and sustained attention to the issue until the 1980s, a time when the municipal government felt pressure citywide to revive the affordable housing market.

When pastors began to address affordable housing shortages in a deliberate manner, they did not do so by merely protesting for more housing or supporting candidates promising at election time to deliver it. They also did not turn to self-help, passing collection plates down their pews on Sundays to raise money from congregants to secure private land, materials, and developers to build houses and apartments on their own. Instead, they developed affordable housing through their churches in partnership with the public and market sectors. It was a point much underlined that Monday in Harlem.

Abyssinian Baptist Church, relying on ADC, developed the Thomas Houses, hiring architects, putting together the financing, managing contractors, and marketing the units for rent. The church and its CDC leveraged their resources, as well as the resources of all three levels of government and an array of commercial institutions, to produce the houses. In particular, public land, funding, and discretion from the Neighborhood Redevelopment Program of the New York City Department of Housing Preservation and Development (HPD) supported the construction.[1]

The development of the Thomas Houses suggests that a public-private partnership may permit churches, through their agencies, to produce tangible physical benefits for their neighborhood. As Reverend Butts, pastor of Abyssinian Baptist Church, intoned on the day ADC opened the houses, "The construction of the Laura B. Thomas Homes stands as a shining example of what we can achieve when government works in close cooperation with communities" (quoted in Geto and DeMilly 2002, 1). Less obvious than the production of buildings for affordable housing was how the process of producing the Thomas Houses empowered the church-associated CDC, along with its sponsor church.

This chapter takes a closer look at how activist African American churches used the resources of the Ten Year Plan to build places like the Thomas Houses. It begins with an overview of four programs HPD designed to administer the plan. Among the programs that permitted the city to administer the Ten Year Plan, these were most pivotal to its performance (Schill et al. 2002; Ellen et al. 2001; Van Ryzin and Genn 1999). The chapter then develops a detailed account of the city government's decision to involve the churches and their CDCs in the execution of the Ten Year Plan. The result was that activist churches and their CDCs obtained influence from and over the implementation of affordable housing policy. Let's consider how the "close cooperation with communities" by government that Reverend Butts spoke about that August day in Harlem allowed activist churches and their CDCs to secure and exercise influence over the planning and implementation of Ten Year Plan programs in the four neighborhoods.

EXECUTING THE TEN YEAR PLAN: FOUR CORE PROGRAMS

HPD, which is under the direct control of the mayor, wields most of the municipal authority for affordable housing production in New York City. It administered the city's Ten Year Plan as well as the affordable housing-production policies of the state and federal governments. The resources HPD possessed to design and administer programs included money, tax-foreclosed properties, and redevelopment powers (e.g., to take private property and to abate and exempt property taxes).

Relying on its fiscal, physical, and legal resources, between 1985 and 2000 HPD catalyzed the construction of 37,000 new housing units, the renovation of 82,000 units in occupied city-owned buildings, the rehabilitation of 47,000 units in vacant city-owned buildings, and the upgrading of 87,000 privately owned apartments for families to rent or purchase (Schill et al. 2002). As of 2003, the city government had divested itself of nearly its entire stock of tax-foreclosed properties in South Jamaica, Bedford-Stuyvesant, Morrisania, and Harlem (Chen 2003). It spent $5.2 billion to do it, funding approximately twenty municipal programs to oversee the process.

The City of New York designed its affordable housing-production experiment to combine delegation, divestment, and displacement. The city government maintained its general responsibility for addressing the affordable housing problem while entrusting to private entities (commercial and civic) responsibility for the production, rental, or sale of affordable housing. HPD obligated nongovernmental organizations and private citizens to use the city's stock of tax-foreclosed properties and public subsidies for affordable housing. To ensure that redeveloped properties functioned as affordable housing, the city relied primarily, but not exclusively, on nonprofit, neighborhood-based organizations to administer the redevelopment and future sales.[2] The Ten Year Plan's process of disposition and development was straightforward, but its ambitions and complexity required more than one program for adequate execution. Four programs formed its core: Partnership New Homes, the Neighborhood Redevelopment Program, Neighborhood Homes, and the Special Initiatives Program.

*Partnership New Homes*

After the Koch administration created Partnership New Homes, this became the program most responsible for altering the opportunity structure of affordable housing in New York City, especially in its low- and moderate-income neighborhoods (Orlebeke 1997; Wylde 1999; Schill et al. 2002). The program, designed and run jointly by HPD and the New York City Housing Partnership, increased the stock of owner-occupied affordable housing by redeveloping municipal land to attract private residential development.[3] It achieved this result by ceding land and providing subsidies to the Housing Partnership. The intermediary then structured the finances, recruited neighborhood-based organizations to sponsor and market redevelopment in their neighborhoods, and identified commercial developers to build housing. From 1983 to 1997, Partnership New Homes facilitated the investment of more than $885 million in some of the city's poorest neighborhoods, yielding approximately 13,500 new units of housing (Orlebeke 1997, 212).[4]

## Special Initiatives Program

Receiving far less attention than Partnership New Homes, the now-defunct Special Initiatives Program of the Koch administration conveyed municipal properties to neighborhood-based organizations to rehabilitate, own, and manage as permanent affordable housing for the homeless. The city government bore all rehabilitation and reconstruction costs for converting buildings to meet the residential needs of its target population. For-profit contractors assumed responsibility for redeveloping the buildings. HPD then identified neighborhood-based organizations to lease, manage, and maintain the renovated buildings. Eventually, the city sold them the buildings, often for one dollar each and after years of management by the neighborhood groups.

Neighborhood-based organizations, after purchasing buildings, received property tax abatements. This served as a subsidy to keep the rents affordable for the homeless. In return for the buildings and subsidies, neighborhood-based organizations designed and administered social service programs for their residents. The services were expected to move residents from dependency (on public assistance as well as on substances such as narcotics or alcohol) to self-sufficiency.

## Neighborhood Redevelopment Program

Ten years after Partnership New Homes began and at the end of the Dinkins administration, HPD created the Neighborhood Redevelopment Program. It transferred to nonprofit organizations the formerly public responsibility for the rehabilitation and management of municipal properties as private rental properties. It also transferred property titles from the city to nonprofit groups.

Additionally, neighborhood-based organizations received construction loans to cover redevelopment costs.[5] HPD also provided the groups with operating subsidies to ensure the long-term affordability of rental units.

An HPD official explained it to me, "You sell it to a not-for-profit, you give them a set amount of money, and you let them figure out who's gonna buy it and what kind of work needs to go into it. The problem is theirs. It's no longer ours, at least directly." The neighborhood-based organizations assumed all remaining costs. They covered them by exchanging low-income housing tax credits for equity from institutional investors (e.g., pension funds and banks) that they leveraged to secure commercial redevelopment loans. Investors received returns on their investments from the rents the neighborhood groups obtained from leasing the redeveloped properties.

## Neighborhood Homes

The Neighborhood Homes program delegated responsibility for affordable housing production to neighborhood-based organizations too. Unlike the Neighborhood Redevelopment Program, it conveyed to them owner-occupant (one-to-four-family) buildings and mixed-use buildings to rehabilitate and sell, not to retain, own, and manage. Additionally, borrowing from prior programs, Neighborhood Homes gave the neighborhood-based organizations public subsidies and construction loans for rehabilitation. Nonprofit organizations taking title to the buildings held them for the duration of rehabilitation, which generally involved weatherization and upgrades to electrical and heating systems, kitchens, and bathrooms. After rehabilitation, they marketed and sold the buildings at below-market value. Buyers were required to reside in the properties for a minimum of ten years.

### RATIONALES FOR THE MUNICIPAL INVITATION TO CHURCHES

Together, the four programs, along with a collection of other programs that relied mainly on for-profit development companies, enabled the municipal government to divest ownership and delegate management of vacant and occupied tax-foreclosed properties to nongovernmental organizations (New York City Department of Housing Preservation and Development 1998). Every conveyance of municipal property and grant of subsidies for rehabilitation and affordability to a nongovernmental organization allowed the city to cede its accountability for tax-foreclosed properties. It also permitted the government to withdraw from its multidecade role as sole owner and manager of the affordable housing problem, especially in the city's low-income black neighborhoods.

The collective objective of the programs went beyond affordable housing production, as HPD made clear early in the experiment: "We're creating more than just apartments—we're re-creating neighborhoods. We're revitalizing parts of the city that over the past two decades had been decimated by disinvestment, abandonment, and arson" (City of New York 1989, 3). Given the designs of the programs, the "we" in the "we're" that HPD referred to included the city government and nongovernmental organizations. The latter included activist African American churches and their CDCs.

By 2000, all but one of the CDCs associated with activist African American churches I studied in New York City was participating in the core programs of the Ten Year Plan. According to unpublished municipal data, African American church–associated CDCs accounted for 16 percent of all neighborhood-based organizations involved in Partnership New Homes as project sponsors and 74 percent of all faith-related agencies participating in the program. In the Neighborhood Redevelopment Program, they constituted approximately 10 percent of the thirty-six neighborhood-based organizations that purchased properties from HPD. And African American church–associated CDCs accounted for 13 percent of the recipients of Special Initiatives Program properties.

Activist African American churches partnered with the city government because their pastors, as I explained in chapter 5, anticipated that partnership would permit them to accomplish a set of political, programmatic, and professional goals. In particular, they saw church-state collaboration as a means of "repositioning the body of Christ in black civil society," as well as creating a new means for community action, advancing black self-initiative, and building capacity to reform neighborhood problems. Pastors believed that partnering their church with the city government would produce positive consequences for their community, the church, and themselves—such as neighborhood revitalization, expanded church-based social services, and improved clergy reputations as omnicompetent leaders, especially vis-à-vis neighborhood politicians.[6]

Yet the contentious history between activist African American churches and the city government, especially during the Koch administration, which I covered in the previous chapter, raises a question: why did the city government permit the African American churches and their CDCs to partner with it? The location of tax-foreclosed properties, the need for effective issue governance, and the overt political calculations of mayoral administrations influenced its decision.

## The Geographic Concentrations of Tax-Foreclosed Properties

The city government intended, as the *New York Times* reported a decade after the start of the Ten Year Plan, to "transform huge swaths of New York's most blighted neighborhoods, including Harlem, the South Bronx, Crown Heights, East New York, Brownsville, and Bedford-Stuyvesant" (Finder 1995). Along with Morrisania and South Jamaica, these neighborhoods were among the poorest neighborhoods in the city, as measured by the proportion of residents receiving public assistance (Schill et al. 2002; Schill and Scafidi 1999; Schwartz and Vidal 1999).

Furthermore, they were among the neighborhoods that had experienced the highest degrees of disinvestment and abandonment by private property owners, as well as the brightest contrails of middle-class flight (Leavitt and Saegert 1990; Bach and West 1993; Oppenheim and Sierra 1994). They had the highest proportions of tax-foreclosed properties and the highest rates of housing vacancies (Van Ryzin and Genn 1999, 804). Housing quality in the neighborhoods was low, while "shelter poverty" (the proportion of residents paying more than 30 percent of income toward housing) remained high (Schill and Scafidi 1999). In the jarring words of one observer, the target neighborhoods were "the wastelands of housing devastation" (Salins 1999, 63).

Yet amid the impoverishment and blight of the Ten Year Plan's target neighborhoods were vibrant remnants of civil society, particularly activist churches and faith-related agencies. They were proximate to the poverty and in many cases had heavily invested in neighborhood property. They demonstrated concern for the prospects of neighborhood residents through their operation of social welfare ministries and faith-related agencies. Robert Carle positions these points within a larger framework of urban ministry in New York City: "Whereas government agencies and [secular] nongovernmental organizations are outsiders in neighborhoods where they seek to effect change, churches bring to the task of community development community roots, hard-earned legitimacy, a solid organizational base, and congregations of members for whom service is not only a duty of citizenship but a responsibility of faith" (1999, 263).

Presence, investment, and programs in impoverished neighborhoods gave churches and their agencies a deeper, perhaps clearer, understanding than government agencies of the solutions required to remove the obstacles to self-sufficiency the poor confronted. If so, it made sense, policymakers and administrators within HPD reasoned, for the city government to work with the churches and faith-related agencies. Perhaps partnerships with them would provide the city government with exceptional opportunities to get its affordable housing initiatives right in black neighborhoods. The inclusion of activist African American churches and their CDCs in the public-private experiment to generate decent and affordable housing seemed appropriate, even necessary. This argument coheres with how scholars understand governance, generally, in American cities.

### Street-Level Governance of Affordable Housing Production

Theoretically, the primary responsibility for the management of collective problems in New York City belonged to public actors (i.e., mayors, city managers, council members, and bureaucrats). On a practical level, however, they held and controlled few resources for achieving effective street-level governance (Bellush and Netzer 1990; Danielson and Doig 1982). To solve entrenched problems like affordable housing shortages, policy makers must use their limited resources and capacities to leverage those of private institutions and organizations (Elkin 1987; Stone 1989 and 1993; Stoker 1998).

In New York City, policy makers directed government agencies to partner with, as well as transfer some of their authority and responsibilities to, nongovernmental groups believed to possess the necessary resource to address problems. Street-level governance to produce affordable housing would occur through the city government's direct cooperation with nongovernmental institutions that possessed strategic resources, that acquired authority and other resources from government to ensure program effectiveness, and that operated across policy spheres to implement programs.

The inclusion of activist churches, especially through CDCs, in the Ten Year Plan rested on their specific capacities, with their resources often determining those capacities. These capacities were important to the city government because by itself it could not carry out the development and rehabilitation of tax-foreclosed property into affordable housing. The city would have to rely on a trilevel "governing regime" to identify, coordinate, and direct resources toward the affordable housing problem (see figure 4).[7]

As in many other cities, an informal coalition of governmental and nongovernmental elites shapes life in New York City. Relationships among its members overarch a multiplicity of informal and formal interactions among a diverse set of intermediate- and low-level public and private actors and agencies

FIGURE 4 Leveling the "governing regime": a look at New York City and affordable housing production

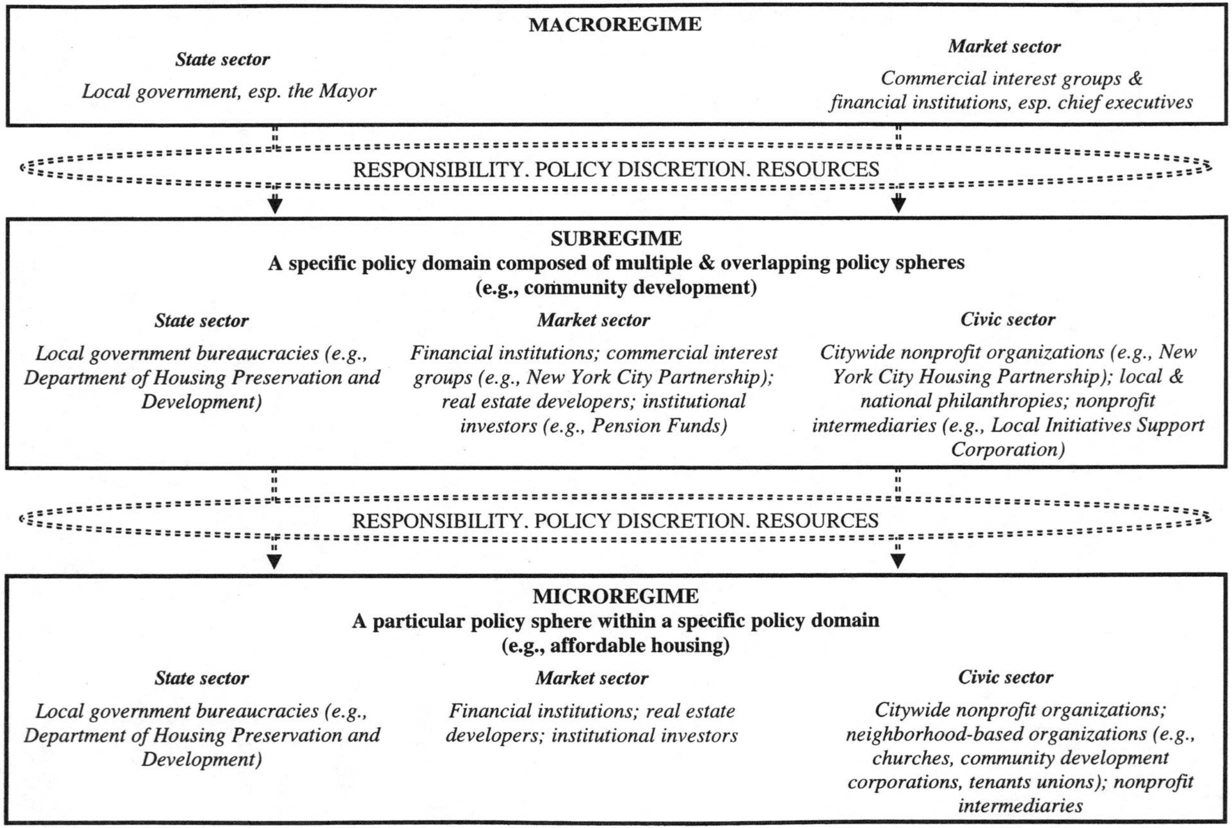

**MACROREGIME**

*State sector*
Local government, esp. the Mayor

*Market sector*
Commercial interest groups & financial institutions, esp. chief executives

RESPONSIBILITY. POLICY DISCRETION. RESOURCES

**SUBREGIME**
A specific policy domain composed of multiple & overlapping policy spheres (e.g., community development)

*State sector*
Local government bureaucracies (e.g., Department of Housing Preservation and Development)

*Market sector*
Financial institutions; commercial interest groups (e.g., New York City Partnership); real estate developers; institutional investors (e.g., Pension Funds)

*Civic sector*
Citywide nonprofit organizations (e.g., New York City Housing Partnership); local & national philanthropies; nonprofit intermediaries (e.g., Local Initiatives Support Corporation)

RESPONSIBILITY. POLICY DISCRETION. RESOURCES

**MICROREGIME**
A particular policy sphere within a specific policy domain (e.g., affordable housing)

*State sector*
Local government bureaucracies (e.g., Department of Housing Preservation and Development)

*Market sector*
Financial institutions; real estate developers; institutional investors

*Civic sector*
Citywide nonprofit organizations; neighborhood-based organizations (e.g., churches, community development corporations, tenants unions); nonprofit intermediaries

(Shefter 1987; Mollenkopf 1994; Sites 1997; Orlebeke 1997). This macrore-gime transfers responsibility, policy discretion, and resources down to lower-level coalitions of governmental and nongovernmental elites that are account-able for orchestrating the specific behaviors and effects of the relevant public, market, and civic sectors. Beneath the macroregime resides a set of "subre-gimes" that employ informal and formal alliances among public and private (for- and not-for-profit) institutions to govern particular policy domains or "games" such as economic development, educational quality, and community development (Swanstrom and Koschinsky 2000). The domains overlap, even if they seem discrete.

In the case of the community development subregime in New York City, relationships among its public and private members constitute what others observe nationally, "a local system of differentiated organizations in which the design and implementation of community development programs are inter-active across organizations" (Yin 1998, 138; see also Ferguson and Stoutland 1999). That is, community development governance in New York takes place through coordination of the resources possessed by public, for-profit and nonprofit members of the subregime. The subregime, however, is constituted by a set of microregimes that influence policy formulation and ensure policy execution in particular spheres (e.g., workforce development or affordable housing production).

Operating within each microregime are multiple, often interdependent, coalitions of public and private actors and agencies that transform the policy aspirations and objectives of higher-level regimes into actions and outcomes. Bringing together all sectors, especially neighborhood-based organizations from the civic sector, microregimes collectively focus on identifying a compre-hensive vision for change to improve the lives and communities of inner-city neighborhoods.[8] They design a machinery of formal and informal relation-ships to implement the vision; they forge a consensus to act on the vision; and they leverage the resources of a diverse set of stakeholders to realize the vi-sion.[9] In the process, microregimes build and strengthen the capacity of their stakeholders—residents, civic associations, market institutions, and public agencies—to define problems well, determine priorities and design appropri-ate responses, leverage assets and opportunities, and produce services for in-dividuals and collectives that encourage and sustain positive changes.

This was evident in the implementation of the Ten Year Plan as HPD sought out activist African American churches and their CDCs and encour-aged them to collaborate with it, along with secular CDCs, financial inter-mediaries (e.g., LISC), banks, and foundations. Together they would construct an effective affordable housing microregime that could function well in the city's low-income black neighborhoods. HPD assumed that the African American churches and church-associated CDCs possessed material and cultural resources that would prove pivotal to the execution and accomplishment of the Ten Year Plan in neighborhoods such as Harlem, Morrisania, Bedford-Stuyvesant, and South Jamaica.

In New York City, activist churches and church-associated CDCs controlled a set of resources that could support and ensure the success of the municipality's affordable housing programs. Legitimacy for social service provision in the city's low-income black neighborhoods was one such resource. They had earned it through or by association with almost a century of presence and the operation of programs oriented toward social uplift in these neighborhoods. Related to their long-standing presence and benevolence in the target neighborhoods was their indigenous knowledge of neighborhood populations, social networks, and group conflicts.

Additionally, the churches and their agencies had access to and influence over mass organizations and communication networks that could produce volunteers, mobilize expertise, raise awareness, and contribute money for supplemental initiatives. Furthermore, they commanded symbols and rhetoric suitable for positively framing the city's affordable housing-development efforts in black neighborhoods as acts of redemption, restoration, and resurrection. Recognizing this, the city government assumed that the churches and their CDCs could apply them in the execution of the Ten Year Plan, thereby transforming governmental aspirations into actions and generating intended consequences.

As the churches used their resources, in conjunction with the resources of other nongovernmental actors and groups within and beyond the low-income black neighborhoods, policy makers expected to increase the city's programmatic flexibility to produce affordable housing. They also anticipated that the city government would be able to reduce its direct service costs and overcome bureaucratic and political constraints to transforming poor black neighborhoods.

While the Koch and Giuliani administrations had political problems with activist black clergy, rooted in race-based distrust and conflict, few neighborhood-based organizations in the areas where the city government would target its resources were as entrenched, as influential, and as responsive to the Ten Year Plan as activist African American churches and their CDCs. Additionally, the mayors, including Dinkins, recognized that the inclusion of such churches and CDCs in the affordable housing microregime might yield greater political support from the residents of black neighborhoods for the city government's affordable housing policies and its broader neighborhood and economic development policies. This idea became apparent during an interview I conducted with an HPD official who served at the pleasure of Koch, Dinkins, and Giuliani:

> I don't think our programs would be as effective without them as community partners. Number one, it's good for any initiative [government] undertakes—it's a good thing to have community support. And more importantly, they build support among the residents of the area, whose support is crucial to having a successful project. HPD, as an administrative agency of the mayor, really isn't in the business of lobbying people. We try to build a consensus. But our time is better suited to doing the work of government and being bureaucrats, and to having a community resident or institution—i.e., an African American church or affiliated CDC—work on gathering support from community boards and from elected officials for the projects that are needed.[10]

The hope, the official acknowledged later on in the interview, was that activist African American churches and their associated CDCs would ensure that the majority of residents in Bedford-Stuyvesant, Harlem, South Jamaica, and Morrisania would support, rather than oppose, the city government's property-redevelopment experiment. Policy makers also believed that the inclusion of the churches and their CDCs in the experiment might permit mayors to increase their electoral chances in black neighborhoods, as well as channel some of the political energy of activist African American churches into routine processes.

### The Political Activities of African American Churches

Activist churches have strong reputations for electoral engagement (Smith and Harris 2005). Figure 5 gives some sense of how involved activist African American churches were in electoral politics in New York City at the end of the 1980s. It suggests that their electoral engagement routinely included activities to mobilize blocs of blacks to influence victories and defeats on Election Day.

An informant from one of the churches, Saint Paul Community Baptist Church in the Brooklyn neighborhood of East New York–Brownsville, which is adjacent to Bedford-Stuyvesant, made the following observation to me:

FIGURE 5   Electoral action: the behavior of activist African American churches in New York
City during the 1980s

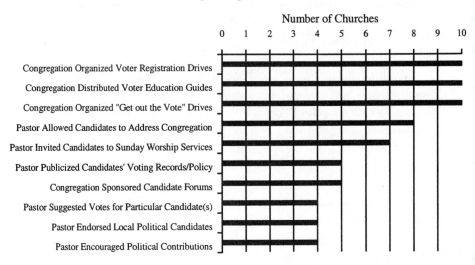

Note: The churches in the sample include Abyssinian Baptist Church, Allen AME Church, Bethany Baptist
Church, Bethesda Missionary Baptist Church, Bridge Street AWME Church, Canaan Baptist Church of
Christ, Concord Baptist Church of Christ, Ebenezer Missionary Baptist Church, Memorial Baptist Church,
and St. Paul Community Baptist Church.

"They knew to watch out for us. We were very involved with voter mobilization. By that I mean not only registration but getting people out to vote. . . .
We knocked on eight thousand doors during election years, and the voter
turnout, if I remember correctly a [statistic] I saw, increased 37 percent."[11]

Aside from their traditional acts of electioneering, a few activist African
American churches recruited and ran their own candidates for elected office.
The Southeast Queens Clergy for Community Empowerment provided the
structure and resources necessary for the pastor of Allen AME Church, Reverend Floyd H. Flake, to win election in 1984 to the U.S. House of Representatives over the wishes of the Queens Democratic Party (Owens 1997a). In
running Flake as a challenger and beating the party, the clergy alliance established a name for itself in neighborhood and city politics: it could create winning coalitions and mobilize resources to defeat incumbents.

Recognizing and fostering their reputations as institutions of electoral
mobilization, activist African American churches like Saint Paul Community Baptist Church and those involved in ministerial alliances like Southeast Queens Clergy for Community Empowerment reminded politicians and

FIGURE 6  Saint Paul's wall: sending a message to politicians and residents. East
New York, Brooklyn, 1999. Photograph by Michael Leo Owens

neighborhood residents that churches could and would use their material and
cultural resources to affect the outcomes of electoral contests (see figure 6).
Because of the churches' potential and actual influence within elections, politicians and policymakers acknowledged that the Ten Year Plan could not ignore them. They did not focus all of their attention on the churches, however.
They attended to their church-associated CDCs, too.

Politicians posited that the CDCs of activist churches were potentially
capacious as electoral actors.[12] They believed that church-associated CDCs
drew strength from their relationships with activist churches, particularly
those that routinely engaged in local electoral politics. Politicians also observed that these CDCs extended the political reach and legitimacy of their
sponsor churches, especially by involving a broad array of community stakeholders in their activities (e.g., on their board of directors) and effectively
representing their target communities to external institutions of power and
authority. They even believed that the CDCs were a means for the churches
to create their own patron-client relationships with neighborhood residents
by exchanging services for votes for favored candidates or a strong showing
at CDC-sponsored events.[13] That is, they saw the CDCs as quasi-political
machines.

Seeing activist churches electioneer, and believing that the potential for electoral engagement by church-associated CDCs was high, politicians and policy makers assumed that inclusion of activist churches in the execution of the Ten Year Plan would improve the electoral margin of mayors up for reelection. This was obvious to Paul Crotty, HPD commissioner in the final years of the Koch administration. He observed that the decade-long affordable housing experiment "started because of the mayoral campaign in [1985] and accomplishments were going to be judged by no later than [1989]" (quoted in von Hoffman 2003, 50). Dinkins, too, recognized the electoral value of partnering with activist churches, especially via their CDCs. Phil Thompson, who served as a housing official in the Dinkins administration, recalls: "Housing development was a real opportunity to marry community development and voting increases in poor communities by directing housing development funds away from [the] city's Department of Housing and Community Preservation's coterie of nonprofit technicians and toward community organizations committed to citizen participation and voter mobilization" (2006, 212). Even Giuliani, according to HPD officials who spoke to me, realized that he could cut some funding for the projects of the churches but he could not cut the churches entirely out of the process. To do otherwise would have unnecessarily increased activist black pastors' antagonism toward the mayor and potentially provided them with a cause for intensifying mobilization against him at the height of his reelection campaign.

Furthermore, politicians and policymakers, especially in the Koch and Giuliani administrations, hoped that allowing activist churches and related CDCs to participate in the execution of the Ten Year Plan might quell their direct challenges to the status quo in public policy and municipal practice. In other words, there was indeed cause for black preachers to fear that collaboration would yield co-optation. By incorporating activists into the routine of pluralist politics and processes, the city government expected to affect their political behavior. As activist churches worked with government to address their concerns through institutional processes and incremental policy change rather than employing contention, confrontation, and electioneering, politicians could better predict electoral outcomes citywide and within districts.

The politicians' expectation was that as the churches obtained access to city government, like interest groups in other cities they would limit their political engagement, abandoning more contentious forms. As they became brokers for their neighborhoods "in bureaucracies and administrative procedures, they were, in turn expected by local officials to use those avenues and not others"; this is a common expectation among urban politicians (Howard,

Lipsky, and Marshall 1994, 154). This is because brokerage via collaboration with government, as I will explain later in this chapter, provided the churches and their CDCs with access to bureaucratic and administrative venues that transferred substantive resources to them.

Politicians believed that the continued exchange of resources would permit them to constrain the political engagement of activist churches and their CDCs on behalf of their constituents. After all, the transfer of public resources through collaboration would continue only if recipients avoided political action against the city governments. Therefore, including activist churches in the Ten Year Plan was, in part, an effort by politicians to co-opt them and their CDCs.

In the end, the inclusion of the churches and the church-associated CDCs was not an apolitical act. It was a conscious decision by mayoral administrations in anticipation of the electoral activity of African American churches and their CDCs. Koch, Dinkins, and Giuliani naturally wanted to retain or gain the electoral support of the residents of black neighborhoods. Also, the mayors were seeking to channel the political energy of activist African American churches in ways that would not complicate the political goals of city hall.

Church-state collaboration, therefore, was one byproduct of activist African American churches' traditional forms of political engagement in New York City.

SUBSTANTIVE RESOURCES OF PARTICIPATION

Regardless of the city government's motivations in permitting African American churches to partner with it, the participation of church-associated CDCs in the Ten Year Plan made them conduits of "substantive" resources from the larger external community to the smaller internal communities of low-income black neighborhoods (Hunter and Staggenborg 1988, 257). These public resources included properties, money, and powers.

*Public Properties*

The substantive resources that church-associated CDCs obtained on behalf of activist African American churches and their neighborhoods included public property. Participation in the execution of the Ten Year Plan allowed these CDCs to acquire ownership of public-owned land and clusters of buildings, often for no more than $500 and sometimes for as little as one dollar. My surveys of CDCs and interviews with HPD officials, along with access to unpublished HPD data, revealed that by 2000 African American church–associated CDCs had taken title to a minimum of 600 housing units. This is a conservative figure. It includes only those units received between 1994 and 2000 through the Neighborhood Redevelopment Program, Neighborhood Homes, and Special Initiatives Program.[14]

Like other neighborhood-based organizations that participated in the programs of the Ten Year Plan, African American church–associated CDCs did not acquire the city government's most select properties for redevelopment. This was because HPD, in the words of one group of scholars who studied its divestment programs, was "interested in realizing a high return from its land holdings and in minimizing the total subsidy required for redevelopment" (Ellen et al. 2001, 189–90). HPD reserved the best sites for commercial developers. Still, the church-associated CDCs used the second-best and even third-best properties to develop rental housing, which they would own and manage on behalf of their churches and target neighborhoods, and owner-occupied housing. As of 2000, in fact, the participation of the African American church–associated CDCs in the four core programs of the Ten Year Plan had yielded at least 2,092 new units of affordable housing in South Jamaica, Bedford-Stuyvesant, Morrisania, and Harlem. The number accounted for 47 percent of all housing units these CDCs had developed, sponsored, or acquired title to before 2000.

*Public Money*

Besides acquiring property, the African American church–associated CDCs that participated in the Ten Year Plan received public funding. Collectively, according to unpublished HPD data, these African American church-associated CDCs that collaborated with the city government to implement the four core programs received approximately $15 million in public subsidies over six years.[15] Bridge Street (AWME) Development Corporation's participation in Neighborhood Homes, for example, brought approximately $3.6 million from the city to subsidize the rehabilitation of conveyed municipal properties for eventual sale as mixed, owner-occupied housing in Bedford-Stuyvesant. Other African American church–associated CDCs received comparable sums for their participation in other programs. Under the Neighborhood Redevelopment Program, for instance, three of these CDCs received approximately $8.6 million in public subsidies to cover the redevelopment costs of the properties.

## Public Powers

Along with money and property, participants in the Ten Year Plan programs received or earned public powers, especially the ability to select redevelopment sites, to name and employ contractors, and to choose apartment tenants and home buyers. The acquisition of such powers by agents of government is a routine consequence of privatization and public-private partnership, as Donald Kettl reminds us: "The sharing of administrative responsibility necessarily means the government shares its power and authority in society with those upon which it relies" (1993, 38). In performing their jobs on behalf of their principals, frontline agents (i.e., those responsible for delivering goods and services to constituents) have significant discretion. They implement government decisions but also make many decisions of their own. As Michael Lipsky comments, "Where well-established bureaucratic rules are developed and in operation, there is often much leeway in the application of rules" (1980, 122).[16]

Once HPD included the church-associated CDCs in the Ten Year Plan programs as agents of the city government, the department expected them to follow its dictates. The CDCs (and their churches) were to observe HPD's mandates with as little deviation as possible from the wishes of policymakers and administrators and the regulations and rules of bureaucrats. Organizations participating in the Neighborhood Redevelopment Program, for example, purchased city-owned properties, but their authority over them as private property was bounded. "There are legal mechanisms in place that regulate[d] their behavior as property owners," an HPD official clarified for me. "Our closing documents are an inch thick about what they can and cannot do with a property, about income levels, rent levels, what they can and cannot do as an owner." This was to ensure, according to the official, that neighborhood-based organizations participating in the program administered properties in ways that preserved access to affordable housing. Nevertheless, HPD's principal-agent relationship with the church-associated CDCs transferred responsibility and opportunities for policy making to the neighborhood groups.

HPD required the church-associated CDCs, along with all other nongovernmental organizations that partnered with it, to assume a set of tasks and obligations (e.g., property management, tenant relocation, and contractor selection) that created spaces for them to influence the affordable housing production programs. As agents of the city government, they could simultaneously implement both HPD's policies and programs and the pastor-guided or community-driven agenda of the churches in the black neighborhoods. The church-associated CDCs could exercise authority over implementation of public policies without always seeking the direct permission of HPD.

The church-associated CDCs that collaborated with HPD did not influence implementation initially. At first, they merely followed the dictates of HPD. Over time, however, as they deepened their relationships with HPD, earned its trust, and gained redevelopment experience, the CDCs acquired and exerted influence in key areas of the development process. Collaboration with government enabled the churches through their CDCs to exploit the Ten Year Plan programs to the benefit of their neighborhoods. Their participation in the Ten Year Plan thus engaged them in more than a simple partnership for producing affordable housing; they were involved in a political process that enabled them to affect the operation of public programs and the allocation of public benefits in black neighborhoods. Picking the locations for affordable housing production, choosing development teams (architects, engineers, and contractors) to build it, and selecting individuals to move into it are examples of ways that churches and CDCs sought and wielded authority as street-level agents of the city government.

*Selecting Sites.* African American church–associated CDCs that participated in the Ten Year Plan influenced the selection of redevelopment sites in their neighborhoods. They affected to some degree where the city decided to invest millions of public dollars, and these decisions encouraged and influenced private investment as well. Their influence, however, varied by HPD program. Usually the influence of African American church–associated CDCs was lowest in those programs where neighborhood-based organizations mainly sponsored and marketed projects for developers (e.g., Partnership New Homes). HPD maintained discretion to grant more or less influence to neighborhood-based organizations for site selection. Generally, neighborhood-based organizations with high institutional capacity that participated in low-influence programs approached HPD to develop a project on land or in a building the city owned. When it was feasible and rational, according to HPD officials, the department gave the groups greater responsibility for selecting redevelopment locations than the program normally allowed.

The CDCs of the activist African American churches sought opportunities to increase their influence over the investment of public resources in black neighborhoods. The best examples of this come from the involvement of Allen NPDC and SQCCE in Partnership New Homes. In their initial dealings with Allen NPDC and SQCCE during the 1980s, the city government and the Housing Partnership either shared or assumed complete responsibility for site selection of the first Partnership New Homes projects in South Jamaica. In subsequent projects associated with the program, however, HPD and the Housing Partnership granted their community partners the responsibility to select the parcels of tax-foreclosed public land in the neighborhoods where housing would be constructed and sold. An Allen NPDC informant recounted the accommodation process for me:

> During the first round [of Guy Brewer Homes], they designated the sites. With this most recent project, Allen Hall Estates, [we] selected the site. It was the one chosen for initial redevelopment by Allen [AM.E Church] twenty years ago, when development of the [Allen AME] Senior Citizens' Center began. Allen NPDC selected the site [which served for years as a used tire and hubcap bazaar], and it was so defiled that two corpses were unearthed as the lot was cleared for development. Our ability to do this stemmed from the good job we did marketing the first project, along with our initiation of independent [commercial and residential] development projects that were extremely successful.

The responsibility for site selection that Allen NPDC assumed from the city government was not the equivalent of eminent domain. Allen NPDC and other church-associated CDCs could not take private property for public purposes or neighborhood benefit.[17] But they could and did identify to HPD dilapidated and abandoned properties that they believed warranted tax-foreclosure proceedings by the city government and transfers to third parties, preferably themselves, for redevelopment as affordable houses and apartments. In acquiring authority over site selection for their development projects, the African American church–associated CDCs achieved what many black organizations had sought during the War on Poverty and its period of community control: they determined, albeit with the consent of city government, the locations of redevelopment in black neighborhoods.

*Selecting Contractors.* Beyond influencing the location of redevelopment, African American church–associated CDCs expanded their influence to determine the complexion, literally, of those who would build affordable housing in black neighborhoods targeted by the Ten Year Plan. When the Bronx Shepherds Restoration Corporation, for instance, closed on the sale of three Neighborhood Redevelopment Program properties for conversion to rental housing that it would manage, the faith-related agency gained responsibility for the overall redevelopment of the public properties, along with $1.4 million from the city's capital budget. Subsequently, the Bronx Shepherds assumed authority for identifying and selecting its architects and other professionals to redesign the municipal properties. There was a time, however, when HPD would have kept the Bronx Shepherds and other African American church-associated CDCs out of the hiring process.

In the beginning of the Ten Year Plan programs, HPD selected the contractors and other redevelopment professionals for projects. A former officer of Harlem Congregations for Community Improvement (HCCI) told me about the results:

> Here in New York, under Koch, the contractors in our community were left out of the loop. The black architects were starving for jobs. There were no opportunities for them because of the limited number of housing development projects that was going their way. It was a damn disgrace to see people redoing our streets and our kids and our grown men standing there looking at some white folks from Bensonhurst [Brooklyn] coming into Harlem, and nobody stops them. Nobody says anything. Meanwhile, our [black] architects, contractors, and construction workers were unemployed, treated like garbage in this city under Koch's leadership.

This state of affairs was problematic for the CDCs and the activist churches that chartered them.

The churches and their CDCs wanted to hire qualified black professionals, contractors, and laborers from the target neighborhoods. From their perspective, according to Rev. Washington of HCCI, the church-associated CDCs were supposed to "employ our people, hire minority contractors, and provide housing for our people" (quoted in Stafford 1997, 42). They also sought to end the catch-22 of trained but green minority professionals, contractors, and laborers' being excluded from employment for their lack of experience. Further, they wanted to create apprenticeships for unskilled laborers. This was perhaps most important. Karen Philips, former executive director of the Abyssinian Development Corporation, expressed this need during a public hearing: "We always insist that the contractor hire from the community. But having people with the skills to actually participate is another issue" (quoted in Stafford 1997, 79).

Like their influence over site selections, hiring discretion by the African

American church-associated CDCs, which would permit them to increase employment opportunities for neighborhood residents, or at least black and Latino entrepreneurs from other parts of the city, grew slowly during the Koch administration. The Dinkins administration, however, was immediately receptive to the CDCs' position, which they broadcast more openly during Dinkins's tenure. The director of a church-associated CDC in Harlem told me, "We said to Dinkins—which we could because he was on our side and we helped him get elected—'We need to be able to hire our own.' It's one of the spoils we as black people had coming to us for wining the mayor's race." They tried to use the "spoils" well.

In due course, the implementation of the Neighborhood Redevelopment Program, designed by the Dinkins administration but administered under Giuliani, transferred much of the responsibility for hiring architects and selecting contractors from the city government to a variety of neighborhood-based organizations. A veteran HPD administrator addressed the issue in an interview, acknowledging the limited influence groups had had in the past over who would build their projects: "We just let the not-for-profits have the opportunity to select that architect as opposed to a number of programs that the city used to have where they didn't have the opportunity to select their architects. It was dictated to them. We may have been serving as the architect for some of the programs. We had people complain, 'You design poorly.' Well, [HPD] says, 'Here is your opportunity to select an architect and design what you need.' We say to them, 'This is your opportunity to take the lead on all of these items.'"

A strong basis for the change, beyond the appeals of the church-associated CDCs and other neighborhood-based organizations for greater hiring autonomy, according to the accounts of other HPD informants, was that the city government was inefficient at selecting and overseeing contractors and other professionals. Inefficiency led to delays and kept buildings decrepit or abandoned, which led to new fights with neighborhood-based organizations over municipal responsiveness. Mayoral administrations could shift the focus of attention by displacing hiring responsibilities to the neighborhood-based organizations. Doing so also satisfied the call of community groups for affirmative action and racial parity in public contracting.

In interviews with me, principals of the African American church-associated CDCs highlighted the change in authority over hiring. The comments of an HCCI informant echoed the general claim that the change made a dramatic difference:

Since [the Koch administration], we've added Latinos in there. All told, eighteen African-American and Latino women architects have worked on our projects. We're the first [African American church–associated CDC] to actually hire African American contractors and take the risks—not Calvin Butts [Abyssinian Development Corporation], not Wyatt T. Walker [Canaan Housing Development Corporation]. We have three black architects—I mean, we have used three black engineers, eighteen black architects, and women and Latinos, and brought thirty-five minority contracting companies into the redevelopment process in our neighborhood.

The implementation of the first phase of the Bradhurst Plan by HCCI cost approximately $25 million, of which nearly 90 percent was distributed to black and Latino contractors and architects (Bernstein 1993). And HCCI may have represented the first African American churches in New York City to hire minority development professionals for government-subsidized redevelopment projects in black neighborhoods, but it was not the last.

The Neighborhood Redevelopment Program was not the only program that enabled activist African American churches and their CDCs to alter the selection of development professionals. Partnership New Homes, too, granted hiring discretion to them. During Allen NPDC's first project in South Jamaica, the 122-unit Guy Brewer Estates, the church and its CDCs were passive concerning the employment of blacks. "Being new to the program," an informant from the CDC remarked, "it chose to study the process rather than try to direct it." In the initial planning phase for its second project, however, Allen NPDC lobbied HPD and the Housing Partnership. It sought the responsibility to identify potential contractors to develop the 100-unit, $10.9 million Allen AME / Hall Estates, which would be located next to the 300-unit Allen AME Senior Citizens Complex, built by the church with federal Section 202 funds in the late 1970s. An officer of Allen AME Church recalled how its CDC, relying on the advocacy of Reverend Flake, pushed HPD and the Housing Partnership to hire a black contractor for the project:

In the initial Guy Brewer Homes, the developer was selected or recommended [by the Housing Partnership]. The developer was Bluestone [a white-owned developer]. But with Allen AME / Hall Estates, we asked the reverend [former U.S. congressman Floyd Flake] to personally recommend [Raleigh W.] Hall to the Housing Partnership, and that's how we got him involved. We wanted a minority developer involved in the redevelopment of the neighborhood, and Hall is not just a minority; he grew up right there near Jamaica Houses [a public housing community in South Jamaica]. He still lives in southeast Queens.

The Housing Partnership acceded to the request, hiring R. W. Hall General Contractors, a minority-operated enterprise based in South Jamaica since 1965. At the time, Allen AME / Hall Estates was the largest project—in size and spending—constructed by a minority contractor under Partnership New Homes. Along with the Hall hire, Allen NPDC influenced the employment opportunities for black craftsmen and laborers: 95 percent of the crew that built Allen AME / Hall Estates were black, and approximately two-thirds of them resided in South Jamaica or another of the majority-back neighborhoods of southeast Queens.

In sum, churches and church-associated CDCs that participated in the Ten Year Plan's implementation transitioned from housing sponsors to housing developers. They went from marketing the projects of others to developing their own projects. The change assured the churches and their CDCs that they would select, with the advice and consent of HPD, the members of their development teams. Hiring blacks and Latinos for their projects, they believed, was vital to their neighborhoods and fair to the process.

*Selecting Tenants and Homebuyers.* The redevelopment of public properties as private properties benefited low- and moderate-income households in South Jamaica, Morrisania, Harlem, and Bedford-Stuyvesant. Until the return of these properties to the private market, affordable homeownership had been but a dream of many working-class families that sought to remain in or return to their neighborhood. As for rental housing, the new properties provided, mainly to single-parent households and families on public assistance, access to decent and safe apartments (Van Ryzin and Genn 1999, 825). HPD preferred that the rental or sale of 50 percent of all units its programs created or rehabilitated go to incumbent residents of the neighborhoods where the units were located. This community preference was intended to increase housing opportunities for residents of the target neighborhoods; it was assumed that this would keep a cap on gentrification pressures related to redevelopment. It might also yield a grateful bloc (or retain the size of the old bloc) of voters for the occupant of Gracie Mansion, the public home of the mayor of New York City.

Information about apartments and houses under development or rehabilitation by the church-associated CDCs, as well as those open for immediate vacancies and purchase, was publicly available. Advertisements were placed in neighborhood and citywide newspapers, and HPD's Affordable Housing Hotline and its website had full listings. Applications were available from the organizations responsible for the redevelopment of the properties. All applicants for apartments and houses produced by the Ten Year Plan had to meet eligibility requirements. Prospective renters of affordable apartments and buyers of houses subsidized by government resources to maintain their affordability were chosen by lotteries. The lotteries were intended to produce a fair distribution of scarce resources. After the lottery drawings, prospective renters and homebuyers were interviewed by the nongovernmental organizations overseeing the projects.

The lottery-based process of awarding affordable housing prevented some "cherry picking" of applicants by the agents of HPD's affordable housing production programs. However, the lottery system generally did not keep agents from affecting the application and receipt of affordable housing. Staff of the CDCs and the churches that chartered them influenced decisions regarding who would and who would not occupy affordable housing, especially rental housing, produced through HPD's programs. Four realities of affordable housing in New York City gave them the ability to do it.

First, the environment of seeking affordable housing affected the search for it.[18] Word of mouth was one of the most important sources of information regarding affordable housing opportunities (New York City Rent Guidelines Board 1998; Marwell 2004). Social networks definitely helped seekers obtain affordable housing information. Generally, community groups were a source of such information, perhaps protecting it as a scarce resource for neighborhood residents. As most of my informants acknowledged after much probing, individuals with ties to the African American church–associated CDCs stood a better chance than those without them to be the first to obtain information about where and when affordable housing would open and what the anticipated rent or price would be.

Although HPD posted housing opportunities in the classified ads of local newspapers, information about upcoming openings in apartments and sales of houses was generally available within the congregations affiliated with the CDCs before it became public knowledge within the larger community. Many of the employees of the church-associated CDCs were congregants of the CDCs' sponsor churches. Their communication with other members quickly spread information about housing opportunities. "You know how gossip spreads through a congregation," noted a CDC director, "and it's not fair, of course, but people talk." Additionally, since the majority of the staff of the church-associated CDCs lived in the target neighborhoods, their social networks with fellow residents transmitted information about upcoming housing availability to housing hunters in the neighborhood before it was broadcast to seekers outside the neighborhood.

The second reality of affordable housing is that only the valid applications are considered during the distribution process (Marwell 2004). One way of improving the chances that winning applicants would be individuals affiliated with the church-associated CDCs or their churches was to increase the number of legitimate applications submitted. According to most CDC informants and pastors, this was achieved through the targeting of members of sponsor congregations or participants in the programs of the CDCs and the churches (e.g., parents of children attending a charter school affiliated with the CDC or the church's religious academy, clients of the church's food pantry, or adult students in the CDC's workforce development training) for application assistance.

A third reality is that only applicants who can afford "affordable" housing can live in it. African American church–associated CDCs made it easier for selected applicants, especially from the working class, to actually purchase a house. In marketing Allen AME / Hall Estates, for example, the Allen NPDC advertised the homes, held information meetings, and screened prospective buyers. The screenings included checking credit histories, verifying employment and earnings, contacting references, and visiting the residences of prospective buyers. Following the screenings, Allen NPDC counseled prospective homebuyers on finances. At the same time, it served as an intermediary between the eventual buyers and mortgage lenders, ensuring that the buyers were well served.

An informant from the church who was instrumental in the development project gave an account, confirmed by mortgage lenders, of how Allen NPDC used its legitimacy as a trusted neighborhood institution and its position as a Partnership New Homes community sponsor to influence how lenders treated and evaluated working-class blacks looking to purchase houses in the new development:

We worked to change the banks' ways of looking at minorities and their qualifications for mortgages. So as opposed to looking at their credit card [history], because you know not many of us [blacks] have credit cards or checking accounts, we convinced them to start looking into less traditional ways of qualifying [prospective homebuyers]. We arranged it so that they could bring a year's worth of phone bills and rent receipts, and that's what they [the banks] judged them on—their ability and frequency to pay. Another good thing was that we invited the banks to come into [Allen NPDC's] office. We set them up in an office over there across the hall. So when homebuyers would come to apply, we would guide them here through the process of getting a mortgage, and that really was helpful.

Moreover, the church-associated CDC calculated, based on household finances and credit, the level of public subsidy that a homebuyer would receive for the property. The level of subsidy would affect the mortgage amount and monthly payments of purchasers: the higher the subsidy, the lower the loan amount and mortgage payment. Those who could receive a higher subsidy were more likely to manage their debt and avoid foreclosure than those who qualified for only a minimal subsidy. In these ways the church-associated CDCs exercised their discretion to allocate benefits from "public" redevelopment in low-income black neighborhoods. They applied their influence to determine who would live in their neighborhoods' new owner-occupied housing.

The final reality of affordable housing in New York City is that rental housing is a privilege; it is not a right. Thousands of families enter the lotteries and sit on waiting lists of HPD and the New York City Housing Authority to receive an opportunity to apply for and possibly win one of the scarce housing units. Ultimately, what determines occupancy?

Income is always a criterion for the award of public-subsidized affordable housing. The apartments owned and managed by the CDCs are located in properties that received public subsidies and tax credit equity. The subsidies and equity terms require that CDCs lease a portion of their apartments to individuals and families who meet income restrictions determined by family size and area median income rates. The CDCs also must maintain rents that are affordable to low-income people. But the decision by the CDCs to rent to prospective tenants can be affected by other factors, too, and the CDCs have discretion in awarding apartments. Although the CDCs must keep the buildings occupied, they do not rent to every applicant whose name is drawn at random or who shows adequate funding.

Assume that there are two prospective tenants for an affordable studio apartment a CDC owns or manages. Both were chosen randomly to apply for housing, and their incomes are equal. However, there is only the single studio for rent. Which applicant will occupy the apartment? In this instance the income limits cannot guide the CDC's decision. It must employ other measures of worthiness to select the winner.

HPD and the CDCs viewed upkeep, safety, and decent behavior as integral to the preservation of affordable housing. Consequently, HPD gave its agents the power to determine which applicants would best contribute to this goal. Who receives an apartment and who does not, as well as who retains an apartment and who vacates the premises, are decisions of the neighborhood-based organizations serving as landlords, not HPD. Principal criteria the church-associated CDCs use to allocate apartments include the employment histories and criminal backgrounds of applicants, as well as the location of their current residence to accommodate the community preference proviso required by the city government. When deciding whether to retain tenants, the CDCs consider tardy rental payments, building infractions such as the doubling up of families in a single unit, and arrests of family members as criteria for evictions. Thus, determining occupancy is perhaps the most significant influence the African American church–associated CDCs acquired over the distribution of affordable housing in their neighborhoods.

### SUBSTANTIVE OUTCOMES: POSITIVE PHYSICAL BUT MARGINAL SOCIAL IMPROVEMENTS

It is evident that collaboration with government provided the church-associated CDCs with public resources, properties, and powers related specifically to the production, placement, and operation of affordable housing in the four black neighborhoods. The substantive resources they acquired gave them, along with their sponsoring churches, opportunities to affect how the municipal affordable housing experiment would unfold. A further important question, however, is whether the substantive resources yielded substantive outcomes, especially real improvements in the targeted neighborhoods.

Evidence from other studies of the execution of the Ten Year Plan in the city's poorest neighborhoods suggests that the experiment has yielded positive physical results. Overall, transformations of public properties into private or community-owned housing through HPD's programs reduced the number of boarded-up buildings and vacant properties in Harlem, Morrisania, South Jamaica, and Bedford-Stuyvesant, as well as other poor neighborhoods in the city (Van Ryzin and Genn 1999). The removal of blight encouraged private investment by for-profit housing and commercial developers and incumbent upgraders near the sites (Schill et al. 2002; Van Ryzin and Genn 1999; Owens 1997b). As private investment increased, blight declined, and household incomes rose in the target neighborhoods, property values began to rise in and around the neighborhoods (Ellen et al. 2001). There is convincing evidence that the public and private investments facilitated increased property values and prices proximate to the sites of the new housing (Schill et al. 2002, 561).

We do not know to what degree the work of activist African American churches and their CDCs accounted for these changes. It is difficult to disaggregate the determinants of revitalization. Yet it is reasonable to conclude that the presence and activities of the churches and CDCs as collaborators with the city government were among the catalysts for the positive physical improvements in the black neighborhoods, as well as for subsequent work by other neighborhood-based organizations and commercial developers to invest in and rebuild the physical environment of the neighborhoods.

The resources and opportunities that the CDCs obtained for their sponsor churches from the Ten Year Plan helped to bring about the positive improvements that have been observed in Harlem, Bedford-Stuyvesant, Morrisania, South Jamaica, and elsewhere throughout the city. Clearly the activities of the church-associated CDCs benefited the residents of the four black neighborhoods, as well as the churches and middle-class congregants who owned property in these neighborhoods. By replacing vacant properties with new owner-occupied housing via the city's programs, the churches altered the administration of public land to the advantage of black middle-class homeowners in their neighborhoods. Neighborhood housing conditions were improved through the removal or reuse of vacant and boarded-up buildings, and this in turn increased property values more generally. Low-income households in the neighborhoods benefited by access to adequate houses and apartments.

Additionally, the sponsorship of low-density, two-family housing or moderate-density rental housing by church-associated CDCs and their affiliated churches on chosen sites spurred private investment near the sites by both incumbent upgraders and for-profit housing developers. Neighborhood residents favored such housing over plans for high-density multifamily buildings. Also by exerting influence over site selection through their CDCs, activist African American churches laid a foundation for implementing a three-part strategy of moderate-income homeownership, incumbent upgrading, and middle-class resettlement that has been instrumental in halting much of the physical decline in their neighborhoods (Owens 1997b).

The products of the churches' involvement in the Ten Year Plan also invited the in-migration of new residents to the target neighborhoods. Evidence from across the city shows that the production of new houses for sale in the target neighborhoods attracted working-class and lower-middle-class households with incomes slightly higher than the neighborhood medians (Ellen et al. 2001). Middle-class residents of black neighborhoods had hoped for such an outcome (Owens 1997b).

We must acknowledge, nevertheless, a limitation of the Ten Year Plan generally and of church-state collaboration specifically. Today the neighborhoods still mirror more of their negative past than had been expected. Walking the streets of the neighborhoods, especially Harlem, one can observe many blocks hosting only facades of residence; buildings on either side of the streets lack tenants, let alone doors, windows, and even roofs. Karen Philips, who once led Abyssinian Development Corporation, testified before a 2001 congressional hearing in Harlem that "nearly two thousand properties scattered around the community are boarded up or in deteriorated conditions with poor tenants that have no services. . . . Many are located on blocks where ADC has properties."

Two years before the testimony, I observed that across the street from the edifice of Abyssinian Baptist Church sat a vacant five-story residential building that the City of New York owned. At the western end of its block, where ADC owns rehabilitated apartments, I saw five to six torched and boarded-up commercial buildings that included approximately fifty walk-up apartments. At the eastern end of the block was a rundown, five-storied mixed-use building. John's Recovery Room, an active bar, occupied the first floor of the building (figure 7). The floors above it had residential units, but they were vacant. A sign on the building bore a message all too familiar for the neighborhood, in capital letters:

THIS IS A PRIVATE PROPERTY OWNED BY 535 LENOX
REALTY CORP.
WHICH PAYS TAXES TO THE CITY OF NEW YORK.
IT IS NOT FOR SALE OR RENT.[19]

Furthermore, two decades after the start of the Ten Year Plan, the demographics of Harlem, Morrisania, South Jamaica, and Bedford-Stuyvesant have not substantially changed. This is true despite signals of commercial revitalization (e.g., openings of Starbucks and The Gap) and claims of widespread gentrification in the neighborhoods (Jackson 2003; M. Taylor 2002; Chinyelu 1999). As of 2000 the proportion of female-headed households with children in the four black neighborhoods was rising, not declining. The mean poverty rate across the neighborhoods was almost 40 percent. Median household income among the neighborhoods' residents was approximately $13,000 less than the median for the city.

FIGURE 7 John's Recovery Room: a sign of selective abandonment and speculation. Central Harlem, Manhattan, 1999. Photograph by Michael Leo Owens

Harlem, Morrisania, South Jamaica, and Bedford-Stuyvesant have yet to become places of social opportunity and economic advancement for the majority of their residents, particularly their poorest residents. None of this is to discount the substantive powers that the CDCs of activist churches, as well as other neighborhood-based collaborators with government, received from their participation in the Ten Year Plan. But we do well to remember that those powers are limited when employed within a larger context of social and economic inequalities and that collaboration with government alone is inadequate to fully resurrect impoverished black neighborhoods in New York City.

### SUMMARY

Executing the Ten Year Plan required the city to design a set of affordable housing-production programs. African American churches and their CDCs participated in them as agents of the local government. In the process, they assisted the city in implementing public policies and programs. That activist churches and their CDCs were located in the impoverished black neighborhoods that contained the bulk of the city-owned properties suitable for redevelopment as affordable housing is part of the reason that the city government permitted them to work with it. Another part of the story is that the city needed, or so it believed, the resources of activist African American churches and their CDCs to govern the affordable housing problem in the target neighborhoods. Beyond the combination of neighborhood contexts and street-level governance of community development, the city government considered the latent and actual political behavior of activist African American churches, especially their engagement in electoral action.

Together, the political reputations of churches, the city's need for effective issue governance, and the location of target properties explain why the city government included activist churches and their faith-related agencies in the Ten Year Plan. In assisting in the implementation of the Ten Year Plan, the church-associated CDCs served as both delegates and trustees of public resources and authority. They executed both the choices of the city governments and their churches' choices concerning the administration of the programs and the allocation of their benefits.

The design of HPD's programs constrained the actions of the CDCs. When it entered contractual agreements with an African American church-associated CDC, the city expected that they would act in a manner that yielded effective collective problem management. At the same time, the design of HPD's programs allowed the church-associated CDCs to influence or make policy on their own. In assisting the municipal government to manage its problems, the CDCs received discretion, which permitted them to influence public policy, especially at the stage of program implementation, on behalf of their churches and neighborhoods.

The particles of power the African American church–associated CDCs derived from participating in the Ten Year Plan's core programs granted them less than absolute authority over community development agendas of the city government. Still, they created opportunities for the CDCs, and their sponsoring churches, to be influential in their neighborhoods. In fact, as street-level agents of the city government, the churches and their CDCs gained bureaucratic enfranchisement. Their roles as developers, managers, and sponsors of affordable housing projects permitted them to exert some influence over and acquire public resources for redevelopment in their neighborhoods. Even if the neighborhood effects thus far are limited to physical improvements, the CDCs of activist African American churches, and the churches' pastors, influenced the selection of sites for public investment in black neighborhoods; they helped increase the hiring of minorities to work on these neighborhood-based projects; and they decided and continue to decide who gets and who does not get to live in public-subsidized affordable apartments and houses.

In the end, the African American church–associated CDCs functioned more independently than administrative automatons following the instructions of public officials. But how autonomous, especially in terms of political engagement, were the CDCs of activist African American churches after they acquired discretion and resources from the city government? It is possible that collaboration empowered the churches and their CDCs to engage in a broader set of political activities to sustain and supplement the resources they acquired through collaboration. Still, why is it that collaboration with government produced more limited substantive effects on the neighborhoods than the churches and CDCs expected? Perhaps it is because collaboration, even if it results in some degrees of empowered cooperation, requires that collaborators reduce their political engagement.

# CHAPTER SEVEN

# Complementing Collaboration

Concord Baptist Church of Christ was abuzz with anticipation the afternoon of April 29, 1999. Those in attendance had not come to hear the Reverend Gary Simpson preach. They were not there to hear the choir sing. Rather, people had come to testify and bear witness at a public hearing coorganized by the Concord Community Development Corporation and two representatives of the neighborhood in the state legislature. Fraud was the topic.

For years, from the community's perspective, mortgage lenders had preyed on the residents of Bedford-Stuyvesant. They tricked the elderly, the working poor, and even members of the middle class into signing mortgages with interest rates and balloon payments they could not afford, leading to foreclosures or perpetual refinancing.[1] The community needed to publicly express its concerns and demand reforms. Accordingly, Concord CDC assisted in creating a venue for issue identification, agenda setting, and future claim making. It also took the lead in mobilizing residents to attend and to speak at the hearing.

The April 29 hearing was one among multiple activities between 1999 and 2002 organized by neighborhood-based and citywide nonprofit organizations to expose mortgage fraud in and beyond Bedford-Stuyvesant. Representatives from activist African American churches and their CDCs participated in these antifraud actions throughout the city. They distributed cautionary fliers, held more hearings, and sponsored scam-recognition workshops. The church-associated CDCs, backed by their clergy, also endorsed a broader campaign to press the city government to enact an anti–predatory lending ordinance. Their devotion of resources to supplement the larger organizing and mobilization by progressive organizations influenced municipal policymakers. On November 20, 2002, by a vote of 40–5, the city council passed a law forbidding the city government from contracting with, depositing funds with, providing subsidies to, or making investments with companies and their affiliates found by the city's comptroller to be predatory lenders. The ordinance took effect February 18, 2003.

Although a court later voided the law on technicalities, the involvement of activist African American churches and their CDCs in the movement for a municipal ordinance raises a set of questions. Was the mobilization against predatory lending anomalous? If not, what acts of political engagement do the church-associated CDCs, with the support of their sponsor churches, generally employ to make sure that black neighborhoods' interests are incorporated into local political decision making? Conversely—and this is my central concern in this chapter—what political actions do they *avoid* and why?[2]

Readers may wonder why this chapter focuses more on the behavior of church-associated CDCs than on that of the activist churches that chartered them. I contend that looking at the political engagement of church-associated CDCs, just like looking at church-state collaboration, extends our understanding of the complexity of the political behavior of activist African American churches. Social scientists often speak as if activist churches engage directly in politics, say protesting public policies or supporting electoral candidates. Of course, some do it. Yet most activist churches merely create opportunities for their members to involve themselves or others in politics, or pastors' actions are equated with their church's actions, or they rely on church-associated, often clergy-based, nonpartisan organizations (Smith and Harris 2005). Therefore, rhetoric and research about the politics of the members, ministers, and agencies of activist African American churches are also talk and studies about the politics of these churches themselves. This is relevant to studying church-associated CDCs as political actors, especially when they perform the brokerage role normally associated with activist churches and their clergy.

What the CDCs of activist churches do politically is symbolic of and a proxy for what their sponsor churches do. This is because they are simultaneously detached from activist churches and unified with them. "The paradox is," a New York City minister who operates a national technical assistance organization for activist African American churches explained to me, "you're dealing with a separate entity that is not really separate; you're dealing with a CDC that is not the church but it *is* the church." Although the agendas of CDCs are developed by governing boards independent of their sponsor churches, the clergy and lay members of activist churches that sponsor and support a CDC often have influence over and within it. This is true of church-associated CDCs affiliated with a single congregation and those manifesting the collective will of an alliance of congregations. Sponsor churches can decide whether and how much a CDC is politically engaged. Thus, if the CDCs of activist churches are politically engaged in activities aside from collaboration with government, it is because the churches, particularly their clergy, permit, even encourage, them to engage in such activities.

With the proliferation of CDCs associated with activist African American churches across the United States, to know the politics of activist African American churches now requires that we also know the behavior of their subsidiaries. Social scientists need to comprehend the extent to which the political behavior of African American church–associated CDCs complement or supplement the sponsoring churches' electoral and contentious engagement. In particular, we need to understand how the politics of church-associated CDCs affect the consideration of black concerns and needs in public policies, programs, and governance. Such study will also help us better understand the potential effects of church-state collaboration on the political behavior of the clergy and congregants of activist churches, especially those that choose to collaborate directly with government (without the use of faith-related agencies such as CDCs).

Though collaboration with government is the core political behavior of CDCs associated with activist African American churches in New York City, I will show in this chapter that these CDCs do carry out other types of political action. Aspects of structure and culture in New York City direct these CDCs toward policy advocacy and constituent education, almost to the complete exclusion of electoral and contentious action to influence public agendas, decisions, and implementation to benefit their neighborhoods.

## COMPETING EXPECTATIONS

Recall from chapter 4 that activist African American churches chartered CDCs in New York City during the 1980s and 1990s to address neighborhood decline. Among other things, they sought to extinguish the fires in Morrisania, reduce poverty in Harlem, halt abandonment in Bedford-Stuyvesant, and build housing for those in South Jamaica who needed it. Such aims were consonant with the political, programmatic, and professional goals of the clergy leading the churches that incorporated the CDCs. These clergy, along with the professionals they hired to manage the CDCs, believed that public policy was implicated in the decline of low-income black neighborhoods and political engagement was required for the reform of their problems.

In my interviews with leaders of the African American church–associated CDCs, these executive directors and principal staff all expressed the view that public policy making was complicit in the concentrated poverty and physical abandonment in their target neighborhoods. In short, they echoed the views of clergy. Without exception, the leaders of the CDCs conveyed awareness that having the voice of their organization, along with those of other blacks, heard in deliberations and decisions about public policies and those who make them is pivotal to gaining government responsiveness to low-income black neighborhoods. A representative of Concord CDC spoke best to the relationships among black neighborhood conditions, public policy, and political engagement in New York City.

> We are reeling and staggering as a community because we've not been diligent in the creation of policy proposals and the impact of public policy. It's really continuously put us in a position of [being reactive], and we remain in a position of being reactive and in crisis. . . . [We] don't understand how everything that goes on in city hall, the city council's meetings, and in Washington affects lives. . . We need to reengage the black community into public policy. We need to not only involve ourselves in public policy, but educate our people in relationship to how public policy is developed and implemented, how it impacts our communities, and how we can impact public policy. I'm not as interested in elected officials as I am in helping our community understand the dynamics of accountability of their elected [and appointed] officials. The Christian Coalition has learned to do this quite well, and they have learned how to intimidate others not to do anything with the [political] process. We need to get off the dime.

Acting on the "needs" would oblige the CDCs of activist African American churches to educate neighborhood residents about politics and policies. It would also require them to expand the representation of their concerns in the policy-making proces, and increase government responsiveness to them. Meeting the objectives would require that activist African American churches obligate their CDCs to engage in political acts alongside or apart from collaboration with government.

Still, most leaders of the church-associated CDCs whom I interviewed agreed that their institution could do a better job of informing community residents and other stakeholders about the policy-making process and their need to track the decisions of their elected and appointed representatives. An informant from Bronx Shepherds Restoration Corporation in Morrisania observed: "We can do more. In order to rise to a new level of political sophistication we must begin to monitor our elected officials, from their votes to their attendance, as well as where their campaign money comes from."

To advance fully the interests of the neighborhoods they serve, the CDCs of activist churches could be expected to mix different forms of and exercise complementary roles in political action to enhance and broadcast their constituents' political voices. We would also expect such CDCs to expand pathways for their constituents to access and exert influence over municipal policy makers. Political engagement beyond collaboration with government would demonstrate the depth of their understanding that a comprehensive redevelopment of low-income black neighborhoods is possible only through increased opportunities for their residents to hold government, especially neighborhood politicians, accountable to them.

We should anticipate that activist churches would encourage their CDCs to engage in extensive actions aside from collaboration with government. Quantitative research employing multivariate analyses shows, for instance, that receipt of government funding, the amount of government funding, percent of revenue form government, and contacts with government increase the political engagement of nonprofits, and particularly of African American churches (Chaves, Stephens, and Galaskiewicz 2004; Berry 2003; LeRoux 2007). Also, there is strong evidence that a positive attitude toward church-state partnership increases a congregation's willingness to seek public funding and affects the proportion of funds that faith-related agencies receive from government (Owens 2006; Ebaugh, Rose, Chafetz, and Pipes 2005).

Yet qualitative research based on case studies and archival analyses presents reasons for one to expect that activist churches would *restrict* the political activities of their CDCs, out of fear of co-optation and concerns about church-state entanglement (Formicola, Segers, and Weber 2003; Harris 2001 and 2005; Walters and Tucker-Worgs 2005; Owens 2004b).

*Positive Expectations*

The CDCs of African American churches that collaborate with government could act politically in comprehensive ways to influence the thoughts and decisions of policy makers, as well as to affect the election of representatives. The public benefits (e.g., land, money, program discretion, and bureaucratic enfranchisement) that churches receive through their CDCs and other agencies may provide incentives for them to broaden the political engagement of their subsidiaries. Benefits are available only to those groups that collaborate with government. Being apolitical, or less political than necessary, may not help to sustain or increase the allocation of governmental resources of collaborators. Instead, it may diminish or stall the acquisition of resources. Therefore, one would expect activist churches to require their CDCs to do all that they can to keep their share of resources and to pressure government to give them more than competing groups. Moreover, the expectation is that ministers and members of churches that have chartered a CDC direct it to take action to retain and increase public resources for the CDC and the neighborhood.

Furthermore, there is the expectation that government reliance on the expertise and legitimacy of African American church–associated CDCs and their sponsor churches to govern public problems grants them leeway to act politically to educate and mobilize their constituents. Recognition by activist churches that their CDCs possess essential resources for government action may politically embolden churches and CDCs alike. Hence, they may engage in any of a broad set of political activities that could influence the election of their representatives and affect governmental decisions about benefits and costs to the group.

There is another reason to expect that the CDCs of activist African American churches in New York City would augment their collaboration with government through political engagement of various kinds. Production, ownership, and management of affordable housing yield a dual constituency for the church-associated CDCs to represent in political processes: apartment tenants and homeowners. The churches and their CDCs could also organize and mobilize this constituency for political participation in support of the churches' neighborhood development agendas and their pursuit of neighborhood-friendly public policies.

Finally, one would expect broad political engagement by African American church–associated CDCs because they are affiliated with politically active churches. These church leaders and their congregants appreciate political action in pursuit of policy responsiveness. They also acknowledge that politics was a catalyst for the creation of their CDC and that the CDC is to be a catalyst for political change on behalf of their neighborhood.

## Negative Expectations

At the same time, there are reasons to expect that the CDCs of activist African American churches would not act politically beyond collaboration. Activist churches believe that the resources their CDCs acquire are vital to neighborhood redevelopment and unobtainable through means other than collaboration with government. They may fear losing favor and material support from the municipal government for church-driven redevelopment, especially for *their* church (that is, they may fear that their resources might be reassigned to other churches or even to secular organizations). Thus, activist churches might limit their CDCs to practicing a mundane set of political acts that foster microchanges at the neighborhood level; such self-limitation is common among secular neighborhood-based organizations receiving public funding in New York City (Mollenkopf 1994; Marwell 2004). Such a decision would heighten the co-optation fear of those black clergy who oppose church-state collaboration. Moreover, it would signal to politicians that they could use church-state collaboration to regulate, and perhaps stop, the political activities of African American churches.

Also, the CDCs of activist churches might not engage in political action other than collaboration with government due to their association with politically active churches. Church-associated CDCs may be less political than one might expect *because* their affiliated churches are political. By that I mean their churches are involved in what Mark Warren describes as "social relations characterized by conflict over goods in the face of pressure to associate for collective action, where at least one party to the conflict seeks collectively binding decisions and seeks to sanction decisions by means of power" (1999, 218). The CDCs may function merely as neighborhood developers, making no waves and backing no losers. This would earn them the trust and support of political elites. Meanwhile, clergy, both as individuals and as representatives of their churches, may press and prod politically for social change.

As the church-associated CDCs collaborate with government and cooperate with the market, pastors can challenge society to serve the needy better and more fairly. This would be consequential in two ways. First, the churches may require less of their CDCs as direct political actors. Second, collaboration need not yield acquiescence to the political status quo, especially regarding the responsibilities and responsiveness of government to the poor in the nation's cities. This would be in contrast to the minister-machine politics of the past, when African American clergy in cities that received public resources faced the expectations of politicians that they squelch their prophetic voices. Therefore, the maintenance of church-associated CDCs that are programmatically subsidiaries of congregations but legally separate from them may be politically strategic for pastors: church-associated CDCs may widen the space for activist pastors to be advocates for social justice and progressive policies on behalf of the urban poor. Pastors can be radical while their CDCs are moderate.

Additionally, political engagement may not be the strength of church-associated CDCs. Like the congregations they are linked with, the church-associated CDCs exist primarily for purposes other than political action, save for collaboration with government. They are professional organizations led by experts in real estate development, city planning, architecture, and finance. Their specialty is putting together the deals that politics creates for them and their sponsor churches. They may therefore devote their skills to designing and implementing programs to meet the needs of their target neighborhoods (e.g., affordable housing) without an eye toward affecting public policy, at least not beyond the domain of affordable housing production.

## ACTIONS BESIDE AND BEYOND COLLABORATION

Do the CDCs of activist African American churches in New York City act politically beyond their collaboration with government? To answer the question, I identify three categories of political action that African American church–associated CDCs could practice to empower their communities and increase governmental responsiveness in conjunction with their collaboration with government. They could (1) encourage others to participate politically, (2) enable them to do it, and (3) take direct political action on behalf of others. *Encouraging others* to participate politically means politicizing others and priming them for mobilization. *Enabling others* to participate politically involves facilitating individuals' engagement in political processes—mobilizing people and channeling their mobilization. *Taking direct political action* refers to an organization's influencing politics and policy makers on behalf of others, which may involve forms of brokerage and mobilization.

Church-associated CDCs may employ four classes of activities to empower and increase the efficacy of their constituents in political arenas. These classes of activities would also enhance and broadcast constituents' political voices and expand their pathways to access and influence public policy makers. They include *constituent education* (informing individuals about political conditions and causes); *electoral assistance* (preparing or permitting individuals to participate in the electoral process); *policy advocacy* (direct interaction with policymakers and bureaucrats to express legislative and regulatory positions); and *contention* (nonviolent but forceful public exhortations, confrontations, and embarrassment of political elites).

Constituent education involves the instruction of current and potential supporters in a collective consciousness for making future claims on government. Through such education groups can spread political values among their constituents, who may then assist them, either independently or collectively, to effect governmental reforms in the distribution of advantages and disadvantages. Constituent education also increases constituents' capacity to advocate on their own behalf for policy changes.

Electoral assistance involves activities that educate and engage the constituents of a group in the electoral process. The intent is to influence constituents' perception of candidates and their mobilization to determine election outcomes.

Policy advocacy involves recommending, even pleading, against or for a legislative or regulatory position or other political cause (Hopkins 1992). "Through advocacy, [civic groups] may instill their group's perceptions of the common good into wider notions of the public good or the public interest" (Reid 1999, 291). Advocacy may also enable a group to "preserve prerogatives and benefits they are currently enjoying, blocking initiatives that they believe would reduce those benefits" (Kingdon 1995, 49).

Contention is deliberate, unconventional public criticism to denounce the effects of public policies for the purpose of fostering change and gaining rewards from elites (Lipsky 1968). Mass-based or individualized, contention involves nonviolent but forceful public acts of exhortation and confrontation, along with overt public embarrassment of political elites. It directs the appeals of a group to mass publics, providing a means, alternative or supplemental to other means, to publicize the concerns it believes requires action through public policy. The aim is to inform public opinion, potentially yielding mass support and allies, the resources groups need to negotiate for greater responsiveness from government.

Organized by the three categories of political action and the four classes of activities, table 5 disaggregates the political engagement of the church-associated CDCs in New York City. Explicitly, it shows that the church-associated CDCs could act in any of twenty different ways to encourage others to participate politically, enable them to do it, and take direct political action on their behalf. All of the activities are *nonpartisan.*

Federal and state statutes do not allow tax-exempt organizations such as CDCs and churches, be they government-funded or not, to engage in partisan electoral activities for the purpose of electing or defeating a particular candidate or party. Within the range of nonpartisan activities, however, there are still multiple ways for tax-exempt groups to engage in politics, especially on behalf of the interests of poor people. Also, my three categories of political

TABLE 5 Complements to collaboration: political engagement by African American church–associated CDCs in New York City, 1998–2001

| CATEGORY OF POLITICAL ENGAGEMENT | CLASS OF ACTIVITIES • Specific activity (number of CDCs engaging in activity) |
|---|---|
| 1. Encouraging others to participate (political mobilization) | *Constituent education* • Organizes the formation of civic associations and block associations (6) • Publishes newsletters and/ or newspapers containing political and policy information (4) • Maintains an organizational website with links to political and policy information (0) *Advocacy* • Encourages individuals, especially neighborhood residents, to lobby public officials (5) *Electoral assistance* • Holds candidate forums and debates in the neighborhood (3) • Publicizes voting records and remarks of political incumbents and challengers (1) |
| 2. Enabling others to participate (political mobilization) | *Constituent education* • Creates opportunities for direct citizen-government interaction (9) • Organizes town hall meetings in the neighborhood related to political and policy issues (5) • Tracks and monitors legislative bills and agency regulations to inform constituents (2) *Advocacy* • Provides advocacy organizations free meeting spaces (6) *Electoral Assistance* • Distributes nonpartisan voter guides (9) • Registers people to vote (3) • Transports registered voters to the polls on election days (1) |
| 3. Taking direct political action on behalf of others (political brokerage and political mobilization) | *Advocacy* • Representatives testify at public hearings (8) • Representatives contact public officials about policies and regulations (7) • Joins advocacy coalitions (6) *Electoral assistance* • Informs electoral candidates, incumbents and challengers, about issues and needs (0) *Contention* • Endorses protests (3) • Challenges bank lending patterns through local, state, and federal community reinvestment mandates (3) • Organizes or cosponsors protests (0) |

action demonstrate that we can expand the concept and measurement of political behavior beyond the protest-electioneering dichotomy that is the basis for most research on religion and politics (Wald 2003; McVeigh and Sikkink 2001), particularly when it focuses on African American congregations, clergy, and church-associated organizations (Morris 1984; Calhoun-Brown 1996; Harris 1999).

The data in table 5 confirm that the CDCs of activist African American churches behave in ways that fit within the three categories of political engagement. Each of the church-associated CDCs during the period of my research (1997–2001) engaged in at least one activity in each category, and a majority of them practiced three activities within each category. The figure provides a sense of the overall level of political engagement by the African American church–associated CDCs that collaborate with government in New York City.

These CDCs are moderately engaged in politics outside of their collaboration with government, if we assume that *high engagement* would correspond to the performance of more than fourteen of the twenty possible political activities, *moderate engagement* is equal seven to fourteen activities, and *low engagement* involves fewer than seven activities. Most of the CDCs had no more than nine acts of political engagement, and seven was the median number of such acts. In other words, the CDCs that activist African American churches used to collaborate with government carried out under one-half of all political activities at their disposal to influence who holds government office and the decisions they make.

Lastly, table 5 reveals that the majority of African American church–associated CDCs choose certain types of activities over others. Specifically, they perform acts of policy advocacy and constituent education over acts of electoral assistance and contention. Activities such as holding candidate forums to educate and engage residents in the electoral process or to influence constituents' perception of candidates and help determine election outcomes are uncommon among the church-associated CDCs. Likewise, nonviolent but forceful public acts of exhortation and confrontation, along with overt public embarrassment of political elites, to influence political decisions (e.g., endorsing protests) are seldom carried out by the church-associated CDCs. Instead, these CDCs are most likely to involve others and themselves in direct interaction with policy makers and bureaucrats to express legislative and regulatory positions (e.g., encouraging lobbying, testifying at public hearings, and contacting public officials).[3] It is common, too, for their acts to involve the civic and political education of constituents and supporters, such as recruiting residents to form civic associations and organizing town hall meetings.

DETERMINANTS OF POLITICAL ENGAGEMENT
BY COLLABORATORS

Overall, the CDCs associated with activist African American churches in New York City are politically engaged. The data suggest that their political engagement, however, involves only a fraction of the range of activities available to nonprofit organizations. Also, it is less inclusive than their low-income black neighborhoods perhaps require for changing the socioeconomic conditions in them. In particular, church-associated CDCs tend to avoid electioneering and contention.

What accounts for these CDCs' political choices and avoidance of activities focused on electioneering and contention? Four factors affect their political engagement, especially their general neglect of electoral assistance and contention, (1) the local patronage context, (2) public regulation of nonprofit organizations, (3) an attitude about "political" organizations, and (4) a negative perception of protest.

*The Local Patronage Context*

New York is a patronage city. It is a place where neighborhood politicians attempt to dominate public resources for political purposes and politically connected neighborhood-based organizations try to win most, if not all, public resources to the benefit of a few (Weir 1999). It is atypical in New York City for neighborhood-based organizations to receive public resources without the sponsorship and approval of local politicians (Hamilton 1979; Mollenkopf 1994; Marwell 2004). Rather, the discretion of politicians, particularly elected neighborhood representatives, determines the award of municipal resources such as city contracts and public land, as well as local allocations of intergovernmental aid (e.g., Community Development Block Grant funds for neighborhood projects). Moreover, administrative rule making strengthens the position of politicians to influence the distribution of resources to neighborhood-based organizations, especially those seeking to collaborate with public agencies to implement policies and programs. Politicians' endorsement of public spending in their districts and their oversight of agency budgets facilitate or hinder the receipt of municipal resources by specific groups.

The CDCs of activist African American churches are not exempt from the political rules of resource allocation in New York City. Their work is embedded in and their outcomes affected by the local political context. Chapters 5 and 6 revealed it, especially through the battle of Harlem Congregations for Community Improvement against the Koch administration. Moreover, the secular realm, particularly the public sector, is the fount of much of the financial support for the church-associated CDCs. As noted in chapter 4, in fact, the public sector is their primary patron. Their continued receipt of public resources is mortgaged to cooperation and enduring patron-client relationships. This does not necessarily mean that the church-associated CDCs, or their churches, are wholly co-opted, especially given that they never renounce their broader political aims and interests. It is true, nonetheless, that the general approach of church-associated CDCs is to sow goodwill among policy makers and administrators in hopes of reaping and sustaining public resources, retaining policy discretion, and earning public recognition for their works.

The church-associated CDCs continually build and protect relationships with neighborhood politicians and agency personnel, according to my informants. A principal staff member of the Abyssinian Development Corporation in Harlem responded to my inquiries about its patron-client relationships.

It's critical to have very solid relationships with elected officials, at all levels, across the political spectrum. That has certainly been our institutional philosophy here, to cultivate and solidify relationships with both elected as well as appointed [officials], and civil service managers within these agencies. It is often they [the bureaucrats] who are left to implement [policies], and it's important to be respectful and mindful of the role that the politicians and the people who are the "lifers" in the agencies can play in determining who gets what from the city. . . . On most applications for government assistance, one of the important questions is "In whose [political] district are you?" or "Can you identify what [political] district these funds will be spent in?" or other similar questions. Frequently you will be asked to, if you are submitting a bid for a competitive RFP [Request for Proposals] or something, you will be asked, or it will be suggested in the RFP, to get a letter of support from a local official. Obviously, there is that [implication] that you should know or have good relationships with your elected officials.

Restating the influence of politicians over resource allocations and the imperative to cooperate, an informant from the Southeast Queens Clergy for Community Empowerment claimed that good relations between their organizations and city hall were critical to their continued collaboration with government. This included their participation in the affordable housing microregime and municipal programs, as well as their continued receipt of public resources.

> To acquire city land, to do work with the city around the development process, nearly all of us do it. But to do it requires maintaining good working relationships with the city politic and with HPD and the banks. Now, I don't know if HPD necessarily keeps an enemy list, though we're all in a love-hate relationship with our city's housing agency. . . . What I'm trying to say is that there is a tradeoff, and so that the groups that do best in any period of time tend to be those groups that are most closely allied with the [mayoral] administration, or at least don't have a a an adversarial role or situation with the city.

This explains why leaders of the church-associated CDCs tended to describe the institutional philosophy of their organization as more cooperative than adversarial or confrontational. An executive director of another church-associated CDC in Harlem remarked to me, "I don't think that we have ever taken a straight-up confrontational position with city officials. That's not to say they haven't taken confrontational positions with us. . . . But ours was not confrontational back; it was just survival. How do we cooperate? We do whatever is necessary to cooperate."

Since the CDCs of activist churches are reliant on politicians who strategically use their control of public resources to their political advantage by rewarding supporters and punishing opponents, cooperation trumps confrontation. Because the church-associated CDCs are dependent on the resources of institutions external to their neighborhood, they are wary of alienating their patrons. Thus cooperation is necessary for organizational survival. It also is critical to neighborhood redevelopment, particularly church-led development.

Conflict rather than cooperation, in the collective view of the executive directors, would exclude their organization from working with government to reform the conditions of poor black neighborhoods. As long as cooperation via collaboration with government continues to provide the church-associated CDCs with the resources they need and allows them to maintain their membership in public-private partnerships, the leaders of the church-associated CDCs are willing to exclude certain types of behavior from their organizations' political repertoires. Specifically, seeking to foster the perception among the neighborhood and citywide politicians that they support these politicians' tenure and administration, the church-associated CDCs tend to refrain from electoral assistance and contention.

Actions and discourse by the church-associated CDCs that political elites construe as oppositional, critical, or confrontational would, according to their executive directors, bring an end to their partnership with public agencies, especially HPD. They would also stall, even stop, they believe, their receipt of municipal resources. An informant from the Association of Brooklyn Clergy for Community Development explained the logic:

> Once a group starts assuming a role in government programs and taking on city funding and gets loans from the banks to do development or almost any programmatic activity of any kind, its ability to get involved in elections or demonstrations tends to be somewhat dulled, partly because—and I think the assumption is quite valid—if you want to do business with the city or the banks, then you really can't get involved in affecting who holds office or be as confrontive as you may want to be on a number of policy matters, public and private.

Clearly, instead of freeing church-associated CDCs to practice comprehensive political engagement, as one would expect of empowered collaborators, collaboration encourages them to neglect, or at least reduce their use of, electoral assistance and contention.

In my interviews, the mention of co-optation raised the ire of most leaders of the church-associated CDCs. One executive director exclaimed, "I don't think they [politicians] should stop a person from speaking their conscience while doing development. The whole mission of CDCs, especially faith-based ones, should be [that we are] the ones who stand up for our communities. We should not be afraid of anything, because I mean really, injustice is something we need more people to speak out against." Quickly but more quietly, however, the respondent admitted, "It's difficult because the politicians watch us like hawks, waiting for us to give them reasons to cut us off and give contracts to other groups. You definitely see that going on with the folks up in Harlem." The best illustrations of this point are the consequences that befell church-associated CDCs following public excoriations of Mayor Giuliani by two Harlem pastors.

At the start of 1998, Canaan Baptist Church of Christ was preparing to become the community sponsor of a $100 million development project on West 116th Street in central Harlem. The project, part of the Alliance for Neighborhood Commerce, Homeownership, and Revitalization (ANCHOR), an HPD program that catalyzes mixed-use development in blighted sections of neighborhoods, anticipated the development of 96,000 square feet of retail space and 778 mixed-income housing units, and it was expected to yield 117 permanent jobs for neighborhood residents.

On January 18, the Reverend Wyatt Tee Walker, then pastor of Canaan Baptist Church of Christ and a board member of Harlem Congregations for Community Improvement, appeared on *Like It Is*, a local black public affairs TV program. Walker vilified Giuliani as a fascist. Subsequently, the Giuliani administration prohibited Canaan Baptist Church and its CDC from participating in the ANCHOR project, even though (1) they were located a block away from the redevelopment site, (2) they were HPD's partners in previous development projects in the neighborhood, and (3) according to HPD informants and representatives of other neighborhood-based organizations in Central Harlem, they had been responsible for the initial revitalization of 116th Street beginning in the late 1970s. The Giuliani administration substituted Malcolm Shabazz Masjid—a black orthodox Muslim mosque with a primarily immigrant African congregation—for Canaan Baptist Church of Christ. The mosque's imam, Izak-El Pasha, had long sought to partner with the city, and he had ingratiated himself with Giuliani, going as far as to call him a "great man" (Mank 2000).

Summing up the episode for me, an informant stated, "Canaan built a lot of housing by working with city hall, but it loses more contracts than it wins. [The 116th Street project] is a glaring example. Walker's politics are too adversarial and his mouth is too big and fast for the church's own good. Everybody in Harlem and HPD knows it."

Five months later, the Reverend Calvin Butts of Abyssinian Baptist Church appeared on *Like It Is*. He clarified a public statement he had made regarding racism in relation to Mayor Giuliani.

The mayor does not like black people and has no regard for the black community. I [have been] asked, was I calling the mayor a racist. I thought long and hard about what I was saying and then I said yes. . . . And this has, this word [*racist*] has stirred up so much of an uproar because a lot of people have been trying to cloak their racism behind what they call policies that are necessary to return us to a sense of stability. But these things are not returning us to a sense of stability. They're creating a society that's not civil. And people are now saying, because they love Giuliani, "Well, if he's calling Giuliani a racist, maybe he's calling me a racist, too," and they don't like this term.

Giuliani responded to Butts's comments in two ways. Rhetorically, he declared, "Reverend Butts engages in using the term 'racist' so loosely that it portrays something substantially wrong in him" (quoted in Noel 1998, 57). Politically, the Giuliani administration opposed a $49 million commercial project for Harlem that the Abyssinian Development Corporation had planned to develop (Lentz 1998). What had happened was obvious to the CDC's representatives: "City hall basically confronted our position in that project based on politics versus on the development [plan of the CDC] and the merits."

Politicians closely watch not only the behavior of church-associated CDCs but also the political actions of the clergy and churches that are associated with them—even when the clergy and congregants act independent of the CDCs, as is almost always the case. When politicians see things they object to, they react swiftly and negatively. The leaders of the church-associated CDCs, however, want policy makers to accept that the political behavior of the clergy and congregations affiliated with them are and always will be separate from their work. They fear that church-associated CDCs will lose opportunities for resources and bureaucratic enfranchisement when clergy linked to them are too outspoken politically. The Harlem examples legitimate the fear.

A director of a church-associated CDC in Bedford-Stuyvesant addressed the issue, touching on the political activities of church-associated CDCs in other parts of the city. "You know that there are some others that are more politically entwined or connected like. I won't name them, but you've been there. I think because they have that entanglement—recently, I have heard some expressions of concern for them—the city might be holding back their funds because they are speaking out against the police or the mayor [Giuliani] and how he reacts. That scares the hell out of us. I guess it makes us think twice about politics, our own and the pastors'." It also makes them bound their political engagement. As collaborators with government, church-associated CDCs feel compelled to practice only a limited set of political activities to influence government officials, both who sits in office and the decisions they make. They tend to avoid electoral and protest mobilization. They understand the potentially harmful effects of opposing politicians or administrative officials, as well as of backing candidates who may become political losers, whether incumbents or challengers. They also recognize the negative consequences of mobilizing voters or sponsoring political events that politicians cannot control, such as protests.

Electoral assistance and contention might merely reduce the margins of victory at the polls by ineffective neighborhood incumbents and intransigent citywide incumbents. Short of defeating incumbents, behaviors by the church-associated CDCs that cut into the political support, or call into question the abilities, personalities, and politics, of incumbents could produce a backlash against the CDCs. Opponents and gadflies of politicians would open themselves, or like-minded neighborhood politicians, to reprisals by more powerful elites, particularly the mayor, who controls the spoils of the municipal bureaucracy. Among other effects, opposition to incumbents could reduce access to discretionary funds for use in the CDCs' neighborhoods, particularly by the church-associated CDCs, and this is not in the short-term interests of low-income black neighborhoods. Accordingly, the patron-client relationships between public representatives (patrons) and the church-associated CDCs (clients), where the former influence and control resources (public money and land) to benefit or protect the latter in exchange for their support or quiescence, endure. That means that the church-associated CDCs tend to adopt a passive politics, characterized by innocuous acts such as distributing voter guides.

Ultimately, the executive directors of the church-associated CDCs would judge that contention and electoral assistance by their organizations would be detrimental to the achievement of substantive goals, even if such actions are strong symbolic gestures and may be appropriate means for addressing the needs of low-income black neighborhoods. Fear and second-guessing their right to political engagement underscore the structural barrier that patronage erects to the church-associated CDCs' broadly encouraging, enabling, and taking political action in and on behalf of low-income black neighborhoods. Consequently, cooperation and collaboration, not confrontation and conflict, are the standard operating practices of these CDCs as political actors. Despite Giuliani's policy stances toward blacks and their neighborhoods, for example, pastors of churches that chartered CDCs (e.g., Floyd Flake of Allen AME Church and Preston Washington of Memorial Baptist Church) endorsed him for reelection as mayor. One pastor explained to me, "Giuliani is not stupid. He knows how to work politically. Anyway, I endorsed him. I endorsed him for business reasons, and he understands that, because the Republicans tend to be pretty cool [i.e., positive] concerning our [neighborhood development] agenda."

The leaders of the church-associated CDCs, like the clergy leading the sponsoring churches, recognize that contesting the decisions and policies of administrative agencies (and private institutions too) could lead to reductions in funding. Hence, their organizations must respect, mind, and, perhaps above all else, value the influence that politicians and their staff wield in discourse and decisions about who gets what, when, how, and where in New York City. Leaders recognize, too, the preemptive power of local politicians and how it influences their actions. Yet the local patronage context is just one factor influencing the political choices and behaviors of church-associated CDCs.

## Public Regulation of Nonprofit Organizations

Public policy can foster political action by nonprofit organizations. After all, the privatization of public resources, along with the contracting of public services, was one of the catalysts for activist African American churches in New York City to charter CDCs. In particular, public policy encourages church-associated CDCs to become advocates for themselves and their neighborhoods. Receipt of public resources by church-associated CDCs after they become collaborators with government is and remains predicated on their ability to lobby for funding, not just their possession of the skills to apply for public support and to execute the policies of government agencies. The pursuit and defense of material and immaterial resources obligate church-associated CDCs to engage in advocacy. Yet public regulation also creates obstacles for political action, preventing nonprofit organizations from engaging freely in the full scope of political activities, especially electioneering.

Federal and state statutes prohibit tax-exempt organizations from carrying out much of the activism one would normally expect of groups working on behalf of the interests of poor people and their neighborhoods (Berry 2003). Again, nonprofit organizations may not engage in *partisan* electoral activities for the purpose of electing or defeating a particular candidate or party.[4] Nonetheless, public regulations, especially the federal Internal Revenue Service Code, permit all tax-exempt, nonprofit organizations, including church-associated CDCs, to engage in electoral activities. Given this, according to a pastor I interviewed in South Jamaica, "one thing that our CDCs should do is to encourage people to vote and show them how their voting influences the monies that come into our communities." The assumption is that neighborhood development funding follows from electoral activity.

Of the pastors I interviewed who were affiliated with church-associated CDCs, the majority agreed that such organizations should be neighborhood-based institutions assisting voters to make rational choices at the polls. That

is, they said that church-associated CDCs should offer residents as much information as possible about candidates for public office and the key issues
of campaigns. Moreover, a majority contended that church-associated CDCs
should persuade the residents of their target neighborhoods, at least those oc-
cupying the buildings owned or operated by the CDCs, to register and vote
in elections, particularly local races for public office. The church-associated
CDCs should even take people to and from the polls, according to most clergy
I interviewed.

Normatively, the CDCs associated with activist African American churches
should be able to engage in all forms of electoral assistance permissible by
public regulation. Empirically, while the African American church–associated
CDCs could register people to vote and mobilize voters during election cycles,
they often do not. The church-associated CDCs could use their Web sites to
provide voter information through links to institutions like the New York City
Voter Assistance Commission, the nonpartisan municipal agency created in
1988 to facilitate voter registration and voter participation in city elections,
but they do not. Church-associated CDCs could invite and present political incumbents and their challengers for public scrutiny at candidate forums
in their neighborhood, but they do not. The status of the church-associated
CDCs as tax-exempt organizations, in the view of their leaders, hinders such
electoral actions.

Consistently, all executive directors and a majority of clergy affiliated with
the church-associated CDCs stated to me that church-associated CDCs cannot involve themselves in the electoral politics of their target neighborhoods
and the city. Electoral engagement, they believe, is legally impermissible for
such nonprofit organizations. The CDCs, in their mind, cannot step a toe into
electoral waters, even if the intent is simply to encourage and enable people
to perform a basic duty of democratic citizenship. To do so, they believed,
would be illegal. "It's correct that we are not as involved in neighborhood
and city electoral politics as we and the 'hoods need us to be," a director acknowledged. "The reason is simple: we need to be mindful of our 501(c)(3)
[tax-exempt] status. We'd be no good to anyone if we didn't have it."[5] Almost
all the executive directors said that they remind the clergy and vice versa that
the church-associated CDCs should shy from acts of electoral assistance and
protest that could be *interpreted* as partisan and therefore detrimental to their
tax status.[6]

Because of public regulation of nonprofit organizations, the church-
associated CDCs engage only in electoral activities that, in the terms of a pastor, allow them to "stay on the good side of the IRS."[7] This explains why the

church-associated CDCs tend to act in ways that encourage electoral action by others, such as distributing voter guides, rather than enable it, for example, by getting voters to the polls on Election Day. The reality, however, is that the CDC leaders' perceptions of public regulation, far more than public regulation itself, proscribe involvement in electoral assistance activities. The church-associated CDCs purposely and honestly, but mistakenly, stand farther outside the electoral arena than public regulation requires of them.

Ultimately, the church-associated CDCs tend to be bystanders to the electoral process in New York City, rather than participants in it. Indeed they are less involved in neighborhood and city elections than residents of low-income black neighborhoods might need and expect them to be.[8] Yet beyond local patronage and misunderstandings about the public regulation of nonprofit organizations, the CDCs have further reasons not to broaden their electoral assistance and contention. Perceptions about what is, and who in relation to the activist churches should be, "political" influence the political repertoires of the church-associated CDCs.

## *Definitions and Expectations of the "Political"*

Based on their lineage and association with politically active African American churches, one would assume that the church-associated CDCs I studied would self-identify as "political" organizations. Their leaders, in fact, did not accept the appellation. Operating in a political environment did not necessarily make their organization political, nor should it, they asserted. As well, they claimed vigorously that the CDCs are something other than political organizations. In particular, they identified their organizations as "faith-based" organizations: "We see the organization as spiritual, not political. I think we're right. We could not have accomplished anything had the spiritual component not been in place. Faith sustains our work and us. We truly have come this far by faith, not politics," a director reasoned. They also did not see themselves as political, because they tend to equate political with electoral. As the executive director of a church-associated CDC in Harlem put it to me: "By default, being initiated by the church, our association with the church puts us in the line of fire, politically. But no, we are not a political institution. I think on our own what we do is not particularly political. I mean . . . we are affected by politics, but in and of itself we are not a political institution, as I define political—I would say an organization whose goal it is to have people elected or change the system of electoral politics—and I don't think the advocacy stuff we say or do is focused on that."

It is not disingenuous for the leaders of church-associated CDCs to claim that their organizations are apolitical, nor is it atypical of what the leaders of most nonprofit organizations, faith-related or secular, would say. Few nonprofit organizations perceive themselves as political institutions, unless their organizational mission states that they are such. Research on nonprofit organizations as interest groups by Jeffrey Berry clarifies the point: "Government relations is usually an afterthought in the initial design and focus of a nonprofit even though necessity requires contact between the government and nonprofits. Many nonprofit leaders still believe that their contact with those in government has no political connotation. Interaction is an immaculate conception—nothing naughty happens, but something productive is expected to gestate" (2003, 25).

Since they do not see their mission as overtly political, the leaders of church-associated CDCs state accurately that their organizations are not "political," regardless of their empowerment rhetoric. Moreover, because these CDCs avoid political activities that would sustain and advance black political participation (e.g., intense electoral assistance and contention), it makes sense that they would describe their organizations as apolitical.

The CDCs of activist African American churches are subject to politics; they must negotiate the political terrains of their neighborhood and the city. Their negotiation need not require them, from the directors' collective perspective, to be involved in elections or protests. They are not required to encourage voters to turn out in high numbers to influence elections or support candidates who share their values and interests. They are not obligated to mobilize and direct collective outrage toward challenging and shaming policy makers to increase governmental responsiveness to their interests and values.

None of the roles of the church-associated CDCs are overtly political, their leaders contend, even if their organization and the communities they serve are buffeted by neighborhood, city, state and federal politics. Furthermore, while the effects of politics on their neighborhood concern the leaders of the church-associated CDCs, they expect electoral mobilization and contentious agitation for social and economic reform to come from the clergy and congregations that chartered them. A representative of the Association of Brooklyn Clergy for Community Development declared during an interview, "The pastors know how to do [politics] best; we're developers, not politicians. We simply focus on the needs and get to work addressing them." The CDC leaders believe that the congregations affiliated with them should and do meet the political needs of their neighborhoods far better than the CDCs ever could.

Throughout the 1980s and into the 1990s, activist African American churches, especially those that incorporated CDCs, were cornerstones of electoral and protest mobilization in the four black neighborhoods, as chapter 6 recounts. Clergy from churches that chartered CDCs, independently or in alliance with clergy from other churches, routinely engaged in or encouraged others to practice various forms of electoral assistance and contention. As long as politicized congregations organize and mobilize black political participation in New York City, the CDCs of activist churches may never have to engage too much in electoral and contentious politics. A question, however, is whether the churches that chartered the CDCs in Morrisania, Harlem, South Jamaica, and Bedford-Stuyvesant remain as engaged in electioneering and protest as they did in the past, before they began to collaborate with government.

Reserving for later whether the churches that chartered CDCs maintain their protest engagement, let us turn to the electoral activities of the churches. Figure 8 shows that the electoral engagement of activist churches in my samples, which here include only those that collaborated with government via church-associated CDCs, increased activity in some modes, remained constant in others, and declined in additional modes from the late 1980s through the late 1990s.[9] Their distribution of voter guides, pastoral endorsements of candidates, and invitations of candidates to Sunday worship services increased during the period in question. Also, the number of churches allowing candidates to address their congregations, mentioning candidate voting records and policy positions in pastoral sermons, and encouraging political contributions remained constant.

We also see, however, that the churches reduced their engagement in other acts of electioneering, activities that church-associated CDCs did not pick up and add to their political repertoires. Specifically, pastors reported that fewer of their congregations organized voter registration and get-out-the-vote drives or sponsored candidate forums in the late 1990s than they had done in the late 1980s. Similarly, during the period in question a smaller number of pastors suggested that congregants vote for particular candidates.

Nonetheless, the key finding is that the churches that collaborate with government engage in the electoral activities their CDCs avoid. This supports the claim that church-associated CDCs need not engage in too much electoral mobilization because the churches they are affiliated with do it.[10] Black politicians' observations regarding church-based electioneering in New York City further buttress the claim. The officials who responded to my survey

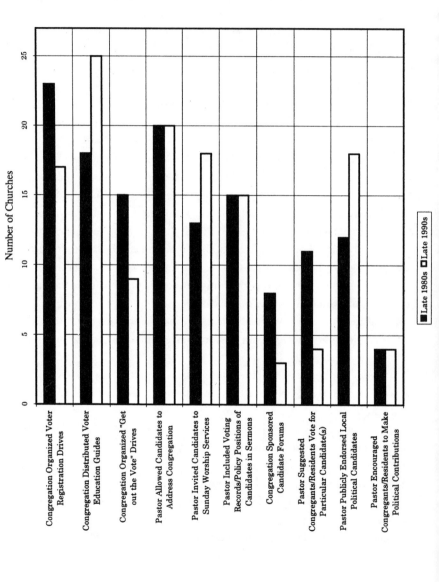

FIGURE 8  Changes in electoral action by activist churches chartering CDCs ($N = 28$)

Number of Churches

■ Late 1980s □ Late 1990s

were given a chance to state their perceptions of the general level of electoral engagement by activist African American churches in their district. I asked them to characterize the engagement of churches, generally, in city and neighborhood politics between the late 1980s and late 1990s. They were instructed to select one of three characterizations: increasing engagement, declining engagement, or no change in engagement. Their responses were consonant with the overall findings from pastor surveys that the electoral engagement of activist churches was varied but constant or increasing: 44 percent of black elected officials agreed that African American churches were more politically engaged in the late 1990s than the late 1980s, 36 percent perceived no change, and the remainder observed that churches were less politically engaged.

Overall, the evidence is strong that, at a minimum, churches with their own CDCs and those supporting alliance-based CDCs encourage and enable the residents of Bedford-Stuyvesant, South Jamaica, Morrisania, and Harlem to participate in electoral activities, regardless of whether their CDCs do it. That is, after more than a decade of collaboration by activist African American churches and their CDCs with the municipal government in New York City, the electoral engagement of such churches remained relatively high; a majority of them engaged in six or more electoral activities. Therefore, the leaders of church-associated CDCs are correct in stating that their organizations may engage in a smaller set of electoral activities without necessarily causing electoral demobilization in the four neighborhoods.

## *The Perception of Protest*

At times there are social problems or policy crises in a neighborhood or city that are not amenable to resolution by neighborhood-based organizations. In those instances, such organizations may resign themselves, or they may press for a governmental response. Seeking to change who holds public office is one valid response to problems, but success may take a long time to arrive. Even if new persons are quickly brought into public office, the government may still not address the problems. An alternative is for neighborhood-based organizations to incorporate public drama with the airing of community frustration and disgust to encourage greater responsiveness from government. Groups can organize demonstrations on behalf of their neighborhoods, publicly demanding a governmental response or denouncing government as unresponsive. Protest may also be carried out if the crisis has a nongovernmental source and the groups seek greater responsiveness from private individuals and institutions, such as predatory lenders.

However, there is a barrier to African American church-associated CDCs' encouraging, enabling, or taking direct contentious actions. It is not the local patronage context, the public regulation of nonprofits, or perceptions about political organizations that pose the greatest obstacle to the use of contention by these CDCs. Instead, it is an attitude that protest is passé and ineffectual at changing public policy to benefit black neighborhoods.

In my interviews with the pastors and executive directors of the church-associated CDCs, as well as in my survey of black elected officials, I asked respondents to rank protest (boycotts and demonstrations), electoral participation (voting and office holding), and lobbying (legislative and regulatory advocacy) according to their ability to influence policy makers to enact policies to better the conditions of low-income blacks in New York City. The majority of pastors (including the thirty pastors in my purposive and random samples) and executive directors (eight of nine), along with 70 percent of elected officials, ranked protest as the least effective means of increasing governmental responsiveness to the lived conditions of low-income blacks. Furthermore, I queried executive directors and pastors about their participation in protest-related activities (e.g., marches, boycotts, rallies) in the previous five years. Three directors had publicly endorsed political causes or events, and the same set of clergy reported that they had participated in at least one protest-type activity in the previous five years.[11] Twenty of the thirty pastors I interviewed answered that they had not engaged in protest.

These are strong indications that the activist churches that have chartered CDCs, as well as those without connections to CDCs and those that did not collaborate with government, tend to avoid protest activity. One pastor opined, "What [blacks] do is continually revert to the protest because that's what we know best. But times have changed. We must develop new instruments of political influence." Implicit in the remarks is a sentiment that protest may have utility under certain circumstance but overall it is an outdated response to contemporary problems. The comments cohered with the general attitude of the black polity in New York City toward protest during the 1990s. Claire Jean Kim estimates that in this period "a sizeable minority of Blacks in New York City strongly supported [protest action], while many more (probably a majority) partially supported it and partially opposed it, and a minority strongly opposed it" (2000, 89).

The sentiment that protest has become less effective than other forms of political engagement fits with the view held by blacks throughout the United States during the last two decades of the twentieth century. Despite interesting illustrations of contentious politics, blacks were moving further away from protest as political participation. In the early 1990s, 71 percent of blacks had not attended a protest meeting or demonstration, and 77 percent had not taken part in a neighborhood march (Dawson 2001, 332). The data do not necessarily contradict the observation of scholars at the time of "interesting political rumblings in urban Black America" and the feeling of "a rebellious mood, usually associated with social change, in the Black community" (Jennings 1992, 12). The "rumblings" and "mood" were real, but they did not denote the dawn of a new episode of contentious black politics rooted in organized demonstrations, marches, and rallies in the cities of the United States. Seven years later, 85 percent of U.S. blacks had not attended a political demonstration or rally (Wuthnow 2000).

In New York City there are class dimensions, too, to the disengagement of blacks from protest. Case studies of black protest events in the late 1980s through the end of the 1990s in New York reveal that the participation of the middle class, especially from the professional ranks, in contention is limited (Joyce 2003; Kim 2000). A minority of its members joined in contentious events such as the marches against white brutality and murders of blacks in Bensonhurst and Howard Beach, as well as the boycotts and pickets against Korean American grocers and Hasidic Jews in Bedford-Stuyvesant, Harlem, and Crown Heights.

Given the demographics of Harlem, Morrisania, South Jamaica, and Bedford-Stuyvesant, the CDCs of activist African American churches in New York City are middle-class organizations "representing" working-class communities. Middle-class professionals, both leaders and staff, govern the decisions and actions of the African American church–associated CDCs. These leaders choose not to devote the resources of their organizations to contention. It is not that they, or the black middle class in New York City, necessarily oppose contention. An individual could decide not to march or demonstrate while endorsing such methods and respecting, even encouraging, the participation of others in protest (Kim 2000, 89).

Even when it does not participate in protest, the black middle class understands why others would employ contention. It recognizes that the intent of speaking loudly and clearly and disturbing the peace, or encouraging and supporting others to do it, is to make political elites aware of important needs or demands and compel them to act (Lipsky 1968). It also accepts the idea that protest permits the recruitment of allies outside and inside government to blunt opposition to radical positions. As bystanders join in on behalf of their neighborhoods, protesters could, working with peers inside the system, use contention as a chip for bargaining with political elites to win more material rewards—or just symbolic ones that appease public sentiment and permit only marginal changes in their neighborhoods.

Still, the primary reason for the limited use of contention, as my interviews with the pastors and executive directors of church-associated CDCs and my survey of black elected officials revealed, was that the black middle class considered it an ineffective form of political engagement in New York City. Rev. Flake, pastor of perhaps the city's largest middle-class African American church, the Greater Allen AME Cathedral, whose CDC (Allen NPDC) has never engaged in contentious activities, said the following about the place of protest in the political involvement of activist African American churches, particularly in public school reform:

> I think my responsibility is to call attention to problems, and clergy's responsibility is to call attention to problems and not necessarily accept the status quo. I think that's what Jesus' ministry was all about. But there are various ways to go about that. You can do it the way Jesse Jackson and Al Sharpton do it—with protest. I don't stand opposed to their method, but you also have to have someone who is the builder and the processor. I think those [are the] two roles of clergy, the protester on the one [hand], the protest leader and the activist, and then the processor, the person who takes the time to really process the arguments that they make and bring about some visible evidence that what they speak about is a possibility. (quoted in Owens 2001, 7)

Flake's perspective as a "processor" is dominant among the leaders of church-associated CDCs. "If others want to protest, that's fine," a director of a CDC in Bedford-Stuyvesant commented, "but that's not what we're we going to do, unless it's absolutely necessary." As a consequence, the CDCs of activist African American churches in New York City consistently avoid the use of contention on behalf of their target neighborhoods, except under extreme situations.

## SUMMARY

To return to the primary question of this chapter, do the CDCs of activist African American churches in New York City act politically beyond their collaboration with government? Yes, but they select some forms of political action over other forms. Their chief political activities involve advocacy. They advocate on behalf of themselves and low-income black neighborhoods to retain and extend the benefits they receive from government. They also make claims for policy and programmatic changes to improve the conditions of their neighborhoods. The church-associated CDCs also act to educate neighborhood residents for future political engagement. Their electoral action, however, is limited, and they leave contention to other actors. We may conclude, then, that the CDCs of activist African American churches in New York City behave like most interest groups in the political system (Walker 1991; Baumgartner and Leech 1998).

Furthermore, the choices of the CDCs associated with activist churches concerning their political action are affected by a set of factors that fit within the structure-culture argument of social movement scholars: just as structure and culture influence the breadth of political engagement by individuals and organizations generally, along with "what they know how to do and what others expect them to do," it affects the political behavior of the leaders of African American church–associated CDCs in the name of low-income black neighborhoods in New York City (Tarrow 1998, 30). On the one hand, collaboration with government, which is mediated through a local patronage environment (structure) that transfers resources from governmental agencies to nongovernmental organizations, encourages church-associated CDCs to engage in advocacy and constituent education to acquire and protect resources and to potentially influence political decisions to the benefit of low-income black neighborhoods. On the other hand, the local patronage environment, along with cultural norms manifested by perceptions of public regulation of nonprofits, narrow definitions and identification of "political" responsibility, and middle-class attitudes toward protest, creates a system of consensual relations that suppresses electoral and contentious challenges to the status quo.

Influencing the thoughts and decisions of policy makers requires a wide-ranging approach to politics, one that begins with efforts to affect who the public elects as policy makers and ends with shaping how the public constructs the decisions of policy makers. The structural and cultural constraints on broad political behavior, which would include a greater use of electioneering and contention, by church-associated CDCs may prevent them from taking full advantage of the access that one would assume collaboration with government grants them to represent well the political interests of low-income black neighborhoods and to see those interests incorporated into political decision making. These CDCs' limited political engagement nonetheless is offset by the continued and varied political engagement of the activist churches that chartered and sustain them.

How should one understand these and other findings of my research in relation to future directions for scholarship on the politics of church-state partnerships? What do my findings mean for assessing the utility of activist African American churches as political and social actors seeking resources and improved conditions for the residents of low-income black neighborhoods in the United States?

Activist African American churches collaborate with government to address the needs of low-income black neighborhoods in cities. Their actions emerge from and continue earlier efforts to resolve racial inequities in cities. We must admire the actions of activist African American churches that work with government, primarily because they are unwilling to disregard any hope that may improve the lives of the urban poor and working class. We must also acknowledge that such churches partner with government, especially city government, as an act of politics. They deliberately participate in formal relationships with public agencies for the explicit purpose of becoming intermediaries to affect public services and public policies in low-income black neighborhoods. Their behavior extends the political engagement tradition of African American churches, especially the long-standing practice of churches and their leaders' brokering the interests of urban blacks and incorporating their preferences in urban policy.

The decision of activist African American churches to collaborate with government is predicated primarily on the political, programmatic, and professional goals their pastors maintain for themselves, their churches, and their communities. Black clergy pursue their goals in a context characterized by a "diminished" position of clergy relative to their onetime "omnicompetent" leadership within black civil society; the endurance of black poverty and the inability of descriptive representation to reduce it; and changes in social welfare policy that invite the participation of religious organizations in "faith-based and community initiatives." Naturally, the occasions and capacity of a given activist African American church to partner with government agencies to provide social welfare in low-income black neighborhoods influence the clergy's choice for their church to embark on such collaboration.

Church-state collaboration in cities, especially in their low-income black neighborhoods, permits activist African American churches, through faith-related agencies, to become agents of government. It transforms them into street-level implementers of public policy, delivering public benefits to citizens on behalf of government agencies. Activist African American churches and their faith-related agencies are interest groups that government elites invite into public-private partnerships. Upon accepting the invitation, a church and its subsidiaries enter policymaking venues to claim, possess, and affect public resources in the name of the black poor. It acquires bureaucratic enfranchisement and material resources for neighborhood development. In the process, churches and their subsidiaries are able to affect to varying degrees how policy is administered in low-income black neighborhoods. Thus, they augment elected officials' articulation of these neighborhoods' political interests.

But activist African American churches and the faith-related agencies that collaborate with government on their behalf face limits. Church-state collaboration may produce only marginal improvements in neighborhood socioeconomic conditions, at least in the short term (two decades or less). Poverty rates may not decline. Employment rates may not rise. Other measures of decline and progress may remain constant. Furthermore, where collaboration is mediated through patron-client relationships, some churches and their agencies may not exercise their full political potential to increase government responsiveness to neighborhood concerns, at least not without jeopardizing patron support. Clergy and others' perceptions about politics and public regulation of groups may further reduce political engagement by these churches and agencies during and beyond the process of church-state collaboration.

None of this is to say that church-state collaboration equals co-optation. What appears to be co-optation might be nothing more than deliberate and strategic choices made by churches: they may restrict the activities of their CDCs, and maybe their own, to ensure their retention of pivotal public resources for neighborhood development. Meanwhile, the churches, or at least their pastors, maintain or increase their electoral engagement and other political activity on behalf of low-income neighborhoods.

Clearly, collaboration with government by activist churches and their faith-related agencies equals political engagement. Even once this is established, there is much more to learn about the utility and process of church-state collaboration and its import to low-income black neighborhoods in the United States. In particular, three subjects emerge from but remain unexamined by my study of church-state collaboration. Two relate to the potential effects of collaboration with government as a means of political engagement by activist African American churches: (1) the political demobilization of residents of low-income black neighborhoods and (2) shifts in partisan support among members of the black polity. The third is whether a larger number of African American churches will be able to increase their collaboration with government on behalf of low-income black neighborhoods.

### POLITICAL DEMOBILIZATION IN LOW-INCOME BLACK NEIGHBORHOODS

Church-state collaboration is a way for African American churches to make a positive difference in low-income neighborhoods. With the assistance of political and financial elites, African American churches can be catalysts for the development and delivery of necessary services and goods in their neighborhood. Generally, such accomplishments result from cooperation, not challenge and conflict, with government. One might argue that the significance, even the elegance, of collaboration with government as political action by activist churches is that it produces results: the delivery of municipal goods and services, without pressure, or with very little pressure. Again, there is no evidence that the absence or reduction in pressure necessarily translates into co-optation. However, activist churches and their agencies may, oddly enough, be participants in the political demobilization of low-income black neighborhoods, "precisely," in the view of Adolph Reed Jr., "by virtue of [their] capacities for delivering benefits" (1999, 185).

Revitalization of low-income black neighborhoods is a process that requires the integration of self-initiative with public and private resources and actions (Ferguson and Dickens 1999; Boston and Ross 1997; Saegert, Thompson, and Warren 2001; von Hoffman 2003). But residents may not perceive the relationship, especially the importance of government participation in the production of the benefits that activist churches and faith-related agencies provide. Government may seem invisible, at least to the eyes of those who are used to seeing government as a direct provider of services and benefits or who often hear the credit given to churches, for instance, for new affordable housing, the opening of charter schools, and the revitalization of commercial strips through church-state partnerships. Residents may assume that the revitalization of their neighborhood is possible without their political participation to push for and sustain public policies directed at neighborhood improvement and the creation of new programs to make it happen.

Additionally, residents of low-income black neighborhoods may believe that the products of activist African American churches and their agencies signal that they compete against and perform better than government in responding to residents' interests, needs, and values. This may further weaken residents' trust in government, which is already low. Also, residents may choose personal inaction, relying on activist churches and their subsidiaries to act as their trustees and provide services to meet their needs. Residents may claim that this is why activist churches exist in the first place, or they may hold to a false hope that such churches alone can transform their neighborhood without greater political participation by residents. Lastly, church-state collaboration may shift residents' attention from the direct pursuit of social justice and racial equity to marginal benefits and gains for poor black neighborhoods, so that they elevate a transactional politics above a transformative politics (Stone 1990; Cohen 2001).

In the end, collaboration with government as a means of political engagement by activist African American churches may equal "community mobilization for political demobilization" or "development for disorganization" (Reed 1999, 188; Stoecker 1997, 101). It is a speculation worthy of scholarship.

### SHIFTS IN PARTISAN SUPPORT

A motivation for politicians to link public agencies to activist African American churches and their agencies through church-state collaboration may be political. From an urban governance perspective, politicians may see church-state partnerships as a means of reforming tough problems in inner cities. If the partnerships they create between public agencies and churches yield reductions in dependence and deviance, the reputations of politicians and their prospects for reelection improve. In the case of white Republican politicians in particular, their successes with church-state partnerships might improve their chances of winning elections and reelections by increasing the number of black votes they receive. Hence, church-state collaboration may transmit meaning from an electoral perspective, too.

The political engagement of and mobilization by activist African American churches have long supported and benefited Democrats in local, state, and national elections. We know, however, that on the national level, Republican calls for "faith-based and community initiatives" and actual funding of activist African American churches by Republican administrations and federal agencies, even if federal funding remains illusory more than substantive, aim to reduce votes for Democrats, especially in competitive elections (Hutchings et al. 2004; Wald 2003; Wuthnow 2004; Formicola, Segers, and Weber 2003; Bositis 2006; Kuo 2006). The calculation is that rhetoric and resources directed at activist African American churches for faith-based initiatives appeal to the political, programmatic, and professional interests of black clergy. They also create opportunities for dialogue and the development of trust between white politicians and black pastors, especially if black clergy perceive Republican politicians to be positive and well-meaning in their policy intentions.

Faith-based initiatives may be accepted despite the GOP's history of race-based appeals to diminish black political incorporation and claims on government responsiveness. And as black clergy become more open to the entreaties of Republicans, perhaps they will become more receptive to policy stances normally associated with Republicans (e.g., school vouchers, work-first for welfare recipients, etc.) that they believe may benefit low-income blacks. Black clergy may shift some of their policy stances and their opinions about Republican candidates, and they may mobilize others to do the same. Thus through public-funded faith-based initiatives, Republican influence may increase and bring about alterations in black political behavior (e.g., vote choice or targets of protest).

There is evidence from New York City and elsewhere that some black clergy, especially those leading activist churches that collaborate with government, are shifting their support from Democrat to Republican candidates, as well as from progressive Democrats to conservative Democrats (Harris 2001 and 2005; Owens 2001). However, social scientists have yet to conduct rigorous analyses of the phenomenon. Moreover, whether public funding of activist African American churches results in shifts in partisan support among these churches' congregants and other members of the black polity has not been determined; it seems unlikely, but the question remains open to empirical investigation. What types of conflicts church-state collaboration may create among black clergy and within the black electorate over support for conservative social welfare policy agendas remains likewise undetermined. A related question is ripe for analysis as well: under what circumstances might public funding of activist churches create policy cleavages between those standing behind pulpits and those seated in pews?

## CONGREGATIONAL CAPACITY FOR NEIGHBORHOOD RESURRECTION

African American churches that provide social services in low-income black neighborhoods practice "programmatic religion"; they express the traditions and theologies of their faith by supporting needy individuals and families (DiIulio 2002). What they provide, however, often does not match the seriousness of problems in low-income black neighborhoods, especially limited educational attainment, high unemployment, frequent exposure to violence, and high incidences of addictive diseases (Wilson 1987 and 1996).

Maybe some of the problems in low-income black neighborhoods endure because the churches do not deliver a comprehensive set of programs to the needy; few churches in poor black neighborhoods attempt to offer services that require high levels of expertise, administration, and funding, such as elementary and secondary education, workforce development, and affordable-housing production (Owens and Smith 2005). Moreover, the social services they provide may not directly increase self-sufficiency among the residents. If this is true, such churches may help people, in the words of social capital theorist Xavier de Souza Briggs, "get by" but not "get ahead" (1998, 178).

It may be instead that activist churches lack *programmatic capacity*, the ability or interest to design, implement, and, more importantly, integrate services across a spectrum of areas to maximize fulfillment of organizational goals and constituent objectives (Glickman and Servon 1998). Maybe activist churches are unable to approach their neighbors' more fundamental problems with a high degree of complexity and comprehensiveness. Or activist churches may lack an interest in expanding their ability to comprehensively address the problems of low-income neighborhoods. After all, congregations, even African American ones, are primarily religious institutions, not social service agencies (Jeavons 2003; Chaves 2004; Cnaan 2002; McRoberts 2004).

Empirically, we do not know if the scale of social services that activist African American churches in low-income black neighborhoods provide and the programmatic areas they cover are driven by their theological bent and practical limitations as institutions of religious worship and education. Nor do we know whether such churches prefer to keep their number of services and programmatic coverage small. Maybe keeping them narrow permits a church to target scarce resources, provide short-term emergency services without worrying about sustainability, allow intense but brief volunteer experiences with those perceived as neediest (i.e., children and the destitute), or prevent duplication of services in its neighborhood.

We need to comprehend better the capacity of activist African American churches in low-income black neighborhoods in relation to their future participation in church-state partnerships, whether for a fee or free. At a minimum, we need to determine whether the low programmatic capacity among activist African American churches is by intent (i.e., churches are disinterested in broader engagement) or default (i.e., churches lack the financial capacity). These are appropriate issues for future social science scholarship, especially if it seeks to inform the policymakers' expectations regarding the potential to increase and expand church-state partnerships in cities.

## THE CONTINUED UTILITY OF ACTIVIST AFRICAN AMERICAN CHURCHES: A CLOSING THOUGHT

Two assets that activist churches generally can bring to politics are a sense of justice and morality, which are bifocals for viewing and critiquing the actions of political elites and society at large (Wood 2002; Wald 2003; Olson 2000; C. Smith 2996). Activist African American churches, in particular, have the potential to call and mobilize for the enactment of more just government policies toward the residents of low-income black neighborhoods, not just to implement government policies directed at them (R. D. Smith 2004; Smith and Harris 2005; Calhoun-Brown 2003b). This is an important point for their pastors and the laity to remember, for poor black neighborhoods need socio-economic transformation, not merely transactions to deliver social services (Cohen 2001; Boston and Ross 1997; McDougall 1993; Thompson 2006). By itself, collaboration with government is insufficient to fully transform their condition.

Activist African American churches, therefore, need to consider supplemental means of articulating and representing the interests of low-income blacks in policy-making venues and processes. They especially need to carry out political practices that will lay "the groundwork necessary for collective mobilization of black people to pressure the government to support an agenda for black community reconstruction" (P. Smith 1999, 265). It requires activist churches to demonstrate "a willingness to experiment with new approaches to organization that could fundamentally alter the relationship of the black community to established power structures" (Green and Wilson 1992, 59).

At a minimum, more African American churches could deliberately attempt to become policy advocates and challengers, rather than just policy implementers (R. D. Smith 2004; McDougall 1993; Orr 2000). Unless African American churches act more politically, especially in alliance with other institutions, they will have only limited success at incorporating the interests of low-income neighborhoods and their residents in government and gaining increased policy responsiveness to them. That would only perpetuate current racial inequalities in U.S. cities.

Between 1997 and 2001 I studied church-state collaboration in New York City. My emphasis was on activist African American churches working with the city government in four black neighborhoods: Bedford-Stuyvesant (Brooklyn), Harlem (Manhattan), Morrisania (the Bronx), and South Jamaica (Queens). Arguably, African American churches in New York City had collaborated with government longer than most of their counterparts in other cities. Moreover, they carried out this collaboration through many of the nation's oldest, largest, and most respected church-associated community development organizations; most of these predated the appearance of similar organizations in other cities. Hence New York City offered strong evidence that activist African American churches perceived church-state collaboration as desirable and that church-state partnerships existed prior to federal social welfare policies under the rubric of "faith-based and community initiatives."

Furthermore, the political conditions in New York City mirrored those of other cities at the end of the twentieth century. The number of black elected representatives had increased, but local government responsiveness to black interests and values, especially those of the black poor, remained weak. Despite increasing descriptive representation of blacks in city government since the late 1980s, the presence of black elected and appointed officials by itself had little effect on the overall allocation of public resources and services in low-income black neighborhoods. Yet at least since the 1970s, the municipal government had regularly partnered with neighborhood-based community development organizations to implement public programs and deliver social services, and this was routine or becoming routine elsewhere across the country during the time of my research.

My acquisition of data on church-state collaboration in New York City involved standard social science approaches. In particular, I employed surveys, elite interviews, archival research, and observation. What follows is a description of the primary and supplemental sources of data that contributed to my comprehension and permitted qualitative and quantitative analyses of church-state collaboration as a political phenomenon intended to transform negative conditions in poor black neighborhoods in the United States.

## ACTIVIST AFRICAN AMERICAN CHURCHES

In *The Struggle for Black Empowerment in New York City* (1992), Charles Green and Basil Wilson identified nineteen activist churches. The list included only churches that used their material and cultural resources as religious institutions to foster political contexts within their congregation to affect political attitudes and behaviors. Moreover, political awareness and activity among leaders and members were central to their congregational identity. In short, the list contained the names of churches most significant to black political mobilization and participation in New York City.

From the list created by Green and Wilson, I contacted a purposive sample of thirteen churches. My sample included only African American churches associated with historically black religious denominations. I mailed letters to this sample, requesting the participation of their senior pastor in interviews and their completion of a survey regarding their church. I explained that I would query pastors about the politics of neighborhood development in New York City. Given my study's potential to produce social harms locally for informants, I also guaranteed pastors anonymity in my use of data from their interviews. In reporting my findings I would not directly attribute any quotes I obtained from them during their interviews with me.

Along with my letters of introduction to the churches, I provided their pastors with letters of endorsement for my research project. Wheeler Winstead, then the director of Faith-Based Programs for the now-defunct National Congress for Community Economic Development, was one of my endorsers. John DiIulio Jr., who at the time led a project for the Brookings Institution to identify and promote church-state partnerships and eventually became the first director of the White House Office of Faith-Based and Community Initiatives, was the other endorser.

Ten of the thirteen senior pastors agreed to participate in my study. They, along with six assistant pastors, from the following churches, allowed me to interview them face to face at least once in their office: Abyssinian Baptist Church, Allen African Methodist Episcopal Church, Bethany Baptist Church, Bethesda Missionary Baptist Church, Bridge Street African Wesleyan Methodist Episcopal Church, Canaan Baptist Church of Christ, Concord Baptist Church of Christ, Ebenezer Missionary Baptist Church, Memorial Baptist Church, and Saint Paul Community Baptist Church.[1] The duration of individual interviews were from thirty-five minutes to ninety minutes. They happened in church offices, cars, and restaurants, as well as during walks along the streets of the neighborhoods that hosted these churches. All of the senior pastors, besides allowing me to interview them, completed a questionnaire about their church. Their information included date of incorporation, size, socioeconomic composition, social welfare services, and political activities of their churches.

My interviews and surveys, which I administered in 1999 and 2000, revealed that my sample of churches varied little on the dimension of collaboration with government. Eight of the churches participated directly in government programs to deliver services, for which they or their nonprofit affiliate received public funding and other government resources. Two churches did not collaborate with government in any way. Recognizing the value of including such churches as a control group, I sought to interview a larger number of pastors from churches that did not collaborate with government. Although I derived a snowball sample of such churches, my repeated efforts to recruit their pastors were unsuccessful. In the end, I was unable to add to my sample other activist churches that avoided collaboration with government altogether. The pastors I did interview, whether their churches collaborated with government or not, offered explanations for why their peers' churches might not partner with government. Although it would be better to have views directly from more pastors whose churches did not partner with government, the perspectives of other pastors are useful and enlightening. I also think they are credible and legitimate sources of information, given the frequent interactions and dialogues among black clergy in New York City.

Nonetheless, in addition to the pastors leading the ten churches in my purposive sample, in 1999 and 2000 I surveyed by telephone a random sample of clergy from twenty activist African American churches known to be politically active and that, in alliance with other African American churches but also with other Christian and Muslim congregations, collaborated with government to improve conditions in the neighborhoods of Morrisania, Bedford-Stuyvesant, Harlem, and South Jamaica through the operation of church-associated CDCs.

My interviews with this random sample allowed me to understand church-state collaboration from the perspective of pastors leading activist churches that indirectly collaborate with government via their community development alliances. My interviews revealed that such churches mainly saw church-state collaboration as a way for resources to flow into their neighborhood, for positive changes (e.g., new affordable housing) to occur, and for "God to get the glory." They also saw collaboration as a means of manifesting their faith, and some perceived the process as a catalyst for becoming more politically engaged. My interviews also shed light on why other churches in their neighborhoods did not collaborate with government.

Ideally, I would have interviewed pastors who led churches that collaborate with government (directly or indirectly) and had ceased engaging in other modes of political action. This type of church, however, is nonexistent in New York City. African American churches that collaborate with government do not cease to be politically active. Historically, as Charles Hamilton reminds us, blacks and the institutions they control participate "where, when, and how they think it matters," with new and varied forms of action to supplement traditional forms of political engagement (1982, xix). Activist African American churches that collaborate with government thus may engage in fewer types of activities, fewer protest and electoral activities in particular, because their clergy have a sense of how new modes of political engagement such as collaboration with government may assist them in achieving the political, programmatic, and professional goals they have for themselves, their church, and their community.

## CHURCH-ASSOCIATED COMMUNITY DEVELOPMENT CORPORATIONS

To fully comprehend and assess the process of church-state collaboration, I studied a set of faith-related agencies that the activist churches in my purposive and random samples chartered to partner and sustain collaboration with government. In particular, I studied their community development corporations (CDCs). At the time of my research, the universe of such CDCs in New York City was undetermined. I developed a sampling frame by identifying African American church–associated CDCs that appeared on mailing lists or membership directories of community development organizations maintained by the New York City Department of Housing and Urban Development, the New York City Housing Partnership, the Alliance for Neighborhood and Housing Development, the Christian Community Development Association, and the National Congress for Community Economic Development. To be included in my study, a church-associated CDC needed to appear on at least two of these lists or directories. Additionally, I asked informants from the congregation-based alliances and the pastors in my purposive sample of ten churches to identify African American churches that chartered their own CDC or allied with other churches to charter a CDC in and beyond their neighborhood.

In the end I identified nine African American church–associated CDCs. Five of them are "independent": they are associated with a particular church. All five were associated with churches in my purposive sample of activist African American churches: Abyssinian Development Corporation, Allen Neighborhood Preservation and Development Corporation, Bridge Street Development Corporation, Canaan Housing Development Corporation, and Concord Community Development Corporation. The remaining four were "alliance-based" church-associated CDCs formed by four of the aforementioned alliances of religious congregations: Association of Brooklyn Clergy for Community Development, Bronx Shepherds Restoration Corporation, Harlem Congregations for Community Improvement, and Southeast Queens Clergy for Community Empowerment, all of which are made up primarily of African American congregations.[2] Combined, the four alliances represented approximately 250 congregations from across the city, including two churches in my purposive sample that lacked independent CDCs: Memorial Baptist Church and Bethesda Missionary Baptist Church.

My sample of African American church–associated CDCs in New York City included some of the oldest and largest of such organizations in the nation (Frederick 2001; Tucker-Worgs 2002; Clemetson and Coates 1992). I interviewed and surveyed (face to face and by telephone) the executive directors of all nine African American church–associated CDCs. My interviews, which occurred in 1999 and 2000 at the headquarters of the CDCs, ranged from sixty to ninety minutes, followed by the completion of a brief survey about the organization and sponsor church(es). I continued to guarantee anonymity to informants. The executive directors permitted me to interview at least one other informant from their organization (i.e., professional staff or members of the board of directors). Subsequently, I interviewed eight other principal staff members and five board members from the church-associated CDCs. I also interviewed fifteen representatives of religious organizations and financial institutions that help the programs of the church-associated CDCs in my sample, including leaders of ecumenical associations, foundation officers, and bank executives.

## BLACK ELECTED OFFICIALS

A complete understanding of collaboration with government by activist African American churches requires attention to the perceptions and behaviors of black politicians. This is because racial residential patterns ensure that the programs of churches that collaborate with government in New York City benefit majority-black electoral districts. To discern the attitudes of black politicians toward church-state collaboration and their opinions about black political incorporation and policy responsiveness, I surveyed by mail a probability sample of twenty-six black elected officials in New York City in 1999. I drew my sample from the universe of thirty-five black elected officials who represented majority-black districts in the New York City Council and New York State Legislature, as well as served as borough presidents. I faxed two reminders and additional copies of the survey to my sample. My methods yielded a response rate of 83 percent.

## SUPPLEMENTAL SOURCES

I obtained supplemental data from (1) interviews of six high-ranking officials in the New York City Department of Housing Preservation who served in the mayoral administrations of Edward Koch, David Dinkins, and Rudolph Giuliani; (2) interviews of ten neighborhood-based community activists, including the leaders of two policy advocacy coalitions that counted African American church–associated CDCs among their members as of 1999; (3) unpublished and published affordable housing development data from the New York City Department of Housing Preservation and Development, New York City Housing Partnership, and New York City Independent Budget Office; (4) unstructured interviews with directors of secular CDCs in New York City and directors of church-associated and secular CDCs in Los Angeles, Atlanta, Detroit, Newark, Philadelphia, Washington, DC, Baltimore, Kansas City, Chicago, and Denver; and (5) an array of public opinion surveys archived by the Inter-university Consortium for Political and Social Research, the Roper Center for Public Opinion Research, and the Association of Religious Data Archives.

# NOTES

## INTRODUCTION

1. Affiliations of African American churches in Gary and Indianapolis (Indiana), Tulsa (Oklahoma), and Memphis (Tennessee) have adopted the agendas and strategies of the Boston Ten Point Coalition. The collective effort of the affiliates, known collectively as the National Ten Point Leadership Foundation, "seeks to build partnerships with community-based, governmental, and private sector institutions which are also committed to the revitalization of the families and communities in which youth must be raised." However, the Boston Ten Point Coalition is now a shell of what it once was, mainly due to conflicts among its members over the control of funding and agenda setting, as well as personal threats and bitterness over publicity (Radin 2006). This suggests that alliances of churches may face a distinct set of difficulties when they partner with government.

2. I use *activist* throughout this book to designate a certain type of church as well as clergyperson. Broadly, I identify "activist" churches as those whose activities correspond to what sociologist Omar McRoberts describes as the "very extroverted forms of religious presence—forms that somehow benefit not only congregation members but people who do not belong to the church" (2003, 100). However, I acknowledge that a dichotomous categorization of churches—activist and nonactivist—is often inadequate, for there are multiple dimensions and continua of activism. Therefore, I adopt the "inward-outward continuum" of James Davidson and Jerome Koch, a conceptual lens that allows us to see that churches "create at least some activities oriented toward the well-being of their members and some policies and programs oriented toward the well-being of society and others who are not members" (1998, 294). "Activist" churches and clergy in my view are those that behave in ways that (1) benefit a mix, albeit an unequal one, of congregants and noncongregants, emphasizing benefits to the latter over the former, and (2) advance a mix of societal and individual change,

one that privileges the former over the latter. Furthermore, I agree with others, especially David Roozen, William McKinney, and Jackson Carroll, that "for the activist [clergy and congregant] achievement of a more just and humane society is a high priority, and the posture toward the existing social and economic order tends to be rather critical" (1998, 35). By definition, all churches that partner with government to address problems in poor neighborhoods are activist churches.

3. African American churches are not the only minority congregations participating in these initiatives. Latino congregations, particularly those affiliated with Pentecostal Christian traditions, partner with government, often through nonprofit organizations chartered by the churches (DeParle 2005; Cnaan 2002).

4. However, many African American churches that partner with government, perhaps the majority of them, do it free or for only nominal compensation (Lincoln and Mamiya 1990). This is a point the extant literature on the federal "faith-based initiative" fails to consider (e.g., Bositis 2006; Kuo 2006).

5. Those churches that receive compensation get grants and contracts to cover their expenses, to earn additional revenue, and to fund new church-based or church-backed social welfare initiatives.

6. "Charitable choice" refers to the collection of federal and state laws, regulations, and rules that encourage government agencies (federal, state, and local) to open fully their competitions for contracts and grants to provide social services and perhaps make awards to a greater proportion of faith-based organizations over secular groups. It was first enacted as part of the Personal Responsibility and Work Opportunity Reconciliation Act of 1996.

7. They also did it as part of the city government's Front Porch Alliance, which uses competitive grants derived from federal Community Development Block Grants to induce congregations, mainly African American churches, to address neighborhood problems in concert with municipal agencies. The problems include blight, drug dealing, low student achievement, and emergency food assistance (Goldsmith 2000).

8. However, we must, and I do, keep in mind a point theologian Samuel K. Roberts makes: "A presumption that is made all too easily, in many of these instances, is that government and faith-based groups share the same perspectives on social issues and on social strategies. Clearly, there are points of convergence, as both faith-based groups and government strive for the common good, but the significant differences in perspectives must always be remembered" (2003, 289). We should not assume that church-state partnerships are necessarily devoid of conflict.

9. In this respect it reflects the larger body of religion and politics research: over-attentiveness to electoral politics and the place of congregations in it is characteristic of the subfield (Wald 2003).

10. Investigations of black protests against municipal police departments during the 1990s, for instance, inadequately explore the contributions made by African American churches to the organization and implementation of marches, pickets, and

boycotts. Research examining the most contentious form of protest, riots, also fails to explore well the place and participation of activist churches in black efforts to channel the anger and energy of riots into righteous rebellion (see, e.g., Jennings 1992; Joyce 2003).

11. For example, Margit Mayer points out that "the number and variety of institutions and projects 'servicing' the marginalized has exploded, and many of them function *within* municipal programs that harness the reform energy of community-based organizations" (1998, 71). Moreover, municipal agencies are increasingly delegating authority and accountability for the success of policies and programs, especially in the domain of community development, to neighborhood-based organizations serving marginalized communities (e.g., community development corporations).

12. The strongest manifestation of co-optation is the abandonment of the opposition's goals and values in exchange for recognition, inclusion, and participation in governmental processes (Selznick 1949; Gamson 1968 and 1990; Gaventa 1980).

13. This makes sense in the U.S. context given that much of government's work is done by complex arrangements (formal and informal) among government agencies, nonprofit organizations, and private businesses (Kettl 1993; Donahue and Nye 2002; Salamon 1995; S. Smith and Lipsky 1993).

14. Influenced by the work of James March and Johan Olsen (1995), I assume that "effective governance" consists of three qualities: efficiency (it makes most or all members of a community better off and minimizes the losses suffered by any particular group), equity (it improves the public welfare and minimizes side-payments to private interests), and capacity (it increases a community's ability to attain collective goals and solve collective problems).

15. Government is rarely ambivalent about collaborating with nongovernmental organizations, especially politicized civic groups. It sees collaboration as a vehicle for "increasing predictability in the timing, process, and content of citizen participation—a narrowing of its scope and impact. As participation [becomes] more prevalent, it also [becomes] more limited" (Howard, Lipsky, and Marshall 1994, 154). Like protest and electoral action, collaboration is a form of political participation that government can regulate. Consequently, government grants spaces for collaboration with politicized civic groups in response to grassroots demands for participation in and influence over public programs that benefit their communities. In doing so, government can bound group political behavior.

16. In relation to religious groups and government, Kenneth Wald refers to this process as "infiltration" (2003, 126–28). Infiltration involves churches' enabling members to hold positions of public authority that influence policymaking and implementation. A common mode of infiltration is the election and appointment to government office (e.g., city council, municipal court, or mayoralty) of individuals representing a religious group to government office. However, as I will argue, collaboration with government is another form of infiltration.

17. At the core of these shifts is the granting of monetary awards and contracting

out of services delivery, whereby governments rely on "cheque-book government" instead of direct action through public organizations (Hood 1983). State and municipal governments use discretionary grants and competitive bids and proposals to foster competition, choice, and efficiency in the delivery of social services, along with a higher degree of flexibility and responsiveness than government can normally offer. There are a host of rational reasons that governments give grants and contracts for the private exercise of public functions (Savas 2000). Governments might not, will not, or cannot perform certain functions. Perhaps they have decided to provide services to a broad clientele but would rather leave the provision of specialized services to a small clientele of private agencies. Governments may be interested in fostering choice or just extending services; increasing flexibility regarding implementation while reducing service costs; overcoming bureaucratic and political constraints while advancing ideological preference; or gaining the support of the private sector.

18. The reliance on nongovernmental organizations "redefines the scope of government but does not eliminate its role altogether, because the [government] externalizes only selected functions to nongovernmental entities" (Kodras 1997, 82; Nathan 1996). "Hence," as Jan Kooiman writes, "it is generally more appropriate to speak of *shifting* roles of government than *shrinking* roles of government" (2000, 139).

19. There is also more collaboration between nongovernmental organizations and local governments than between nongovernmental organizations and state governments, because the local level is more empowering (S. Smith 2000). Nongovernmental organizations have a better chance of affecting municipal policymakers through electioneering, protest, and advocacy than they do influencing state policymakers. Plus, nongovernmental organizations have an easier time mobilizing local constituencies for local policy change than they would for statewide policy change.

20. Studying church-state collaboration also illuminates the functions of congregations in contemporary society and how they practice certain acts of alms. At a minimum, examining the partnerships between African American churches and government agencies permits social scientists to expand the taxonomies of "faith-based poverty relief" (Bartkowski and Regis 2003), to develop further the causal explanations of such relief and the lack thereof (McRoberts 2003; Chaves and Tsitsos 2001), and to better describe and clarify the processes by which relief operates and produces positive effects (Ammerman 2005). Additionally, studies of church-state collaboration enlighten our understanding of the social welfare potential of government initiatives to award public funds to faith-based organizations (Dionne and Chen 2001; Monsma 2004; Farnsley 2003), as well as identify for policymakers the limited capacities of faith-based organizations (congregations and otherwise) to collaborate with government, stemming from theological, racial, class, and organizational barriers (Chaves 1999 and 2004; Chaves and Tsitsos 2001; Farnsley 2001 and 2003; McRoberts 2003; Bartkowski and Regis 2003; Monsma 2004; Owens 2004b and 2006).

21. Governing coalitions differ from electoral coalitions. The latter are those interests that aid in the victories of electoral candidates; the former are composed of

those interests (commercial and civic) that assist mayors and other elected officials in addressing the problems of cities. Governing coalitions, then, are the informal associations of public institutions and private interests that blend their capacities to govern cities, where to "govern" involves making and executing decisions that affect individual and collective problems (Stone 1989).

22. Although the incorporation literature tends to focus on "official" or elected and appointed government representatives in the policymaking process (Browning, Marshall, and Tabb 1984), it also considers the place of "unofficial" representatives of minority interests and values such as community activists, clergy, and social entrepreneurs to influence the decisions and outcomes of urban governments and the process of governance (Stone 1989; Orr 1999; Henig et al. 1999).

CHAPTER ONE

1. This fact would eventually influence the outcomes of Reverend Borders's work as a lobbyist, including his successful advocacy, in conjunction with other members of the ACRC such as Martin Luther King Sr., Benjamin Mays, and John Wesley Dobbs, for the city's hiring of blacks as police officers in 1947 and firefighters in 1962 (Bayor 1996, 174–82).

2. Wheat Street was not alone. Other churches sought partnerships with government to tackle poverty in cities (Schaller 1967; Fish 1973). Wheat Street was, however, among those that succeeded, forming a vanguard of nonprofit organizations collaborating with government in the post–World War II period. Few Protestant churches in the United States, and especially few African American churches, participated in the programs of the nascent War on Poverty. Nevertheless, by the middle of the 1960s, churches participating in the FHA Section 236 program had developed, according to one estimate, approximately twenty thousand units of affordable housing for the elderly (Schaller 1967, 46). From 1959 to 1966, more than one-half of the nonprofit organizations participating in HUD's Section 202 program were affiliated with congregations of various racial compositions and denominations (Schaller 1967, 47).

3. It was not the first time Wheat Street Baptist Church chartered a subsidiary to advance the aims of the church and its surrounding community. In 1956 it created a church-based credit union, one of the first among African American churches, to advance thrift and economic development in black Atlanta (English 1967).

4. Research suggests that between 55 and 71 percent of African American churches operate, participate in, or support some form of social services in their community (Chaves 1998; Billingsley 1999; Owens and Smith 2005; Lincoln and Mamiya 1990; Tsitsos 2003).

5. This perspective places them at odds with most of their white peers, who see in poverty a moral failure and personal irresponsibility (Day 2002; Olson 2000; Emerson and Smith 2000).

6. Moreover, not all African American churches that are politically active aid in

reforming the conditions of black communities. The history of city politics is full of examples of black clergy who have placed the interests of their church ahead of the interests of poor blacks (Gosnell 1935; Wilson 1960; Katznelson 1973; Keiser 1997; Harris 2005). When the Reverend Martin Luther King Jr. took his call for a poor people's campaign to Chicago, "anti–civil rights black ministers" connected to the Daley machine repelled his march. Conservative black ministers such as Reverend Joseph Jackson of Olivet Baptist Church benefited by defending the interests of the machine and its allies who held the mortgages and controlled code inspections of their buildings (Cohen and Taylor 2000, 359). Opposing the political agenda of the machine, which preserved the status quo of power and responsiveness, could mean the eviction of a congregation from its church or the nailing shut of church doors for code violations.

7. Of course, inaction can be considered a form of action. In the words of the Reverend Arthur Brazier, "at a fundamental level every church is participating all the time in the oppressive status quo, either to change it or to uphold it or some mixture of the two" (1969, 133).

8. One explanation for the perceived lack of political fervor among African American churches since the civil rights movement, despite dramatic increases in the number of blacks in political offices, focuses on the commitment of African American churches to the struggle of blacks. Following the 1960s, according to religious studies scholar Anthony Pinn, "the vast majority of the nation's black churches lost their commitment to social activism" (2002, 15). That line of argument claims that politicized African American churches traded their progressivism and concern for the poor for conservatism and "individual pietism that promised heaven but did little to change the existential situation of black Americans" (Pinn 2002, 18–19). Moreover, there is evidence that many African American churches preach a privatistic gospel of materialism over a collective gospel of social change. Among such churches "the message has moved," according to Fredrick C. Harris, "from community empowerment to individual prosperity" (quoted in Hadnot 2004). Not discounting the role of "commitment" and "prosperity gospel," another explanation of the decline in activism among African American churches is that churches today lack the ability to be activists given the imperatives of institutional change. "The role that African American churches play in politics," Allison Calhoun-Brown argues, "has diminished since the 1960s not because churches are unwilling to participate or preaching prosperity but because declines in important political resources over the last thirty years have diminished their capacity" (2003b, 16). She claims that diminishment of three key resources influences the contemporary politics of African American churches: membership, clergy leadership and moral authority in black communities, and attachment to and reliance on a theology of black liberation. Unfortunately, these explanations remain speculative, primarily due to inadequate data for empirical testing and theoretical confirmation.

9. I use the material-cultural dichotomy, a perspective that is more common in the

sociology of religion literature (Pattillo-McCoy 1998; Wood 1994a and 1994b) than in the political science scholarship (Harris 1999), of which the latter identifies "macro" (i.e., material) and "micro" (symbolic) resources. The macro-micro distinction is useful but does not immediately convey a sense of the types of resources churches possess.

10. The use of material and cultural resources by churches is well documented in the research on social movements, community organizing, and urban politics (see, e.g., Morris 1984; McDougall 1993; Wood 2002; Warren 2001; Pattillo-McCoy 1998).

11. Black public opinion supports African American churches' employing their resources toward political ends, as well as translating community concerns into action through politics. Sixty-eight percent of blacks believe African American churches should be involved in politics (Brown, Dawson, and Jackson 1994). Moreover, 65 percent of blacks agree that churches should publicly express their views on social and political questions (Pew Research Center for the People and the Press 2001b). Support for political engagement by churches is even higher among those in the black pulpit than among the laity: 80 percent of clergy agree that African American churches should engage in politics (Smith 2003a, 299). African American congregations, in fact, have been more likely than other congregations to offer their attenders opportunities to have their political attitudes, preferences, and actions influenced (Beyerlein and Chaves 2003).

12. As a style that began as early as Reconstruction, brokerage spread broadly across the North by southern preachers migrating to the region ahead of or trailing congregants (Montgomery 1993, 156–57). Black preachers who adopted it, whom Charles Hamilton (1972) classifies as *church-based activists*, advocated political diplomacy over conflict, electoral or otherwise. Their means and goals were often conservative, buttressing the racial ordering of residential opportunities and government responsiveness to groups. In seeking to develop and maintain a persona of respectability and trustworthiness in the eyes of whites, clergy of this ilk opposed and disavowed mass participation by blacks.

13. No single type of clergy has been identified with brokerage. This is mainly because there is no single type of black clergy who can be profiled as a political activist (Hamilton 1972).

14. At the national level, the political reasoning behind white politicians' seeking church-state partnerships seems more transparent and is more researched. During the 2000 presidential election, for instance, "Republican elites thought that faith-based [policy rhetoric] might allow them to attract a few more highly religious African American and Hispanic voters; gaining only a few more percentage points [at the polls from] these groups would assure a GOP victory" (Black, Koopman, and Ryden 2004, 12).

15. It is more perceptible in national political rhetoric but is applicable to local politics as well. Before a gathering of religious leaders in New Orleans in 2003, George W. Bush remarked, "Problems that face our society are oftentimes problems that require

something greater than just a government program or a government counselor to solve" (Bush 2003).

16. This is so despite the polity's concerns about which religious groups government should work with in tackling the problems of the poor, especially the afflicted and addicted among them (Pew Research Center for the People and the Press, 2001a; Wuthnow 2004).

17. Faith-related agencies are distinct from congregations. The former are groups with "a formal funding or administrative arrangement with a religious authority or authorities; a historical tie of this kind; a specific commitment to act within the dictates of a particular established faith; or a commitment to work together that stems from a common religion" (S. Smith and Sossin, 2001, 652). Such agencies include nonprofit subsidiaries of individual congregations and faith-based social service coalitions, with the latter sometimes being ecumenical institutions but almost always possessing resources and governance structures distinct from those of congregations, partnering with secular groups and agencies, and pursuing and receiving government funding to operate their programs (Ebaugh, Chafetz, and Pipes 2005).

18. In doing their work, faith-related agencies rely more on paid professionals and less on amateur volunteers than do congregation-based programs, and the former place more laypersons in positions to serve as representatives of churches than the latter (Walker 1994; Ebaugh, Chafetz, and Pipes 2005). Faith-related agencies also tend to rely less on coreligionists to deliver services (Monsma 2004). Thus faith-related agencies work similarly to secular nonprofit social agencies, partnering with government to improve the general welfare of neighborhoods.

19. For example, First African Methodist Episcopal Church (FAME) is the oldest African American church in Los Angeles and one of the few designated by President George H. W. Bush as one of his one thousand Points of Light in 1990 (Billingsley 1999, 151). FAME, which is among the largest churches in America, claiming a congregation of eighteen thousand that once included the first and only black mayor of Los Angeles, has a well-earned reputation for political action, mobilizing thousands from south central Los Angeles on Election Day (Wood 1997). It uses its FAME Renaissance/Assistance Corporation (FAC) to acquire or leverage millions of dollars in public resources from municipal, state, and federal agencies to address the concerns of residents in the neighborhoods torn and burned during the 1992 riots (Clemetson and Coates 1992; Frederick 2001). In fiscal year 2001, FAC received approximately $5 million in government grants (Miranne and Amato-Von Hemert 2001).

20. The bias toward activist churches also exists because of the survey methods chosen by scholars. Generally, gathering data on African American churches involves in-person queries of black clergy at denominational gatherings of ministers and pastors or the use of telephone and mail surveys without generating a random sample of churches from a random sample of blacks (Lincoln and Mamiya 1990; Billingsley 1999; Smith 2003a; McDaniel 2004; Dash and Rasor 2001–2002).

21. Compare these provisional findings to an earlier finding from a survey of black

clergy during the 1980s: only 6 percent of respondents, along with 8 percent of urban respondents, affirmed that their churches participated in government programs that publicly funded the administration of church-based social welfare services such as early childhood development, homeless outreach, and job skills development (Lincoln and Mamiya 1990, 155). Also, compare it to the approximately 3 percent of all congregations in the United States (Chaves 2004, 231). Clearly, there may be racial differences in relation to church-state collaboration. When African American churches attempt to resolve social problems in their community, they are significantly more likely than white churches to collaborate with government and other secular organizations (Chaves and Tsitsos 2001). The reason is that African American churches are more likely than white churches to provide social services in areas favoring church-state collaboration—e.g., community development, public health education, workforce development, and substance abuse counseling. This is true even though African American congregations are no more likely to provide social services than white congregations are (Chaves and Higgins 1992; Tsitsos 2003). By the end of the 1990s, approximately 40 percent of African American churches that partnered with other institutions to address community problems collaborated with government, compared to 34 percent of white mainline Protestant congregations like Presbyterians and 26 percent of conservative Protestant congregations such as Southern Baptists (Ammerman 2002, 145).

22. Research does identify a set of factors that may predict which congregations, *regardless of racial composition and racial-denominational history*, generally will work with government in exchange for public funding (Chaves 1999; Chaves and Tsitsos 2001; McDaniel 2004; Owens 2006). It includes attitudinal predictors (i.e., congregations with liberal theological and political orientations; clergy with low fears of church-state entanglement; clergy with high hopes that faith-based organizations can be more compassionate than government and secular nonprofit agencies in providing services), attributional predictors (i.e., congregations with middle-class attenders, college-educated clergy, large annual revenues, large numbers of congregants), and behavioral predictors (i.e., congregations that provide social welfare services).

23. The findings also reveal that the fears of clergy, generally, regardless of race and holding other factors constant, are more influential than their hopes for predicting whether their congregation will seek public funding to provide social welfare to the poor. Specifically, clergy fears of government entanglement with religion and upsetting church-state separation have negative and significant effects. Additionally, the results show that congregations with a mainline Protestant affiliation, congregations that provide social welfare, and congregations that partner with secular (nongovernmental) organizations to address community problems are most likely to avail themselves of public funding. Clergy age is another significant predictor: a congregation with older clergy is less likely to seek public funding. These data are from the 2002 Faith and the City Survey of Metropolitan Atlanta Clergy (FATC), a telephone survey of a random sample of congregations in the metropolitan area of Atlanta, inclusive

of the twenty counties ringing its central city. The sample size was 400 congregations with an 81 percent response rate. I use the FATC for my analysis rather than the
National Congregations Study data because the former was administered fourteen
months after the creation of the White House Office of Faith-Based and Community
Initiatives and its initial efforts to increase the flow of public funds to congregations
and faith-related agencies, as well as six years after the enactment of welfare reform in
1996. Thus, the FATC data provide responses from a sample of clergy who had had
adequate time to consider the potential positive and negative effects of church-state
partnerships. The weakness of the FATC is that the data are from a sample of clergy
leading congregations in a single metropolitan are, and thus not necessarily representative of the national population of congregations (Owens 2006).

24. Generally, public opinion supports the faith-based initiatives of governments
to collaborate with religious institutions. A majority of the public supports the idea of
governments' looking to churches, in particular, to do more with and on behalf of the
public to address poverty: 75 percent of adults favor the transfer of public money to
congregations to aid the poor, and 44 percent of adults favor public funding of congregations even if the money supports overt religious messages during the delivery of
services (Pew Research Center for the People and the Press 2001a).

25. Data are from the 2001 Religion and Public Life Survey (Pew Research Center
2001b), which administered telephone interviews among a nationwide sample of 2,041
adults (eighteen years of age or older). The survey, conducted between March 5 and
March 18, 2001, by Princeton Survey Research Associates, included an oversample
of 197 African-Americans that was combined with the national sample and weighted
to national parameters. The dataset is publicly available from the American Religion
Data Archive (http://www.theARDA.com).

26. Borrowing from Michael C. Dawson, I employ *ideology*, which is used syn-
onymously here with *ethos*, to mean "a world view readily found in the population,
including sets of ideas and values that cohere, that are used publicly to justify political
stances, and that shape and are shaped by society. Further, political ideology helps
define who are one's friends and enemies, with whom one would form political coalitions, and furthermore, contains a causal narrative of society and the state" (Dawson
2001, 4).

27. Community nationalism sounds conservative to some social scientists, who
perceive it solely as a "call for individual, voluntarist, private, and community-based
approaches to the usual litany of black social problems—poverty, unemployment,
crime, drug abuse, teenage parenthood" (P. Smith 1999, 258; Reed 1999). In their
ears, community nationalism sounds like an appeal to retain the status quo of inequality and to put aside political claims of social justice on behalf of blacks. Preston Smith,
for instance, hears the "call" as black acceptance and parroting of white conservative
rhetoric: "Black people should stop looking to the state for aid and solutions to their
problems. They must instead look within their own communities for the solutions
and, increasingly, for the source of their problems as well" (1999, 257). But as Glen

Loury would argue (along with Harris-Lacewell 2004, 60–67), community nationalism "is not a substitute for government provision but rather an essential complement to it" (Loury 1995, 80–81). Community nationalism, from my perspective, advocates a central role for civil society in the resurrection of black neighborhoods. It is about empowering communities to be agents of their own change, change that is self-determined and community directed through neighborhood institutions. This explains why it is not synonymous with an appeal for massive government activism, at least not large-scale direct government interventions staffed by public sector employees. Yet the ideology does not imply that government has no responsibility or role to play in the redemption of black communities. Thus a call for black community action that encompasses cooperation with government by African American churches is not a retreat from the state.

28. In contrast, self-help is characterized by *independence*. It supports the "politics of parallelism, in which self-help organizations [independent of other organizations] pull themselves together to fill vacuums created by the inability or unwillingness of government to provide or create the essential conditions of social life—housing, employment, education, public safety, civic guidance" (McDougall 1993, 11–12). If, for example, a community needs daycare centers but none exist, a self-help response is for black civil society to use its own resources to open centers. It asserts, as the separatist nationalism of the 1960s proclaimed, "Mr. Charlie, we'd rather do it ourselves" (Carmichael and Hamilton 1967, 182).

29. It results from the American democratic identity of blacks. "African Americans are citizens of the United States and thus affected by government policies, the legal system and social institutions. It makes sense for them to make claims on the state. A self-help strategy in and of itself is not adequate, although the building of internal strength [and institutions] is necessary and sensible" (R. Bush 1999, 50). This perspective is accepted and expressed by blacks on the right and the left, clergy and lay (Woodson 1998; Dawson 2001; Loury 1995; Flake and Williams 1999; R. Smith 1996; Simpson 1998; Harris-Lacewell 2004; Owens 2001). It is particularly appealing now amid the pressing needs of urban black neighborhoods for social and economic reform despite increased rates in black electoral representation since the 1960s. As Dawson (2001) asserts, the ideology resurrects itself in times of heightened governmental neglect of black values, wants, and needs. The late 1960s are illustrative. Blacks sought community control in response to a War on Poverty that seemed to offer nothing more than what Alan Altshuler described as "a fillip to ghetto aspirations and a mechanism through which demands might be more effectively articulated," not necessarily addressed (1970, 111). Moreover, the call for community control arose at a time when policymakers disregarded the values of black neighborhoods in the formulation of public policies and overlooked their interests in the administration of public programs, despite a federal mandate of "maximum feasible participation" in key national programs with local effect. So blacks narrowed their political focus to their immediate communities and advocated community nationalism in the form of

"community control." Although community control corresponded to Black Power, there was a distinction. "Where Black Power calls generally for Blacks to take back power over their own lives, community control calls more specifically for Blacks to take back control over institutions in their own (segregated) neighborhoods, such as schools, banks, political offices, and stores. We might think of community control as a place-specific application of the Black Power frame" (Kim 2000, 61). In advocating community control in the 1960s, blacks advocated for complete participation in public decisions and actions that affected their lives and the conditions of their neighborhoods, thus supporting the two faces of community control—community control as a normative democratic practice and community control as an institution for minority group advancement (Carmichael and Hamilton 1967; Hamilton 1973; Fainstein and Fainstein 1976).

30. "Linked fate" is the notion that a member of a social or racial group perceives their destiny or life chances to be connected to the fate of their group as a whole in such a way that self-interests are viewed through group-interests (Dawson 1994, 76).

31. Replicating previous factor and regression analyses of community nationalism (Brown and Shaw 2002; Davis and Brown 2002), support for community nationalism—the dependent variable—is a single factor comprising beliefs that tap core political and economic principles of community nationalism: blacks should have control over the government in mostly black communities; blacks should have control over the economy in mostly black communities; blacks should rely on themselves and not others; and black people should shop in black-owned stores whenever possible. The independent variables measure *ideology* (very conservative = 0, very liberal = 1); *family income* (pretax amount); *education* (number of years); *membership in a black organization* (no = 0, yes = 1); *black linked fate* (what happens to blacks generally affects you [either] not at all = 0 [or] yes, a lot = 1); *age* (number of years); *gender* (male = 0, female = 1); *region* (outside the South = 0, South = 1); *community-oriented religiosity* (attend a church that provides community outreach programs: no = 0, yes = 1); *positive attitude toward church involvement in politics* (African American churches should be involved in political matters: strongly disagree = 0, strongly agree = 1); and *perceived race of the interviewer* (white = 0, black = 1). The perceived race of the interviewer is included in the model as a control variable because extant research finds that the perception that an interviewer is white influences levels of support for Black Nationalism and controversial racial attitudes (Brown and Shaw 2002; Gurin, Hatchett, and Jackson 1989; Davis 1997). My results confirm and extend the findings of Brown and Shaw 2002, without discounting rival model specifications and findings (Davis and Brown 2002). I thank Robert Brown and Todd Shaw for sharing their coding scheme and assisting me in reconstructing their community nationalism index for my analysis.

32. Such an approach, which serves as a first principle, overlaps with the negation of racial separatism that is central to community nationalism. It also stands in opposition to the separatism of Black Christian Nationalism, whose practitioners, in the

words of its principal philosopher and agent, the Reverend Albert Cleage, are "unashamedly separatists" (1972).

33. In many respects black support for community nationalism accords with the Catholic principle of "subsidiarity," which instructs the church and society to define the relationship of the state to other sectors of society, along with establishing how the state should assist the other sectors to fulfill their missions (Hehir 2000).

CHAPTER TWO

1. There are caveats to relying on clergy-centered models of church agency in terms of decision making and behavior by churches. Focusing on clergy raises concerns about the location of power and influence within congregations, as well as assumes that clergy goals necessarily overlap with the goals of their congregation, which may or may not be true (Ammerman 2002; Chaves 2004; Bedford 2004; Woolever and Bruce 2002; Harris-Lacewell 2004; Owens 2006). Still, regarding whether to engage in certain practices as a congregation, research suggests that congregations look to their clergy for guidance and decisions, mainly because they have "pragmatic authority," deep knowledge of their congregation's resources, and respect based on their theological expertise (Ammerman 2001, 51–54; also Cnaan 2002; McRoberts 2003).

2. "Own" here includes, as the research on both group consciousness and linked fate suggests, the preferences and values of individuals as individuals and individuals qua members of social groups (Shingles 1981; Conover 1984; Dawson 1994; Tate 1993).

3. They may also be the motives that influence a church's broader decision to provide social welfare or serve as a "community-outreach" church in its neighborhood, whether through congregation-based "social welfare ministries," a faith-related agency associated with the church, or both (Chaves 2004; Ammerman 2001; Cnaan 2002; McRoberts 2003; Harris 1987).

4. Because I recognize the limits to rationality, my assumption about clergy behavior includes the possibility that they may "satisfice" and limit themselves to accomplishing what they perceive as adequate or "good enough," making decisions that cohere with their objectives, given their limitations of choice (Simon 1956; Eckstein 1991).

5. They may also have played a role in advancing the attitude, whether it is valid or not, of a black pulpit that is socially irrelevant in relation to secular organizations. At present, clergy's diminished reputation, as well as the split between and influence among church-associated and non–church-associated black elites, remains more than perceptual, especially from the perspective of civil rights activists, including those ordained to preach the gospel. For instance, when George W. Bush met with black clergy in Austin, Texas, in 2000 to discuss the plans of his administration regarding social welfare policy, the Reverend Jesse Jackson Sr. of Rainbow/PUSH observed derisively, "Meeting with political leaders is one thing and meeting with ministers is

another" (quoted in Milbank and Harris 2000; see also Adams 2000). His comment suggests that under certain circumstances the latter are less influential and legitimate than the former.

6. A majority of blacks who attend church report not hearing from their clergy about inequality, and a large minority have heard nothing about social welfare policy in an era of government retrenchment. Data from the 2000 Religion and Politics Survey reveals that 53 percent of black church attenders have not heard a sermon concerning the widening gap between rich and poor, and 48 percent of black church-goers have not heard a sermon on government policies toward the poor (Wuthnow 2000). The data are from a telephone survey of a probability sample of adults in the continental United States, yielding 5,603 responses, including 507 from self-reported black respondents. The specific question, asked of those respondents who attended church at least a few times a year and identify themselves as members of churches, was as follows: "During the last year, have you heard a sermon, lecture, or group discussion in your congregation that dealt with any of the following?" The choices, which were not mutually exclusive, included "the widening gap between rich people and poor people" and "the government's policies towards the poor." The dataset is publicly available from the Association of Religious Data Archives (www.theARDA.com).

7. The migration also yielded deleterious effects on those left behind, including family dissolution and lack of family formation, social alienation, crime, fear, and decreased rates of civic and political engagement (W. J. Wilson 1987; Venkatesh 2002; Anderson 1990; Cohen and Dawson 1993).

8. "It is possible," in fact, as Isaac Laudarji and Lowell Livezey speculate, "that most of the very poor do not go to church in [their neighborhood] and may not attend any church anywhere" (2000, 92; see also Nelsen and Kanagy 1993). Seeking to confirm and understand the challenge of the social disconnect between churches and the poor at the start of the new millennium, the Faith Communities and Urban Families Project (FCUFP) examined the institutional relationships between churches and residents in seven low-income neighborhoods across four cities. Specifically, it gathered quantitative and qualitative data from a random sample of congregations located in seven public housing neighborhoods in Camden, Denver, Hartford, and Indianapolis. It also surveyed 1,206 public housing residents in the seven neighborhoods. The study found that most (71 percent) of public housing residents were not church members, most residents (67 percent) had never "been contacted by any churches and asked to participate in their activities," and a majority (61 percent) of those who attended church did not have a "particular place where [they] usually attended services" (R. D. Smith 2003b, 40). This was the case despite the presence of churches in each of these neighborhoods (Owens and Smith 2005; R. D. Smith 2001 and 2003b). Consistent with these data, 90 percent of the clergy leading churches in the seven neighborhoods reported that the majority of their followers resided outside the neighborhood where their church stood, a phenomenon common in low-income U.S. neighborhoods, especially public housing neighborhoods (Owens and Smith

2005; Laudarji and Livezey 2000). Nevertheless, a majority (72 percent) of the clergy surveyed claimed that their congregation provided at least one social welfare program, and a majority (69) claimed that the programs served the broader community, not just church members (Owens and Smith 2005). How do we square the findings? It demonstrates a truth articulated by Laudarji and Livezey: "Unfortunately, the literature on urban churches [and faith-based initiatives] tells us more about church programs to benefit the poor than about interactions with the poor, including the participation of the poor in the churches" (2000, 89).

9. Furthermore, there is the issue of the narcissistic, even haughty, return of some middle-class blacks to inner-city churches on Sundays for church (Laudarji and Livezey 2000). This is the view of a resident of one low-income neighborhood: "When people move out of the community and move somewhere else, they never come back to see exactly what is going on. Their church might be across the street from us, but they don't pay any attention to what's going on with us over here. They come to church on Sunday, attend services, and they go home" (quoted in Smith 2003b, 12). This perspective is inherent in findings from the 1993 National Black Politics Survey, which asked blacks their opinions about the black middle class. Most respondents agreed that middle-class blacks have not done enough to assist the poor in the neighborhoods many of them departed: a majority (61 percent) of blacks averred that the prosperous among them had done little to improve the socioeconomic position of impoverished blacks. A high proportion of middle-class blacks who attended church even found fault with their class, with 68 percent of them agreeing that prosperous blacks have done too little for the black poor (Brown, Dawson, and Jackson 1994).

10. Both assumptions are challenged and refuted by sociologists (e.g., Pattillo-McCoy 2000; Young 2004).

11. How many black clergy have joined the choir singing a redemptive song by urging their peers to reposition themselves as omnicompetent leaders and their churches as socially relevant to the plight of the black poor specifically and the race generally is undetermined. There are no quantitative data to measure the phenomenon. Although there are considerable quantitative data from surveys of the perceptions, attitudes, and behaviors of black clergy, none of them systematically address the positional-reputational status of churches and clergy. Scholars, especially those interested in religion and politics, as well as African American politics, need to ask new questions in their surveys of clergy (regardless of race) and to further test my theory of positional-reputational influence through rigorous multivariate analyses with proper controls and test for interaction effects.

12. As measured by federal income standards, 24.7 percent of blacks report pretax incomes below the poverty line—$9,214 for a single person and $14,269 for a family of three (U.S. Census Bureau 2006).

13. The pursuit of this goal may be rooted mainly in congregations' seeking to expand the pool of resources available to them to address collective problems. Yet the pursuit may also be rooted in the pursuit of racial equity, with some black clergy

contending that government has favored white congregations, denominations, and faith-related agencies over those led by blacks (Farnsley 2003).

14. This point came up in interviews I conducted with an informant from a national organization that provides technical assistance to African American congregations involved in community development: "[There are] black and minority religious institutions, which are overwhelmingly Christian and Protestant, struggling the hardest and fighting with the least resources in a larger sea of faith-based community development that generally allows money only to the mainline religious denominations, predominated by nonminorities, whites, who have for four hundred years had access to resources. Since the founding of the Republic Catholic hospitals, the YMCA, Catholic Charities, Episcopal charities, Lutheran charities have had that kind of access and are now moving rapidly in large numbers to claim the faith-based movement, and in the process I'm afraid that the institutions comprised of the people who are the faces at the bottom of the well will be lost in the shuffle. [Religious] institutions of people of color and communities of people of color here before had been and may continue to be denied access to public and private resources" (quoted in Owens 2004b).

15. John DiIulio Jr. contends that there are multiple "faith factors" or ways religious organizations can "work" or improve the lives of the poor (2002). Religious organizations can contact the needy directly through the cultural resources of churches, especially via religious culture and motivation; they can influence the impoverished indirectly through religious organizations that affect members of their social networks; and through the work of religious organizations they can affect the social milieu of the poor and their neighborhoods in ways that recover and rehabilitate individuals, families, and communities from physical, social, and economic afflictions and addictions.

16. Although there is little empirical evidence that this is true of all types of clergy and not just black pastors, the literature is suggestive (Cnaan 2002; Formicola and Morken 2001; Bartkowski and Regis 2003).

17. Thus, a congregation may grow even larger, and as its membership grows because of its social services, church revenues (tithes, offerings, and charitable contributions) and the operating budget may increase. Consequently, the prestige of the pastor increases, and this further increases the growth of the church.

18. Between 1996 and 2001, the Faith Communities and Urban Families Project (FCUFP) gathered quantitative and qualitative data on congregations located in seven public housing neighborhoods. The Annie E. Casey Foundation funded the applied research project to discern lessons for strengthening the ties between the residents and religious institutions in and around its Making Connections sites. *Making Connections* is a ten-year comprehensive community initiative. It seeks to improve socioeconomic outcomes for families and children in a select number of low-income neighborhoods in ten cities: Denver, Des Moines, Hartford, Indianapolis, Louisville, Milwaukee, Oakland, Providence, San Antonio, and Seattle. The initiative invests in community-driven projects that create opportunities for adults to earn a decent living and build assets; connect and strengthen ties among families, neighbors, religious

institutions, and civic associations; and design and implement neighborhood-based social services systems. I was a senior research consultant for the FCUFP, which was designed and led by my colleague R. Drew Smith of the Leadership Center at Morehouse College (Owens and Smith 2005; R. D. Smith 2003b).

19. In addition to a telephone survey of a random sample of congregations in the metropolitan area of Atlanta, the 2002 Faith and the City Survey of Metropolitan Atlanta Clergy (FATC) surveyed by telephone a random sample of divinity students at three Atlanta-based seminaries: Interdenominational Theological Center, Candler School of Theology (Emory University), and Columbia Presbyterian Seminary. The sample size was three hundred seminarians with a 100 percent response rate across the three schools.

20. In the early 1960s, the federal government began to transform public approaches to poverty in U.S. cities. It also considered and applied ways of fostering greater community engagement in collective problem solving. Policymakers amended laws and regulations to accommodate a services-oriented approach to poverty reduction, one operating primarily through community-based nonprofit organizations that implemented new antipoverty programs such as the Community Action Program at the local level (Kershaw 1970; Derthick 1975; S. Smith and Lipsky 1993; Greenstone and Peterson 1976). The subsequent War on Poverty strategy of services provision used public contracts and grants to increase the participation of nonprofit organizations, inclusive of churches and faith-related agencies such as the Salvation Army, Lutheran Family Services, and Catholic Charities, in public-funded initiatives (Schaller 1967; Fish 1973).

21. "These results do not reflect the full extent of Federal funding awarded to faith-based organizations," the White House Office of Faith-Based and Community Initiatives (2006) acknowledges. This is because the amounts include only nonformula, discretionary grant programs administered by the Departments of Housing and Urban Development, Health and Human Services, Education, Justice, Labor, and Agriculture, and seventeen program areas at the Agency for International Development.

22. Faith-based organizations with international missions accounted for the bulk of the growth in federal discretionary funds going to faith-based organizations between 2003 and 2005.

23. This finding comes from an independent study that looked at discretionary grants across the seven agencies identified in the White House report, as well as the Corporation for National and Community Service and Department of Commerce (Montiel and Wright 2006).

24. Sherman based her findings on content analysis of media stories and interviews with government officials and leaders of faith-based organizations in the late 1990s.

25. The telephone and mail surveys of 389 faith-based organizations (congregations and faith-related agencies), conducted by the Bliss Institute in 2002, relied on a sample of 587 leaders of congregations and faith-related agencies with government contracts in fifteen states: Arkansas, California, Colorado, Florida, Illinois, Indiana,

Massachusetts, Michigan, Mississippi, New York, Ohio, Oklahoma, Texas, Virginia, and Wisconsin. All contracts between the organizations and government were funded by federal programs under the scope of charitable choice. It is unclear how the implementation of the programs by state governments affected the funding.

26. Seventy percent of them reported contracts valued at less than $50,000 (Green and Sherman 2002, table 3). Another survey also suggests that African American churches, in particular, are not the primary recipients of federal "faith-based and community initiative" funds (Bositis 2006). However, this finding has not been replicated through a probability sample of African American churches.

27. My consideration of institutional capacity draws from the research by Norman Glickman and Lisa Servon (1998; also Nye and Glickman 2000) on the five abilities—organizational, programmatic, resource, network, and political—that determine and measure the capacity of community development organizations to foster physical and social change in disadvantaged neighborhoods. Elsewhere I examine these abilities in relation to the general research on both institutional capacity for community development and faith-based organizations, especially congregations (Owens 2004a).

28. By one estimate, the universe of church-associated CDCs, regardless of racial affiliation, operating in the United States at the end of the 1990s was 420, accounting for approximately 14 percent of all CDCs in the nation (Vidal 2001). The growth in church-associated CDCs outpaced all other types of CDCs in the United States, and African American churches yielded the bulk of new church-associated CDCs (National Congress for Community and Economic Development 1999).

29. Government resources, particularly funding and land, often assist church-associated CDCs to construct, improve, manage, and otherwise provide housing and complementary social and economic initiatives invested with a public interest (Mares 1994; Vidal 2001; Clemetson and Coates 1992).

30. Research on secular CDCs suggests that the political utilities of church-associated CDCs may be limited (Berndt 1977; Kelly 1977; Twelvetrees 1989; Blakeley and Aparicio 1990; Stoecker 1997). I examine the political utilities of African American church-associated CDCs in chapters 5, 6, and 7.

CHAPTER THREE

1. Social scientists commonly measure segregation by the isolation index, which is an average of the extent to which members of one group of people live within areas that are predominantly of that group (Massey and Denton 1993). A value of 100 percent would suggest complete segregation of that group from other groups. By comparison with New York, at least one-half of Chicago's black population in 1900 was concentrated spatially in the wards of the Black Belt. Not until 1920 did black New Yorkers make up more than 50 percent of a single ward (Morsell 1950, 6). This disadvantaged black New Yorkers, setting them decades behind black Chicagoans in achieving political incorporation.

2. White responses ranged from passivity, such as looking to local real estate boards to defend their interests, to direct action, such as forming landlord associations and neighborhood improvement associations (e.g., the Save-Harlem Committee and the Gates Avenue Association in Bedford-Stuyvesant) to employ public policies, as well as private decisions, to push black migrants to settle in black neighborhoods (Osofsky 1996; Connolly 1977). Direct action also included the enforcement of restrictive covenants, the individual and communal purchase of black-owned properties, and the giving of cash to black renters to move. Whites lobbied the city government to ban the operation of rooming houses in white neighborhoods and boycotted real estate agencies and other businesses that accepted blacks as clients.

3. The geography of black New York City contributed as much to the slow pace of black electoral incorporations as did the strength of the Democratic machine and white resistance to political change. Martha Biondi summarizes the difficulties created by the geography of black neighborhoods in the postwar period: "The struggle for black empowerment in New York entailed a series of separate struggles in the boroughs of Brooklyn, the Bronx, Manhattan, and Queens. Moreover, the city's growing black middle-class neighborhoods in Queens were spatially and politically cut off from the largest black neighborhoods in Harlem and Bedford-Stuyvesant. The political and residential landscape of discrete black constituencies distinguished New York from other cities such as Chicago and Detroit, where black populations were more concentrated in one location" (2003, 208). Moreover, as J. Phillip Thompson explains, the existence of borough-specific political machines created "borough-based [i.e., county-based] political arenas . . . ; black politicians competed to adopt strategies of survival in their boroughs," not citywide (2006, 166–67).

4. I say "most" because there were black neighborhoods in New York City that belied the "trope of the black ghetto" (Gregory 1998, 12). Not all black neighborhoods were poor. A few of them, such as St. Albans, Addisleigh Park, East Elmhurst, and Corona in Queens, were predominantly middle class. Their rates of homeownership, married households, college graduates, and civic and political participation were far higher than those of the poor black neighborhoods (Gregory 1998; Nathan, Chow, and Owens 1995). Such neighborhoods still exist in New York City, as well as other parts of the New York metropolitan area and other metropolitan areas in the United States (Wright, Patillo, and Montiel 2006; Owens and Wright 1998).

5. Commissioned by the Ford Foundation and conducted by Lou Harris and Associates to evaluate black-Jewish relations, the 1969 New York City Racial and Religion Survey was administered by telephone to a random sample of 1,041 blacks, 635 Jewish whites, and 511 non-Jewish whites (Harris and Swanson 1970). Data are available for each subgroup from the Association of Religious Data Archives at www.theARDA.com.

6. The intensity of perceived discrimination, disadvantage, and disillusionment among blacks responding to the survey was so high that 40 percent of them supported a radical notion, one that ran counter to the objectives of the civil rights movement and the 1954 constitutional ruling of *Brown v. Board of Education*—blacks in

New York City should seek *separate but equal* rights and opportunities (Harris and Associates 1969).

7. In some black neighborhoods, however, especially Bedford-Stuyvesant, voter registration was high but voter turnout, especially among the working class, in local elections never rose above 50 percent (Center for Urban Education 1967, 94).

8. The welfare rolls grew from 328,000 in 1960 to approximately 1.25 million in 1972 (Cannato 2001, 539). Putting this in stark perspective, Fred Siegel explains that the number of people in New York City receiving public assistance exceeded the population of fifteen states (1997, 49).

9. In 1975 the city government spent more than $2 billion, or 23 percent of its budget, on social services (Savitch 1990, 265).

10. Because of municipal rent control laws, however, affordable housing was largely spared (Shefter 1987, 135).

11. The effects of the municipal policies were exacerbated by the effects of federal policies. The start of the Koch administration coincided with a modest growth in federal government assistance to poor citizens and declines in social and human services grants to city governments and neighborhood organizations. Generally, this period in U.S. history witnessed the first dramatic cuts in federal grants-in-aid, especially in the area of housing and community development (Judd and Swanstrom 1998; Eisinger 1998). Federal expenditures for housing, for instance, declined from $30 billion in 1981 to $8 billion in 1988 (Bockemeyer 2003, 179). The era of Reagan also began a trend of reduced federal support for cities, breaking with an intergovernmental funding regime that had existed since the 1940s (Judd and Swanstrom 1998, 238). Federal aid accounted for 24 percent of New York City's municipal budget in 1978, the highest in the city's history (Savitch 1990, 261). But federal assistance began to decline in ensuing years. In 1983 federal funding accounted for 16 percent of the municipal budget, subsequently dropping to 9 percent by 1990 (Savitch 1990, 264; Biles 2001, 139). Also, the amount of federal Community Development Block Grants going to New York City declined from $249 million in 1985 to $155 million in 1987 (Bockemeyer 2003, 180). Federal reductions in entitlement and other social welfare programs, along with the political and economic pressures to return New York City to solvency following the fiscal crisis of the late 1970s, constrained municipal policymaking (Shefter 1987). One observer decried the actions of the federal government as "savaging housing and neighborhood programs designed to help cities and their poor" (Wood 1991, 230).

12. This was not new. During the fiscal crisis of the 1970s, for instance, when the city government cut twenty-five thousand jobs in 1975 alone, policymakers reduced by 35 percent the number of black municipal workers, and they deliberately curtailed social services programs perceived as primarily benefiting blacks (Shefter 1987, 125). Furthermore, throughout the 1980s the Koch administration routinely hamstrung black politicians. It ignored the counsel of black political elites regarding municipal appointments of black administrators, it reorganized the welfare bureaucracy without

considering the effects on recipients, and it proposed to close city hospitals in black neighborhoods (Shefter 1987, 179). Regrettably, blacks in the city council, as well as in the bureaucracy, were in no position to veto or alter, let alone influence, mayoral decisions. In the end, according to Martin Shefter, black politicians were "obligated to accept compromises that left their constituents at the bottom of the city's social structure" (1987, 180).

13. The ability of blacks to exert political influence was also hampered by the decline in electoral development within their neighborhoods. Excluding the surge of black electoral activism surrounding the presidential bids of Jesse Jackson, political scientist Charles Hamilton observes, black neighborhoods during the 1980s were marked by "political quiescence" (1990, 379). Much of the calm came from the almost complete disappearance of political clubs, which had once flourished in the black neighborhoods and throughout the rest of New York City (Thompson 1990; Peel 1935; Adler and Blank 1975). At their height, political clubs connected blacks to the Democratic Party and its remnants of the Tammany political machine. They also trained blacks in the practical arts of politics: candidate recruitment and grooming, the organization of blocks, precincts, and districts for voter registration and turnout, and the distribution and withholding of patronage. Political clubs offered some blacks a ladder up from poverty to prosperity; the most loyal and committed members gained stable and well-paid employment in the public sector. Over time, however, blacks bolted from political clubs. Aside from the limited employment prospects of club participation, blacks left the clubs mainly because the club model was outdated and out of step with the black politics of the day. Influenced by Black Power ideology, many blacks sought to participate in organizations that favored protest over accommodation and that advanced black political development outside the confines of white-led parties. As Thompson points out, "most Black clubs [were] in the machine tradition, they [did] not organize around issues in the community, hold forums on controversial issues, or train young people on the foundations and intricacies of politics" (1990, 100).

14. With poverty high, the underground economy boomed. The crack trade grew deadly as gangs fought for control of street corners. Quickly, large portions of the neighborhoods became blighted. There were stable blocks within the low-income black neighborhoods, but most residential properties wanted for upkeep, care, and new owners. Landlords of commercial and residential units stopped investing in their properties. Some abandoned them outright. Others evicted tenants and held on to the properties as empty shells for land speculation. Beyond abandonment, arson was a problem (Bach and West 1993). Poverty, abandonment, and arson exacerbated crime in the neighborhoods, which was already serious.

15. Dinkins also came into office at a time when cities were feeling sharp cuts in federal aid. A 1989 survey of city financial officers found that 86 percent of them reported that their city government received less federal aid than it had at the start of

the 1980s (Biles 2001). Across the nation, more than one-third of city governments eliminated various municipal services and cut workforces as a consequence of federal urban divestment.

16. Financially, Dinkins was faced with the same problem, albeit to a lesser degree, that Koch faced in his first term as mayor. Fiscal constraints and unbalanced budgets required mayoral attention above all other issues (Arian et al. 1991, 29).

17. Though blacks constituted 25 percent of the city's population in 1990, their share of the municipal government workforce was 35 percent (Waldinger 1996). In some municipal agencies and departments, blacks held a majority share of jobs. Of the thirty-nine agencies under the direct control of the mayoralty in 1993, eight had majority-black workforces (Institute for Puerto Rican Policy 1994). In departments such as Juvenile Justice, Social Services, and Human Resources Administration, blacks accounted for more than half of all employees. In another seven departments such as Aging, Mental Health, and Personnel, blacks fell short of a majority but made up a plurality of employees.

18. By the end of the Dinkins administration, there were municipal agencies with a significant presence of blacks, but blacks occupied mainly "lower-status positions" such as building services and clerical jobs (Institute for Puerto Rican Policy 1994).

19. High rates of black descriptive representation in municipal bureaucracies has long been expected to produce what Peter Eisinger describes as routine occasions "to shape and establish choices on which elected officials act, to implement laws passed by elected bodies, and to shape the very character of the public work force through internal procedures for recruitment, hiring, and promotion" (1982b, 769). This was especially anticipated in New York City. After studying its municipal bureaucracy in the 1970s, Joseph Viteritti concluded that blacks in New York City "who sit in positions of authority at the top" and who occupy slots at the mid- and street levels "of our government bureaucracies exercise a direct impact on public policy" (1979, 89). Since then, however, case studies of New York City and other cities have contradicted these expectations and anticipation (Thompson 2006; Mollenkopf 1994; Browning, Marshall, and Tabb 2003).

20. This theme was frequent in the public announcements of Giuliani at the beginning of the administration. Early on, he asserted: "The City economy that I inherited in January 1994 presented a significant imbalance between a bloated government and a diminished private sector" (Office of the Mayor 1995, 2). Moreover, he claimed that the municipal priorities of his administration symbolized "more than just a change in direction; it is a change in vision to get government out of the way of the economy, and support the policies and programs that stabilize and expand the private sector" (Office of the Mayor 1995, 2).

21. Evidence of this comment is captured well in how Dinkins responded to conditions in East New York–Brownsville, a majority-minority neighborhood located east of Bedford-Stuyvesant and one of the grittiest and violent sections of the city. According to journalist Samuel Freedman (1993), the Dinkins administration was unable to

carry out rudimentary decisions that would improve the conditions in the neighborhood such as keeping open its only park during the summer. Aside from an inability to provide basic neighborhood services, the Dinkins administration seemed to have a tin ear for more serious neighborhood problems. In response to a spate of crossfire shootings of children in East New York–Brownsville, for instance, the mayor did nothing more than visit the neighborhood for a press conference.

22. Black politicians understood the problems in their districts. They framed neighborhood problems, maintained attitudes, and favored policy alternatives in the same way as their constituents in Harlem, Morrisania, Bedford-Stuyvesant, and South Jamaica, including the pastors of neighborhood churches. In my survey of black elected officials and interviews of clergy, I asked them to identify and rank the three chief problems of their neighborhoods at the end of the 1990s. There was an absence of variance in my findings; the elected officials and clergy agreed on the same set and order of problems in their neighborhoods. All respondents identified employment, public education, and affordable housing, in that order, as the primary needs of impoverished black neighborhoods in New York City. Generally, this set and ordering of problems patterned black public opinion in New York City during the 1990s (WCBS-TV and New York Times 1990).

23. This is a sentiment among black clergy elsewhere. In Philadelphia, for instance, Katie Day observes from her study of activist black clergy that they "concluded that accessing power [i.e., getting blacks elected] had not gotten their constituent communities very far down the path of economic development. They felt demoralized by the poverty and discrimination that persists despite the gains of the civil rights movement" (2001, 98).

24. Black elected officials evaluated themselves differently. My survey results show that a majority of black elected officials believed that their individual career in public office had made positive differences in their district. They judged themselves effective on a number of dimensions. Using the data from my survey of politicians, I constructed a self-perceived effectiveness index consisting of seven items: increased resident satisfaction; increased interaction between constituents and government; increased housing opportunities; increased resident participation in community affairs; increased voter participation; increased employment opportunities; and increased self-sufficiency among district residents (alpha = 0.681). Multivariate analysis (not shown) identified two statistically significant factors that seem to affect politicians' perceived effectiveness. Tenure is one of them, but the relationship was negative ($p$ = 0.06). The longer politicians served in office, the lower their index score. The other factor, whether a politician believed that a black mayor necessarily increases the amount of resources allocated to black neighborhoods, reduced the effectiveness scores of politicians ($p$ = 0.057).

25. Black elected officials believed that churches' continued involvement in electioneering was a good thing because it might increase the number of blacks in elected office. According to 88 percent of the black elected officials responding to my survey,

more public resources would go to black people in New York City if there were more black elected officials. As for the potential effect of a black mayor, 74 percent agreed that a black mayor would make a difference to their district.

26. Sometimes, of course, black elected officials did "deliver." In the winter of 1998, for instance, charter school legislation was up for a vote in the New York State Assembly. Leaders of the church-associated CDCs and other neighborhood-based groups were quite concerned about the possibility that black assemblymen would oppose the legislation despite strong black support for public school reform, including various forms of parental choice (Hartocollis 1998; Stafford 2001; Morken and Formicola 1999; Owens 2001). The concern arose from a political fact. Teachers' unions contributed financially to the reelection campaigns of black politicians, and the unions generally opposed charter schools as public policy. But the majority (83 percent) of black assemblymen representing Bedford-Stuyvesant, Harlem, Morrisania, and South Jamaica voted in favor of the bill, and the legislature subsequently passed the legislation and the governor signed it into law.

CHAPTER FOUR

1. Black Christian Nationalism was a variant of the separatist nationalism that was in vogue during the 1960s and early 1970s. Cleage and other adherents pushed an unorthodox interpretation of Christianity, one that identified a black Christ, equated white religious institutions with racism, and advanced revolutionary consciousness as the first step toward black theological liberation from white domination.

2. Operation Breadbasket, named in hopes of bringing "bread, money, and income into the baskets of Black and poor people," was a radical jobs program of the Southern Christian Leadership Conference (Sanford 2002, 154). Initiated in Atlanta 1962, Operation Breadbasket exerted pressure on local businesses in cities to hire black laborers, especially in the fields of construction and retail. Its tactics included boycotts, pickets, and other contentious activities (King 1967; Sanford 2002; Jones 1979, esp. 76–112).

3. By 2000, the mean number of years that the ten churches I studied in depth had been in their current location was fifty-two years. The edifices of seven churches (Abyssinian Baptist, Allen AME, Bethany Baptist, Bridge Street AME, Canaan Baptist, Concord Baptist, and Memorial Baptist) had stood in their current neighborhood for more than fifty years. The other three (Bethesda Missionary Baptist, Ebenezer Missionary Baptist, and Saint Paul Community Baptist) had been in their current neighborhoods for at least thirty years. The neighborhood tenure of the churches was not atypical. Sociologists of the Black Church have found that tenure of more than twenty-five years in a neighborhood is common among urban black churches. C. Eric Lincoln and Lawrence Mamiya report, based on a survey of 1,531 urban black churches during the 1980s, that the mean number of years churches have been in their present neighborhood is 46.5 years. They attribute such long tenures to residential

segregation: "For many black urban churches, residential segregation has meant that their locations have been relatively constant, almost to the point of permanence" (Lincoln and Mamiya 1990, 137, 158).

4. Often the churches perceived migrants from the South as most needy, especially in terms of morality and thrift. This was a common assessment among northern blacks, especially the churchgoing and members of the emerging middle class. They perceived migrants as uncouth, embarrassing, and a hindrance to white support of black progress (Sernett 1997; Tolnay 2001). Even the eminent sociologist W. E. B. Du Bois thought low enough of his southern brethren to claim that the "level of intelligence and efficiency in these newcomers is almost inevitably below that of the Negro already established in the North" (1923, 540). Such social conventions held despite the fact that the literacy rates, employment, and family situations of black southern migrants in the 1920s were equal to or better than those of black northerners (Tolnay 2001).

5. I thank Eric McDaniel for sharing the data with me.

6. As of 1999, thirteen years was the median age of these organizations, compared to the national median of fifteen years for all types of CDCs, secular and church-associated (National Congress for Community Economic Development 1999). At the time of my research, the sizes of the African American church–associated CDCs in New York City varied in terms of the number of employees. Staff sizes ranged from two to fifty-two full-time staff. Thirteen was the median staff size, double the national median for all types of CDCs.

7. Only three of the African American church–associated CDCs—Harlem Congregations for Community Improvement, Abyssinian Development Corporation, and Bridge Street Development Corporation—routinely develop commercial properties, encourage private commercial investment, and foster entrepreneurship in their neighborhoods through partnerships with other institutions. The limited focus on economic development is not because the CDCs or their affiliated churches discount its importance or discourage it in their neighborhood. Rather, many African American churches in New York City engage in economic development through their church directly or by entities other than their CDC. Actually, CDCs tend to be one among a set of nonprofit, even for-profit, subsidiaries of activist African American churches. Furthermore, a church-associated CDC may focus less on economic development than housing because it is still establishing a successful record of housing development to leverage into larger economic development projects. External funding streams are another reason they tend to focus less on economic development and more on housing, as well as human and health services.

8. All of the executive directors were black. Ten years was the mean length of time they had been employed by their CDCs, which was longer than the tenure of executive directors of other African American church–associated CDCs in the United States (Frederick 2001). While they worked in their neighborhood, often for years, executive directors tended to not live in it. A minority of executive directors, com-

pared to a majority (75 percent) of their staff, lived in the neighborhood served by their church-associated CDC. A majority of the executive directors (six of nine) and full-time staff (69 percent) were women, which is common among community development organizations in the United States, be they secular or faith-based (Gittell, Ortega-Bustamante, and Steffy 1999; Tucker-Worgs 2002).

9. The organization patterned itself after extant grassroots groups such as the Southeast Bronx Community Organization, the People's Development Corporation, the Banana Kelly Community Improvement Association, and the Mid-Bronx Desperadoes, which opened their doors on the streets of the South Bronx in the late 1960s through the middle years of the 1970s. These organizations grew or were growing from narrow groups of concerned and activist residents with a list of complaints to institutions with broad agendas for reforming conditions in South Bronx neighborhoods, often in collaboration with government agencies (Gonzalez 2004; von Hoffmann 2003).

10. It is true that church-associated CDCs are not religious institutions. Church-associated CDCs do not necessarily incorporate religious education, overt worship, and appeals for redemption and salvation into their activities. Nonetheless, their existence and activities are imbibed with religious spirit. Also, in the minds of their founders and staff, more than a temporal authority regulates their behavior. Additionally, their activities express fidelity to religious traditions and deity devotion, with their staff often working in an "atmosphere of religiosity" (Briggs, Mueller, and Sullivan 1997, 91).

11. The degree to which faith directs and sustains the missions, behaviors, and objectives of church-associated CDCs is open to contention and validation. This holds for most faith-related agencies (Chambre 2001; S. Smith and Sossin 2001; Jeavons 1994). Religious adherence, however, is not a criterion for hiring employees in the nine church-associated CDCs I studied. None of them require prospective and current employees to attend their sponsor churches or even to be Christians. But this is atypical of African American church–associated CDCs in the United States (Frederick 2001). Still, most executive directors whom I interviewed identified themselves to me as members of a (or the) congregation affiliated with their organization.

12. It may be that the works of church-associated CDCs perform an evangelical function, albeit obliquely—conversion. Some of the persons who observe or benefit from the works of the church-related CDCs may voluntarily convert to the faith(s) associated with the CDCs. I deliberately use "faith(s)" here. All of the independent church-associated CDCs are affiliates of Christian churches. However, the congregations supporting the alliance-based CDCs include a small set of Muslim masjids and Jewish congregations. Still, the common assumption of observers is that the alliance-based CDCs are primarily Christian faith-related agencies. There is no empirical evidence of conversions occurring because of the work of these CDCs, even if there is evidence from studies of other types of faith-related agencies (Wuthnow 2004).

13. The brochure for the Abyssinian Development Corporation, for example, iden-

tifies empowerment as a fundamental aspect of its mission: "To develop, among the population we serve, an empowered citizenry, capable of constructively organizing and governing themselves, and requiring that institutions vested with the public trust (i.e., city agencies, community boards, school boards, landlords, etc.) fulfill their legal and moral obligations to the community." Empowerment rhetoric is explicit and implicit in the missions of all African American church–associated CDCs in New York City.

14. The average resident of the neighborhoods cannot participate directly as staff or officer of a CDC. Therefore, most residents will not acquire knowledge about and experience with neighborhood planning, public funding, and advocacy. They also will not learn to design and administer projects, nor will they acquire new skills such as idea formulation, deliberation, negotiation, or consensus-building. Moreover, they will not gain a heightened sense of political efficacy or increase their social capital, both of which are vital to improving the conditions of individuals and solving collective problems.

15. Lay representation is prominent on the boards of directors of the CDCs, except for the three CDCs where pastors govern alone. Combined, 140 neighborhood stakeholders govern the six church-associated CDCs with lay representation. The leadership and influence of pastors is prominent, even when they are absent from the board of a black church–associated CDC. Executive directors acknowledged the important roles that the pastors of their sponsor churches play in the work of the CDCs. These roles range from fundraiser to lobbyist to deal maker, as the director of one CDC observed: "Reverend [name withheld for confidentiality], as pastor of the church, is an advocate. He is the founder. He is an advocate. He is a fundraiser. He is an adviser. Those roles are very big, and very necessary to the survival, reputation, and success of our organization." Some pastors, however, are more active in the work of church-associated CDCs. As of 2000, pastors were the executive directors of the Association of Brooklyn Clergy for Community Development, Harlem Congregations for Community Improvement, and Southeast Queens Clergy for Community Empowerment. Having pastors rather than lay professionals head the alliance-based CDCs may allow their member churches to transfer some of their moral authority and political capital to the CDCs. This may be useful to the CDCs when they make claims on the state or private actors for policies and resources that benefit the CDCs and their neighborhoods. An executive director observed: "We certainly stand on the shoulders of our member churches, some of whose names most certainly resonate historically and in a contemporary sense in this city in terms of sort of institutional strength and certainly because of the prominence and sort of charismatic leadership of their pastors. Some of our members' churches have names that are recognized in New York City, and we try to use that to our advantage and to the benefit of the community." Having clergy as directors may also strengthen the connections that the public, and especially policymakers, make between the CDCs and the power of the churches as institutions of community concern and care. Furthermore, it may demonstrate a preference among clerics for leadership and accountability by their peers.

16. The CDCs select board members who have the requisite skills for effective governance of their organizations, who provide access to financial, political, or social networks to facilitate new or expand current programs, and who possess the aptitudes that advance the organization's institutional capacity. An executive director of a church-associated CDC in Bedford-Stuyvesant commented thus on the selection of board members: "We target people. We always look for people who have some skill that we think will be valuable to the corporation, whether its business skill or architectural, professional skills, being an architect, a banker, educator, or manager. We look for people who either live in Bed-Stuy or serve Bed-Stuy because they own a business or run an institution that serves Bed-Stuy. Initially we looked for members of the church who met all of those criteria. Within the last year and a half we cast our net more broadly to include people who are not members of the church, and the focus has been on attracting people who are residents of the community and who have skills that would benefit the community through the corporation or have access to resources that would benefit the community through the corporation." Interviews with the other executive directors revealed that the aforementioned criteria are common.

17. Determining which stakeholders within low-income neighborhoods benefit the most from churches' collaborating with government is difficult. In particular, it is difficult to determine whether residents should benefit more than the members of the collaborating churches. The difficulty is amplified because there is often little overlap between the residents of low-income neighborhoods and the congregants of churches in them (Smith 2001; Laudarji and Livezey 2000). Members of local congregations associated with the CDCs are a key segment of the "community" in the neighborhoods. Aside from determining who should benefit more, deciding which *parts* of low-income communities will benefit before others is also knotty. Collaboration produces benefits that are often pegged to a specific locale within a neighborhood. In the long run, an entire neighborhood may benefit from the products of collaboration, but in the short run the production of benefits is a zero-sum game. Ambiguity over "community" as residents and "community" as congregants may lead to resentment between the two groups. Likewise, ambiguity over "community" as a the geographic whole and "community" as a subset of space within it may create resentments over the decisions of CDCs to build in one area rather than another.

18. It may also explain why black elected officials see value in the church-associated CDCs. According to my survey of black elected officials in New York City, 76 percent of them agree that it was necessary for blacks to develop independent service-delivery systems such as CDCs, be they church-associated or secular, to increase services in black neighborhoods. A majority (84 percent) of them also agreed that CDCs could supplement black representatives' ability to increase the allocation of public benefits in black neighborhoods. However, politicians may have held positive views toward the church-associated CDCs precisely because they did not perceive the latter as actual competitors for representing the interests of the four neighborhoods. Given the composition of their leadership and staff, the church-associated CDCs did not

necessarily have a broad constituency. Also, whereas the politicians by their election had a democratic mandate to serve as representatives, the church-associated CDCs did not.

19. Also, CDCs provided a few churches with an overarching management organization to monitor and assist their other faith-related agencies. Concord Baptist Church initially intended to use its CDC solely to manage and monitor the work of eight faith-related agencies of the church. In response to the needs of residents, especially congregants, who wanted to become homeowners, Concord CDC began emphasizing housing development, increasing prospective homeowners' access to lenders, and attacking redlining (i.e., the exclusion of financial services by banks and insurers in low-income neighborhoods). Similarly, Bridge Street AWME Church created its CDC to provide the church with an instrument for guiding the operation and growth of its other nonprofit subsidiaries and addressing housing-related problems in the vicinity of the church.

20. Historically, black clergy have participated in informal ministerial alliances or conferences, which are venues for discussion, civic action, and political engagement (Newman 1994; Owens 1997b). In New York City from the late 1970s and to middle 1980s, multiple ministerial alliances such as the Metropolitan Ministers Conference and the African People's Christian Organization appeared in black neighborhoods (Green and Wilson 1992). Clergy used them to decide how their churches could cooperate to identify common problems, publicize neighborhood needs, and mobilize their communities for political action. Some used their ministerial alliances to assume broader missions, create bureaucracies, and perform roles that went beyond providing venues for black clergy to vent their concerns and improvise community-based responses. Such alliances became staging areas for the development of the alliance-based church-associated CDCs.

21. This was to the consternation of many black clergy in New York City. Reverend Wyatt Tee Walker, pastor emeritus of Canaan Baptist Church of Christ in Harlem and former executive director of the Southern Christian Leadership Conference, spoke to this assessment of the funding context during an interview with me for another project: "Look at Catholic Charities and the tax dollars that go to them as compared to the numbers of blacks and Latinos in this community [Harlem]. The Catholic Charities probably gets fifty times the tax dollars that all of the black [church] enterprises like mine and the others might receive" (quoted in Owens 2004b, 96).

22. Moreover, they sought to use CDCs to financially shield the churches against unintended costs and liabilities of providing social and community development services. This is because the CDCs are legally (i.e., financially and administratively) separate from their congregations. Thus, church-associated CDCs assist churches in being good stewards, protecting what pastors and the laity deem "divine resources"— the tithes and offerings of attenders (Mares 1994).

23. As of 1999, the budgets of the African American church-associated CDCs in New York City were larger than those of the typical CDC (faith-related or secular) in

the United States. The median operating budget of the nine church-associated CDCs was $550,000, compared to $200,000-399,000 for all CDCs nationally (National Congress for Community Economic Development 1999).

24. This seems to apply to African American church–associated CDCs in other cities (Frederick 2001).

25. The remainder of their external resources, which I detail elsewhere (Owens 2003), comes from banks (7 percent), intermediaries such as LISC-NY (8 percent), corporations (4 percent), and philanthropic foundations (10 percent). Formed in 1979, LISC-NY (i.e., the Local Initiatives Support Corporation) provides low-cost financing and technical support to housing-development organizations in New York City. It raises private equity investments for development projects by its nonprofit clients (von Hoffman 2003).

26. Nongovernmental organizations (both commercial and nonprofit) were the initiative's beneficiaries, with the organizations rehabilitating and managing or selling residential properties.

CHAPTER FIVE

1. The plan would address simultaneously the weak affordable housing supply, along with housing abandonment and neighborhood decline. It would transfer responsibilities, authority, and resources to nongovernmental organizations. From a rational actor perspective, this was a conscious and logical decision. Mayor Koch, backed by public opinion and the business community, perceived nongovernmental organizations as more efficient and effective than municipal agencies at delivering services. Dependence on nongovernmental organizations also had the potential to increase municipal flexibility regarding how to implement the policy while fostering competition and choice, weakening bureaucratic and political constraints, and advancing ideological preferences for smaller government. Additionally, it ensured the support of the private sector for particular policies.

2. Victor Bach and Sherece West (1993; see also Marcuse 1986 and Listokin 1985) defined abandonment during this period as an "owner no longer exercis[ing] an active material interest in the property, even to the point of risking losing title to the property without further compensation, as through tax foreclosure or mortgage foreclosure." Strict municipal zoning and building regulations, along with regulation of rents in the private housing market, also affected the supply of affordable housing (Salins 1999).

3. This phenomenon of "tax-driven abandonment," Peter Salins and Gerard Mildner note, was related to the finding from a set of cities in the United States that properties in low-income neighborhoods were "assessed at significantly higher rates relative to market value than those in better-off neighborhoods" (1992, 157).

4. Their behavior was strange. Nathan Glazer notes that it was a "striking phenomenon—one never seen in any American city, or perhaps other cities, since the decline

of the urbanism of the ancient world—[that] appeared in New York: the abandonment of sound housing" (cited in Orlebeke 1997, 24).

5. The taking of abandoned properties was permissible under local law, especially a new law enacted in the mid-1970s to take properties that had been in tax arrears for one year (Listokin 1985; Braconi 1999).

6. When the city government acquired occupied buildings, HPD assumed the day-to-day management and maintenance of them. "It spent a lot of time making sure there was hot water, the boilers worked, and that people were getting what they needed," according to an HPD official.

7. Privatization shifts the provision of public services from a system based on public agency responsibility to a system where nongovernmental organizations implement public policies and programs. Commonly, it takes one of three forms—divestment, delegation, or displacement (Savas 2000). When governments *divest,* they sell or donate public-owned assets to nongovernmental organizations for their use, presumably in the interest of the public. When governments *delegate,* they transfer responsibility for the production of a function or purpose to nongovernmental organizations by means of material incentives (contracts, franchises, grants, vouchers, loans) or mandates, while maintaining their responsibility for ensuring the continuance of a public function or achievement of a purpose. When governments *displace,* they relinquish absolutely their responsibilities in a given physical or policy domain.

8. This demonstrates how long it can take for initial ideas to become municipal policies. Charles Orlebeke (1997) recounts that Koch, upon taking office in 1978, sought to devise a program that would build owner-occupied housing on vacant public land. This was three years after a housing official in the previous Beame administration had proposed a mixed federal-municipal program to build rental housing on vacant city land.

9. Eventually, in 1993, the City of New York stopped taking direct control of tax-foreclosed properties, distressed or otherwise, as municipal assets. Amendments to the local foreclosure law in 1996, however, permit the city government, with the approval of the city council, to transfer distressed properties directly from delinquent private owners to third parties for rehabilitation and use as affordable or market-rate rental or owner-occupied housing, all without the city government's ownership, management, or sale of the properties (Allred 2000).

10. Alex Schwartz reports that the city's housing expenditures rose from $25 million to $850 million between 1985 and 1989 (Schwartz 1999, 840). The amount was astonishing, especially given that municipal spending for housing and community development in New York City had not increased in the three years preceding the plan's announcement (Abramson and Salamon 1986, table 5.1). Another reason to find municipal expenditures for the experiment surprising was that the city government tended to use grants-in-aid from the federal government to deliver affordable housing to low- and moderate-income families and individuals (Schwartz 1999, 842). Yet at one point the city government channeled so much money into affordable hous-

ing production that it spent almost four times as much as the next fifty largest American cities combined (Berenyi 1989).

11. Community Development Block Grants are federal funds provided to cities as entitlement grants for the purpose of improving low- and moderate-income neighborhoods (Rich 1993).

12. Low Income Housing Tax Credits, introduced during the federal tax reforms of 1986, are used by cities and states to induce companies to invest in low-income rental housing by taking a tax credit for the entire investment over a ten-year period. HOME, which started in 1990, provides flexible block grants to states and cities for housing targeted to low- and moderate-income families.

13. Its efforts at leveraging financial resources from the private sector were assisted greatly by the Community Reinvestment Act (CRA). Enacted into law in 1977, the CRA requires banks and lending institutions to serve the credit needs of their service areas, including low- and moderate-income areas.

14. As of 2005, the city's inventory of tax-foreclosed properties consisted of 2,285 units: 999 in occupied buildings and 1,286 in vacant buildings (New York City Department of Housing Preservation and Development 2005). It also included 240 vacant lots, down from a high of 5,000, and the city offered these remaining lots for sale to developers who would be willing to build more affordable housing units than the minimum required by past subsidy programs (Steinhauer 2005). Overall, the city is set to dispose of its inventory of foreclosed buildings by 2011 (Housing First 2005).

15. Scholars judge the Ten Year Plan for the development of affordable housing for low- and moderate-income individuals and families a success (Schill et al. 2002; Van Ryzin and Genn 1999; Schwartz 1999).

16. Generally, municipal governments looked at nongovernmental organizations through bifocals. They saw such organizations as competitors of government, providing a critique and challenge to public action and effectiveness. Alternatively, they observed nongovernmental organizations to be complements of government, providing resources for public action and effectiveness. Although academic scholars and policymakers made much of the first lens during the period, emphasizing market-based solutions to public problems, the bulk of municipal social welfare services would be provided by noncommercial organizations. In short, cities adopted the "nonprofitization" of municipal services (Nathan 1996).

17. Following a review of reports issued by the New York City comptroller, John Mollenkopf reported that the city increased its contracting in the areas of aging, social services (e.g., foster care and adoption services), health, youth services, and housing by 109 percent, 79 percent, 55 percent, 39 percent, and 14 percent, respectively (1994, 157).

18. Nonprofit organizations received just 2 percent of all municipal expenditures for housing and neighborhood development in 1982, while they received 78 percent, 69 percent, and 43 percent of all municipal spending for employment and training, social services, and health care, respectively (Abramson and Salamon 1986, 35).

19. The Community Management Program would become a forerunner of similar municipal programs that relied on community-based organizations to rehabilitate and manage formerly city-owned properties (Orlebeke 1997; Leavitt 1980; Leavitt and Saegert 1990). I describe the four most important of these programs, particularly in relation the city's black neighborhoods, in chapter 6, which details the involvement of activist African American churches and their CDCs in the implementation of the programs.

20. Doug Turetsky reminds us, however, that inclusion of community-based groups in these municipal initiatives was not the original choice of the municipal government (1993, 21). Rather, it came in response to community agitation for the inclusion of neighborhood voices in public policy–making processes to redress neighborhood neglect. In particular, the protest mobilization of blacks during the mayoralty of Robert Wagner, especially the Harlem Rent Strikes of 1962 and 1963, influenced the decisions of the subsequent mayoral administration of John Lindsay about the implementation of the Model Cities program in New York City (Lipsky 1970; Schwartz 1986).

21. Recall from the Introduction of this book that the Section 202 Elderly Housing program was one of the federal initiatives that introduced churches in the United States to the advantages of working with government to produce housing in its community. It was also the program that appears to have influenced the original involvement of faith-based organizations, especially ecumenical associations such as the Council of Churches, in the creation of nonprofit housing development corporations and church-based sponsorship of affordable housing projects in New York City (J. Schwartz 1986).

22. Ideologically, black pastors in New York City are socially moderate or liberal (Carnes 2001). Moreover, their Democratic partisanship is deep. Although some pastors believe, as one commented in an interview with me, that "some black Republicans" were needed "in there somewhere," and although a few of them (e.g., Rev. Floyd Flake of Allen AME Church) do project and maintain Republican personas and relationships, the majority of the pastors of activist African American churches in New York City are Democrats.

23. The pastor's words are informed by chapter 1 of the book of Daniel in the Old Testament. Daniel, a prophet, was a captive of the Babylonian kingdom, following the overthrow of the kingdom of Judah. Nebuchadnezzar, the Babylonian king, identified him and a small set of other Judeans as sages. He trained them to serve his court and its interests, and he expected all captives who served him to renounce their religious practices and beliefs. During the course of the training, Nebuchadnezzar presented food from his table to Daniel, who declined to eat it. In referencing Daniel's decision, the pastor I interviewed interpreted the act to be an instruction to clergy like him—those placing themselves within the prophetic tradition—that they should not allow government or any other institution to co-opt their beliefs and values as men of the true God.

24. The pastor's remarks are another biblical reference to standing firm in one's be-

liefs and values and avoiding co-optation. The phrase "minions of Caesar" recalls the time during the first century when some Jews were favored and rewarded by Tiberius Caesar Augustus, the emperor of Rome, for their willingness to serve his interests regardless of how they might conflict with the Torah. Their pragmatic strategy raised the issue of whether Jews could serve two masters, Caesar and God. The dilemma is best represented in the Gospels of Mark (12:13–17), Matthew (22:14–17), and Luke (20:20–26), where Jesus is queried by his opponents about whether it is right for Jews to pay taxes to Caesar. He responded that Jews were to give each master his due. But according to some interpretations, Jesus implied that when one is forced to choose between them, the correct choice is to obey God regardless of the consequences.

25. Consequently, black pastors, regardless of whether their churches partnered with government, were wary of appearing too close to city hall's conservative occupants. For example, following the 1993 defeat of Mayor Dinkins, black clergy from across the city, including the Baptist Ministers Conference of Greater New York, pressured their peers to shun Mayor Giuliani. This was a response adopted by congregants, too. One congregation fired its senior pastor, Rev. John Brandon, for aligning with Giuliani and allowing him into the church following his victory over Dinkins (Kirtzman 2000, 182).

26. Overall, the majority of black clergy I interviewed, those whose churches do not collaborate with government and those whose churches do, doubted that whites, even liberal Democrats, are concerned about the conditions of black neighborhoods. As a Harlem pastor fumed during an interview: "You not gonna change white folks. The spirit of white America is demonic. I don't have any optimism about their ability to do what is right by us."

27. The pastors' choice of residence also kept the clergy hidden from the public spaces of black neighborhoods: most pastors opted to live outside them. A majority of pastors I interviewed did not reside in the neighborhood where they shepherded their flock.

28. Of course, this was often a false dichotomy, particularly in New York City: it was not uncommon for pastors to be politicians and for clergy to be elected or appointed officials.

29. Focusing on the decline in church membership among black men during the 1990s, Robert Franklin takes a longitudinal perspective: "A generation ago, four out of every five inner city black men had some contact with church or Sunday School. Today, studies show three out of five have no church contact whatsoever" (quoted in Pinn 2002, 20).

30. The state dissolved HUDC in 1995 in response to findings of mismanagement of public funds and tax violations (New York 1998). It was reconstituted as the Harlem Community Development Corporation, a public authority governed by gubernatorial appointees and heads of state administrative agencies, including the Empire State Development Corporation.

31. This point was directed primarily at Congressman Charles Rangel. A few years

later, Rev. Butts of Abyssinian Baptist Church made it known in a 1992 *Jet* magazine story that he and other pastors continued to hold Rangel accountable for the thwarted development of Harlem: "Social and economic conditions in Harlem have declined substantially during Mr. Rangel's tenure in Congress" (anonymous 1992). Interestingly, the criticism of Rangel by black pastors dovetails with the criticisms of the congressman by former mayor Koch (1984).

32. Haskell Ward, who served as Koch's commissioner of the Human Resources Administration, the city's chief welfare and family services department, was one of them. He also was a political competitor of Harlem's U.S. representative, Charles Rangel.

33. This account counters the revisionist claim that the Koch administration "would work with any housing producer who came to them with a reasonable offer—which included putting money on the table" (von Hoffman 2003, 50).

34. In exchange for their participation, the five churches received, indirectly through a collection of faith-related agencies they created, approximately $25 million in government loans at below-market interest rates to develop and own 693 units of affordable rental housing for the elderly in their neighborhoods. This data comes from unpublished data I obtained from the U.S. Department of Housing and Urban Development. I thank William Kooper for his assistance in obtaining the data.

35. The resources fed the growth in numbers of community-based housing organizations in New York City. In turn, the expanding universe of such organizations increased the number of groups the city could partner with. Felice Michetti, a deputy housing commissioner under Koch and chief housing commissioner in the Dinkins administration, acknowledged the connection: "When the Ten Year Plan began, there were about twelve not-for-profits in the City of New York that were actively involved in housing. . . . By the time I left HPD, there were over a hundred not-for-profits involved in the Ten Year Plan, and involved not in the traditional federal role of sponsoring projects, but actively involved [in development]" (quoted in Schill et al. 2002, 535).

CHAPTER SIX

1. Equity generated by the local affiliate of the Local Initiatives Support Corporation from the federal Low Income Housing Tax Credit Program and capital raised from private financial institutions also supported the development of the houses.

2. Six of HPD's programs conveyed property and resources solely to nonprofit organizations. From 1986 to 1997, the City of New York transferred 57,823 units of vacant and occupied housing from the public sector to the private sector (Schwartz 1999, 851, 865). Nonprofit organizations received approximately one-half of these properties.

3. The New York City Partnership and Chamber of Commerce established the Housing Partnership in 1982 to address the city's shortage of affordable housing and

the lack of private investment in its low-income neighborhoods (Orlebeke 1997). It became one of the foremost not-for-profit intermediaries in the New York City afford- able housing production experiment. Epitomizing a "governing nonprofit" (Hula, Jackson, and Orr 1997), the Housing Partnership advocated nongovernmental, espe- cially market-based, development of affordable housing, incentive-based affordable housing policies, and regulatory repeals.

4. Annually, the program developed approximately 1,200 new single-family town- houses and two- and three-family homes, condominiums, and cooperatives in New York City for sale to buyers with annual incomes below $71,000 (New York City Housing Partnership 1999, 2). The city's investment in Partnership New Homes was $1.5 billion (Wylde 1999, 82–83).

5. The loans were funded from the city's capital budget, federal Community De- velopment Block Grants, and proceeds from federal Low Income Housing Tax Credit sales.

6. Black politicians supported church-state collaboration. My survey found that 88 percent of black elected officials supported the city government's inclusion of ac- tivist African American churches in the delivery of public services in black neighbor- hoods, especially affordable housing production.

7. *Governing regime* is the term that scholars of urban politics apply to the informal interactions and resource arrangements between government and nongovernmental actors for the management of collective problems, where governmental and nongov- ernmental actors share financial and programmatic responsibilities (Elkin 1987; Stone 1989). Since the emergence of the governing regime perspective in urban politics re- search, scholars have attended to the highest level of interactions and informal arrange- ments for local governance by coalitions of governmental and nongovernmental actors (e.g., Ferman 1996; Orr 1999). But focusing on that level, which I term the macro- regime, ignores the presence and utility of lower-level sets of governing coalitions that make up the larger corpus of a governing regime. Much, if not most, of the transforma- tion of policy into action and collective problem management is the responsibility of informal arrangements and formal partnerships (especially contractual relationships) among governmental and nongovernmental organizations interacting at the street level in cities. I term these street-level arrangements and partnerships *microregimes,* and I have argued elsewhere that they are pivotal to the success of urban governing regimes, just like the "subregimes" others identify as residing between macroregimes and microregimes (Owens 2000 and 2002; Swanstrom and Koschinsky 2000).

8. The designs of some federal community-development programs basically man- date the inclusion of neighborhood-based groups in affordable housing-production microregimes. The Low Income Housing Tax Credit, HOME Investment Partner- ship Grant, and McKinney Homelessness Assistance programs encourage, even re- quire, that nonprofit organizations participate in packaging the finances for, design- ing and building, and owning, managing, and marketing housing units (O'Regan and Quigley 2000; Orlebeke 2000; Schill 1994).

9. At first glance, a microregime may appear to be nothing more than a traditional subsystem for a particular policy sphere, especially when one considers the role of formal relationships via contracting. Edward Goetz and Mara Sidney observe in their research on the local/neighborhood-level politics of community development that "subsystem actors enjoy privileged access to the policy process for that issue and some degree of hegemony over development of policy alternatives. Typically, they control most of the routine decision making in a particular policy area" (1997, 491). But policy subsystems need not involve regimes, while regimes necessarily involve policy subsystems. Influenced by Paul Sabatier (1993, 16–17), I define a subsystem as "the interaction of actors from different institutions [public and private] who follow and seek to influence government decisions in a policy area," within an intergovernmental context, permeated by a dominant "belief system" composed of "value priorities." But when street-level governance of a policy domain or sphere is nested within the subsystem framework, characterized by two competing coalitions, the usefulness of describing it as a subsystem falls short.

10. New York City has a decentralized system of neighborhood participation and input in land use, budget, and service delivery decisions, built around fifty-nine community boards whose members are nominated by the city council and appointed by borough presidents (Pecorella 1994).

11. Empirical evidence suggests that the informant's church and others like it indeed had reputations for electoral action. But the electoral mobilization of Saint Paul Community Baptist Church and other churches associated with East Brooklyn Congregations, an affiliate of the Industrial Areas Foundation that operates in East New York–Brownsville, is less effective than the informant suggested. The electoral mobilization by the churches had modest or null effects on voter turnout and the election of favored candidates (Ross 1996). Nevertheless, in politics perceptions are as important as reality.

12. This matched with earlier theorizing by political scientists such as Reginald Earl Gilliam Jr. (1975) and Theodore Cross (1984) that *secular* CDCs could serve black neighborhoods as electoral institutions and interest groups to increase black incorporation in local government and responsiveness of municipal politics.

13. Looking at Latino-serving CDCs in New York City, sociologist Nicole Marwell found that they function as quasi-political machines that organize electoral action by neighborhood residents (2004, 269). The finding does not, however, strongly and persuasively contradict two decades of empirical research that concludes that the political utilities of secular CDCs are weak (Berndt 1977; Kelly 1977; Gittell 1980; Twelvetrees 1989; Blakeley and Aparicio 1990; Stoecker 1997).

14. For example, the city government in 1999 conveyed to three of the nine African American church–associated CDCs participating in the Neighborhood Redevelopment Program eleven buildings (225 housing units) for rehabilitation, ownership, and management as rental housing. The transfers accounted for 6 percent of the 4,049 units the city government transferred to nonprofits via the program. Under the Spe-

cial Initiatives Program of the 1980s, HPD conveyed 28 properties (370 units) to five African American church–associated CDCs. These represented 7 percent of 5,144 vacant residential units that the program transferred to neighborhood-based organizations citywide.

15. Federal HOME Investment Partnership Grant funds accounted for 62 percent of the total public subsidies the church-associated CDCs received, with the city's capital budget and CDBG funds accounting for 27 percent and 11 percent, respectively. In addition, the African American church–associated CDCs received $625,000 to $1.25 million in administrative fees to cover initial management and maintenance responsibilities during their lease periods. Participants in the Neighborhood Redevelopment Program and Neighborhood Homes, for example, earned development fees of $2,400 to $5,000 for every unit they rehabilitated. They also received administrative cost allowances for their management of HPD properties during the rehabilitation phase. Furthermore, their revenues ensured the continued operation of their organizations: filling vacancies and collecting rents often raised enough income for the CDCs to start and sustain social services and economic development programs such as workforce development or microenterprise lending.

16. This is a common externality of city governments' transferring responsibilities and resources to neighborhood-based organizations, especially those with politicized origins. In U.S. cities during the 1980s and 1990s, Margit Mayer writes, city governments "institutionalized the involvement of nongovernmental, community-based groups . . . in both policymaking and policy implementation. They . . . delegated responsibility for the implementation of a variety of tasks to their private and voluntary sector groups" (1991, 17; see also Clavel, Pitt, and Yin 1997; Eisinger 1998; Ferman 1996). This expressed a consensus among Democrats and Republicans that the public sector must cooperate with neighborhood-based organizations to manage and reform collective problems (Grogan and Proscio 2000; Goldsmith 2000; Siegel 2002). An effect of the institutionalization of neighborhood-based organizations in government has been the transfer of "fragments of governmental power" from the public sector to neighborhood-based organizations (Judd and Swanstrom 1998, 410).

17. It may surprise some readers that I would imply that neighborhood-based organizations could ever hope to hold the reins of eminent domain. Such groups rarely acquire eminent domain authority, but some have obtained it. This is evidenced by the joint administration of eminent domain authority by the City of Boston and the Dudley Street Neighborhood Initiative during the 1980s (Medoff and Sklar 1994).

18. It is a common finding about the search for goods such as public schools (Schneider, Teske, and Marschall 2000).

19. Such signs of speculation were not new to Harlem or elsewhere in New York City. They were visible on buildings during the 1980s, according to Jacqueline Leavitt and Susan Saegert, when "certain locations became hot real estate markets and targets of gentrification, landlords paid their taxes, emptied their buildings of poor people,

and 'warehoused' the units until they could convert them to luxury collaborators and condominiums" (1990, 111).

CHAPTER SEVEN

1. Moreover, some mortgage lenders surreptitiously acquired signatures from residents to open credit card accounts with exorbitant interest rates, to issue insurance policies with pricey premiums, and to lease automobiles with high monthly payments. Some home repair contractors incorporated such ruses as well. Contractors offered residents home refinancing to cover house and apartment repairs. Others took cash deposits from homeowners for future work but never returned to do it. A few contractors even began work on houses without owners' permission, only to later demand payment for their unwanted services.

2. My questions have been asked regarding other institutions of black civil society, especially in cities (Cohen 1999; Orr 2000; Johnson and Sanford 2003). They have also been directed at civil society organizations generally in the United States (Berry 2003; Medoff and Sklar 1994; Hula and Jackson-Elmoore 2000; Cuoto 1999).

3. The policy advocacy of the African American church–associated CDCs in New York City is no different from that of secular CDCs generally in the United States. Studies suggest that 60 percent of secular CDCs engage in legislative-regulatory advocacy (Vidal 1992). Moreover, secular CDCs tend to participate in advocacy coalitions to identify collective interests and lobby for increased government responsiveness (Goetz 1993).

4. Public policy also sets annual limits on nonprofit organizations' legislative lobbying. Moreover, policy makers have attempted to curtail further the lobbying of nonprofit organizations. During the 1990s the U.S. Congress and various state legislatures debated bills that ranged from making nonprofits ineligible for government funds if they engaged in advocacy to limiting how much money they could spend on lobbying activities. There also were attempts to legislate "prior permission" clauses for nonprofit organizations, barring nonprofits from political activities without the consent or permission of their donors.

5. Tax-exempt status facilitates fundraising. It is an incentive for individuals to make tax-deductible private donations to a nonprofit organization. It also serves as a means of assuring prospective donors that the organization is legitimate, as it is chartered by the government.

6. A few informants recognized that their organization could not engage in partisan activities, but they pointed out that its leaders could be partisans in their "private" lives. "We cannot actively advocate for one political candidate or another as a CDC. As individuals, we can. I supported [Republican George] Pataki because I thought that what he was doing was better than what [Democratic Governor Mario] Cuomo did for our community for the most part. A lot of his other stuff I don't go for, too

tough, but you know that's as an individual. But I could not say we as [a CDC] endorse X, because then we would disqualify ourselves as a nonprofit that is engaged in a partisan activity." Another director explained: "I could endorse the mayor. I just can't do it on the steps of city hall or as the director of [this organization]. I got to protect the organization, you know? In fact, I did endorse him in El Barrio and in my own neighborhood. And let me tell you, I thought the Spanish newspapers would pick it up, not the white media, and doggone it if the *Daily News* didn't have my name and the affiliation with [our organization]."

7. In light of recent IRS investigations of nonprofits, especially congregations, for political engagement, their perceptions are rooted squarely in reality (Internal Revenue Service 2006; Cooperman 2005; Allen 2004).

8. They are not alone, for misunderstanding and misstatement of the public rules of political engagement by nonprofit organizations in the United States are extensive among their leaders (Berry 2003). The majority of nonprofit organizations incorrectly limit their ability to represent well and to the fullest the interests of their constituents.

9. The data are from the survey responses of twenty-eight clergy in my purposive and random samples. Their churches, either alone or in alliance with other churches, collaborated with government through church-associated CDCs to serve Morrisania, Bedford-Stuyvesant, Harlem, and South Jamaica. The remaining two churches in my study did not collaborate with government, either directly or indirectly, and are excluded from the analysis.

10. Even if the churches that chartered CDCs decrease some of their electoral engagement, other activist churches in the four neighborhoods may maintain a significant level of electoral activism. For instance, two churches that neither chartered CDCs nor collaborated with government in any way sustained or increased their electoral engagement in the ten political activities over the decade. However, given the small number of churches in my sample that did not charter CDCs or collaborate with government, rigorous comparisons cannot be made between those churches that chartered CDCs and activist churches that did not. Accordingly, I cannot generalize about the political engagement of all activist African American churches in the four neighborhoods from the late 1980s through late 1990s.

11. The three directors generally endorsed demonstrations related to the lack of jobs, low wages, and housing affordability. They also sanctioned events focused on race and police misconduct. For example, in 1999 public demonstrations occurred over the death of Amadou Diallo, an innocent and unarmed West African immigrant shot by police officers in a Bronx neighborhood. The directors marched to support an investigation of the killing and changes to the enforcement practices of the New York Police Department in black communities. Similarly, they were involved in the protests following the 1997 torture of Haitian immigrant Abner Louima in a police precinct. One director commented, "Normally, I stay out of protests because they

can get out of hand. There is a time, you know, however, when you got to stand up for what's right. I mean the police were running wild that night they brutalized that man [Louima]. The least I could do was show my support and be a face in the crowd."

1. The ten churches are "very political," according to the five-measure index of political action that Allison Calhoun-Brown (1996) devised: (1) there are discussions in the church among members about politics; (2) church members talk about politics; (3) clergy encourage attenders to become more involved in politics; (4) political candidates and public officials speak during church services; and (5) clergy suggest that congregants engage in specific acts such attending political meetings, going to protest marches, or contacting officials. All of the churches in my purposive sample scored a 5 on the index.

2. I identified other alliance-based church-associated community development organizations in New York City. However, I excluded them for two reasons. One, they did not self-identify themselves to me as church-associated CDCs when I contacted them. Two, their founders were not African Americans or leaders of churches affiliated with historically black religious denominations. Among the exclusions were Industrial Areas Foundation affiliates such as East Brooklyn Congregations, South Bronx Churches, and Upper Manhattan Together, as well as other faith-based community organizations such as BEC New Communities.

REFERENCES

Abramson, Alan, and Lester Salamon. 1986. *Government Spending and the Nonprofit Sector in New York City.* Washington, DC: Urban Institute Press.

Adams, John Hurst. 2000. "Forgotten Black Ministers." *Washington Post,* December 22, A32.

Adler, Norman, and Blanche Davis Blank. 1975. *Political Clubs in New York.* New York: Praeger.

Allen, Mike. 2004. "NAACP Faces IRS Investigation." *Washington Post,* October 29, A8.

Allred, Christopher. 2000. "Breaking the Cycle of Abandonment: Using a Tax Enforcement Tool to Return Distressed Properties to Sound Private Ownership." New York: New York City Department of Housing Preservation and Development.

Altshuler, Alan A. 1970. *Community Control: The Black Demand for Participation in Large American Cities.* New York: Bobbs-Merrill.

Ammerman, Nancy. 2001. *Congregation and Community.* New Brunswick, NJ: Rutgers University Press.

———. 2002. "Connecting Mainline Protestant Churches with Public Life." In *The Quiet Hand of God: Faith-Based Activism and the Public Role of Mainline Protestantism,* edited by Robert Wuthnow and John H. Evans. Berkeley: University of California Press.

———. 2005. *Pillars of Faith: American Congregations and Their Partners, Building Traditions, Building Communities.* Berkeley: University of California Press.

Anderson, Elijah. 1990. *Streetwise: Race, Class, and Change in an Urban Community.* Chicago: University of Chicago Press.

———. 1999. *Code of the Street: Decency, Violence, and the Moral Life of the Inner City.* New York: W. W. Norton.

Andrews, Dale P. 2002. *Practical Theology for Black Churches: Bridging Black Theology and African American Folk Religion.* Louisville, KY: Westminster John Knox.

Andrews, Kenneth T. 2002. "Social Movements and Policy Implementation: The Mississippi Civil Rights Movement and the War on Poverty, 1965 to 1971." *American Sociological Review* 66:71–95.

Anonymous. 1992. "Pastor Abandoned by Perot Exit in Politics." *Jet,* August 13, 53–54.

Arian, Asher, Arthur S. Goldberg, John H. Mollenkopf, and Edward Rogowsky. 1991. *Changing New York City Politics.* New York: Routledge.

Arete Corporation. 1997. *Winners and Losers: Impacts of Budget Changes on Social Services and Community Districts in New York City, 1993–1996.* New York: Arete Corporation.

Arrow, Kenneth J. 1951. *Social Choice and Individual Values.* New Haven, CT: Yale University Press.

Ashcroft, John. 2003. Transcript of remarks delivered at the White House Faith-Based Conference, Tampa, Florida, December 5.

Assensoh, Akwasi, and Yvette Alex-Assensoh. 2003. "Black Political Leadership in the Post–Civil Rights Era." In *Black Political Organizations in the Post–Civil Rights Era,* edited by Ollie A. Johnson and Karin L. Sanford. New Brunswick, NJ: Rutgers University Press.

Bach, Victor, and Sherece Y. West. 1993. *Housing on the Block: Disinvestment and Abandonment Risks in New York City Neighborhoods.* New York: Community Service Society of New York.

Bacote, Clarence. 1955. "The Negro in Atlanta Politics." *Phylon* 69:333–50.

Baer, Hans A., and Merrill Singer. 1992. *African-American Religion in the Twentieth Century: Varieties of Protest and Accommodation.* Knoxville: University of Tennessee Press.

Banaszak, Lee Ann. 2002. "Inside and Outside the State: Movement Insider Status, Tactics, and Public Policy Achievements." Paper prepared for the Workshop on Social Movements and Public Policy, Laguna Beach, CA, January 11–13.

Banaszak, Lee Ann, Karen Beckwith, and Dieter Rucht. 2003. *Women's Movements Facing the Reconfigured State.* Cambridge: Cambridge University Press.

Barna, George, and Harry Jackson. 2004. *High-Impact African-American Churches: Leadership Concepts from Some of Today's Most Effective Churches.* Rev. ed. Ventura, CA: Regal.

Barnes, Sandra. 2004. "Priestly and Prophetic Influences on Black Social Services." *Social Problems* 51:202–21.

Barrett, Wayne. 2000. *Rudy! An Investigative Biography of Rudolph Giuliani.* New York: Basic Books.

Bartkowski, John P., and Helen A. Regis. 2003. *Charitable Choices: Religion, Race, and Poverty in the New Post-Welfare Era.* New York: New York University Press.

Baumgartner, Frank, and Beth Leech. 1998. *Basic Interests: The Importance of Groups in Politics and in Political Science.* Princeton, NJ: Princeton University Press.

Bayor, Ronald H. 1996. *Race and the Shaping of Twentieth-Century Atlanta.* Chapel Hill: University of North Carolina Press.

Bedford, Ian. 2004. "Some Issues Which Modify the Way Congregations Approach Their Community Involvement." Paper presented at the annual meeting of the Association for Research on Nonprofit Organizations and Voluntary Action Research, Los Angeles.

Bellush, Jewel, and Dick Netzer, eds. 1990. *Urban Politics New York Style.* Armonk, NY: M. E. Sharpe.

Berenson, William M., Kirk W. Elifson, and Tandy Tollerson III. 1976. "Preachers in Politics: A Study of Political Activism among the Black Ministry." *Journal of Black Studies* 6:373–92.

Berenyi, Eileen B. 1989. *Locally Funded Housing Programs in the United States: A Survey of the Fifty-one Most Populated Cities.* New York: Community Development Research Center, New School for Social Research.

Berndt, Harry Edward. 1977. *New Rulers in the Ghetto: The Community Development Corporation and Urban Poverty.* Westport, CT: Greenwood.

Bernstein, Emily M. 1993. "Neighborhood Report: Harlem." *New York Times,* September 12 (late Sunday ed.).

———. 1994. "A New Bradhurst: Harlem Trades Symbols of Decay for Symbols of Renewal." *New York Times,* January 6, B1.

Berrien, Jenny, Omar McRoberts, and Christopher Winship. 2000. "Religion and the Boston Miracle: The Effect of Black Ministry on Youth Violence." In *Who Will Provide? Religion and Social Welfare in America,* edited by Mary Jo Bane, Brent Coffin, and Ronald Thiemann. Boulder, CO: Westview.

Berry, Jeffrey M. 2003. *A Voice for Nonprofits.* Washington, DC: Brookings Institution Press.

Beyerlein, Kraig, and Mark Chaves. 2003. "The Political Activities of Religious Congregations in the United States." *Journal for the Scientific Study of Religion* 42:229–46.

Biles, Robert. 2001. "Mayor David Dinkins and the Politics of Race in New York City." In *African-American Mayors: Race, Politics, and the American City,* edited by David Colburn and Jeffrey Adler. Urbana: University of Illinois Press.

Billingsley, Andrew. 1999. *Mighty like a River: The Black Church and Social Reform.* New York: Oxford University Press.

Biondi, Martha. 2003. *To Stand and Fight: The Struggle for Civil Rights in Postwar New York City.* Cambridge, MA: Harvard University Press.

Black, Amy, Douglas Koopman, and David Ryden. 2004. *Of Little Faith: The Politics of George W. Bush's Faith-Based Initiative.* Washington, DC: Georgetown University Press.

Blakely, Edward J., and Armando Aparicio. 1990. "Balancing Social and Economic Objectives: The Case of California's Community Development Corporations." *Journal of the Community Development Society* 21:115–28.

Bobo, Lawrence, and Franklin D. Gilliam Jr. 1990. "Race, Sociopolitical Participation, and Black Empowerment." *American Political Science Review* 84:377–94.

Bockmeyer, Janice. 2003. "Devolution and the Transformation of Community Housing Activism." *Social Science Journal* 40:175–88.

Bositis, David A. 2006. "Black Churches and the Faith-Based Initiative: Findings from a National Survey." Washington, DC: Joint Center for Political and Economic Studies.

Boston, Thomas D., and Catherine L. Ross. 1997. *The Inner City: Urban Poverty and Economic Development in the Next Century.* New Brunswick, NJ: Transaction.

Braconi, Frank. 1999. "In Re *In Rem:* Innovation and Expediency in New York's Housing Policy. In *Housing and Community Development in New York City: Facing the Future,* edited by Michael Schill. Albany: State University of New York Press.

Branch, Taylor. 1988. *Parting the Waters: America in the King Years, 1954–63.* New York; Simon and Schuster.

Brandt, Nat. 1996. *Harlem at War: The Black Experience in WWII.* Syracuse: Syracuse University Press.

Bratt, Rachel G. 1989. *Rebuilding a Low-Income Housing Policy.* Philadelphia: Temple University Press.

Brazier, Arthur. 1969. *Black Self-Determination: The Story of the Woodlawn Organization.* Grand Rapids, MI: Eerdmans.

Briggs, Xavier de Souza. 1998. "Brown Kids in White Suburbs: Housing Mobility and the Many Faces of Social Capital." *Housing Policy Debate* 9:177–221.

Briggs, Xavier de Souza, and Elizabeth J. Mueller, with Mercer Sullivan. 1997. *From Neighborhood to Community: Evidence on the Social Effects of Community Development.* New York: Community Development Research Center, New School for Social Research.

Brown, Ethan. 2005. *Queens Reigns Supreme: Fat Cat, 50 Cent, and the Rise of the Hip Hop Hustler.* New York: Anchor.

Brown, Robert, and Todd Shaw. 2002. "Separate Nations: Two Attitudinal Dimensions of Black Nationalism." *Journal of Politics* 64:22–44.

Brown, Ronald, Michael Dawson, and James Jackson. 1994. *National Black Politics Study, 1993: Data File and Codebook.* Available from Inter-university Consortium for Political and Social Research, University of Michigan, Ann Arbor.

Browning, Rufus P., Dale Rogers Marshall, and David H. Tabb. 1984. *Protest Is Not*

*Enough: The Struggle of Blacks and Hispanics for Equality in Urban Politics.* Berkeley: University of California Press.

——. 1986. "Protest Is Not Enough: A Theory of Political Incorporation." *PS* 19:576–81.

——, eds. 2003. *Racial Politics in American Cities.* 3rd ed. New York: Longman.

Bunche, Ralph J. 1973. *The Political Status of the Negro in the Age of FDR.* Chicago: University of Chicago Press.

Burns, Peter. 2006. *Electoral Politics Is Not Enough: Racial and Ethnic Minorities and Urban Politics.* Albany: State University of New York Press.

Bush, George W. 2001. *Rallying the Armies of Compassion.* Washington, DC: White House Office of Faith-Based and Community Initiatives.

——. 2003. Transcript of prepared remarks delivered at the National Religious Broadcasters' Convention, Nashville, February 10.

Bush, Rod. 1999. *We Are Not What We Seem: Black Nationalism and Class Struggle in the American Century.* New York: New York University Press.

Butts, Calvin O. 1998. Transcript of remarks during taping of *Like It Is,* show 1108, aired May 31.

Calhoun-Brown, Allison. 1996. "African American Churches and Political Mobilization: The Psychological Impact of Organizational Resources." *Journal of Politics* 58:935–53.

——. 2003a. "What a Fellowship: Civil Society, African American Churches, and Public Life." In *New Day Begun: Black Churches, Public Influences, and American Civic Culture,* edited by R. Drew Smith. Durham, NC: Duke University Press.

——. 2003b. "Will the Circle Be Unbroken: The Political Involvement of Black Churches since the 1960s." In *Black Political Organizations in the Post–Civil Rights Era,* edited by Ollie A. Johnson and Karin L. Sanford. New Brunswick, NJ: Rutgers University Press.

Cannato, Vincent J. 2001. *The Ungovernable City: John Lindsay and His Struggle to Save New York.* New York: Basic Books.

Capeci, Dominic. 1977. *The Harlem Riot of 1943.* Philadelphia: Temple University Press.

Carle, Robert. 1999. "Shelter in the Time of Storm: The Black Church in New York City." In *Signs of Hope in the City: Ministries of Community Renewal,* edited by Robert D. Carle and Louis A. DeCaro Jr. Valley Forge, PA: Judson.

Carlson-Thies, Stanley. 2001. "Charitable Choice: Bringing Religion Back into American Welfare." *Journal of Policy History* 13:109–32.

Carmichael, Stokely, and Charles Hamilton. 1967. *Black Power.* New York: Vintage.

Carnes, Tony. 2001. "A Profile of New York City's African American Church Leaders." In *New York Glory: Religions in the City,* edited by Tony Carnes and Anna Karpathakis. New York: New York University Press.

Center for Urban Education. 1967. *Community Attitudes in Bedford-Stuyvesant: An Area Study.* New York: Center for Public Education.

Chambre, Susan. 2001. "The Changing Nature of 'Faith' in Faith-Based Organizations: Secularization and Ecumenicism in Four AIDS Organizations in New York City." *Social Service Review* 75:435–55.

Chaskin, Robert J., Prudence Brown, Sudhir Venkatesh, and Avis Vidal. 2001. *Building Community Capacity.* New York: Aldine de Gruyter.

Chaskin, Robert J., and Sunil Garg. 1997. "The Issue of Governance in Neighborhood-Based Initiatives." *Urban Affairs Review* 32:631–61.

Chaves, Mark. 1998. *National Congregations Study: Data File and Codebook.* Tucson: University of Arizona, Department of Sociology. Available from the American Religion Data Archive, www.theARDA.com.

———. 1999. "Religious Congregations and Welfare Reform: Who Will Take Advantage of 'Charitable Choice'?" *American Sociological Review* 64:836–46.

———. 2004. *Congregations in America.* Cambridge, MA: Harvard University Press.

Chaves, Mark, and Lynne Higgins. 1992. "Comparing the Community Involvement of Black and White Congregations." *Journal for the Scientific Study of Religion* 31:425–40.

Chaves, Mark, and William Tsitsos. 2001. "Congregations and Social Services: What They Do, How They Do It, and With Whom?" *Nonprofit and Voluntary Sector Quarterly* 30:660–83.

Chaves, Mark, Laura Stephens, and Joseph Galaskiewicz. 2004. "Does Government Funding Suppress Nonprofits' Political Activity?" *American Sociological Review* 69:292–316.

Chen, David W. 2003. "One Housing Woe Gives Way to Another: New York Is No Longer Awash in Abandoned Buildings, Now the Issue Is Supply." *New York Times,* December 21, B1.

Chinyelu, Mamadou. 1999. *Harlem Ain't Nothin' but a Third World Country.* Los Angeles: Mustard Seed.

Chong, Dennis. 1991. *Collective Action and the Civil Rights Movement.* Chicago: University of Chicago Press.

Chrislip, David D., and Carl E. Larson. 1994. *Collaborative Leadership: How Citizens and Civic Leaders Can Make a Difference.* San Francisco: Jossey-Bass.

Cisneros, Henry. 1996. "Higher Ground: Faith Communities and Community Building." *Cityscape* 2:71–84.

Citizens Budget Commission. 1997. *The State of Municipal Services in the 1990s: Social Services in New York City.* New York: Citizens Budget Commission.

City of New York. 1989. *The Ten-Year Plan.* New York: Department of Housing Preservation and Development, City of New York.

Clark, Kenneth B. 1967. *Dark Ghetto: Dilemmas of Social Power.* New York: Harper Torchbooks.

Clark, Shelton Leroy. 1978. "The Black Clergy as Agents of Social Change: With an

Emphasis on the Life of Adam Clayton Powell." Ph.D. diss., Rutgers University, State University of New Jersey.

Clarke, Susan E. 2000. "Governance Tasks and Nonprofit Organizations." In *Nonprofits in Urban America,* edited by Richard C. Hula and Cynthia Jackson-Elmoore. Westport, CT: Quorum.

Clavel, Pierre, Jessica Pitt, and Jordan Yin. 1997. "The Community Option in Urban Policy." *Urban Affairs Review* 32:435–58.

Cleage, Albert, Jr. 1972. *Black Christian Nationalism: New Directions for the Black Church.* New York: William Morrow.

Clemetson, Robert A., and Roger Coates. 1992. *Restoring Broken Places and Re-building Communities: A Casebook on African-American Church Involvement in Community Economic Development.* Washington, DC: National Congress for Community Economic Development.

Cnaan, Ram A. 1999. *The Newer Deal: Social Work and Religion in Partnership.* New York: Columbia University Press.

———. 2002. *The Invisible Caring Hand: American Congregations and the Provision of Welfare.* New York: New York University Press.

Cohen, Adam, and Elizabeth Taylor. 2000. *American Pharaoh: Mayor Richard J. Daley—His Battle for Chicago and the Nation.* Boston: Little, Brown.

Cohen, Cathy J. 1999. *The Boundaries of Blackness: AIDS and the Breakdown of Black Politics.* Chicago: University of Chicago Press.

———. 2001. "Social Capital, Intervening Institutions, and Political Power." In *Social Capital and Poor Communities,* edited by Susan Saegert, J. Phillip Thompson, and Mark R. Warren. New York: Russell Sage.

Cohen, Cathy J., and Michael Dawson. 1993. "Neighborhood Poverty and African American Politics." *American Political Science Review* 87:286–302.

Colburn, David, and Jeffrey Adler. 2001. *African-American Mayors: Race, Politics, and the American City.* Urbana: University of Illinois Press.

Connolly, Harold X. 1977. *A Ghetto Grows in Brooklyn.* New York: New York University Press.

Conover, Pamela. 1984. "The Influence of Group Identification on Political Perception and Evaluation." *Journal of Politics* 46:760–85.

Cooperman, Alan. 2005. "IRS Reviews Church's Status." *Washington Post,* November 19, A3.

Countryman, Matthew J. 2006. *Up South: Civil Rights and Black Power in Philadelphia.* Philadelphia: University of Pennsylvania Press.

Coy, Patrick G., and Timothy Hedeen. 2005. "A Stage Model of Social Movement Co-optation: Community Mediation in the United States." *Sociological Quarterly* 46:405–35.

Crawford, Sue, and Laura Olson. 2001. "Clergy as Political Actors in Urban Contexts." In *Christian Clergy in American Politics,* edited by Sue E. S. Crawford and Laura Olson. Baltimore: Johns Hopkins University Press.

Cross, Theodore. 1984. *The Black Power Imperative: Racial Inequality and the Politics of Nonviolence.* New York: Faulkner.

Culhane, Dennis P., Stephen Metraux, and Susan M. Wachter. 1999. "Homelessness and Public Shelter Provision in New York City." In *Housing and Community Development in New York City: Facing the Future,* edited by Michael H. Schill. Albany: State University of New York Press.

Cuoto, Richard A. 1999. *Making Democracy Work Better: Mediating Structures, Social Capital, and the Democratic Prospect.* Chapel Hill: University of North Carolina Press.

Daniels, C. Mackey. 2001. "President of the Progressive National Baptist Convention, Inc., Compares Charitable Choice Initiative to 'Thirty Pieces of Silver.'" Press release of the Progressive National Baptist Convention, February 14.

Danielson, Michael N., and Jameson W. Doig. 1982. *New York: The Politics of Urban Regional Development.* Berkeley: University of California Press.

Dash, Michael I. N., and Stephen C. Rasor. 2001–2002. "ITC/FaithFactor Project 2000: An Affirmation for the Journey Inward and Outward." *Journal of the Interdenominational Theological Center* 29:9–24.

Davidson, James D., and Jerome R. Koch. 1998. "Beyond Mutual and Public Benefits." In *Sacred Companies: Organizational Aspects of Religion and Religious Aspects of Organizations,* edited by N. J. Demerath, Peter Dobkin Hall, Terry Schmitt, and Rhys. H. Williams. New York: Oxford University Press.

Davis, Darren W. 1997. "Nonrandom Measurement Error and Race of Interviewer Effects among African Americans." *Public Opinion Quarterly* 61:183–207.

Davis, Darren W., and Ronald E. Brown. 2002. "The Antipathy of Black Nationalism: Behavioral and Attitudinal Consequences of an African American Ideology." *American Journal of Political Science* 46:239–53.

Dawson, Michael. 1994. *Behind the Mule: Race and Class in African-American Politics.* Princeton, NJ: Princeton University Press.

———. 2001. *Black Visions: The Roots of Contemporary African-American Political Ideologies.* Chicago: University of Chicago Press.

Day, Donna C. (Katie). 2001. "The Construction of Political Strategies among African American Clergy." In *Christian Clergy in American Politics,* edited by Sue E. S. Crawford and Laura R. Olson. Baltimore: Johns Hopkins University Press.

Day, Katie. 2002. *Prelude to Struggle: African American Clergy and Community Organizing for Economic Development in the 1990s.* Lanham, MD: University Press of America.

DeParle, Jason. 2005. "Hispanic Group Thrives on Faith and Federal Aid." *New York Times,* May 3, A1.

Derthick, Martha. 1975. *Uncontrollable Spending for Social Service Grants.* Washington, DC: Brookings Institution Press.

Detroit News. 1991. "lack American Perspectives [United States]: The Future of

Civil Rights, November 11–25."Computer file, ICPSR version. Rochester, NY: Gordon S. Black Corporation.

DeVita, Carol J. 1999. "Nonprofits and Devolution: What Do We Know?" In *Nonprofits and Government: Collaboration and Conflict,* edited by Elizabeth T. Boris and C. Eugene Steuerle. Washington, DC: Urban Institute Press.

DiIulio, John J., Jr. 2002. "The Three Faith Factors." *Public Interest* 129:50–64.

Dinkins, David. 1992. Transcript of remarks during taping of *Like It Is,* show 838, aired January 12.

Dionne, E. J., and Ming Hsu Chen, eds. 2001. *Sacred Places, Civic Purposes: Should Government Help Faith-Based Charity?* Washington, DC: Brookings Institution Press.

Donahue, John D., and Joseph S. Nye Jr. 2002. *Market-Based Governance: Supply Side, Demand Side, Upside, and Downside.* Washington, DC: Brookings Institution Press.

Du Bois, W. E. B. 1923. "The Hosts of Black Labor." *The Nation,* May 9, 540–41.

Eaton, Leslie. 1999. "Banks Put Their Faith in Building Churches." *New York Times,* January 10, B1.

Ebaugh, Helen Rose, Janet S. Chafetz, and Paula Pipes. 2005. "Funding Good Works: Funding Sources of Faith-Based Social Service Coalitions." *Nonprofit and Voluntary Sector Quarterly* 34:448–72.

Eckstein, Harry. 1991. "Rationality and Frustration in Political Behavior." In *The Economic Approach to Politics,* edited by Kristen Renwick Monroe. New York: HarperCollins.

Eisinger, Peter K. 1982a. "Black Employment in Municipal Jobs: The Impact of Black Political Power." *American Political Science Review* 76:380–92.

———. 1982b. "The Economic Conditions of Black Municipal Employment." *American Journal of Political Science* 76:754–71.

———. 1998. "City Politics in an Era of Federal Devolution." *Urban Affairs Review* 33:308–25.

Elkin, Stephen L. 1987. *City and Regime in the American Republic.* Chicago: University of Chicago Press.

Ellen, Ingrid Gould, Michael H. Schill, Amy Ellen Schwartz, and Scott Susin. 2001. "Building Homes, Reviving Neighborhoods: Spillovers from Subsidized Construction of Owner-Occupied Housing in New York City." *Journal of Housing Research* 12:185–216.

Emerson, Michael O., and Christian Smith. 2000. *Divided by Faith: Evangelical Religion and the Problem of Race in America.* New York: Oxford University Press.

English, James W. 1967. *Handyman of the Lord: The Life and Ministry of Rev. William Holmes Borders Jr.* New York: Meredith.

Evers, Adalbert. 1995. "Part of the Welfare Mix: The Third Sector as an Intermediate Area." *Voluntas* 6:159–82.

Fainstein, Norman I., and Susan S. Fainstein. 1974. *Urban Political Movements: The*

*Search for Power by Minority Groups in American Cities.* Englewood Cliffs, NJ: Prentice-Hall.

———. 1976. "The Future of Community Control." *American Political Science Review* 70:905–23.

Fainstein, Susan S., and Norman I. Fainstein. 1982. "Neighborhood Enfranchisement and Urban Redevelopment." *Journal of Planning Education and Research,* Summer, 11–19.

Fainstein, Susan S., Norman I. Fainstein, and P. Jefferson Armistead. 1983. "Bureaucratic Enfranchisement under the Community Development Block Grant Program." *Journal of Urban Affairs* 5:123–39.

Farnsley, Arthur E., Jr. 2001. "Can Faith-Based Organizations Compete?" *Nonprofit and Voluntary Sector Quarterly* 30:99–111.

———. 2003. *Rising Expectations: Urban Congregations, Welfare Reform, and Civic Life.* Bloomington: Indiana University Press.

Farris, Anne. 2004. "Kerry Lays Out Faith-Based Platform." Available from the Roundtable on Religion and Social Welfare Policy, www.religionandsocialpolicy.org/news/article.cfm?id=1687.

Ferguson, Karen. 2002. *Black Politics in New Deal Atlanta.* Chapel Hill: University of North Carolina Press.

Ferguson, Ronald F., and William T. Dickens, eds. 1999. *Urban Problems and Community Development.* Washington, DC: Brooking Institution Press.

Ferguson, Ronald F., and Sarah E. Stoutland. 1999. "Re-conceiving the Community Development System." In *Urban Problems and Community Development,* edited by Ronald F. Ferguson and William T. Dickens. Washington, DC: Brookings Institution Press.

Ferman, Barbara. 1996. *Challenging the Growth Machine: Neighborhood Politics in Chicago and Pittsburgh.* Philadelphia: Temple University Press.

Finder, Alan. 1995. "New York Pledge to House Poor Works a Rare, Quiet Revolution." *New York Times,* April 30, A1.

Fish, John Hall. 1973. *Black Power/White Control: The Struggle of the Woodlawn Organization in Chicago.* Princeton, NJ: Princeton University Press.

Flake, Floyd, and Donna Marie Williams. 1999. *The Way of the Bootstrapper: Nine Action Steps for Achieving Your Dreams.* New York: HarperCollins.

Formicola, Jo Renee, and Hubert Morken. 2001. *Religious Leaders and Faith-Based Politics: Ten Profiles.* Lanham, MD: Rowman and Littlefield.

Formicola, Jo Renee, Mary Segers, and Paul Weber. 2003. *Faith-Based Initiatives and the Bush Administration: The Good, the Bad, and the Ugly.* Lanham, MD: Rowman and Littlefield.

Fosler, R. Scott. 2002. *Working Better Together: How Government, Business, and Nonprofit Organizations can Achieve Public Purposes through Cross-Sector Collaboration, Alliances, and Partnerships.* Washington, DC: Three Sector Initiative.

Franklin, Robert Michael. 1994. "The Safest Place on Earth: The Culture of Black

Congregations." In *American Congregations*, vol. 2, *New Perspectives in the Study of Congregations*, edited by James Wind and James Lewis. Chicago: University of Chicago Press.

———. 1997. *Another Day's Journey: Black Churches Confronting the American Crisis*. Minneapolis: Augsburg Fortress.

———. N.d. "Crisis in the Village: Restoring Hope to African American Communities." Manuscript.

Frazier, E. Franklin. 1964. *The Negro Church in America*. New York: Schocken.

Frederick, Gloria B. 2001. "Organizing around Faith: The Roots and Organizational Dimensions of African American Faith-Based Community Development Corporations." Ph.D. diss., Rutgers University, State University of New Jersey.

Freedman, Samuel G. 1993. *Upon This Rock: The Miracles of a Black Church*. New York: HarperCollins.

French, Howard. 1988. "Restoring Abyssinian Church's Stature." *New York Times*, February 27, B33.

Fuchs, Esther. 1992. *Mayors and Money: Fiscal Policy in New York and Chicago*. Chicago: University of Chicago Press

Gamson, William A. 1968. *Power and Discontent*. Homewood, IL: Dorsey.

———. 1990. *The Strategy of Social Protest*. 2nd ed. Belmont, CA: Wadsworth.

Gartell, Leland, and Nick Herman. 1971. "Participation of Religious Institutions in Non-profit Housing Corporations, New York City." New York: Council of Churches of the City of New York.

Gaventa, John. 1980. *Power and Powerlessness: Quiescence and Rebellion in an Appalachian Valley*. Champaign: University of Illinois Press.

Gelb, Joyce. 1970. "Blacks, Blocs, and Ballots: The Relevance of Party Politics to the Negro." *Polity* 3:44–69.

Geto and De Milly. 2002. "Innovative Community-Government Partnership Reclaims Seven Classic Harlem Buildings." Press release, August 19.

Gilbreath, E. 1995. "The Pulpit King." *Christianity Today* 39:25–26.

Gilliam, Reginald Earl. 1975. *Black Political Development: An Advocacy Analysis*. Port Washington, NY: Dunellen.

Gittell, Marilyn. 1980. *Limits to Citizen Participation: The Decline of Community Organizations*. Beverly Hills, CA: Sage.

Gittell, Marilyn, Isolda Ortega-Bustamante, and Tracy Steffy. 1999. *Women Creating Social Capital and Social Change: A Study of Women-Led Community Development Organizations*. New York: Howard Samuels State Management and Policy Center, Graduate School and University Center, City University of New York.

Giugni, Marco G. 1998. "Introduction: Social Movements and Change: Incorporation, Transformation, and Democratization." In *From Contention to Democracy*, edited by Marco G. Giugni, Doug McAdam, and Charles Tilly. Lanham, MD: Rowman and Littlefield.

Giugni, Marco G., and Florence Passy. 1998. "Contentious Politics in Complex

Societies: New Social Movements between Conflict and Cooperation." In *From Contention to Democracy*, edited by Marco G. Giugni, Doug McAdam, and Charles Tilly. Lanham, MD: Rowman and Littlefield.

Glazer, Nathan, and Daniel Patrick Moynihan. 1963. *Beyond the Melting Pot: The Negroes, Puerto Ricans, Jews, Italians, and Irish of New York City.* Cambridge, MA: MIT Press.

Glenn, Charles. 2002. *The Ambiguous Embrace: Government and Faith-Based Schools and Social Agencies.* Princeton, NJ: Princeton University Press.

Glickman, Norm, and Lisa Servon. 1998. "More Than Bricks and Sticks: Five Components of Community Development Corporation Capacity." *Housing Policy Debate* 9:497–540.

Goetz, Edward G. 1993. *Shelter Burden: Local Politics and Progressive Housing Policy.* Philadelphia: Temple University Press.

Goetz, Edward G., and Mara S. Sidney. 1994. "Revenge of the Property Owners: Community Development and the Politics of Property." *Journal of Urban Affairs* 16:319–34.

Goldsmith, Stephen. 2000. "Having Faith in Our Neighborhoods: The Front Porch Alliance." In *What's God Got to Do with the American Experiment?* edited by E. J. Dionne Jr. and John J. DiIulio Jr. Washington, DC: Brookings Institution Press.

———. 2003. "City Hall and Religion: Why, When, and How to Lead." Cambridge, MA: Kennedy School of Government, Harvard University.

Gonzalez, Evelyn Diaz. 2004. *The Bronx.* New York: Columbia University Press.

Gopnik, Adam. 2002. "Saving Paradise: The Preservationist, the Pastor, and a Night Club in Harlem." *New Yorker*, April 20–29, 76–86.

Gosnell, Harold F. 1935. *Negro Politicians: The Rise of Negro Politics in Chicago.* Chicago: University of Chicago Press.

Gramby-Sobukwe, Sharon. n.d. "Who Cares for the Urban Poor? Changing Race, Class, and Religious Dynamics in the Role of the African-American Church in Civil Society." Manuscript.

Green, Charles, and Basil Wilson. 1992. *The Struggle for Black Empowerment in New York City: Beyond the Politics of Pigmentation.* New York: McGraw-Hill.

Green, John, and Amy Sherman. 2002. *Fruitful Collaborations: A Survey of Government-Funded Faith-Based Programs in Fifteen States.* Charlottesville, VA: Hudson Institute.

Green, Larry. 1979. "Harlem in the Great Depression." Ph.D. diss., Columbia University.

Greenberg, Cheryl Lynn. 1991. *Or Does It Explode? Black Harlem in the Great Depression.* New York: Oxford University Press.

Greenstone, J. David, and Paul E. Peterson. 1976. *Race and Authority in Urban Politics: Community Participation and the War on Poverty.* Chicago: University of Chicago Press.

Gregory, Steven. 1998. *Black Corona: Race and the Politics of Place in an Urban Community.* Princeton, NJ: Princeton University Press.

Grimshaw, William J. 1992. *Bitter Fruit: Black Politics and the Chicago Machine, 1931–1991.* Chicago: University of Chicago Press.

Grogan, Paul, and Tony Proscio. 2000. *Comeback Cities: A Blueprint for Urban Neighborhood Revival.* Boulder, CO: Westview.

Gurin, Patricia, Shirley Hatchett, and James Jackson. 1989. *Hope and Independence: Blacks' Response to Electoral and Party Politics.* New York Sage Foundation.

Hadnot, Ira. 2004. "Some Black Churches Shun Politics." *Dallas Morning News,* August 4.

Hamilton, Charles V. 1972. *The Black Preacher in America.* New York: William Morrow.

———. 1973. "Neighborhood Control and Urban Governance." In *Neighborhood Control in the 1970s: Politics, Administration, and Citizen Participation,* edited by George Frederickson. New York: Chandler.

———. 1979. "The Patron-Recipient Relationship and Minority Politics in New York City." *Political Science Quarterly* 94:211–27.

———. 1982. Foreword ro *The New Black Politics: The Search for Political Power,* edited by Michael B. Preston, Lenneal J. Henderson Jr., and Paul Puryear. New York: Longman.

———. 1990. "Needed, More Foxes: The Black Experience." In *Urban Politics New York Style,* edited by Jewel Bellush and Dick Netzer. Armonk, NY: M. E. Sharpe.

Harris, Fredrick C. 1999. *Something Within: Religion in African-American Political Activism.* New York: Oxford University Press.

———. 2001. "Black Churches and Civic Traditions: Outreach, Activism, and the Politics of Public Funding of Faith-Based Ministries." In *Can Charitable Choice Work? Covering Religion's Impact on Urban Affairs and Social Services,* edited by Andrew Walsh. Hartford, CT: Pew Program on Religion and the News Media and Greenberg Center for the Study of Religion in Public Life.

———. 2005. "Black Churches and Machine Politics in Chicago." In *: Clergy Influence, Organizational Partnership, and Civic Empowerment,* edited by R. Drew Smith and Fredrick C. Harris. Lanham, MD: Rowman and Littlefield.

Harris, James. 1987. *Black Ministers and the Laity in the Urban Church.* Lanham, MD: University Press of America.

Harris, Louis, and Associates. 1969. *New York City Racial and Religious Survey, No. 1925: Data File and Codebook.* Available from the American Religion Data Archive, www.thearda.com.

Harris, Louis, and Bert E. Swanson. 1970. *Black-Jewish Relations in New York City.* New York: Praeger.

Harris-Lacewell, Melissa. 2004. *Barbershops, Bibles, and BET: Everyday Talk and Black Political Thought.* Princeton, NJ: Princeton University Press.

Hartocollis, Anemona. 1998. "Religious Leaders Plan Schools with Public Funds in New York," *New York Times,* December 29, A1.

Haynes, Bruce. 2001. *Red Lines, Black Spaces: The Politics of Race and Space in a Middle-Class Black Suburb.* New Haven, CT: Yale University Press.

Hays, Sharon. 1994. "Structure and Agency and the Sticky Problem of Culture." *Sociological Theory* 12:57–72.

Hehir, J. Bryan. 2000. "Religious Ideas and Social Policy: Subsidiarity and Catholic Style of Ministry." In *Who Will Provide? Religion and Social Welfare in America,* edited by Mary Jo Bane, Brent Coffin, and Ronald Thiemann. Boulder, CO: Westview.

Henig, Jeffrey, Richard Hula, Marion Orr, and Desiree Pedescleaux. 1999. *The Color of School Reform: Race, Politics, and the Challenge of Urban Education.* Princeton, NJ: Princeton University Press.

Hevesi, Alan. 1999. *Fiscal Year 1999: Report on New York City Contracts.* New York: Office of the Comptroller, City of New York.

———. 2000. *Fiscal Year 2000: Report on New York City Contracts.* New York: Office of the Comptroller, City of New York.

Hevesi, Alan, and Ira Millstein. 2001. *Nonprofit Governance in New York City.* New York: Office of the Comptroller, City of New York.

Higginbotham, Evelyn Brooks. 1993. *Righteous Discontent: The Women's Movement in the Black Baptist Church, 1880–1920.* Cambridge, MA: Harvard University Press.

Hood, Christopher. 1983. *The Tools of Government.* London: Macmillan.

Hopkins, Bruce. 1992. *Charity, Advocacy, and the Law.* New York: John Wiley and Sons.

Housing First. 2005. "A Home for All New Yorkers: Housing First! A 2005 Policy Update." New York: Housing First.

Howe, Marvine. 1992. "Black Clergy Urges Boycott in 'Day of Absence.'" *New York Times,* June 16: B3.

Howard, Christopher, Michael Lipsky, and Dale Rogers Marshall. 1994. "Citizen Participation in Urban Politics: Rise and Routinization." In *Big-City Politics, Governance, and Fiscal Constraints,* edited by George E. Peterson. Washington, DC: Urban Institute Press.

Huckfeldt, Robert, Eric Plutzer, and John Sprague. 1993. "Alternative Contexts of Political Behavior: Churches, Neighborhoods, and Individuals." *Journal of Politics* 55:365–81.

Hula, Richard C., and Cynthia Jackson-Elmoore. 2000. "Nonprofit Organizations, Minority Political Incorporation, and Local Governance." In *Nonprofits in Urban America,* edited by Richard C. Hula and Cynthia Jackson-Elmoore. Westport, CT: Quorum.

Hula, Richard C., Cynthia Jackson, and Marion Orr. 1997. "Urban Politics, Governing Nonprofits, and Community Revitalization." *Urban Affairs Review* 32:459–89.

Hutchings, Vincent L., Nicholas A. Valentino, Tasha Philpot, and Ismail K. White.

2004. "The Compassion Strategy: Race and the Gender Gap in American Politics." *Public Opinion Quarterly* 68:512–41.

Imbroscio, David L. 1997. *Reconstructing City Politics: Alternative Economic Development and Urban Regimes.* Thousand Oaks, CA: Sage.

Institute for Puerto Rican Policy. 1994. "The Giuliani Budget Cuts and People of Color: Disproportionate Employment Impact." New York: Institute for Puerto Rican Policy.

Internal Revenue Service. 2006. Project 302: Political Activities Compliance Initiative. Washington, DC: Internal Revenue Service.

Jackson, John. 2003. *Harlemworld: Doing Race and Class in Contemporary Black America.* Chicago: University of Chicago Press.

Jackson-Elmoore, Cynthia, and Richard C. Hula. 2000. "Introduction: An Overview of Emerging Roles of Nonprofits in Urban America." In *Nonprofits in Urban America,* edited by Richard C. Hula and Cynthia Jackson-Elmoore. Westport, CT: Quorum.

Jargowsky, Paul A., and Rebecca Yang. 2006. "The 'Underclass' Revisited: A Social Problem in Decline." *Journal of Urban Affairs* 28:55–70.

Jeavons, Thomas H. 1994. *When the Bottom Line Is Faithfulness: Managing Christian Service Organizations.* Bloomington: Indiana University Press.

———. 2003. "The Vitality and Independence of Religious Organizations." *Society,* January/February, 27–36.

Jennings, James. 1992. *The Politics of Black Empowerment: The Transformation of Black Activism in Urban America.* Detroit: Wayne State University Press.

———. 2005. "Black Faith-Based Coalitions in Boston: Civic Advantages and Challenges." In *Black Clergy and Local Politics: Clergy Influence, Organizational Partnerships, and Civic Empowerment,* edited by R. Drew Smith and Fredrick Harris. Lanham, MD: Rowman and Littlefield.

Johnson, Ollie A., and Karin L. Sanford, eds. 2003. *Black Political Organizations in the Post–Civil Rights Era.* New Brunswick, NJ: Rutgers University Press.

Jones, Lawrence N. 1999. "The Black Churches: A New Agenda." In *African American Religious History: A Documentary Witness,* 2nd ed., edited by Milton C. Sernett. Durham, NC: Duke University Press.

Jones, William A. 1979. *God in the Ghetto.* Elgin, IL: Progressive Baptist.

Jones-Correa, Michael, ed. 2001. *Governing American Cities: Inter-ethnic Coalitions, Competition, and Conflict.* New York: Russell Sage Foundation.

Joyce, Patrick D. 2003. *No Fire Next Time: Black-Korean Conflicts and the Future of America's Cities.* Ithaca, NY: Cornell University Press.

Judd, Dennis R., and Todd Swanstrom. 1998. *City Politics: Private Power and Public Policy.* New York: Longman.

Katznelson, Ira. 1973. *Black Men, White Cities: Race, Politics, and Migration in the United States, 1900–30, and Britain, 1948–68.* Chicago: University of Chicago Press.

———. 1981. *City Trenches: Urban Politics and the Patterning of Class in the United States.* Chicago: University of Chicago Press.

Keiser, Richard A. 1997. *Subordination or Empowerment? African-American Leadership and the Struggle for Urban Political Power.* New York: Oxford University Press.

Kelly, Rita Mae. 1977. *Community Control of Economic Development: The Boards of Directors of Community Development Corporations.* New York: Praeger.

Kennedy, Sheila Suess, and Wolfgang Bielefeld. 2006. *Charitable Choice at Work: Evaluating Faith-Based Job Programs in the States.* Washington, DC: Georgetown University Press.

Kershaw, Joseph A. 1970. *Government against Poverty.* Washington, DC: Brookings Institution.

Kettl, Donald F. 1993. *Sharing Power: Public Governance and Private Markets.* Washington, DC: Brookings Institution Press.

Kilson, Martin. 1971. "Political Change in the Negro Ghetto, 1900–1940s." In *Key Issues in the Afro-American Experience,* edited by Nathan I. Huggins, Martin Kilson, and Daniel M. Fox. San Diego: Harcourt Brace Jovanovich.

———. 1987. "The Weakness of Black Politics: Cursed by Factions and Feuds." *Dissent,* Fall: 523–29.

Kim, Claire Jean. 2000. *Bitter Fruit: The Politics of Black-Korean Conflict in New York City.* New Haven, CT: Yale University Press.

King, Martin Luther King, Jr. 1967. *Where Do We Go from Here? Chaos or Community.* Boston: Beacon.

Kingdon, John W. 1995. *Agendas, Alternatives, and Public Policies.* New York: HarperCollins.

Kirtzman, Andrew. 2000. *Rudy Giuliani: Emperor of the City.* New York: William Morrow.

Klein, Joe. 1997. "In God They Trust." *New Yorker,* June 16, 40–48.

Koch, Edward I., with William Rauch. 1984. *Mayor.* New York: Simon and Schuster.

Kodras, Janet E. 1997. "Restructuring the State: Devolution, Privatization, and the Geographic Distribution of Power and Capacity in Governance." In *State Devolution in America: Implications for a Diverse Society,* edited by Lynn A. Staeheli, Janet E. Kodras, and Colin Flint. Thousand Oaks, CA: Sage.

Kooiman, Jan. 2000. "Societal Governance: Levels, Modes, and Orders of Sociopolitical Interaction." In *Debating Governance: Authority, Steering, and Democracy,* edited by Jon Pierre. Oxford: Oxford University Press.

Kuo, David. 2006. *Tempting Faith: An Inside Story of Political Seduction.* New York: Free Press.

Laudarji, Isaac B., and Lowell W. Livezey. 2000. "The Churches and the Poor in a 'Ghetto Underclass' Neighborhood." In *Public Religion and Urban Transformation,* edited by Lowell W. Livezey. New York: New York University Press.

Lawson, Ronald. 1986. "Tenant Responses to the Urban Housing Crisis, 1970–

1984." In *The Tenant Movement in New York City, 1904–1984,* edited by Ronald Lawson and Mark Naison. New Brunswick, NJ: Rutgers University Press,

Leavitt, Jacqueline. 1980. "Resident and Community Receivership Programs in New York City." In *Housing Form and Public Policy in the United States,* edited by Richard Plunz. New York: Praeger.

Leavitt, Jacqueline, and Susan Saegert. 1990. *From Abandonment to Hope: Community-Households in Harlem.* New York: Columbia University Press.

Lentz, Philip. 1998. "Giuliani Blocks Harlem Project in Butts Feud," *Crains,* February 1–7, 1.

LeRoux, Kelly. 2007. "Nonprofits as Civic Intermediaries: The Role of Community-Based Organizations in Promoting Political Participation." *Urban Affairs Review* 42:410–22.

Lewinson, Edwin. 1974. *Black Politics in New York City.* New York: Twayne.

Lieberson, Stanley. 1980. *A Piece of the Pie: Blacks and White Immigrants since 1880.* Berkeley: University of California Press.

Lincoln, C. Eric, and Lawrence Mamiya. n.d. *The Black Church in the Black Experience Study: Urban Church Data Set and Codebook.* Hartford, CT: Center for Social and Religious Research, Hartford Seminary.

———. 1990. *The Black Church in the African American Experience.* Durham, NC: Duke University Press.

Lipsky, Michael. 1968. "Protest as a Political Resource." *American Political Science Review* 62:1144–58.

———. 1970. *Protest in City Politics.* Chicago: Rand McNally.

———. 1980. *The Street-Level Bureaucrat.* New York: Russell Sage Foundation.

Listokin, David. 1985. *Housing Receivership and Self-Help Neighborhood Revitalization.* New Brunswick, NJ: Center for Urban Policy Research, Rutgers, and State University of New Jersey.

Little, Rivka Gewirtz. 2002. "The New Harlem: Who's behind the Real Estate Gold Rush and Who's Fighting It?" *Village Voice,* September 18–24.

Littrell, Donald, and Daryl Hobbs. 1989. "The Self-Help Approach." In *Community Development in Perspective,* edited by James A. Christenson and Jerry W. Robinson Jr. Ames: Iowa State University Press.

Logue, Edward. 1980. "The Future for New Housing in New York City." In *Housing Form and Public Policy in the United States,* edited by Richard Plunz. New York: Praeger.

Loury, Glen C. 1995. *One by One from the Inside Out: Essays and Reviews on Race and Responsibility in America.* New York: Free Press.

Lupu, Ira C., and Robert Tuttle. 2003. *State of the Law 2003: Developments in the Law concerning Government Partnerships with Religious Organizations.* Albany, NY: Roundtable on Religion and Social Welfare Policy, Nelson A. Rockefeller Institute of Government.

Mamiya, Lawrence H. 1998. "A Social History of the Bethel African Methodist Episcopal Church in Baltimore: The House of God and the Struggle for Freedom." In *American Congregations*, vol. 1, *Portraits of Twelve Religious Communities*, edited by James P. Wind and James W. Lewis. Chicago: University of Chicago Press.

Mank, Rob. 2000. "Harlem's Un-Sharpton." Salon.com, April 6.

Marable, Manning. 1983. *How Capitalism Underdeveloped Black America: Problems in Race, Political Economy, and Society*. Boston: South End.

———. 1990. "A New Black Politics." *Progressive* 54 (August): 18–21.

March, James, and Johan Olsen. 1995. *Democratic Governance*. New York: Free Press.

Marcuse, Peter. 1986. "Abandonment, Gentrification, and Displacement: Linkages in New York City." In *Gentrification of the City*, edited by Neil Smith and Peter Williams. Boston: Allen and Unwin.

Mares, Alvin S. 1994. "Housing and the Church." *Nonprofit and Voluntary Sector Quarterly* 23:139–57.

Marschall, Melissa, and Anirudh V. S. Ruhil. 2006. "The Pomp of Power: Black Mayoralties in Urban America." *Social Science Quarterly* 87:828–50.

Martin, Douglas. 2003. "Preston R. Washington, 54, Minister in Harlem, Is Dead." *New York Times*, July 4, B8.

Marwell, Nicole P. 2004. "Privatizing the Welfare State: Nonprofit Community-Based Organizations as Political Actors." *American Sociological Review* 69: 265–91.

Massey, Douglas S., and Nancy A. Denton. 1993. *American Apartheid: Segregation and the Making of the Underclass*. Cambridge, MA: Harvard University Press.

Matloff, Judith. 2002. "Sacred Ground: As Churches Make Real Estate Part of Their Mission, Some Harlem Residents Pray for Relief." *City Limits*, July/August.

Mayer, Margit. 1991. "Politics in the Post-Fordist City." *Socialist Review* 21:105–24.

———. 1998. "The Changing Scope of Action in Urban Politics: New Opportunities for Local Initiative and Movements." In *Possible Urban Worlds: Urban Strategies at the End of the Twentieth Century*, edited by Richard Wolff. Basel, Germany: Birkhauser Verlag.

Mays, Benjamin Elijah, and Joseph William Nicholson. 1933. *The Negro's Church*. New York: Institute of Social and Religious Research

McAdam, Doug. 1999. *Political Process and the Development of Black Insurgency, 1930–1970*. 2nd ed. Chicago: University of Chicago Press.

McClerking, Harwood K., and Eric L. McDaniel. 2005. "Belonging and Doing: Political Churches and Black Political Participation." *Political Psychology* 26:721–33.

McDaniel, Eric L. 2004. "Black Clergy in the 2000 Election." *Journal for the Scientific Study of Religion* 42:533–46.

McDougall, Harold A. 1993. *Black Baltimore: A New Theory of Community*. Philadelphia: Temple University Press.

McKnight, John. 1989. "Why 'Servanthood' Is Bad." *The Other Side* 25:38–41.

McRoberts, Omar M. 2001. "Black Churches, Community, and Development." *Shelterforce: The Journal of Affordable Housing and Community Building* 23:8–11.

———. 2003. *Streets of Glory: Church and Community in a Black Neighborhood.* Chicago: University of Chicago Press.

McVeigh, Rory, and David Sikkink. 2001. "God, Politics, and Protest; Religious Beliefs and the Legitimation of Contentious Tactics." *Social Forces* 79:1425–458.

Mead, Lawrence M. 2003. "A Biblical Response to Poverty." In *Lifting Up the Poor: A Dialogue on Religion, Poverty, and Welfare Reform,* edited by Mary Jo Bane and Lawrence M. Mead. Washington, DC: Brookings Institution Press.

Medoff, Peter, and Holly Sklar. 1994. *Streets of Hope: The Fall and Rise of an Urban Neighborhood.* Boston: South End.

Metis Associates. 2003. *ADC Community Vision—Neighborhood Partners Initiative: Report on the 2001 Community Survey.* New York: Metis Associates, Center for Human Environments, City University of New York Graduate Center.

Meyer, David S., and Sidney Tarrow. 1998. "A Movement Society: Contentious Politics for a New Century." In *The Social Movement Society,* edited by David S. Meyer and Sidney Tarrow. Lanham, MD: Rowman and Littlefield.

Michetti, Felice. 1993. "New York City Capital Program for Affordable Housing." In *Housing America: Mobilizing Bankers, Builders, and Communities to Solve the Nation's Affordable Housing Crisis,* edited by Jess Lederman. Chicago: Probus.

Milbank, Dana, and Hamil Harris. 2000. "Bush, Religious Leaders Meet: President-Elect Begins Faith-Based Initiative, Reaches for Blacks." *Washington Post,* December 21, A6.

Millner, Denene. 1995. "Activists Fear for Harlem Project." *New York Daily News,* May 14, 20.

Miranne, Kristine B., and Katherine Amato-Von Hemert. 2001. "Putting Flesh on the Word: Churches and Welfare Reform." *Journal of Poverty* 5:21–43.

Mollenkopf, John Hull. 1986. "New York: The Great Anomaly." *PS* 19:591–97.

———. 1994. *A Phoenix in the Ashes: The Rise and Fall of the Koch Coalition in New York City Politics.* Princeton, NJ: Princeton University Press.

———. 1997. "New York: The Great Anomaly." In *Racial Politics in American Cities,* 2nd ed., edited by Rufus P. Browning, Dale Rogers Marshall, and David H. Tabb. New York: Longman.

———. 2003. "New York: Still the Great Anomaly." In *Racial Politics in American Cities,* 3rd ed., edited by Rufus P. Browning, Dale Rogers Marshall, and David H. Tabb. New York: Longman.

Monsma, Stephen V. 1996. *When Sacred and Secular Mix: Religious Nonprofit Organizations and Public Money.* Lanham, MD: Rowman and Littlefield.

———. 2004. *Putting Faith in Partnerships: Welfare-to-Work in Four Cities.* Ann Arbor: University of Michigan Press.

Montgomery, William. 1993. *Under Their Own Vine and Fig Tree: The African American Church in the South, 1865–1900.* Baton Rouge: Louisiana State University Press.

Montiel, Lisa. 2002. *The Use of Public Funds for Delivery of Faith-Based Human Services.* Albany, NY: Roundtable on Religion and Social Welfare Policy, Nelson A. Rockefeller Institute of Government.

Montiel, Lisa, and David J. Wright. 2006. *Getting a Piece of the Pie: Federal Grants to Faith-Based Social Service Organizations.* Albany, NY: Roundtable on Religion and Social Welfare Policy, Nelson A. Rockefeller Institute of Government.

Moorer, Talise D. 2003. "A Home-Going Fit for a King: Community Bids Farewell to Beloved Rev. Preston R. Washington Sr." *Amsterdam News,* July 10, 30.

Morken, Hubert, and Jo Renee Formicola. 1999. *The Politics of School Choice.* Lanham, MD: Rowman and Littlefield.

Morris, Aldon. 1984. *The Origins of the Civil Rights Movement.* New York: Free Press.

———. 1996. "The Black Church in the Civil Rights Movement: The SCLC as the Decentralized Radical Arm of the Black Church." In *Disruptive Religion: The Force of Faith in Social Movement Activism,* edited by Christian Smith. New York: Routledge.

Morsell, John Albert. 1950. "The Political Behavior of Negroes in New York City." Ph.D. diss., Columbia University.

Murphree, David W., Stuart A. Wright, and Helen Rose Ebaugh. 1996. "Toxic Waste Siting and Community Resistance: How Cooptation of Local Citizen Opposition Failed." *Sociological Perspectives* 39:447–63.

Murray, Charles. 1994. *Losing Ground: American Social Policy, 1950–1980.* 10th ed. New York: Basic Books.

Nathan, Richard P. 1996. "The Nonprofitization Movement as a Form of Devolution." In *Capacity for Change? The Nonprofit World in the Age of Devolution,* edited by Dwight F. Burlingame, William A. Diaz, Warren Ilchman, and associates. Bloomington: Center on Philanthropy, Indiana University.

Nathan, Richard P., Julian Chow, and Michael Leo Owens. 1995. "The Flip Side of the Underclass: Minority Working and Middle Class Neighborhoods." *Rockefeller Institute of Government Bulletin,* 14–22.

National Congress for Community Economic Development. 1999. *Coming of Age: Trends and Achievements of Community-Based Development Organizations.* Washington, DC: National Congress for Community Economic Development.

Needleman, Martin, and Carolyn Emerson Needleman. 1974. *Guerillas in the Bureaucracy.* New York: John Wiley and Sons.

Nelsen, Hart, and Conrad Kanagy. 1993. "Churched and Unchurched Black Americans." In *Church and Denominational Growth,* edited by David A. Roozen and C. Kirk Hadaway. Nashville: Abingdon.

Nelson, William E., Jr. 2000. *Black Atlantic Politics: Dilemmas of Political Empowerment in Boston and Liverpool.* Albany: State University of New York Press.

Newman, Harvey C. 1994. "Black Clergy and Urban Regimes: The Role of Atlanta's Concerned Black Clergy." *Journal of Urban Affairs* 8:23–33.

New York, State of. 1998. *An Investigation into the Creation of the Harlem Urban Development Corporation and Its Operations from 1981–1995.* Albany: Commission of Investigation, State of New York.

New York City Department of City Planning. 1992. *Demographic Profiles: A Portrait of New York City's Community Districts.* New York: New York City Department of City Planning.

———. 1993. *Socioeconomic Profiles: A Portrait of New York City's Community Districts.* New York: New York City Department of City Planning.

New York City Department of Housing Preservation and Development. 1998. *Breaking New Ground: A Guide to the Programs and Services of the Department of Housing Preservation and Development.* New York: New York City Department of Housing Preservation and Development.

———. 2005. "H.O.M.E.S.: Housing Operations Management System Fact Sheet, December 2005." New York: New York City Department of Housing Preservation and Development.

New York City Housing Partnership. 1999. *Revitalizing Neighborhoods through Affordable Housing and Community Involvement.* New York: New York City Housing Partnership.

New York City Nonprofits Project. 2002. *New York City's Nonprofit Sector.* New York: New York City Nonprofits Project.

New York City Rent Guidelines Board. 1998. *Recent Movers Study.* New York: New York City Rent Guidelines Board.

Newfield, Jack. 2002. *The Full Rudy: The Man, the Myth, the Mania.* New York: Thunder's Mouth Press and Nation Books.

Noble, Gil. 1992. Transcript of remarks made during *Like It Is,* show 838. Aired January 12.

Noel, Peter. 1998. "The Battle for Harlem." *Village Voice,* June 2:53–54.

Nye, Nancy, and Norman Glickman. 2000. "Working Together: Building Capacity for Community Development." *Housing Policy Debate* 11:163–98.

Office of the Mayor. 1995. *Mayor's Executive Budget.* New York: Office of the Mayor, City of New York.

Olasky, Marvin. 1992. *The Tragedy of American Compassion.* Washington, DC: Regnery.

———. 1997. *Renewing American Compassion: How Compassion for the Needy Can Turn Ordinary Citizens into Heroes.* Washington, DC: Regnery.

Olson, Laura. 2000. *Filled with Spirit and Power: Protestant Clergy in Politics.* Albany: State University of New York Press.

Olson, Mancur. 1965. *The Logic of Collective Action*. Cambridge, MA: Harvard University Press.

Onishi, Norimitsu. 1997. "As Cathedral Opens, Preacher-Politician Looks Ahead." *New York Times*, July 28, B1.

Oppenheim, Vicki Ann, and Luis Sierra. 1994. *Building Blocks: Community-Based Strategies to Counteract Housing Disinvestment and Abandonment in New York City*. New York: Community Service Society of New York.

Orbell, John, and Toru Uno. 1972. "A Theory of Neighborhood Problem Solving: Political Action vs. Residential Mobility." *American Political Science Review* 66:471–89.

O'Regan, Katherine M., and John M. Quigley. 2000. "Federal Policy and the Rise of Nonprofit Housing Providers." *Journal of Housing Research* 11:297–317.

Orlebeke, Charles J. 1997. *New Life at Ground Zero: New York, Homeownership, and the Future of American Cities*. Albany, NY: Rockefeller Institute Press.

———. 2000. "The Evolution of Low-Income Housing Policy, 1949 to 1999." *Housing Policy Debate* 11:489–520.

Orr, John. n.d. "County Strategic Models: Los Angeles County–The Collaboration Council." Los Angeles: Center for Religion and Civic Culture, University of Southern California.

Orr, Marion. 1999. *Black Social Capital: The Politics of School Reform in Baltimore, 1986–1998*. Lawrence: University Press of Kansas.

———. 2000. "Baltimoreans United in Leadership Development: Exploring the Role of Governing Nonprofits." In *Nonprofits in Urban America*, edited by Richard C. Hula and Cynthia Jackson-Elmoore. Westport, CT: Quorum.

Osofsky, Gilbert. 1996. *Harlem: The Making of a Ghetto*. 2nd ed. Chicago: Ivan R. Dee.

Owens, Michael Leo. 1997a. "Local Party Failure and Alternative, Black Church–Based Nonparty Organizations." *Western Journal of Black Studies* 21:162–72.

———. 1997b. "Renewal in a Working-Class Black Neighborhood." *Journal of Urban Affairs* 19:183–206.

———. 2000. "Black Church–Affiliated Community Development Corporations and the Coproduction of Affordable Housing in New York City." In *Nonprofit Organizations in Urban America*, edited by Richard Hula and Cynthia Jackson-Elmoore. New York: Quorum.

———. 2001. "The Reverend Floyd Flake: African Methodist Episcopal Church Minister for School Choice." In *Religious Leaders and Faith-Based Politics*, edited by Jo Renee Formicola and Hubert Morken. Lanham, MD: Rowman and Littlefield.

———. 2002. "Nonprofitization and the Membership of Black Churches in Urban Micro-Regimes." Paper presented at the annual meeting of the Urban Affairs Association, Boston, March 20–23.

———. 2003. "Doing Something in Jesus' Name: Black Churches and Community Development Corporations." In *New Day Begun: Black Churches, Public Influences, and American Civic Culture,* edited by R. Drew Smith. Durham, NC: Duke University Press.

———. 2004a. "Capacity Building: The Case of Faith-Based Organizations." In *Building the Organizations That Build Communities: Strengthening the Capacity of Faith- and Community-Based Development Organizations,* edited by Roland V. Anglin. Washington, DC: Office of Policy Development and Research, U.S. Department of Housing and Urban Development.

———. 2004b. "Contestant, Advocate, Implementer: Social Services and the Policy Roles of African American Churches." In *The Long March Ahead: African American Churches and Public Policy in Post–Civil Rights America,* edited by R. Drew Smith. Durham: Duke University Press.

———. 2006. "Which Congregations Will Take Advantage of Charitable Choice? Explaining the Pursuit of Public Funding by Congregations." *Social Science Quarterly* 87:55–75.

Owens, Michael Leo, and Michael J. Rich. 2003. "Is Strong Incorporation Enough? Black Empowerment and the Fate of Atlanta's Low-Income Blacks." In *Racial Politics in American Cities,* 3rd ed., edited by Rufus P. Browning, Dale Rogers Marshall, and David H. Tabb. New York: Longman.

Owens, Michael Leo, and R. Drew Smith. 2005. "Congregations in Low-Income Neighborhoods and the Implications for Social Welfare Policy Research." *Nonprofit and Voluntary Sector Quarterly* 34:316–39.

Owens, Michael Leo, and David Wright. 1998. "The Diversity of Majority-Black Neighborhoods." *Rockefeller Institute of Government Bulletin,* 78–86.

Pagano, Michael A., and William Barnes. 1991. *City Fiscal Conditions in 1991.* Washington, DC: National League of Cities.

Pateman, Carole. 1970. Participation *and Democratic Theory.* Cambridge, UK: Cambridge University Press

Patillo-McCoy, Mary. 1998. "Church Culture as a Strategy of Action in the Black Community." *American Sociological Review* 63:767–84.

———. 2000. *Black Picket Fences: Privilege and Peril among the Black Middle Class.* Chicago: University of Chicago Press.

Pecorella, Robert F. 1994. *Community Power in a Postreform City: Politics in New York City.* Armonk, NY: M. E. Sharpe.

Peel, Roy V. 1935. *The Political Clubs of New York City.* New York: G. P. Putnam's Sons.

Perry, Huey L. 1996. *Race, Politics, and Governance in the United States.* Gainesville: University Press of Florida.

Peterson, Paul. 1981. *City Limits.* Chicago: University of Chicago Press.

Pew Research Center for the People and the Press. 2001a. "Faith-Based Funding Backed, but Church-State Doubts Abound." Washington, DC: Pew Research Center for the People and the Press.

———. 2001b. *Religion and Public Life Survey: Data File and Codebook.* Available from the American Religion Data Archive, www.thearda.com.

———. 2002. *Religion and Public Life Survey: Data File and Codebook.* Available from the American Religion Data Archive, www.thearda.com.

Pierre, Jon, and B. Guy Peters. 2000. *Governance, Politics, and the State.* New York: St. Martin's.

Pinn, Anthony B. 2002. *The Black Church in the Post–Civil Rights Era.* Maryknoll, NY: Orbis.

Plunz, Richard. 1990. *A History of Housing in New York City: Dwelling Type and Social Change in the American Metropolis.* New York: Columbia University Press.

Pollard, Alton B. 2005. "Black Churches, Black Empowerment, and Atlanta's Civil Rights Legacy." In *Black Clergy and Local Politics: Clergy Influence, Organizational Partnership, and Civic Empowerment,* edited by R. Drew Smith and Fredrick Harris. Lanham, MD: Rowman and Littlefield.

Pomerantz, Gary. 1996. *Where Peachtree Meets Sweet Auburn: A Saga of Race and Family.* New York: Penguin.

Pratt, Henry. 2004. *Churches and Urban Government in Detroit and New York, 1895–1994.* Detroit: Wayne State University Press.

Pristin, Terry. 2000. "In Bedford-Stuyvesant a Boom Remains a Bust." *New York Times,* May 29, B1.

Quimby, Ernest. 1977. "Black Political Development in Bedford-Stuyvesant as Reflected in the Origin and Role of the Bedford-Stuyvesant Restoration Corporation." Ph.D. diss., City University of New York.

Radin, Charles A. 2006. "A Shattered Alliance." *Boston Globe,* February 14, B1.

Ragan, Mark, Lisa Montiel, and David Wright. 2003. *Scanning the Policy Environment for Faith-Based Social Services in the United States: Results of a Fifty-State Study.* Albany, NY: Roundtable on Religion and Social Welfare Policy, Nelson A. Rockefeller Institute of Government.

Ragan, Mark, and David Wright. 2005. *The Policy Environment for Faith-Based Social Services in the United States: What Has Changed Since 2002? Results of a Fifty-State Study.* Albany, NY: Roundtable on Religion and Social Welfare Policy, Nelson A. Rockefeller Institute of Government.

Ramsay, Meredith. 1998. "Redeeming the City: Exploring the Relationship between Church and Metropolis." *Urban Affairs Review* 33: 595–626.

Raymond and May Associates. 1968. *Vest Pocket Housing in Bedford-Stuyvesant: A Summary Report to the Community and City on Some of the First Steps in New York's Model Cities Program.* White Plains, NY: Raymond and May Associates.

Reed, Adolph L., Jr. 1986. *The Jesse Jackson Phenomenon: The Crisis of Purpose in Afro-American Politics.* New Haven, CT: Yale University Press.

———. 1999. *Stirrings in the Jug: Black Politics in the Postsegregation Era.* Minneapolis: University of Minnesota Press.

————. 2000. *Class Notes: Posing as Politics and Other Thoughts on the American Scene.* New York: New Press.

Reed, Gregory J. 1994. *Economic Empowerment through the Church: A Blueprint for Progressive Community Development.* Grand Rapids, MI: Zondervan.

Reid, Elizabeth J. 1999. "Nonprofit Advocacy and Political Participation." In *Nonprofits and Government: Collaboration and Conflict,* edited by Elizabeth T. Boris and C. Eugene Steuerle. Washington, DC: Urban Institute Press.

Rhodes, R. A. W. 1996. "The New Governance: Governing without Government." *Political Studies* 44:652–57.

————. 1997. *Understanding Governance: Policy Networks, Governance, Reflexivity, and Accountability.* Maidenhead, UK: Open University Press.

Rhomberg, Chris. 2004. *No There There: Race, Class, and Political Community in Oakland.* Berkeley: University of California Press.

Rich, Michael. 1993. *Federal Policymaking and the Poor: National Goals, Local Choices, and Distributional Outcomes.* Princeton, NJ: Princeton University Press.

Rich, Michael, Micheal Giles, and Emily Stern. 2001. "Collaborating to Reduce Poverty: Views from City Halls and Community-Based Organizations." *Urban Affairs Review* 37:184–204.

Rivers, Eugene. 1995. "Beyond the Nationalism of Fools: Toward an Agenda for Black Intellectuals." *Boston Review* 20:16–18.

————. 2001. "Effectiveness over Ideology: Church-Based Partnerships." In *Sacred Places, Civic Purposes: Should Government Help Faith-Based Charity?* edited by E. J. Dionne and Ming Hsu Chen. Washington, DC: Brookings Institution Press.

Roberts, Samuel K. 2003. "On Seducing the Samaritan: The Problematic of Government Aid to Faith-Based Groups." In *New Day Begun: African American Churches and Civic Culture in Post–Civil Rights America,* edited by R. Drew Smith. Durham, NC: Duke University Press.

Rock, JoAnn. 2002. *Stepping Out on Faith: New York City's Charitable Choice Demonstration Program.* Albany, NY: Roundtable on Religion and Social Welfare, Nelson A. Rockefeller Institute of Government.

Rock, JoAnn, and Richard Roper. 2001. *An Evaluation of the Start-Up Phase of the New York City Charitable Choice Demonstration.* Albany, NY: Roundtable on Religion and Social Welfare Policy, Nelson A. Rockefeller Institute of Government.

Roistacher, Elizabeth, and Emanuel Tobier. 1984. "Housing Policy." In *Setting Municipal Priorities: American Cities and the New York Experience,* edited by Charles Brecher and Raymond D. Horton. New York: New York University Press.

Roozen, David A., William McKinney, and Jackson W. Carroll. 1988. *Varieties of Religious Presence: Mission in Public Life.* New York: Pilgrim Press.

Rosenstone, Steven J., and John Mark Hansen. 1993. *Mobilization, Participation, and Democracy in America.* New York: Longman.

Ross, Timothy. 1996. "The Impact of Industrial Areas Foundation Community Organizing on East Brooklyn: A Study of East Brooklyn Congregations." Ph.D. diss., University of Maryland.

Sabatier, Paul A. 1993. "Policy Change over a Decade or More." In *Policy Change and Learning: An Advocacy Coalition Approach*, edited by Paul A. Sabatier and Hank C. Jenkins-Smith. Boulder, CO: Westview.

Saegert, Susan, J. Phillip Thompson, and Mark R. Warren, eds. 2001. *Social Capital and Poor Communities*. New York: Russell Sage.

Salamon, Lester. 1973. "Leadership and Modernization: The Emerging Black Political Elite in the American South." *Journal of Politics* 35:615–66.

———. 1995. *Partners in Public Service: Government-Nonprofit Relations in the Modern Welfare State*. Baltimore: Johns Hopkins University Press.

———. 2002. *The Tools of Government: A Guide to the New Governance*. New York: Oxford University Press.

Salins, Peter D. 1999. "Reviving New York City's Housing Market." In *Housing and Community Development in New York City: Facing the Future*, edited by Michael H. Schill. Albany: State University of New York Press.

Salins, Peter D., and Gerard C. S. Mildner. 1992. *Scarcity by Design: The Legacy of New York City's Housing Policies*. Cambridge, MA: Harvard University Press.

Salvatore, Nick. 2005. *Singing in a Strange Land: C. L. Franklin, the Black Church, and the Transformation of America*. New York: Little, Brown.

Sanford, Karin. 2002. "Reverend Jesse Jackson and the Rainbow/PUSH Coalition: Institutionalizing Economic Opportunity." In *Black Political Organizations in the Post–Civil Rights Era*, edited by Ollie A. Johnson and Karin L. Sanford. New Brunswick, NJ: Rutgers University Press.

Savas, E. S. 2000. *Privatization and Public-Private Partnerships*. New York: Seven Bridges.

Savitch, Hank. 1990. "The Federal Impact on City Politics." In *Urban Politics New York Style*, edited by Jewell Bellush and Dick Netzer. Armonk, NY: M. E. Sharpe.

Sawyer, Mary R. 1994. *Black Ecumenism: Implementing the Demands of Justice*. Valley Forge, PA: Trinity Press International.

———. 2001. "Theocratic, Prophetic, and Ecumenical: Political Roles of African American Clergy." In *Christian Clergy in American Politics*, edited by Sue E. S. Crawford and Laura Olson. Baltimore: Johns Hopkins University Press.

Schaller, Lyle E. 1967. *The Churches' War on Poverty*. Nashville: Abingdon.

Scheiner, Seth M. 1965. *Negro Mecca: A History of the Negro in New York City, 1865–1920*. New York: New York University Press.

Schill, Michael H. 1994. "The Role of the Nonprofit Sector in Low-Income Housing Productions: A Comparative Perspective." *Urban Affairs Quarterly* 30:74–101.

———, ed. 1999. *Housing and Community Development in New York City: Facing the Future*. Albany: State University of New York Press.

Schill, Michael H., and Benjamin P. Scafidi. 1999. "Housing Conditions and Problems in New York City." In *Housing and Community Development in New York City: Facing the Future,* edited by Michael H. Schill. Albany: State University of New York Press.

Schill, Michael H., Ingrid Gould Ellen, Amy Ellen Schwartz, and Ioan Voicu. 2002. "Revitalizing Inner-City Neighborhoods: New York City's Ten-Year Plan." *Housing Policy Debate* 13:529–66.

Schneider, Mark, Paul Teske, and Melissa Marschall. 2000. *Choosing Schools: Consumer Choice and the Quality of American Schools.* Princeton, NJ: Princeton University Press.

Schwartz, Alex. 1998. "Bank Lending to Minority and Low-Income Households and Neighborhoods: Do Community Reinvestment Agreements Make a Difference?" *Journal of Urban Affairs* 20:269–301.

———. 1999. "New York City and Subsidized Housing: Impacts and Lessons of the City's $5 Billion Capital Budget Housing Plan." *Housing Policy Debate* 10:839–77.

Schwartz, Alex, and Avis Vidal. 1999. "Between a Rock and a Hard Place: The Impact of Federal and State Policy Changes on Housing in New York City." In *Housing and Community Development in New York City: Facing the Future,* edited by Michael H. Schill. Albany: State University of New York Press.

Schwartz, Joel. 1986. "Tenant Power in the Liberal City, 1943–1971." In *The Tenant Movement in New York City, 1904–1984,* edited by Ronald Lawson and Mark Naison. New Brunswick, NJ: Rutgers University Press.

Scotland, Roger N. 1999. "Raising Lazarus: The Resurrection and Transformation of Harlem." In *Signs of Hope: Ministries of Community Renewal,* edited by Robert D. Carle and Louis A. DeCaro Jr. Valley Forge, PA: Judson Press.

Segal, Julie A. 1999. "A 'Holy Mistaken Zeal': The Legislative History and Future of Charitable Choice." In *Welfare Reform and Faith-Based Organizations,* edited by Derek Davis and Barry Hankins. Waco, TX: J. M. Dawson Institute of Church-State Studies, Baylor University.

Selznick, Philip. 1948. "Foundations of the Theory of Organization." *American Sociological Review* 13:25–35.

——— 1949. *TVA and the Grass Roots: A Study in the Sociology of Formal Organization.* Berkeley: University of California Press.

Sengupta, Somini. 1995. "Meshing the Sacred and the Secular; Floyd Flake Offers Community Development via Church and State." *New York Times,* November 23, B1.

Sernett, Milton. 1997. *Bound for the Promised Land: African American Religion and the Great Migration.* Durham, NC: Duke University Press.

Shefter, Martin. 1987. *Political Crisis/Fiscal Crisis: The Collapse and Revival of New York City.* New York: Basic Books.

———. 1988. "Political Incorporation and Containment: Regime Transformation in New York City, 1897–1953." In *Power, Culture, and Place: Essays on New York City,* edited by John H. Mollenkopf. New York: Russell Sage Foundation.

Sherman, Amy. 2000. *The Growing Impact of Charitable Choice.* Washington, DC: Center for Public Justice.

Shingles, Richard. 1981. "Black Consciousness and Political Participation: The Missing Link." *American Political Science Review* 79:293–304.

Shipp, E. R. 1991. "Harlem Battles over Development Project." *New York Times,* July 31, B1.

Siegel, Fred. 1997. *The Future Once Happened Here: New York, DC, LA, and the Fate of America's Big Cities.* New York: Free Press.

———. 2002. "The Death and Life of America's Cities." *Public Interest* 248:2–22.

Simon, Herbert A. 1956. "A Behavioral Model of Rational Choice." *Quarterly Journal of Economics* 69:129–38.

Simpson, Andrea Y. 1998. *The Tie That Binds: Identity and Political Attitudes in the Post–Civil Rights Generation.* New York: New York University Press.

Sites, William. 1997. "The Limits of Urban Regime Theory: New York City under Koch, Dinkins, and Giuliani." *Urban Affairs Review* 32:536–57.

Skocpol, Theda. 1979. *States and Social Revolutions.* Cambridge: Cambridge University Press.

———. 2003. *Diminished Democracy: From Membership to Management in American Civic Life.* Norman: University of Oklahoma Press.

Smith, Christian. 1996. *Disruptive Religion: The Force of Faith in Social Movement Activism.* New York: Routledge.

Smith, Preston H. 1999. "Self-Help, Black Conservatives, and the Reemergence of Black Privatism." In *Without Justice for All: The New Liberalism and Our Retreat from Racial Equality,* edited by Adolph L. Reed Jr. Boulder, CO: Westview.

Smith, R. Drew. 2001. "Churches and the Urban Poor: Interaction and Social Distance." *Sociology of Religion* 62:301–13.

———. 2003a. Appendix to *New Day Begun: Black Churches, Public Influences, and American Civic Culture,* edited by R. Drew Smith. Durham: Duke University Press.

———. 2003b. *Beyond the Boundaries: Low-Income Residents, Faith-Based Organizations, and Neighborhood Coalition Building.* Baltimore: Annie E. Casey Foundation.

———, ed. 2004. *The Long March Ahead: African American Churches and Public Policy in Post–Civil Rights America.* Durham, NC: Duke University Press.

———. 2005. "Black Clergy and the Governmental Sector during George W. Bush's Presidency." In *Black Churches and Local Politics: Clergy Influence, Organizational Partnerships, and Civic Empowerment,* edited by R. Drew Smith and Fredrick C. Harris. Lanham, MD: Rowman and Littlefield.

Smith, R. Drew, and Fredrick C. Harris. 2005. *Black Clergy and Local Politics: Clergy Influence, Organizational Partnerships, and Civic Empowerment.* Lanham, MD: Rowman and Littlefield.

Smith, R. Drew, and Corwin Smidt. 2003. "System Confidence, Congregational

Characteristics, and Black Church Civic Engagement." In *New Day Begun: Black Churches, Public Influences, and American Civic Culture,* edited by R. Drew Smith. Durham, NC: Duke University Press.

Smith, Robert. 1996. *We Have No Leaders: African Americans in the Post-Civil Rights Era.* Albany: State University of New York Press.

Smith, Steven Rathgeb. 2000. "Nonprofit Organizations in Urban Politics and Policy." In *Nonprofits in Urban America,* edited by Richard C. Hula and Cynthia Jackson-Elmoore. Westport, CT: Quorum.

Smith, Steven Rathgeb, and Michael Lipsky. 1993. *Nonprofits for Hire: The Welfare State in the Age of Contracting.* Cambridge, MA: Harvard University Press.

Smith, Steven Rathgeb, and M. R. Sossin. 2001. "The Varieties of Faith-Related Agencies." *Public Administration Review* 61:651–70.

Spear, Allan. 1967. *Black Chicago: The Making of a Negro Ghetto.* Chicago: University of Chicago Press.

Stafford, Walter W. 1997. *Black Civil Society and the Black Family in New York City: A Struggle for Inclusion in Decision Making.* New York: Manhattan Borough President's Office.

———. 2001. "The New York Urban League Survey: Black New York—On Edge, but Optimistic." In *State of Black America.* Washington, DC: National Urban League.

Steinhauer, Jennifer. 2005. "Coming Full Circle, City to Sell Blighted Lots." *New York Times,* August 19, B1.

Stewart, Carlyle Fielding. 1994. *African American Church Growth: Twelve Principles of Prophetic Ministry.* Nashville: Abingdon.

Stoecker, Randy. 1994. *Defending Community: The Struggle for Alternative Redevelopment in Cedar-Riverside.* Philadelphia: Temple University Press.

———. 1997. "The CDC Model of Urban Development: A Critique and Alternative." *Journal of Urban Affairs* 19:1–22.

Stoker, Gerry. 1998. "Regime Theory and Urban Politics." In *Theories of Urban Politics,* edited by David Judge, Gerry Stoker, and Harold Wolman. London: Sage.

———. 2000. "Urban Political Science and the Challenge of Urban Governance." In *Debating Governance: Authority, Steering, and Democracy,* edited by Jon Pierre. Oxford: Oxford University Press.

Stone, Clarence N. 1989. *Regime Politics: Governing Atlanta, 1946–1988.* Lawrence: University Press of Kansas.

———. 1990. "Transactional and Transformational Leadership: A Re-examination." Paper presented at the annual meeting of the American Political Science Association, San Francisco, August 30–September 2.

———. 1993. "Urban Regimes and the Capacity to Govern: A Political Economy Approach." *Journal of Urban Affairs* 15:1–28.

Strozier, Matthew. 1999. "Holy Owned Subsidiaries." *City Limits,* March.

Swanstrom, Todd, and Julia Koschinsky. 2000. "Rethinking the Partnership Model

of Government-Nonprofit Relations: The Case of Community Development." In
*Nonprofits in Urban America,* edited by Richard C. Hula and Cynthia Jackson-
Elmoore. Westport, CT: Quorum.

Sweeting, Catherine O. 1999. "This Far by Faith: Allen African Methodist Episcopal
Church." In *Signs of Hope in the City: Ministries of Community Renewal,* edited
by Robert DeCarle and Louis A. DeCaro Jr. Valley Forge, PA: Judson Press.

Tabb, William K. 1986. *The Long Default: New York City and the Urban Fiscal Crisis.* New York: Monthly Review.

Tarrow, Sidney. 1998. *Power in Movement: Collective Action, Social Movements, and
Politics.* Cambridge: Cambridge University Press.

Tate, Katherine. 1993. *From Protest to Politics: The New Black Voters in American
Elections.* New York: Russell Sage Foundation; Cambridge, MA: Harvard University Press.

Taylor, Clarence. 1992. "The Black Churches of Brooklyn from the Early Nineteenth
Century to the Civil Rights Movement." Ph.D. diss., Columbia University.

———. 1994. *The Black Churches of Brooklyn.* New York: Columbia University Press.

Taylor, Lucy. 1997. "Privatising Protest: NGOs and the Professionalization of Social
Movements." Paper presented at the annual meeting of the Latin American Studies Association, Guadalajara, Mexico, April 17–19.

Taylor, Monique M. 2002. *Harlem: Between Heaven and Hell.* Minneapolis: University of Minnesota Press.

Taylor, Robert Joseph. 1987. "Black Americans' Perceptions of the Sociohistorical
Role of the Church." *Journal of Black Studies* 18:123–38.

Thomas, June Manning, and Reynard N. Blake Jr. 1996. "Faith-Based Community
Development and African-American Neighborhoods." In *Revitalizing Urban
Neighborhoods,* edited by W. Dennis Keating, Norman Krumholz, and Philip Star.
Lawrence: University Press of Kansas.

Thompson, J. Phillip. 1990. "The Impact of the Jesse Jackson Campaigns on Local Black Political Mobilization in New York City, Atlanta, and Oakland." Ph.D.
diss., City University of New York.

———. 1996–1997. "The Failure of Liberal Homeless Policy in the Koch and Dinkins
Administration." *Political Science Quarterly* 111:639–61.

———. 2006. *Double Trouble: Black Mayors, Black Communities, and the Call for
Deep Democracy.* New York: Oxford University Press.

Tolnay, Stewart E. 2001. "The Great Migration Gets Underway: A Comparison of
Black Southern Migrants and Nonmigrants in the North, 1920." *Social Science
Quarterly* 82:235–53.

Toussaint, Pamela Ann. 1999. "Concord Baptist Church: Taking Care of Business in
Bed-Stuy." In *Signs of Hope in the City: Ministries of Community Renewal,* edited
by Robert D. Carle and Louis A. DeCaro Jr. Valley Forge, PA: Judson Press.

Tsitsos, William. 2003. "Race Differences in Congregational Social Service Activity."
*Journal for the Scientific Study of Religion* 42:205–15.

Tucker-Worgs, Tamelyn. 2002. "Bringing the Church 'Back In': A Study of Black Megachurches and Their Community Development Activities." Ph.D. diss., University of Maryland–College Park.

Turetsky, Doug. 1993. *We Are the Landlords Now: A Report on Community-Based Housing Management.* New York: Community Service Society of New York.

Twelvetrees, Alan. 1989. *Organizing for Neighborhood Development.* Brookfield, VT: Averbury.

U.S. Census Bureau. 2006. *Current Population Survey, 2004 to 2006: Annual Social and Economic Supplements.* Washington, DC: U.S. Census Bureau.

Van Ryzin, Gregg, and Andrew Genn. 1999. "Neighborhood Change and the City of New York's Ten-Year Housing Plan." *Housing Policy Debate* 10:799–838.

Venkatesh, Sudhir. 2000. *American Project: The Rise and Fall of a Modern Ghetto.* Cambridge, MA: Harvard University Press.

Verba, Sidney, and Norman Nie. 1972. *Participation in America: Political Democracy and Social Equality.* New York: Harper and Row.

Vidal, Avis C. 1992. *Rebuilding Communities: A National Study of Urban Community Development Corporations.* New York: Community Development Research Center, New School for Social Research.

———. 2001. *Faith-Based Organizations in Community Development.* Washington, DC: U.S. Department of Housing and Urban Development.

Viteritti, Joseph P. 1979. *Bureaucracy and Social Justice: The Allocation of Jobs and Services to Minority Groups.* Port Washington, NY: Kennikat.

Von Hoffman, Alexander. 2003. *House by House, Block by Block: The Rebirth of America's Urban Neighborhoods.* New York: Oxford University Press.

Wald, Kenneth D. 2003. *Religion and Politics in the United States.* 4th ed. Lanham, MD: Rowman and Littlefield.

Wald, Kenneth D., Dennis Owen, and Samuel Hill Jr. 1988. "Churches as Political Communities." *American Political Science Review* 82:531–48.

Waldinger, Roger. 1996. *Still the Promised City? African-American and New Immigrants in Postindustrial New York.* Cambridge, MA: Harvard University Press.

Waldman, Amy. 2001. "Bush's Call to Churches Is Discussed with Skepticism." *New York Times,* March 23, B6.

Walker, Darren. 2001. "Faith in Harlem: Community Development and the Black Church." In *Sacred Places, Civic Purposes: Should Government Help Faith-Based Charity?* edited by E. J. Dionne and Ming Hsu Chen. Washington, DC: Brookings Institution Press.

Walker, Jack. 1991. *Mobilizing Interest Groups in America.* Ann Arbor: University of Michigan Press.

Walker, Wyatt Tee. 1994. *The Harvard Paper: The African-American Church and Economic Development.* New York: Martin Luther King Fellows Press.

———. 1998. Transcript of remarks made during taping of *Like It Is,* show 838. Aired January 18.

Walter, John. 1989. *The Harlem Fox: J. Raymond Jones and the Tammany, 1920–1970*. Albany: State University of New York Press.

Walters, Ronald, and Tamelyn Tucker-Worgs. 2005. "Black Churches and Electoral Engagement in the Nation's Capital." In *Black Clergy and Local Politics: Clergy Influence, Organizational Partnership, and Civic Empowerment*, edited by R. Drew Smith and Fredrick C. Harris. Lanham, MD: Rowman and Littlefield.

Warf, B. 1990. "The Reconstruction of Social Ecology and Neighborhood Change in Brooklyn." *Environment and Planning D: Society and Space* 8:73–96.

Warren, Mark. 1999. "What Is Political?" *Journal of Theoretical Politics* 11:207–31.

———. 2001. *Dry Bones Rattling: Community Building to Revitalize American Democracy*. Princeton, NJ: Princeton University Press.

Washington, Preston Robert. 1986. *From the Pew to the Pavement: Message on Urban Outreach*. Morristown, NJ: Aaron.

Watkins, Alan. 1998. "Faith-Based Community Development Corporations in Impoverished Communities." New York: Chase Manhattan Foundation of the Chase Community Development Group.

WCBS-TV and New York Times. 1990. *Race Relations Poll, New York City*. Study USWCBSNYT1990-JUNENYC. Storrs, CT: Roper Center.

Weikart, Lynne E. 2001. "The Giuliani Administration and the New Public Management in New York City." *Urban Affairs Review* 36:359–81.

Weir, Margaret. 1999. "Power, Money, and Politics in Community Development." In *Urban Problems and Community Development*, edited by Ronald F. Ferguson and William T. Dickens. Washington, DC: Brookings Institution Press.

Welty, William. 1969. "Black Shepherds: A Study of the Leading Negro Clergymen in New York." Ph.D. diss., New York University.

White, Andrew. 1992. "Dollars and Change." *City Limits* 17 (December): 16–21.

White House Office of Faith-Based and Community Initiatives. 2005. *Grants to Faith-Based Organizations, Fiscal Year 2004*. Washington, DC: White House Office of Faith-Based and Community Initiatives.

———. 2006. *Grants to Faith-Based Organizations, Fiscal Year 2005*. Washington, DC: White House Office of Faith-Based and Community Initiatives.

Wilder, Craig Steven. 2000. *A Covenant with Color: Race and Social Power in Brooklyn*. New York: Columbia University Press.

Williams, Grant. 2003. "Preaching beyond the Choir: Boston Minister Promotes Vision for Expanding Faith-Based Charity." *Chronicle of Philanthropy*, January 23, 21–23.

Williams, Juan. 2003. "The Faithful's Wayward Path." *New York Times*, January 20, A19.

Wilmore, Gayraud. 1983. *Black Religion and Black Radicalism*. Rev. ed. Maryknoll, NY: Orbis.

Wilson, Basil, and Charles Green. 1988. "The Black Church and the Struggle for

Political Empowerment in New York City." *Afro-Americans in New York Life and History*, January, 51–79.

Wilson, James Q. 1960. *Negro Politics: The Search for Leadership*. Glencoe, IL: Free Press.

Wilson, William Julius. 1987. *The Truly Disadvantaged: The Inner City, the Underclass, and Public Policy*. Chicago: University of Chicago Press.

———. 1996. *When Work Disappears: The World of the New Urban Poor*. New York: Alfred A. Knopf.

Windhoff-Heritier, Adrienne. 1992. *City of the Poor, City of the Rich: Politics and Policy in New York City*. Berlin: Walter de Gruyter.

Wineburg, Bob. 2001. *A Limited Partnership: The Politics of Religion, Welfare, and Social Service*. New York: Columbia University Press.

Winship, Christopher. 2001. "Maintaining Legitimacy: Church-Based Criticism as a Force for Change." In *Sacred Places, Civic Purposes: Should Government Help Faith-Based Charity?* edited by E. J. Dionne and Ming Hsu Chen. Washington, DC: Brookings Institution Press.

Wood, Brent Alan. 1997. "First African Methodist Episcopal Church and Its Social Intervention in South Central Los Angeles." Ph.D. diss., University of Southern California.

Wood, R. 1991. "Cities in Trouble." *Domestic Affairs* 1:221–38.

Wood, Richard. 1994a. "Faith in Action: Religious Resources for Political Success in Three Congregations." *Sociology of Religion* 55: 397–417.

———. 1994b. "Religious Culture and Political Action." *Sociological Theory* 17: 307–32.

———. 2002. *Faith in Action: Religion, Race, and Democratic Organizing in America*. Chicago: University of Chicago Press.

Woodson, Robert L. 1998. *The Triumphs of Joseph: How Today's Community Healers Are Reviving Our Streets and Neighborhoods*. New York: Free Press.

Woolever, Cynthia, and Deborah Bruce. 2002. *A Field Guide to U.S. Congregations: Who's Going Where and Why?* Louisville, KY: Westminster John Knox.

Worth, Robert. 1999. "Guess Who Saved the South Bronx? The Silent Partner in Community Development." *Washington Monthly* 31 (April): 26–33.

Wright, David, Mary Patillo, and Lisa Montiel. 2006. *The Flip Side of the Underclass: Unexpected Images of Social Capital in Majority–African American Neighborhoods*. Albany, NY: Rockefeller Institute Press.

Wuthnow, Robert. 2000. *Religion and Politics Survey: Data File and Codebook*. Princeton, NJ: Princeton University, Department of Sociology. Available from the American Religion Data Archive, www.thearda.com.

———. 2004. *Saving America? Faith-Based Services and the Future of Civil Society*. Princeton, NJ: Princeton University Press.

Wylde, Kathryn. 1999. "The Contributions of Public-Private Partnerships to New York City's Assisted Housing Industry." In *Housing and Community Develop-

*ment in New York City: Facing the Future,* edited by Michael H. Schill. Albany: State University of New York Press.

Yates, Douglas. 1973. *Neighborhood Democracy: The Political Impact of Decentralization.* Lexington, MA: Lexington.

Yin, Jordan S. 1998. "The Community Development System: A Case Study of Politics and Institutions in Cleveland, 1967–1997." *Journal of Urban Affairs* 20:137–57.

Young, Alford, Jr. 2004. *The Minds of Marginalized Black Men.* Princeton, NJ: Princeton University Press.

Youngblood, Johnny Ray. 1992. *Where the Hope Is: The Wriston Lecture.* New York: Manhattan Institute.

*Note:* The letter *f* following a page number denotes a figure; the letter *t* denotes a table.

Allen AME/Hall Estates, 159, 162–63,
   165–66
Allen AME Neighborhood Preservation
   and Development Corporation
   (Allen NPDC)
   founding of, 94, 99–100
   goals of, 103
   independent status of, 215
   non-contention policy of, 200
   Partnership New Homes and,
      158–59, 162–63, 165–66
Allen AME Senior Citizens' Center, 159,
   162–63
Allen AME Women's Resource Center
   (AWRC), 94, 135
Allen Temple Baptist Church (East
   Oakland), 2
Alliance for Neighborhood and Hous-
   ing Development, 215
Alliance for Neighborhood Commerce,
   Homeownership, and Revitaliza-
   tion (ANCHOR), 187–88
Allred, Christopher, 112
Altshuler, Alan, 227n29
Ammerman, Nancy, 32
Anderson, Elijah, 50
Annie E. Casey Foundation, 232n18
Antioch Missionary Baptist Church
   (Chicago), 2
Assensoh, Akwasi, 47
Association of Brooklyn Clergy for
   Community Development
   (ABCCD), 120, 187, 194
   alliance-based status of, 104, 105,
      213–14, 215
   founding of, 94, 98–99
   leadership of, 243n15
   property redeveloped by, 131–32
Association of Religious Data Archives,
   216, 230n6, 235n5
Atlanta, Georgia, 21–24, 35, 36t
Atlanta Negro Voters League, 22
Atlanta Transit Company, 22
Azusa Christian Community, 53

Bach, Victor, 246n2
Bacote, Clarence, 21
Baer, Hans A., 41
Banana Kelly Community Improvement
   Association, 242n9
Baptist African American congrega-
   tions, 31
Baptist Ministers Conference of Greater
   New York, 250n25
Barrett, Wayne, 79, 121
Bartkowski, John P., 220n20
Battery Park City, development of, 115
Beame (Abraham) mayoral administra-
   tion, 72–73
BEC New Communities, 257n3
Bedford-Stuyvesant (Brooklyn neigh-
   borhood)
   activist churches in, 81–108, 211
   black population decline in, 72, 146,
      175
   black population growth in, 69
   black poverty and unemployment in,
      72, 80–81, 98, 239n22
   Coalition for Community Empower-
      ment, 124–25
   community development corpo-
      rations in, 94–96, 98–99, 105,
      131–32, 137, 156, 173–74, 187, 195,
      196f, 197, 199–200
   during Dinkins administration, 76
   during Giuliani administration, 80
   during Koch administration, 73, 75
   mortgage fraud in, 173–75, 255n1
   property values in, 167–69, 171
   resident dissatisfaction in, 71
   residents' views of churches'
      relevance in, 125–27
   voter turnout in, 236n7
Berenson, William M., 25, 28, 47
Berry, Jeffrey, 194
Bethany Baptist Church (Bedford-
   Stuyvesant, New York)
   activism of, 88, 124, 213
   age of, 240n3